ID0984803

Grave of a Dozen Schemes

Grave of a Dozen Schemes

British Naval Planning
and the War Against Japan,
1943–1945

H. P. WILLMOTT

NAVAL INSTITUTE PRESS — ANNAPOLIS, MARYLAND

Library of Congress Cataloging-in-Publication Data
Willmott, H. P.
      Grave of a dozen schemes : British naval planning and
   the war against Japan, 1943–1945 / H. P. Willmott.
            p.   cm.
      Includes bibliographical references (p.) and index.
      ISBN 1-55750-916-6 (alk. paper)
      1. World War, 1939–1945—Naval operations, British.   2. Strategy.
   3. World War, 1939–1945—Japan.   I. Title.
   D777.W55   1995
   940.54'5941—dc20   95-23496

Printed in the United States of America on acid-free paper ∞

03 02 01 00 99 98 97 96   9 8 7 6 5 4 3 2
First printing

To the Memory of

_____

Donald Arthur Frederick Willmott
and
Olive Edna Willmott

CULVERIN—bold sounding name,
    Abortive hope, grave of a dozen schemes.
Where brave commanders might have made their names
    And able planners realized their dreams.
Enchained you stand, fast hard to Tojo's ken,
    Your secrets hid by mangroves, fringed by waves,
You will not feel the tread of countless men,
    Your breast will not be scarred by nameless graves.
Your face will not be marred, allay your fears,
    By ruthless hordes of airfield engineers.

CULVERIN—dream of release.
    Loved home of Achins and the coast Malay,
Suffer for yet awhile your chained peace.
    Revel in sunsets over Langsa Bay.
One day, who knows, perhaps not very far we
    Shall break our dreams and plan fierce battles when
Assault brigades will land at Lhoksomawe
    While others surge ashore at Bireuen,
To drive your cruel gaolers from Japan
    South, via Idi, Brandan and Medan.

CULVERIN—sleep in peace.
    You will not be the scene of warlike deeds.
Sleep on until all earthly strife shall cease,
    Or to the day when AXIOM succeeds.
Worship your ancient gods. Nippon endure.
    Suppress your rightful wrath. Reserve your anger.
Let cannibals feast on in Simalur
    And, alas, dream of trade at Samalanga.
One day, I promise you shall have your Queen,
    Your own, Imperial exile, Wilhelmine.

Undated and unsigned memorandum that closed the CULVERIN
planning file in April 1944: W.O. 203.1624.19.

Contents

British Defense Planning Organization
1943

MEMBERSHIP

The Foreign Office provided one counselor as Chairman of the Joint Intelligence Sub-Committee and one as member of the Strategical Planning Staff: it also provided a First Secretary with the Joint Intelligence Staff. The Ministry of Economic Warfare provided its Deputy Director General for the Joint Intelligence Sub-Committee, and an Assistant Secretary and Principal for the Joint Intelligence Staff and a Principal for the Intelligence Section (Operations). The Political Warfare Executive and the Ministries of Economic Warfare, Home Security, and War Transport also provided liaison officers for the three sections of the Joint Planning Staff, as did other departments when circumstances demanded. The Joint Intelligence Sub-Committee was staffed, at two-star level, by the Directors of Intelligence: the Joint Planning Staff, at one-star level, by the Directors of Plans and a half-colonel secretary from the War Cabinet Secretariat.

The Strategical Planning Section was staffed by one captain and two commanders; one half-colonel and two majors; and one group captain and two wing commanders: the Executive Planning Staff by one captain and three commanders, one half-colonel, three majors, and one captain, and one wing commander and one squadron leader: the Future Operational Planning Section by one captain and two commanders, one half-colonel and one major, and one group captain and one wing commander. The Joint Intelligence Staff had the same military establishment as the Future Operational Planning Staff. The Inter-Service Security Board and Intelligence Section (Operations) were staffed, respectively, at the half-colonel and major levels.

The Chief of Combined Operations was not a member of the Chiefs of Staff Committee but attended meetings as business demanded.

DRAMATIS PERSONAE

BRITISH

Attlee, Clement. Deputy Prime Minister; also Dominions Secretary until

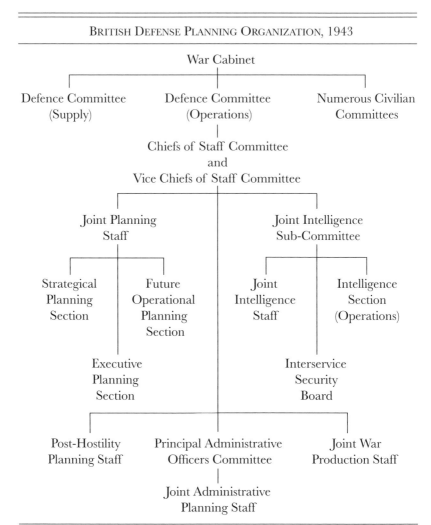

BRITISH DEFENSE PLANNING ORGANIZATION, 1943

War Cabinet

Defence Committee (Supply) — Defence Committee (Operations) — Numerous Civilian Committees

Chiefs of Staff Committee and Vice Chiefs of Staff Committee

Joint Planning Staff — Joint Intelligence Sub-Committee

Strategical Planning Section — Future Operational Planning Section — Joint Intelligence Staff — Intelligence Section (Operations)

Executive Planning Section — Interservice Security Board

Post-Hostility Planning Staff — Principal Administrative Officers Committee — Joint War Production Staff

Joint Administrative Planning Staff

All names, ranks and positions are contemporaneous. Entries are relevant to 1943–44 only.

September 1943 and thereafter Lord President of the Council.

Brooke, Field Marshal Sir Alan. Chief of the Imperial General Staff.

Churchill, Winston. Prime Minister and First Lord of the Treasury, and Minister of Defence.

Cunningham, Admiral of the Fleet Sir Andrew. First Sea Lord after October 1943.

Dill, Field Marshal Sir John. Head of Joint Staff Mission.

Eden, Anthony. Foreign Secretary and Leader of the House of Commons.

Fraser, Admiral Sir Bruce. Successively Commander-in-Chief of the Eastern and British Pacific Fleets.

Ismay, General Sir Hastings. Chief of Staff, Minister of Defence, and Deputy Military Secretary to the War Cabinet.

Jacob, Col. Ian. Military Assistant Secretary to the War Cabinet.

Leathers, Lord. Minister of War Transport.

Lumsden, Lt. Gen. Herbert. British liaison officer, South West Pacific Command.

Lyttleton, Oliver. Minister of War Production.

Mallaby, Lt. Col. George. Secretary of the Joint Planning Staff and Member of the Military Secretariat of the War Cabinet.

Mountbatten, Admiral Lord Louis. Supreme Allied Commander, South East Asia.

Noble, Admiral Sir Percy. Head of British Admiralty Delegation, Joint Staff Mission.

Portal, Air Chief Marshal Sir Charles. Chief of the Air Staff.

Pound, Admiral of the Fleet Sir Dudley. First Sea Lord until October 1943.

Pownall, Lieutenant-General Sir Henry. Chief of Staff, South East Asia Command.

Somerville, Admiral Sir James. Commander-in-Chief Eastern Fleet.

Sugden, Brigadier Cecil. Director of Plans (Army).

Non-British

Arnold, Commanding General Henry H. U.S. Army Air Force.

Chiang Kai-shek, Generalissimo. President of the Republic of China.

Curtin, John. Prime Minister of Australia.

Fraser, Peter. Prime Minister of New Zealand.

King, Adm. Ernest J. Commander-in-Chief U.S. Fleet and Chief of Naval Operations.

Leahy, Adm. William D. Chief of Staff to the President of the United States.

MacArthur, Gen. Douglas A. Supreme Allied Commander, South West Pacific Command.

Marshall, Gen. George C. Chief of Staff, U.S. Army.

Nimitz, Adm. Chester W. Commander-in-Chief U.S. Pacific Fleet and Pacific Ocean Areas.

Roosevelt, Franklin D. Thirty-second President of the United States of America.

Stilwell, Lt. Gen. Joseph. Deputy Supreme Allied Commander, South East Asia; Chief of Staff to Chiang Kai-shek; and Commanding General China-Burma-India theater with executive authority over the Northern Combat Area Command and the 10th and 14th Army Air Forces.

Wedemeyer, Maj. Gen. Albert C. Deputy Chief of Staff, South East Asia Command.

Explanatory Notes

SOURCES

All primary material is given in endnotes first by reference and then by document. Wherever possible, references have been standardized in the interests of simplicity and clarity with class and file numbers and file number and individual document separated by periods.

The full details of all primary and secondary sources are listed in the appropriate sections of the bibliography.

CONFERENCES

EUREKA: Conference of the three major Allied powers, Britain, the United States, and Soviet Union, held in Tehran between 28 November and 1 December 1943.

OCTAGON: Anglo-American conference held in Quebec, 13–16 September 1944.

QUADRANT: Anglo-American conference held in Quebec, 14–24 August 1943.

SEXTANT: Two-part Anglo-American conference held in Cairo, the first, involving consultations with the Chinese, 22–25 November, the second 4–6 December 1943.

TRIDENT: Anglo-American conference held in Washington, 12–25 May 1943.

Dates correspond to first and last plenary sessions.

PLANNING AND OPERATIONS

ANAKIM: Plan of campaign for the reconquest of Burma, first considered in 1942. It was to involve an overland offensive into Upper Burma, amphibious landings in the Arakan, and an assault on Rangoon, the latter being followed by advances into Lower and central Burma with the intention of completing the encirclement and annihilation of the enemy.

ANVIL: Allied landings in southern France in August 1944: initially considered in 1943 and executed under the code name DRAGOON.

BUCCANEER: Plan for landings in and reconquest of the Andaman Islands. Considered in 1943 and in 1944.

BULLFROG: Plan for landings on and reconquest of Akyab Island. Considered in 1943 and canceled in January 1944. Successor to CANNIBAL, which was a 1942 plan. Akyab was reoccupied in January 1945 in the course of Operation TALON, the naval side being given the code name LIGHTNING.

CAPITAL: Plan for an offensive into Upper Burma, and initially known as CHAMPION. Considered first in 1943 and at SEXTANT, when cancellation led to its being followed by a scaled-down version, TARZAN, and then, briefly, by GRIPFAST, which envisaged an advance limited to the line of the Chindwin.

CHAMPION: See CAPITAL.

CUDGEL: Plan for an overland offensive in the Arakan: considered in 1943 and 1944 as an alternative to an offensive involving amphibious operations.

CULVERIN: Plan for successive landings in northern Sumatra and Malaya. First considered in late 1942. In 1943 and 1944 a number of variants were considered under a variety of names. FIRST CULVERIN was the code name applied to plans for landings in northern Sumatra and SECOND CULVERIN for landings in Malaya, but confusingly some plans for these separate operations retained the CULVERIN name and CULVERIN was the code name also applied to such variants as the Simalur operation, which, in 1943, had been one small part of the northern Sumatra plan. In addition, a reduced CULVERIN was known as JUNIOR CULVERIN. It seems that in spring 1944 some five different plans, each named CULVERIN, were under consideration at different times, and perhaps as many as ten different plans were prepared under its auspices.

DRACULA: See VANGUARD.

DRAKE: American plan to bomb the Japanese home islands and areas on the mainland under Japanese control with B-29 Superfortresses operating from bases in southwest China and supplied by B-24 Liberators operating from northeast India. MATTERHORN was a similar plan but involved the Superfortresses ferrying their own supplies from India.

HUSKY: The invasion of Sicily in July 1943.

NEPTUNE: The naval side of the Normandy landings, June 1944.

OCTOPUS: Plan for landings in the area of the Sunda Strait. Considered in 1944.

OVERLORD: The name given to the Anglo-American campaign in northwest Europe: technically, its dates are June 1944 and January 1945.

PIGSTICK: Plan for an offensive in the Arakan involving both amphibious and overland operations. Considered in 1943, canceled in January 1944.

SCEPTRE: Plan for landings on the Kra Isthmus. Considered in 1943, it was reexamined in 1944 and, under the code name CLINCH, in 1945.

TARZAN: See CAPITAL.

VANGUARD: Plan for an assault landing at Rangoon. Considered in 1944, it was subsequently renamed LIMELIGHT and then DRACULA, and under the latter code name was executed, on a much-reduced scale, in May 1945.

Individual naval operations in the Far East are cited appropriately.

Acknowledgments

It would be pleasing to record that this book first saw the light of day as a result of the conviction that the story of the British contribution to the war against Japan in 1944–45, and specifically the story of the British Pacific Fleet, deserved an account that did both justice. Unfortunately, this author cannot honestly make such a claim. This study took shape as a result of the realization that a doctorate, and with it admission to the most mysterious Masonic order in the Western world, would be required if the author was to work in the United States.

It was in the course of working on the third volume of the author's Pacific war history in 1982–84 that this work assumed substance, the realization of the need for a doctorate coinciding with the awareness that the Public Record Office had generously yielded material sufficient for several theses on the subject of British strategic policy in the last two years of the Second World War. The situation thus produced was not without ironies: the third volume remains to be completed, and the inevitable delays that attended registration with King's College, London, meant that the thesis could have been presented on the day of enrollment. In the event, the thesis was written within the space of three months, but not until the third year and not without the patient advice and help of various individuals in no way accountable for the final product's errors and omissions. My most grateful appreciation is directed to Professor Geoffrey Till, who, as my supervisor, was responsible for the insight, forbearance, and tolerance that softened otherwise harsh judgments in the drafts and ensured that the final product was one that Professor Brian Rampf and Dr. David French could consider worthy of a doctorate without too great a struggle with their consciences. My thanks are also directed to certain individuals who contributed the best of their knowledge even though they could be sure that what they told me was certain to be remembered, altered, and used mendaciously. Most immediately, this includes two colleagues and friends, Professor Ian Beckett and Dr. A. H. leQ. Clayton, the latter being indefatigable—and indeed personally formidable, illustrious, implacable, indomitable but, alas, never victorious—in his knowledge of British naval and imperial history. There were various people engaged in research on related subjects at the Public Record Office with me whose friendship and help were much appreciated: one would single out John Ferris for specific gratitude. Outside Kew Michael H. Cole, Vice Adm. Kaye Edden, and the two Dr. Sweetmans, Jack of Annapolis and John of Camberley, all gave freely of their knowledge, and I acknowledge their contributions and thank them for all their various kindnesses.

But particular acknowledgment is due to three people. Anthony Gorst, having completed his master's degree on the subject of the British Pacific Fleet, welcomed a fellow student at the start of his studies and unselfishly provided critical encouragement at all stages of study and writing. The final product is confirmation of the debt that he is owed by the author and, one trusts, a worthy supplement to his own writings. No less significantly, David Brown provided the same, and never more so than during the process by which thesis was supplemented and converted into a book: the chronologies and orders of battle represented an enormous and selfless contribution that was as welcome as it was freely given. My final thanks to individual members of academia, alas, are given in memoriam. Col. Riley Sunderland, the co-author of the CBI series, was a source of inspiration and encouragement in the preparation of this work, and his advice and friendship, his gentleness and tolerance, are missed. I trust that the final product is worthy of his scholarship and learning.

Finally, four acknowledgments need to be made, first to the various libraries and offices that over the years provided facilities and support, specifically the Public Record Office staff, the members of the Army and Navy Historical Branches, the Ministry of Defence, and the long-suffering library staffs of various places that I frequented in preparing this text—the Royal Military Academy Sandhurst; the Staff College and the Ministry of Defence; the British Museum; King's College, London; the National Maritime Museum; and Churchill College, Cambridge. Second, I wish to thank the various members of faculties of which I have been a member since 1989 and who assisted me immensely in so many ways in the preparation of this book. Most obviously, this goes to colleagues from Tennessee, where the thesis was written, and also, for their tolerance, attention, and critical assessments, to those who have attended the various presentations I have given on related subjects. My specific thanks in this regard are rendered to Mike MccGwire, Paul B. Kincade, and Robin Hugham. Third, I thank my wife, Pauline, my children, Gaynor and Stephen, and the dogs, who have endured much during the wanderings of the last few years. I hope that all was not in vain and that this poor screed is some small recompense for their endurance and stoicism. Fourth, I thank the staff of the Naval Institute Press for the confidence that they expressed in commissioning the book and, along with copyeditor Therese D. Boyd, rendering it suitable for publication. To all, and many more, I express my sincere appreciation: one trusts the final product does justice to your attention and to the subject itself.

Grave of a Dozen Schemes

The Gathering of Strands
War, Paradox, and Relative Positions

A couple of books, the occasional article and thesis, and *en passant* references in accounts of the final stages of the Pacific war more or less represent the sum of attention paid by History to the British Pacific Fleet: even in the otherwise admirable official histories of Woodburn Kirby and Stephen Roskill the British Pacific Fleet seems to figure only as a sad, embarrassing endpiece to the story of more heroic endeavors made elsewhere. No single year seems to pass without some new addition if not to knowledge then to some already threadbare aspect or episode of the Second World War, but since the files on the British Pacific Fleet were opened to inspection at the Public Record Office in 1972 an unholy alliance of historians and publishers would seem to have conspired to ensure that Admiral Sir Bruce Fraser's command remains "The Forgotten Fleet." Such a state of affairs is somewhat surprising. With no fewer than five fleet, four light fleet and seven escort carriers, four fast battleships, eight light cruisers, 28 destroyers, 33 escorts, an auxiliary anti-aircraft ship, three fast minelayers and 22 submarines under command and on station at the time of its enemy's unconditional surrender, the British Pacific Fleet was the most powerful single strike force assembled by Britain in the course of the Second World War and, relative to its own time, was probably as powerful a force as any raised by the Royal Navy at any stage in its long history.

One committed such comments to paper nearly ten years ago, and if in the meantime a series of fiftieth anniversary commemorations have ensured a number of books on Britain, the war against Japan, and the British Pacific Fleet, one remains convinced that the last still awaits its historian.

War and Paradox

From an American perspective the story of the war against Japan is told in terms of a journey across the Pacific marked by signposts that, over years of repetition, have become all but very familiar friends. Over some four decades Pearl Harbor, the battles in the Coral Sea, off Midway Islands, and in the Solomons, the landings on Tarawa and in the Marshalls, the Great Marianas Turkey Shoot, Leyte and Luzon, Iwo Jima and Mount Suribachi, and finally the B-29 raids, have provided the standard framework upon which the narrative of the Pacific war has rested, irrespective of the story of this war being told in terms of events, service, or personality.

In one obvious sense, that histories of this war should be so structured is right, and on two counts. First, the issue of war is invariably decided upon the battlefield. In the present century no war between great powers has been decided without either the reality of a military decision—on land, at sea, and in the air—having been reached or the recognition by one side either of its inability to secure victory by military means or of the inevitability of its military defeat. The history of any war, including the war against Japan, cannot be told without reference to its military dimensions, and those campaigns that together resulted in the destruction of Japan's ambition form the rightful terms of reference of this war's story. Second, this destruction of Japan's ambition was American-induced and was accomplished primarily in the Pacific.

But in another sense an account of the war against Japan that employs such terms of reference is necessarily flawed because it cannot provide more than a partial and incomplete account and interpretation of events. Just as the Second World War was two partially concurrent wars that were, at one and the same time, largely separated but related to one another, so the war against Japan was militarily two conflicts. The war on the Asian mainland was no less important than the war in the Pacific, if not in terms of the outcome of the war against Japan then in the shaping of the postwar order in eastern and Southeast Asia. But no less significantly the history of the present century reveals that wars between great powers necessarily involve nonmilitary dimensions that, though hard to quantify and assess, nevertheless provide the wider context of armed struggle. This century's world wars have been total wars, and acknowledgment of the totality of war is to admit that military matters cannot account for more than a part of war, to admit that aspects of military victory and defeat cannot explain more than a single part of the result of a war. Thus for Japan defeat in 1945 embraced every aspect of its war effort but one, and such was the nature of the war it initiated that even in that one aspect of its war effort that remained unbroken—the willingness of its armed forces to resist and to accept death as the means of continuing resistance—there was no compensation for a defeat that was otherwise comprehensive and total. It was a defeat that embraced its armies in Burma, northern China, and Manchuria, and the more important of its garrisons in the Pacific. It was a defeat that reduced the Japanese navy to impotent irrelevance. It was a defeat made obvious in the summer of 1945 by American control of the skies over the home islands. It was a defeat that was political in at least two respects: that Japan had but weak, dependent associates with which to oppose an alliance the leading members of which were individually much more powerful than Japan itself; that Japan had singularly failed to secure active and genuine endorsement on the part of the various peoples that had come under its control since 1937. It was a defeat that had obvious financial and industrial dimensions and such, by August 1945, was Japan's economic exhaustion that even if the Allied powers had then halted all air, naval, and amphibious operations against the home islands it is doubtful if Japan could have sustained itself into spring 1946.

Such was the totality of Japan's defeat in war that little purpose is served by trying to assess the relative importance of its various aspects. It cannot be doubted, however, that there was an interdependence of these different aspects of defeat, that they fed off one another. Moreover, it cannot be doubted that, even though the Soviet Union's entry into the war was critical in Japan's decision to end the war in order to avoid the prospects of Soviet occupation and social revolution, the major agent of Japan's defeat was the United States: equally it cannot be doubted that the most immediately apparent aspects of Japan's national failure were the all-but-total destruction of the Imperial Navy and Japan's industrial prostration. But understanding the various aspects of Japan's defeat is rendered difficult by the fact that evidence suggests that, unlike Germany in the Second World War, Japan never had any realistic prospect of not being defeated in the war that it initiated, that the Pacific war from its start was for Japan something akin to a national *kamikaze* effort. Such an assessment poses obvious problems of interpretation: if Japan's defeat was unavoidable, then no single aspect of that defeat was decisive and no single battle or campaign was of singular importance.

Such an argument is seductive and its logic hard to dispute. Short of the United States of America slipping beneath the surface of the sea under the weight of the war material it produced between 1940 and 1945, there seems to have been no means by which Japan could have saved itself from defeat in the Second World War. Clearly, and indisputably, Japan's defeat stemmed from its fundamental failure to understand the nature of the war that it had initiated, if not in summer 1937 then in December 1941. Nations so mismatched that the defeat of one is as assured and predictable as the victory of the other normally arrange their affairs accordingly, and by means other than war.

This interpretation of events presents a problem for historians that is seldom recognized by those whose explanation of events is mere description: How does one *explain* an inevitable defeat? Put another way, When did Japan's cause pass recall? The obvious answer is on 7 December 1941, with the Japanese success in uniting American public opinion behind a total war effort that could result only in either total victory or total defeat for the United States in the Pacific. Perhaps more accurately, the answer should be three days earlier, on 4 December, when the 1st Carrier Striking Force received confirmation of its orders to proceed with its attack on Pearl Harbor: this was perhaps the moment of truth, the last opportunity to have shaped events to a different end. But as individuals we tend to find such interpretation aesthetically unpleasing, preferring to look instead at battlefield events as marking the point when Fortune changed sides, when the issue of success and failure was decided. Under such terms of reference several battles and dates commend themselves for consideration wherein Japan's fate was sealed, the most obvious being when the cutting edge of Japanese naval power was destroyed off Midway Islands on 4 June 1942. But the idea of a "decisive battle" cannot be reconciled to that of an inevitable outcome: if the defeat of Japan was assured from the time that its carriers struck the U.S. Pacific Fleet, Midway could only be a milestone on a road, not a signpost where the road divided. But the very idea of "decisive battle," in which the Imperial Navy believed until it ceased to exist, is flawed. At this time navies, no less than armies and air forces, were so large and diverse, and possessed such immense powers of recuperation, that no single defeat could be decisive. In terms of the Pacific war one looks not to a single battle, Midway, but to the series of actions fought between May and November 1942 that resulted in the wresting of the initiative from the Japanese.

In this there is a matter of very considerable historical interest because it raises the fundamental question of the basis of war. If one considers naval warfare in its historical context then one cannot but admit the primacy of the British naval experience: for good or ill, British naval power and the British experience of war at sea have shaped our perspective of naval warfare. Yet that perspective is generally impaired in the sense that conventional wisdom suggests that British naval victories were the cause of British naval supremacy, whereas they were the result. Clearly, the relationship between victory and supremacy is two-way, but in the making of British naval supremacy the advantages conferred by geographical position, depth of financial resources, superiority of manpower, and skills of seamanship were the basis of victories that confirmed that supremacy. The Pacific war is interesting in part because it was perhaps the only occasion when ownership of the Trident passed from owner to successor without their fighting one another for its possession, but the Pacific war is also interesting in part because the relationship between victory and supremacy most obviously changed in its course. To borrow and amend a saying, after Midway the initiative was like a gun lying in the street: it was there for either side to pick up and use. The United States seized and then fought to retain the initiative, and it did so with a series of victories that provided supremacy after November 1942. But after September 1943, and with a wartime fleet that had in large measure replaced the prewar fleet that had won the critical battles of the previous year, victory was the product of supremacy. Lest this be doubted, a consideration of Japanese shipping losses, specifically in July 1945 but more generally in the last four months of the war, reveals the obvious: these losses were not the cause but the reflection of Japan's defeat. In real terms, however, the end of the Pacific war can be dated with the American descent upon the Gilbert Islands in November 1943. In terms of the certainty of the outcome of events, the decision of the war had been reached by the time that the Americans gathered for Operation GALVANIC task forces that were so powerful that the outcome of this enterprise, indeed the outcome of the war itself, was assured: thereafter, the advances across the Pacific were primarily a matter of technique, the application of supremacy, and the only questions that remained to be settled after Tarawa were the manner and timing of Japan's final defeat and the cost that would be exacted in the making.

RELATIVE POSITIONS

Such was the extent of Japan's misunderstanding of the nature of the war that was unleashed on 7 December 1941, and of the American society against which it pitted itself, and such was the discrepancy of power between Japan and its enemies, that it is difficult, indeed impossible, to see how, after the outbreak of war, events could have been shaped to a different end. But if only in two respects, it is possible to see how events could have been shaped differently. The first may be considered with reference to a historical experience that is seldom recalled by Western historians. The years 1407–8 saw Chinese naval forces invade Sumatra and exact tribute from the peoples that lived along the Strait of Malacia, while between 1408 and 1411 Chinese forces invaded and conquered Ceylon. Between 1412 and 1415 Chinese forces established themselves on the Strait of Hormuz, and as late as 1431–33 were active in the Red Sea and exacted tribute from Mecca. One wonders what would have been the effect had the Japanese at Easter 1942 followed the Chinese example instead of conducting a one-off raid against Ceylon even as divisions not needed to complete the occupation of Burma were in the Indian Ocean en route to Rangoon. One instinctively dismisses the suggestion that Britain could have been forced from the war after the United States had entered it, but a Japanese occupation of Ceylon and rampage through the western Indian Ocean could well have brought down the Raj, severed the only route to a theater where the Allied powers were in overland contact with one another, cut Britain's access to its oil supplies, and broken Britain's supply lines with its forces in Egypt. There was precious little that the British could have done to counter a Japanese move in what was perhaps *the* Allied "center of gravity" at a time of crippling weakness, and it may be that a Japanese effort in this theater, by adding to the defeats of the previous four months, would have driven Britain from the war. The counterarguments to this view need little in the way of elaboration. The enormous distances involved in such an effort, the need to have coordinated this endeavor with a corresponding German undertaking in the eastern Mediterranean, and the fact that even a success in driving Britain from the war would have availed Japan little if anything in terms of the prosecution of the war in the Pacific present themselves as such formidable objections to an Indian Ocean alternative in April 1942 that the latter may be dismissed from serious practical consideration. But a second alternative may not be so lightly dismissed, and it is the reverse image of the first, not a British elimination from the war but a major British involvement in the Pacific war in 1944–45.

The opportunity for such an involvement presented itself but fleetingly in late 1943 and is but little known. Over the last decade or so a series of works have added much to our understanding of the formation of Allied strategy in the course of the Second World War, but the war against Japan is one that remains, at least for the British, a somewhat neglected and little understood conflict. Certainly the cause of understanding has not been helped by the way in which policy, and particularly British policy, evolved. The threads of continuity are not easy to discern amid the interminable intricacies of Anglo-American conferences, the rustle of forms in triplicate, and the maze of places with unpronounceable names throughout the Far East. One suspects, moreover, that for the British another factor has been at work, that with the removal by infirmity and death of those involved in these proceedings, the contraction of British power and influence in the Far East has been attended by a contraction of interest. Not altogether surprisingly, the British dimension to the Pacific war is little known to, and of even less interest to, the United States, particular five decades after the event.

This book concerns itself with the wartime formation of British policy, specifically the search, after the summer of 1943, for a strategy for the war against Japan. As Ismay, Churchill's chief of staff, noted at the time, this story is not an edifying one. It is also a very complicated one, and the purpose of this introduction is to set out the terms of reference, the events, and the various problems that attended this British search for a strategy, thereby providing a guide to the process whereby policy was settled after September 1943. The remainder of this introduction thus divides into two parts: a basic definition of the problems that beset the formation of policy and an examination of the main features of policy as it evolved. But in noting the problems one must begin by noting that in the evolution of British policy there are two quite distinct phases, the watershed between them being September 1943. In the first phase, between December 1941 and September 1943, the British were forced to respond to events beyond their control and to fight where they were rather than where they would. This meant, in effect, the border between India and Burma. In the second phase, during and after September 1943, an element of choice entered British calculations because the surrender of the Italian fleet, and the crippling of the *Tirpitz*, freed British naval forces from home waters and the Mediterranean for service in the Far East at the very time when the British command turned its attention to the question of when, in which theater, and with what forces Britain should expand its effort against Japan. In the event this question came to revolve upon the issue of the employment of the fleet, in large measure because the element of choice seemingly available to the British high command in late 1943 proved largely illusory.

With respect to the period between December 1941 and September 1943, the basic terms of reference for the British settling of policy were determined by the events of the first six months. Between December 1941 and May 1942, the Allied powers suffered a series of defeats throughout Southeast Asia: Britain, specifically, incurred defeats on Borneo, at Hong Kong, in the southwest Pacific, and in Malaya and Burma. These defeats brought home certain inescapable facts: that despite a global presence Britain lacked global power; that the British operational timetable for the war against Japan had to wait upon events in the German war; that the Mediterranean theater had second claim upon British resources and attention; that, by extension, the Indian Ocean and Southeast Asia held no more than a tertiary position in the British order of priorities, and that the Pacific, in effect, had no position whatsoever. It was within this context that the negative British view of Burma took shape. For the British high command, Burma possessed no intrinsic military, economic, or political value that made reconquest mandatory. Britain's view, ironically, was a mirror image of that of the enemy. For the British and the Japanese alike the Chindwin and the Bay of Bengal were a line of mutual exhaustion, convenient to both. Neither had the means to undertake major offensive operations in these theaters, and both Japan and Britain would have preferred, if left to their own devices, to have accepted a standoff here in order to devote their resources and attentions to other, more important theaters.

Burma, however, possessed a value for the Allies that made obligatory the commitment that the British did not want. The point, often forgotten, was that Britain, in terms of its position in China and freedom of action in the Far East, was one of the real losers at Pearl Harbor.[1] The United States entered the war as the dominant force or at least influence in Asia, and it possessed the means to force Britain to conform to its will with regard to the prosecution of the war in eastern Asia. It entered the war with the belief that Japan's defeat had to be comprehensive and embrace both mainland Asia and the Pacific: there could be no question of Japan's being defeated unless its armies in Manchoutikuo, China, and French Indo-China were engaged and defeated in battle. To this end the United States harbored a dual intention toward China: to prepare the Chinese army for large-scale offensive operations on the mainland, and to ready southwestern China as a base for air operations against Japanese-occupied territories on the mainland and against the Japanese home islands. To Washington, China was essential to the Allied cause, and for China to play an effective part in that cause it was essential that overland communications with Chungking be restored. These overland communications had to pass through Burma because only through

Burma could the Nationalist armies of Chiang Kai-shek be supplied by road on the scale necessary to play the role assigned them in the American scheme of things. Burma, therefore, had to be reconquered in order to reestablish overland communications with the Chinese Nationalists.

Leaving aside the fact that Britain did not agree with the American view of the value of China to the common cause, American attitudes gave rise to three sets of related problems. The two strands of American policy—the military and air designs for China—were supposedly complementary but were in fact in rivalry; there was the problem of ordering priorities; and there were difficulties directly associated with the reestablishment of overland communications with China. These second and third problems had their basis in the geography and conditions of northeast India and Burma. In terms of the problems of defining priorities, northeast India lacked the administrative infrastructure to maintain an attempt to invade Burma and it lacked the administrative infrastructure to maintain an airlift into China. The needs of an offensive into Burma and an airlift into China were mutually exclusive, but the effort needed to develop northeast India for either or both could not take precedence over two efforts that had to be made immediately and simultaneously. There was, in short, a clash between political imperative and military necessity that was never properly resolved.

In terms of the problems associated with the reestablishment of overland communications with China, these crystallized at different levels. As far as the British high command was concerned, there was no prospect of significant deliveries to China being possible before 1946 or 1947, by which time the impact of China upon events could not be anything other than marginal. With only some 6 percent of all Allied ground troops in Southeast Asia in the engineers compared to 16 percent in the southwest Pacific, the service support that was needed to meet different and conflicting commitments in India was not available. Even discounting the engineering resources needed to develop the transportation infrastructure of northeast India and the airlift, the assault engineers needed in the vanguard of an advance into Burma were the same engineers needed to develop the lines of communication that would support the advance—and, of course, engineers cannot be relied upon to accomplish one task, still less two. Moreover, as the British planning staffs made their calculations, it transpired that if a road through Upper Burma was secured but the enemy remained intact in central Burma, then the logistical requirements of the forces needed to guard the road to China would equal the carrying capacity of the road itself. These various considerations convinced the British high command that the whole idea of pushing a road south from Ledo to join the old Burma Road around Bhamo was nonsense,[2] but in reality such a view was as much a rationalization as a reason because the British high command had no particular interest in any campaign in Burma per se. For the British high command, a campaign in Burma represented a most hazardous and uncertain undertaking because it would involve a long and exhausting approach to contact by forces moving through the mountains and forests of the border area against an enemy that had the choice of where, when, and how to counterattack, and to make these choices on the basis of possession of good and secure lines of communication through the Irrawaddy and Sittang Valleys.

The obvious counter to these advantages, as the Americans argued, was to mount converging attacks along external lines of communication but, as the British high command noted, this solution depended for success upon an effective Chinese contribution from Yunnan. But the Chinese armies in Yunnan could only contribute effectively to the clearing of Upper Burma if first supplied by the very road that their efforts were designed to open. This Catch-22 situation was but one aspect of the phenomenon whereby for every American solution there was an unanswerable British objection,[3] but this conundrum was but one aspect of insoluble Allied problems. If the British moved into Upper Burma and went over to the defensive, then the resultant commitment would be greater than the existing commitment in Assam and Manipur and could not be sustained on the basis of present and planned resources. Moreover, the only alternative to a long-term defensive commitment in Upper Burma was to attempt the overland reconquest of Burma from the north. Until October 1944 this was rejected by Allied planners as unrealistic. Even if a road south from Ledo to Bhamo was opened, it would extend no further than 250 of the 750 miles to Rangoon and Allied planners accepted that an advance of 500 miles without any effective line of communication was not a feasible proposition.

Given this calculation, the British believed that the only way that Burma could be reconquered was by a campaign that involved holding operations in Upper Burma, securing the Arakan for its airfields, and an assault landing at Rangoon followed by an advance through the Irrawaddy and Sitting Valleys and a battle of encirclement and annihilation in central Burma (Operation ANAKIM). The conceptual problem here, however, was that if Britain indeed acquired the means to conduct ANAKIM then it had every incentive not to do so. For Britain there were other more prestigious and valuable targets than Rangoon in Southeast Asia, and if the Japanese held Burma in strength, as indeed they did, then there was every reason for the British to bypass rather than attempt to reconquer Burma.

Such was the basis of the CULVERIN alternative, the idea of landings in northern Sumatra and Malaya that were to end with the recapture of Singapore. But the idea, while sound, was never a practical proposition. Most certainly in the first phase of the British search for a strategy the army in India, at least before February 1944, was of very uncertain quality and could not be reinforced from Europe. Neither amphibious nor naval forces could be made available on the scale necessary for such an enterprise until Germany and Italy were defeated, and, crucially, the Americans would not accept any proposed amphibious strategy that left the Burma situation unchanged.[4] Moreover, India could not maintain either the amphibious shipping or the naval forces required for this operation in addition to its existing and planned commitments. By any standard, however unexacting, when it came to the formation of policy for the war against Japan, the British found themselves snookered.

In the second phase of policymaking, after September 1943, the British high command found that its attitude toward the United States was thrown into confusion, and its strategic deliberations all but wrecked, by a quickening tempo of the war in the Pacific which forced a choice between mutually exclusive alternatives. For Churchill there was a fear of the uses to which American power could be put in the reordering of the postwar world, and he most clearly resented Britain's dependence upon the United States and his country's loss of the power of decision: in this period much of Churchill's behavior conformed to the de Gaulle syndrome, which is the penchant for increasingly divisive activity as the power of decision diminishes. Churchill believed that, because the Americans could defeat Japan, and could defeat Japan without the support of any ally, and because American primacy in the Pacific left Britain without a role in that theater, Britain had to make its effort in Southeast Asia in order to expunge the shame of defeat: Britain had to recover its lost colonies by its own efforts and not be dependent for their return upon American largess. The British Chiefs of Staff, on the other hand, regarded the United States as an ally that had to be supported rather than a power against which provision had to be made. They believed that Britain's priority had to be the fastest possible end to the Japanese war and that recovering lost colonies after the war's end was as good as fighting for them. The service heads believed that making the British effort in the main theater of operations offered the best prospect of the earliest possible end to the war, that a naval commitment in the Pacific would be cheaper in manpower terms than any other effort, and that making an all-out effort in the Pacific would stand Britain well when it came to securing postwar American loans.

The views of Churchill and the Chiefs of Staff were mutually exclusive because there was no single base from which British forces could operate in both the Indian Ocean and the Pacific. But, as they considered policy, both sides to this argument were forced to admit the imperial connection. It was increasingly recognized, by both parties, that India could not be expected to shoulder any increased commitment, and that Canada had no wish to be involved in any imperial effort as it sought to forge its own bilateral arrangements in the Pacific with the United States. In addition, both Churchill and the Chiefs of Staff knew that New Zealand was unable to provide effective support for any British effort and that, in short, there was a reversal of the traditional relationship whereby Britain had been able to rely upon imperial support. In 1943–44 India and the Dominions looked to Britain to support them by sending forces that would lighten the load upon themselves. But while the British high command sympathized with India's problems, was prepared to indulge the Canadians, and was willing to support New Zealand, Australia was in a category of its own. Indeed, a reading of Anglo-Australian exchanges in 1943 and 1944 prompts the thought that the Bodyline Tour had never ended.[5]

These exchanges were riddled with ambiguity, but an ambiguity laced with considerable suspicion and dislike that was an inauspicious background to the consideration of matters of national and alliance priorities. There can be little doubt that Churchill viewed all things Australian with loathing, especially when they came in the shape of John Curtin. Churchill's antipathy to the Dominion extended to a refusal even to inform Australia of the SEXTANT agreement, to enter into any form of policy discussion with the Australians, and even, at the Dominions Prime Ministers' Conference in May 1944, to pass the relevant discussion papers to the Australians except at a time when they could not be read before meetings. Fueling this animosity was a British Treasury that insisted that Australia should pay through the nose for everything and denied terms that were available to Canada and New Zealand. The Chiefs of Staff and the Royal Navy were not beyond trying to treat Australia as a colony that would do what it was told. The Chiefs of Staff had no regard for the Australian prime minister, whom they regarded as MacArthur's stool pigeon, but if they possessed a rasping contempt for Blamey then at least they demonstrated inestimable good taste on that particular score.

On the matter of strategic policy, moreover, Anglo-Australian relations were somewhat schizophrenic. For their part, the Australians deeply resented their exclusion from the policymaking process, but while Curtin sought to ensure MacArthur's South West Pacific Command against any attempted takeover by the British, other members of the Australian high command saw a British return to the Pacific as essential to counterbalance their being casually and ungraciously discarded by the Americans as the battle moved away from their country's shores. These Australians, indeed even Curtin, believed that their country had carried the imperial banner in the Pacific since 1942 and they wanted a British and imperial effort in order to compensate for Australia's progressive weakening as the Second World War entered its fifth year.

The British Chiefs of Staff, and even Churchill in his more reasoned moments, were aware of the immense effort that Australia had made and the manpower and financial problems that it faced in 1944. Yet, unfortunately if unavoidably, London in 1944 saw Australia as a land of plenty, which the latter manifestly was not. The year opened with the British staff planning to send six divisions, lift for three divisions, a fleet with fifteen carriers and eight battleships, and 140 Royal Air Force squadrons to the Pacific, some 675,000 military personnel plus labor and support workers being penciled in for movement to Australia. The year also opened with the British high command casually assuming that Australia could accommodate and provide for such numbers, but as the year progressed two matters became clear: that everything that was required for these forces from building materials to prime movers, from hospital equipment to every form of general and specialist labor, would have to be sent to Australia, and that Britain did not have such resources to send. At the same time, the Royal Navy calculated that shortages of air groups would mean that no more than three fleet carriers could be maintained in the Pacific, and it was forced to deal with the difficulties presented by the lack of an oceanic fleet train. But in order to prestock an Australian base in readiness for the arrival of the fleet and to have an oceanic fleet train on hand, merchantmen would have to be taken from service—for refitting and the run to Australia—at a time when Britain's merchant fleet could not meet minimum import requirements. This was at a time, too, when the demands on the merchant fleet would increase with the invasion of Europe, and when it was realized, for the first time, that paradoxically demands on British shipping would increase still further with the surrender of Germany. To compound these problems, in 1944 British planning was based on the assumption that it would take between eleven and eighteen months to prepare a base in Australia, yet in the course of 1944 Britain found itself squeezed between a lengthening of the German war into 1945 at the same time as the planning end of the Japanese war was moved forward at least into 1945 if not into 1946.

The shortage of imperial and British resources of all descriptions was, however, only one aspect of the problems that in the course of 1944 resulted in the major change in British policy. In the course of this year the army commitment all but disappeared: it seems MacArthur indicated that he would not accept Indian Army divisions in the southwest Pacific and the British high command realized that postwar occupation duties in Europe precluded any significant reinforcement of the Far East. The sheer scale of American air power in the Pacific meant that the RAF in effect was discounted from serious consideration. A fleet train was improvised but only at the cost of abandoning any amphibious ambitions, although in part this was unavoidable anyway: British amphibious shipping was largely shore-to-shore rather than ship-to-shore as required in the Far East. The postponement of OVERLORD, the subsequent failure to secure a working port until November, and the inability to raise 125,000 seamen needed to provide a corps-sized lift in the Far East conspired to kill the amphibious option. In the course of 1944, therefore, the Royal Navy, in the form of its carriers, changed from being the first of the services that were to arrive in the Far East to being the only one likely to arrive in any significant strength before the defeat of Japan was accomplished, with all the political and psychological investment that fact entailed. This, combined with the fact that there was no base common to an Indian Ocean strategy and a Pacific strategy, was to explain why the struggle within the British high command over policy was so difficult, so bitter, and so protracted. Lest the point be missed, the Chiefs of Staff at their meeting of 21 February 1944 determined upon collective resignation if Churchill tried to insist upon a Southeast Asia commitment for political reasons. In effect, the service chiefs claimed to be the better judges of national interest than the duly appointed head of government—an engaging state of affairs given the long-established principle of civilian control of the military in Britain. Perhaps two points emerge from this little-known episode: specifically, the danger of seeing Churchill and the British high command as one and the same, and, generally, the confusion of political, economic, and military issues in the sense that distinction between these aspects of governance is blurred to the point of being meaningless at this level of command.

Such were the problems that at various times beset the British search for a strategy for the war against Japan and which largely explain why this search became, specifically, a search for a naval strategy. Lest the story of this search be compromised by an examination of events in this introduction, note at this time need only be taken of certain aspects, specific to the first phase of British deliberations, of developments.

In terms of the unfolding of events, the period between May 1942 and May 1943 was marked by the frantic build-up in northeast India and the start of the airlift, the development of the ANAKIM plan and its acceptance by the Americans and Chinese as the basis of strategic policy in February 1943, and the disastrous first Arakan offensive. The latter is the dominant event and it is often argued that it was the failure of first Arakan that pushed the British into CULVERIN. This was partly true, but in reality the CULVERIN proposal was on the table in September 1943 before the first Arakan offensive began. It had taken shape and commanded considerable support well before disaster overwhelmed the 14th Indian Division in the Arakan. CULVERIN gained support on five counts. First was the realization that the Arakan offensive would fail. Second was the desire to cut the lines of communication between Singapore and Rangoon. Third was the belief, which subsequent calculations suggested was wrong, that CULVERIN would involve fewer resources than ANAKIM, this misapprehension being combined with the natural desire to seek out the more weakly held objective. Finally, and least credibly, was the idea of a double envelopment of the southern resources area. The landings in Sumatra and Malaya were to be accompanied by landings on Timor.

With or without the Timor absurdity, the whole CULVERIN concept was nonsense. If northern Sumatra had been occupied Britain would have been left with two open-ended commitments at a time when it could not meet one. A plan to secure northern Sumatra as a base for air operations made little sense when no heavy bombers were available for operations. The plan could not be effected before the end of the war in Europe, and it did nothing to solve the problem of Burma. Critically, however, the CULVERIN idea left the

British with no proposals for the 1943–44 campaigning season in Burma, and this became patently obvious in the period between TRIDENT and QUAD-RANT. Between these conferences the British high command abandoned CULVERIN as impracticable, but at QUADRANT, by accepting the American offer to provide air support for a Chindit operation, the British found themselves tied to an Upper Burma commitment. But at QUADRANT, too, the British accepted, as the basis of future planning, the American insistence that the defeat of Japan should follow within one year of the defeat of Germany, which was set for October 1944. The implications of this timetable were quickly appreciated by British planners. If the Americans were to arrive in the western Pacific in early 1945, as would be necessary if Japan was to be defeated by October 1945, then China, and the efforts to be made in and from that country, ceased to have any relevance. If China could be discounted from serious consideration then so, too, could Burma. Therefore, within three months of having discarded CULVERIN as impracticable, the British high command found itself thrown back upon CULVERIN or some amphibious alternative in Southeast Asia, but not ANAKIM, as the only strategic possibility that presented itself in this theater. It is with this appreciation, and the predictable American failure to agree with this analysis, that the first chapter of this book opens.

The subject of these pages is the second phase of the British search for a strategy for the war against Japan, from the time, in the immediate aftermath of QUADRANT, that the Twelve-Month Plan presented itself to the time, in October 1944, when decisions held over from OCTAGON were made and which ended the British quest: the end of the Japanese war in August 1945 in effect meant that British decisions made in and after November 1944 could not be implemented before Japan's surrender in August 1945. *Grave of a Dozen Schemes* traces the evolution of British policy through various obscure episodes such as the formulation of the XYZ/WXYZ options, the AXIOM Mission, the deployment of the Japanese fleet to Singapore in February 1944 and the dispatch of the *Saratoga* and *Richelieu* to the Indian Ocean as a result, the development of the Middle Strategy and then the Modified Middle Strategy, and the emergence, and then the disappearance, of an ANAKIM variant as part of an incongruous British policy proposal that survived OCTAGON but not the month that followed.

In so doing this book provides, in this introduction, comment on Burma, commitment and campaign, sufficient to explain why Burma formed the point of reference in British strategic deliberations. Burma, at one and the same time, was both central and marginal to the British search for a strategy for the war against Japan. Burma represented the inescapable commitment, the one to which all British arguments had to return, but British deliberations between September 1943 and October 1944 for the most part were concerned with options outside Burma that were not wholly dependent upon Burma. Thus the Burma dimension to British deliberations has been described, in this introduction, in some detail in order that it should not intrude upon the wider story of British policymaking and thereby further complicate a story that is confused enough even without it.

In so doing, this book tells the story of the British search for a strategy for the war against Japan in terms of the problems and aspirations that vied with one another for attention during the deliberations of the British high command. At issue, between September 1943 and August 1944, was the question whether an expanded British effort in the Far East should take the form of an amphibious undertaking in Southeast Asia or a naval commitment in the Pacific. But, inevitably, the summary of the issue is more easily related than its unfolding, beset as the latter was by intractable problems that reflected national exhaustion and which forced all but constant adjustment, with its attendant confusion, upon a harassed, distracted British high command. Relations with Commonwealth partners, problems of manpower, the ordering of priorities as a result of conflicting claims of amphibious formations and naval forces, the mutually exclusive virtues of various operations, the abstract requirements of national prestige and questions of administrative margins, and the realization that these Commonwealth partners could not provide the facilities and support that were essential if Britain was to expand its war effort in the Far East—these were the more important of the intractable problems that bore down upon the British high command and which shaped British decisions. Each of these problems was complicated, in its detail and its unfolding, in large measure because none presented itself complete at any single stage of proceedings but rather moved erratically to center stage on separate and successive occasions and in some way slightly but significantly different from its previous guise. *Grave of a Dozen Schemes* makes no attempt to trace the individual stories of these very different and deep-rooted problems and is content to afford them consideration only on those occasions when, individually, they forced themselves to the forefront of British deliberations. At its end this record of events does not examine these problems but merely recounts the record of military developments after October 1944 to set against the attitudes and calculations of those responsible for the conduct of the nation's affairs. These various problems that emerged at different times to confound British calculations and proceedings are each worthy of full and proper consideration in their own right, and no doubt future students will afford them such treatment and, in setting out these stories and their conclusions, force revision of these pages. But that it a matter for the future: it is with the aftermath of QUAD-RANT that *Grave of a Dozen Schemes* presently concerns itself.

CHAPTER ONE

A Very Dangerous Condition

From QUADRANT to SEXTANT

*T*he most significant of the decisions made at the QUADRANT conference
was the higher priority afforded the conduct of the war against Japan.
While the Germany-first principle was reaffirmed, the implementation of an
offensive strategy against Japan was no longer to wait upon the defeat of
Germany but was to be put into effect even as the Anglo-American effort in
Europe reached its peak. After QUADRANT, in the words of one American
historian, "there was no longer any talk of holding a line in the Pacific until
Germany should be defeated."[1] The corollary, of course, was obvious: the
increased priority accorded the war against Japan demanded the definition of a
coherent strategy because improvisation could no longer form the basis of policy.

But like the TRIDENT conference before it, QUADRANT left unresolved more
than it settled, and the shift in favor of a more active prosecution of the
Japanese war could not disguise the fact that there was no agreement either
within the American high command or between Washington and London on
how this was to be achieved. Given the stage of planning reached on both sides
of the Atlantic before QUADRANT, such a state of affairs was unavoidable; this
QUADRANT acknowledged with the decision that the planners continue their
various studies in order to develop proposals that would allow the Combined
Chiefs of Staff to settle the main features of policy at the next Anglo-
American conference. Thus the planners were instructed to draw up a plan
for a strategic air offensive against Japan and to conduct no fewer than six
studies based on the assumption that Germany would be defeated on or by
1 October 1944. One of these studies was to provide an overall plan for the
defeat of Japan within one year of that of Germany, the remaining five concerned options in Southeast Asia. These options were defined as a landing in
northern Sumatra in May 1944 (FIRST CULVERIN); an advance southward
from Upper Burma after November 1944 (TRIUMPHANT); landings, at times

17

that remained unspecified, at Moulmein and on the Kra with a view to advancing on Bangkok (SCEPTRE); a "direct assault" on Singapore on the assumption that northern Sumatra had already been secured (CULVERIN/SECOND CULVERIN); and landings on Akyab (BULLFROG) and Ramree (LYNCHPIN). These options were to be examined in relation to one another, and BULLFROG and LYNCHPIN were to be examined in relation to planned operations in Upper Burma.[2]

On the last day of the QUADRANT conference, 24 August, the combined planners, in order to eliminate unnecessary duplication of effort, agreed upon a division of duties, schedules, and liaison arrangements that would ensure the proper coordination of their studies. The American planners were to work on the Twelve-Month and bombing plans, and three British officers from the Joint Staff Mission were to help in the preparation of the latter. This plan was to be completed by 15 September,[3] but while the Twelve-Month Plan was to be submitted by 15 October the combined planners agreed that the two plans should be prepared in conjunction.[4] This seemingly awkward if not impossible arrangement was one that the Combined Chiefs of Staff were to approve on 17 September[5] at their first meeting after a draft plan for the strategic air offensive against Japan was presented by the Army Air Force (AAF) staff to the combined planners in Washington.[6] The British planners, with the help of two American officers seconded from Washington, were to examine the Southeast Asia options and complete their reports by 1 October.[7]

The British planners who had remained in London during QUADRANT were informed of these decisions on 25 August,[8] and on the basis of these arrangements divided the study of these options between the different sections of the staff.[9] Subsequently their original demarcation of duties was revised and supplemented,[10] though in the process the BULLFROG and LYNCHPIN studies appear to have fallen by the wayside.[11] BULLFROG remained approved and scheduled for the next campaigning season, but its planning was beset by a number of imponderables that made its cancellation likely: its prospects could not have been helped by India Command's recommendation that study of this operation be deferred until the end of the monsoon and the acquisition of fresh intelligence on which to finalize a plan of campaign. The authorities in Whitehall chose to order India Command to send two officers to London for consultations and to continue planning on the basis that its work could be made available to Mountbatten when South East Asia Command was activated.[12] The Joint Planning Staff in London, however, was to examine problems that bore directly upon BULLFROG, such as India's capacity to handle naval and amphibious forces that might be sent to the Indian Ocean[13] and schedules for the release of forces from the Mediterranean theater for operations across the Bay of Bengal. These arrangements, which in effect made Delhi primarily responsible for the BULLFROG study,[14] suggest that the Akyab option did not figure too highly in London's calculations. The remaining studies, however, were another matter. The final demarcation of duties within the Joint Planning Staff gave the Executive Planning Section responsibility for the examination of FIRST CULVERIN[15] and the Future Planning Section for CULVERIN and TRIUMPHANT,[16] the Joint Intelligence Staff being ordered to collaborate in these studies. The Strategical Planning Section was given the task of considering SCEPTRE,[17] and despite the division of responsibility for CULVERIN variants it was also instructed to examine the possibilities of mounting a full CULVERIN option at any time of year and not simply within its favored second-quarter slot.[18] In addition, the S. Section was to provide the British contribution to the Twelve-Month Plan and was to draw up proposals before certain of its members went to Washington in the first week of October for discussions with their American counterparts and the finalization of this particular plan.[19]

Between August 1943 and August 1944 the British planning effort for the war against Japan was plagued by distractions, confusion, and fundamental policy differences. Indeed, in this year it proved impossible for the British high command to settle national policy for the war against Japan. In effect, the only British decisions were formal cancellation of options that had passed by default. An inability to agree upon national priorities at the highest level of command was the most important single factor in the paralysis of the decisionmaking process. The fact that Churchill and the Chiefs of Staff could not decide between the conflicting claims of the Indian Ocean and the Pacific theaters lay at the heart of British difficulties. The higher priority of other theaters, and the dependence of policy for the war against Japan upon events in these other theaters, also contributed to the difficulties that attended British deliberations. But crucial in confusing the decisionmaking process in the autumn of 1943 was the national demarcation of duties agreed by the combined planners at QUADRANT. By this decision British planning attention was refocused on options in Southeast Asia that, for the most part, had been discounted before the conference, and it did so at a time when in effect the British planners were excluded from the preparation of the Twelve-Month Plan, yet forced to decide among the various options within Southeast Asia without knowing how these options might be reconciled to the Twelve-Month Plan. In some measure this would have happened anyway: the creation of South East Asia Command forced the British high command to define its mission and to do so outside the terms of reference that were to be supplied by the Twelve-Month Plan. But this apart, the QUADRANT decision had the effect of diverting British planning attention into a political and strategic cul-de-sac at a time when there was, very briefly, an opportunity to develop a combined Anglo-American approach to the war against Japan, and with it the possibility of a real British contribution to the war in the Pacific. In the event the British high command failed even to recognize this opportunity, and thereafter it was condemned to months of futile argument about options in Southeast Asia that were ever less relevant with the quickening of the American advances into the western Pacific.

The planning effort on both sides of the Atlantic began immediately after QUADRANT. In Washington this took the form of devising a new framework for the war, the Twelve-Month Plan, and defining how operations in the Pacific could be accelerated and a bombing effort so arranged as to fit within its terms of reference. All three aspects of this effort presented formidable problems. The initiative that had been won in the Pacific, and the local superiority that the United States commanded in each of its three main operational areas, presented not only opportunity but the dilemma of choice. Any attempt to accelerate the pace of the Pacific war automatically involved definition of priorities and of two relationships. The conflicting claims of the northern, central, and southwest Pacific areas had to be resolved, and in this process the interests of Nimitz's Pacific Ocean Areas and MacArthur's South West Pacific Command, and of the Army and Navy departments in Washington, had to be reconciled. In addition, the development of the air plan raised the problem of where an independently minded AAF fitted into a scheme in which the Army and Navy had already established their own spheres of influence.[20] American planning also necessarily involved a definition of relations with Britain and China. In setting about its planning, therefore, the American staffs faced problems with ramifications for interservice and alliance relations that were so obvious as to need no further elaboration.

In comparison the British should have had a much simpler task in preparing their studies, most of which were well advanced even before QUADRANT, but from the outset their efforts were dogged by problems that the physical dispersal of the high command after QUADRANT did nothing to ease. After QUADRANT Brooke and Portal took a short leave before returning to London while Churchill, his personal staff, and Pound, who was dying, traveled to Washington to stay as Roosevelt's guests at the White House. As a result, the Chiefs of Staff did not formally meet in full session in London after QUADRANT until 14 September, and Churchill, who returned to Britain in the *Renown*, did not arrive in London until the twentieth.[21] Thus the British high command did not reconvene until just ten days before the studies of options in Southeast Asia were to be completed, but by the time it did so events had conspired in a manner that served to confuse and misdirect the British planning effort.

This state of affairs flowed from two sources. The first was the Twelve-Month Plan. The initial study of this plan by the Strategical Planning Section raised the critical question of the place that operations in Southeast Asia occupied in the overall plan for the defeat of Japan. On 11 September the Strategical Planning Section sent a signal to the American staff to the effect that if, in accordance with the twelve-month schedule, Japan was to be defeated by October 1945, then it followed that Honshu would have to be invaded at that time and that a strategic bombing campaign would have to begin in mid-1945. Working from this premise, the S. Section stated that because such a timetable meant that either Hokkaido or Kyushu would have to be secured in the summer of 1945 and that Formosa would have to be secured in the spring, China would cease to figure in Allied calculations because there was no possibility it would be able to provide air and naval bases for Allied forces in time to meet such a schedule. Given the implications of such a line of reasoning for the British position in India and future operations in Burma, the British planners asked Washington for clarification and elaboration of American attitudes.[22]

The American reply to this request was made in three parts. In the first of the combined staff papers devoted to the Twelve-Month Plan to appear after QUADRANT, the American planners on the thirteenth acknowledged that a strategic air offensive could not be mounted in time to meet an October 1945 deadline. But they asserted that this was the result of a shortage of aircraft and shipping which could not be overcome. By using this particular, if not peculiar, argument, the American planners sought to sidestep the British intimation that a timetable devised under the Twelve-Month Plan and the plan to bomb Japan from bases in China could not be reconciled. The American planners, with the AAF reluctant to abandon its China plan because existing plans for the advance across the Pacific precluded securing bases from which to wage a strategic air offensive before 1947, dismissed the British observation with the assertion that "supplies to China when translated into military effort will pay enormous dividends to the United Nations in the war against Japan."[23]

At an informal meeting with British planners in Washington on the fourteenth, however, the American planners argued that while the defeat of Germany by 1 October 1944 was unlikely, this made no difference to the intention to secure the defeat of Japan as soon after victory in Europe as possible.[24] But in a signal to London on the same day the American planners adopted yet another line, arguing that the alternatives that now presented themselves were either an invasion of Japan without the preliminary aerial bombardment that had been envisaged or an invasion as scheduled but preceded by an air offensive mounted from bases in the Pacific.[25]

These exchanges took place when American planning was still tentative and when the U.S. staffs had been brought to the realization that their air plan, as it stood, was unworkable on a number of counts.[26] The first AAF paper setting out a plan for a strategic air offensive based upon the Marianas was presented to the American joint planners on the sixteenth,[27] just ten days after the same planners were presented with a timetable for operations that included the Marianas on the list of proposed American objectives for 1944.[28] But these matters notwithstanding, what was clear from this collective presentation of American arguments on the thirteenth and fourteenth was its disregard of the fact that the British planners, in their signal of the eleventh, had pinpointed the two weaknesses inherent in American strategic thinking: that the timings of the twelve-month schedule and the air plan did not hang together, and that the various administrative and operational aspects of the air plan were inconsistent. The different lines of reasoning employed by the American planners in the attempt to discount the British argument of the eleventh were a backhanded confirmation of its accuracy. Overall, however, the American argument was something more, namely notice to Britain that the United States intended to have its way over the air plan, irrespective of its present details. This became obvious, in the course of a somewhat tense exchange between American and British planners on the fifteenth,[29] the British not being slow to draw the appropriate conclusion. Despite their continuing belief that the air plan was riddled with inconsistencies and was incapable of being put into effect,[30] the British representatives at the meeting of the Combined Chiefs of Staff on the seventeenth made no attempt to oppose the American air plan,[31] a redrafted version of which had been submitted to the Joint Staff Mission on the previous day.[32] The available record gives no indication why on this occasion the British followed the line of least resistance in dealing with so flawed a proposal as this particular plan. It may be, however, that, with London not having settled proposals of its own, the British delegates saw no good reason to earn American resentment by opposing a draft plan when the problems that would confound American intentions would argue for themselves soon enough.[33]

These exchanges were crucially important in the British planning process but for a reason that is not immediately obvious. Before QUADRANT the British high command, in a hesitant and reluctant way, had come to recognize that an amphibious strategy in the Indian Ocean, whether in the form of ANAKIM or CULVERIN, was unrealistic. The QUADRANT studies breathed new life into these options, and the Twelve-Month Plan brought the amphibious options to the forefront of British attention for exactly the reasons that the Strategical Planning Section had set down in its signal of the eleventh: if China was shorn of a strategic role as a result of the Twelve-Month Plan then Burma fell from consideration *en passant*, and an amphibious strategy in the Indian Ocean reemerged despite itself as the only option available to the British in Southeast Asia. Moreover, the creation of a South East Asia Command under British auspices, with a British supreme commander in this British area of responsibility, reinforced this development: the only justification for such a command was operations on a scale and of a nature previously unknown in this theater.[34] By definition these had to be amphibious because there was no good reason to have such a command if its operational role was confined to Upper Burma. But by refusing to accept the logic of the Twelve-Month Plan with respect to China the Americans kept open every option in Southeast Asia, whether amphibious or otherwise. Burma, therefore, retained its place in the Allied strategic jigsaw with one result: the British planners in September 1943 were faced with a Burma option, an amphibious option, and an option that involved supporting operations in the Arakan without any definition of priority. Moreover, to compound these difficulties, the studies ordered at QUADRANT by mid-September had produced depressingly familiar conclusions. London and Delhi were divided on the question of what should be attempted in Upper Burma[35] and the Arakan studies were stymied. In addition, the initial examination of SCEPTRE revealed that one of the problems that had plagued earlier CULVERIN plans, namely the relationship between secondary operations and the main endeavor, threatened to jeopardize this option. In this case the problem was presented by the Andamans, the planners' calculation being that the group could not be bypassed and that its garrison therefore had to be eliminated before a landing on the Kra was attempted. An Andamans operations, however, represented an effort complete in its own right, and if executed would mean that a landing on the Kra could not take place in the same season. As a result of this discouraging conclusion, the Joint Planning Staff on 16 September halted the SCEPTRE study[36] and ordered the Future Planning Section to examine the question of an Andamans operation.[37] In this way one more amphibious option in the Indian Ocean was added to the QUADRANT list.

Equally discouraging for the British high command was the fact that by 16 September its remaining CULVERIN options had foundered on two quite separate counts. First, after QUADRANT the Joint Planning Staff ordered a review of the forces needed to execute the various CULVERIN options then under consideration. By the eleventh it had become clear that neither could Britain provide nor could India maintain forces on the scale needed if an operation such as FIRST CULVERIN was to proceed.[38] The Executive Planning Section, therefore, was ordered to review the whole question of the forces that could be required, their availability, and the administrative margins on which they would function. On the sixteenth it reported that the fleet that could be assembled in the Indian Ocean in the spring of 1944 could not exceed three capital ships, three fleet and six escort carriers, ten cruisers, and twenty-five destroyers.[39] Given such numbers it was clear that such an operation as CULVERIN, which would involve the use of twenty-five escort carriers, twelve cruisers, and 134 destroyers and escorts, plus 1,458 landing ships and craft,[40] could not proceed. Second, the detailed examination of operational aspects of FIRST CULVERIN proved distinctly pessimistic because not only would an invasion of northern Sumatra involve having to maintain the equivalent of five divisions across open beaches during the monsoon, but Sabang itself could not be assaulted. Intelligence estimates, which were the subject of dispute between London and Delhi,[41] credited the Japanese with a 9,000-strong garrison on the island. With Sabang's two beaches that were suitable for assault each limited to a brigade frontage, an attack on the island was clearly problematical.

As a result of its findings, the Executive Planning Section took the unusual step of submitting an incomplete report on 16 September with the observation that it could see "little profit in preparing a further outline plan which it is most unlikely can be implemented."[42] Evidently the Executive Planning Section was instructed, in no uncertain manner, to do what it was told and that the question of whether or not FIRST CULVERIN could be implemented was not its to decide. Later that same day a full report, with its predictable conclusion that this operation did not appear a practical proposition on the basis of existing and planned resources, was finalized.[43]

Thus by the sixteenth every QUADRANT option had been either discounted by the planners or reduced by circumstances to the status of the impractical, but the need for some decision on the QUADRANT studies was pressing. Exactly this point was made on the sixteenth by a report on operations in Upper Burma, this paper noting that there was clearly a need for a decision on policy in Burma before Mountbatten left to take up his appointment in Southeast Asia.[44] The Directors of Plans, therefore, reported the state of planning to the Chiefs of Staff at their routine meeting on the sixteenth. In making their report the Directors noted that they and India Command could not agree on the form of TRIUMPHANT; that irrespective of its final form, the needs of TRIUMPHANT and of BULLFROG appeared mutually exclusive; and that FIRST CULVERIN appeared a very dubious proposition. Somewhat surprisingly in view of this latter conclusion, the Directors told the Chiefs of Staff that the planners were presently considering operations in the Sunda Strait.[45] But what was even more surprising was what the Directors do not appear to have told the Chiefs of Staff: first, that for the first time doubts were being expressed about BULLFROG on the grounds that possession of Akyab was not deemed essential to the success of operations in Upper Burma; second, that SCEPTRE appeared dubious because of the need to secure the Andamans; third, that an Andamans operation seemed unlikely; and, fourth, that the planners had taken upon themselves responsibility for an examination of a full ANAKIM option.[46] At the same time, however, the Directors advised the Chiefs of Staff of their view that the terms of reference of the Twelve-Month Plan rendered irrelevant any effort in Southeast Asia other than the continuation of the airlift to China, an observation that represented a significant shift of the British position since the eleventh and which no doubt was prompted by the revelation of American views on this question.

It is somewhat difficult to see how these various parts of the planning effort hung together. If indeed TRIUMPHANT and BULLFROG were mutually exclusive, then ANAKIM, with its amphibious landings in the Arakan and airborne landings in the delta, debarred itself from serious consideration, and why London should concern itself with ANAKIM while Delhi considered a TRIUMPHANT alternative would seem to be a somewhat unsound arrangement. Moreover, if BULLFROG, SCEPTRE, an Andamans operation, and any

CULVERIN variant were each unlikely on the basis of available resources, then a Sunda Strait option could hardly present itself as a practical proposition, especially in light of a report from India Command that credited the Japanese with a battle squadron at Singapore.[47] Why and on what authority the ANAKIM, Andamans, and Sunda Strait options were allowed to emerge to complicate British deliberations is unclear.

But what was truly extraordinary about these proceedings was that while the Directors of Plans asked the Chiefs of Staff for guidance in their future studies, on the sixteenth the Americans were informed by London that a campaign in Upper Burma in conjunction with either BULLFROG or FIRST CULVERIN represented Britain's provisional preference for future operations in Southeast Asia.[48] Even allowing for the conditional nature of this definition and the possibility that it was given in readiness for the next day's meeting of the Combined Chiefs of Staff,[49] this statement of national choice would seem to be wholly incomprehensible, given the state of British planning and a QUADRANT schedule that made no provision for such a definition of priorities at this stage of proceedings.

Clearly, therefore, British planning had become somewhat confused by mid-September, and indeed in an obvious sense this was perhaps unavoidable because the British planners were trying to square a circle. The British planners had grasped the nettle presented by the Twelve-Month Plan, namely that all operations in Southeast Asia, not just those in Burma, were marginal to the prosecution of the war against Japan. In this situation all the QUADRANT options threatened to fall into the void. For obvious political reasons this could not be allowed to happen, but unless the next Anglo-American conference discounted all the QUADRANT options the British high command faced an unenviable choice between the futile and the impossible.

It was small wonder, therefore, that British deliberations were somewhat confused, but, as noted elsewhere, the Twelve-Month Plan was only one of two sources from which this confusion flowed. The second, the liaison and reporting procedures that had been agreed at QUADRANT, both caused and compounded confusion, in part because of the nature of the reply provided by the Chiefs of Staff to the Directors of Plans' request for guidance.

Brooke provided the guidance that the Directors sought in the form of the statement that "it was obviously unsound to decide time before strategy. The best method of defeating Japan must be decided upon and thereafter an estimate must be made of the time it would take to accomplish our objective."[50] Consistent with the pre-TRIDENT opinion that an overall plan of campaign, not an amalgam of otherwise unrelated staff studies, was what was needed for the effective prosecution of the war against Japan,[51] this guidance in effect amounted to an instruction to prepare studies for operations, complete in their own right, that could be settled into an overall plan of campaign at a later date.[52] Such, therefore, was the state of British planning as judged by the first American officer to arrive in London, on this of all days, in accordance with the QUADRANT liaison arrangements.[53] But Brooke's guidance also amounted to an explicit repudiation of the twelve-month schedule as set down at QUADRANT, and in setting down these guidelines Brooke imposed upon the planners a form of business that would have been correct in any situation except the one in which the British found themselves *vis-à-vis* the Americans and the Twelve-Month Plan. What was wrong in this instance was the fact that the Americans were intent upon the Twelve-Month Plan and held the power of decision. It made no sense for Brooke to impose a "strategy-before-time" formula upon British planning when reality dictated that Britain had to conform to the dictates of the Twelve-Month Plan, despite its uncertainties and inconsistencies.

A final matter that contributed to the confusion of the British planning effort at this time arose from the fact that at the meeting of 16 September the Directors proposed that their American opposite numbers be invited to London in October to discuss British findings once studies were completed. As an alternative to this proposal they suggested that the studies be completed and recommendations made by the Chiefs of Staff before being passed to the American and combined planners.[54] The danger of raising policy issues to Chiefs of Staff level before their being raised with the American planners was recognized, and the Joint Staff Mission objected strongly to such a course of action.[55] But the alternatives were placed before, and the second accepted by, the American high command.[56] Given the fact that neither the British nor the Americans could spare their Directors before the next Anglo-American conference, American acceptance of the second alternative was more or less inevitable, but so were the consequences for the British decisionmaking process. To date the British had advised the Americans that their provisional preference in Southeast Asia was a military operation, the details of which could not be settled, plus one of two amphibious operations, neither of which was a practical proposition. Now, the final British consideration of options in Southeast Asia was raised to Combined Chiefs of Staff level before the American planners were consulted fully and before the British knew the details of the Twelve-Month Plan.[57] This the British did in mid-September while tied to the 1 October deadline. In short, the British high command had set itself an all-but-impossible task and an all-but-impossible schedule. And it had done so with respect to operations in a theater that the planners had come to dismiss as tertiary in importance, and from a base that could not maintain the forces that would be needed to mount these thus-far-undetermined efforts.[58]

The situation in which the British planning effort found itself by mid-September bordered upon the absurd. But what added a further element of unreality to proceedings was the fact that, having set itself so difficult a problem and schedule, the British high command showed little inclination to define priorities and policy for the war against Japan. Such a sin of omission, however, was in large measure the result of the demands of other issues upon the time and attention of the service chiefs and planners. The most important of these was OVERLORD, but the most immediate concerned the situation in the Mediterranean following the surrender of Italy. Of these matters the British high command found itself confronted not simply by the magnitude of the problems that demanded immediate solution about OVERLORD, but the fearfully complicated issues involved in defining the relationship, first, between OVERLORD and ANVIL and, second, between ANVIL and the campaign in peninsular Italy. These matters also concerned the Americans, but what added a peculiarly British dimension to these questions was the fact that the Mediterranean was a theater of specific British interest and influence, and operations then in hand in this theater involved resources that would be needed for an Indian Ocean amphibious effort. Likewise, the creation of South East Asia Command produced a series of immediate problems that made inroads on the time and attention that could be allowed consideration of questions of policy of the Japanese war by the British high command. The need to define the hopelessly entangled relationship between this new command and India, to fill senior appointments within South East Asia Command, and to try to bring some form of order to Stilwell's invariably confused relations with all and sundry in eastern and Southeast Asia produced a short-term attention to detail at the expense of long-term consideration of policy. The extent to which these various matters encroached upon the deliberations of the British high command to the detriment of policy questions can be gauged by the fact that of the 284 items on the agenda of the Chiefs of Staff meetings in September 1943 just 36 concerned India and South East Asia Commands. Most of the latter involved decisions on demarcation disputes between these authorities. On those few occasions when policy issues were before the Chiefs of Staff, moreover, British deliberations focused upon two separate but related matters. First, though the need to issue a directive to Mountbatten before South East Asia Command was activated was recognized, the task of doing so encountered the obvious circular problem: a directive could not be framed until strategic policy was settled, and strategic policy could not be settled until the terms of the directive were determined. Second, in the absence of a post-QUADRANT directive, India Command interpreted its QUADRANT summaries to mean the diversion of manpower and resources from airfield construction to the provision of lines of communication needed for operations into Upper Burma, to the immediate and very considerable irritation of the Americans. The British Chiefs of Staff were thus left with the task of placating the Americans and defining India's administrative priorities, and to deal with the problem that the offensive for which India sought to prepare for the forthcoming campaigning season accorded with the modest aims that had been embraced at TRIDENT but not the more ambitious perspective adopted at QUADRANT. It was small wonder, therefore, that such relatively minor matters as overall policy for the war against Japan and Southeast Asia study options were left at the September starting gate. Indeed the proceedings of the sixteenth barely merited a mention in Brooke's daily summary of proceedings.[59] Clearly the vexed question of policy for this war was not one that greatly exercised the British high command's attention at this time.

Given this unfolding of events, it was unavoidable that after mid-September the main British consideration of policy for the war against Japan would involve Southeast Asia. The Upper Burma, Arakan, and amphibious options thus vied with one another for adoption, yet even as they did so another option intruded upon British deliberations. This was the Pacific. It is not certain whether the Pacific option originated with the Americans or the British, but the available record suggests that it originated in Washington, where two sets of negotiations that involved a British contribution to the Pacific war were in hand. Options in the northern Pacific were the subject of discussions between the local theater commanders and the planning staffs at this time,[60] and part of these deliberations was the suggestion that British naval and amphibious forces should proceed to the northern Pacific in order to take part in operations against Hokkaido.[61] At about the same time as these talks, Churchill raised the question of British involvement in the Pacific war when he was in Washington between 1 and 12 September.

What prompted Churchill's taxing his hosts on this subject was the prospect of the surrender of the Italian fleet. For three years the Italian navy had employed a "fleet-in-being" strategy, but, as the British high command realized, with the Italian surrender Britain would be "in a position of a man who had suddenly succeeded into two fortunes: the Italian fleet and the British fleet which had been containing it for so long." As far as Churchill was concerned, the Italian surrender would enable Britain to give "positive proof of [its] resolve to participate in the Far Eastern war," and rather than let British forces "loaf around in the Indian Ocean until our amphibious operations in 1944 are due,"[62] Churchill proposed that a British squadron proceed to the Bay of Bengal via the Panama Canal and a four-month tour of duty with the U.S. Pacific Fleet. Despite King's opposition, the American high command agreed that "it was indeed most desirable" that a British formation should make its way to the Indian Ocean via the Pacific.[63]

But in making this offer Churchill bypassed the Admiralty, where the question of naval deployment after Italy's surrender had been under consideration since June.[64] With no fleet base east of Malta and the total repair facilities of the Indian subcontinent less than those of either Rosyth or Southampton,[65] the Admiralty planned to put in hand a major refitting program before units moved to the Indian Ocean. This program had been deferred for HUSKY and by September could not be delayed. In making his proposal Churchill either ignored or was ignorant of this, and when ordered to make the arrangements necessary to allow a formation to move to the Pacific the Admiralty could suggest only that a single squadron, which would include the *Queen Elizabeth* and *Illustrious*, should leave for the Pacific on 15 October. It noted, however, that with other units earmarked for the

Indian Ocean unable to leave before November and December and thus obliged to proceed via the Mediterranean in order to be on station by 1 February 1944 as planned, the effort involved in sending such a squadron to the Pacific was out of proportion to any result that might be achieved. The Admiralty therefore advised Churchill to abandon his proposal and allow the refitting program to proceed as arranged.[66]

Churchill was more than a little irritated by this advice and lost no time in so informing the Admiralty,[67] but over the next two weeks the prime minister came to accept the logic of its argument. But acceptance of argument did not get around the awkward problem of how to withdraw an offer freely made and, much worse, freely accepted by the American high command[68] and, moreover, favorably received by American commanders in the Pacific.[69] With Churchill unable to abandon his offer formally,[70] instructions were sent to the Joint Staff Mission for its members to stress in their talks with the Americans the short time that a British formation could serve in the Pacific and the pressing need to increase the antiaircraft armament of British warships bound for the Far East.[71] Thereafter British negotiators ensured that the British offer became entangled in details of movements, arrivals, logistical requirements, and operational plans until, on 8 October, the Americans suggested that the time the British intended to spend in the Pacific might be better used in rearming their ships.[72] Since Churchill had abandoned any thought of sending a naval force to the Pacific in the coming months,[73] and the Americans had ensured that blame could not be laid at their door for any failure of the British to appear in the Pacific,[74] this statement of the obvious enabled the two sides to bury Churchill's ill-considered proposal.[75]

By the time they did so, however, the question of a British naval involvement in the Pacific had arisen in a more substantial form as a result of American consideration of the Twelve-Month Plan. In seeking ways to ensure the end of the Japanese war by October 1945 the Americans seem to have examined options from two perspectives: by the acceleration of existing plans and schedules, and by working backwards, both in time and by geography, from the need to invade Honshu in late 1945. Either way, the American planners came to a conclusion that would seem to be extraordinary: that a British naval presence in the Pacific was essential if the twelve-month requirement was to be realized.[76] The speed and relative ease with which the U.S. Navy took the war from the Gilberts and Solomons in November 1943 to Honshu by March 1945 has served to obscure the fact that before November 1943 American planners, very conscious that every carrier battle in the Pacific to date had resulted in American losses, had to plan for "worst-possible" eventualities, hence the perceived need for the British.

By itself this development had obvious implications for British planning and interests: British involvement in the Pacific was an alternative to, perhaps an escape from, Southeast Asia, at least in part. Inevitably, however, the unfolding of events proved more complicated than their summary.

American deliberations threw up a series of options for the British, and in the process the latter were presented with two possible roles, with all too predictable a consequence for the British policymaking process. These two roles, made known after 7 October to the British officers sent to Washington to work on the Twelve-Month Plan, presented a choice between involvement in main force operations in the Pacific in 1945 and the conduct of independent but secondary operations in the Indian Ocean followed by, or as a diversion for, operations in the western Pacific.

The first role initially envisaged British participation in the invasion of either Formosa or Hokkaido in 1945. At the outset of talks the American planners had not decided which of these islands, if not both, should serve as the stepping-stone to Honshu. By 18 October, however, the British planners were able to inform London that though the American planners considered Hokkaido superior to Formosa as the penultimate objective before Honshu, the fact that Hokkaido could not be invaded in 1944, possibly not even in 1945, meant that the northern Pacific option had faded from serious consideration.[77] Although the Hokkaido option remained on file, Formosa, for reasons of timing, was considered its superior, and also superior to its MacArthur-sponsored rival, Luzon, which in its turn was deemed superior to any southern Philippines option and to a Ryukyus option (that is, Okinawa).[78] Within another week "the senior U.S. team" had decided that the British should be involved in the invasion of Formosa in spring 1945, but American planners, in the belief that British naval forces were "necessary . . . to improve the prospects of destroying the Japanese fleet, of completing the capture of the Mandates and of taking the Marshalls,"[79] wanted a British carrier force in the Pacific in mid-1944 in order to support the assault on the Marianas.[80] Because the planners believed that British naval and amphibious forces, "small though they may be initially, may make all the difference to timely completion of approved operations . . . and to decisive fleet action,"[81] they were prepared to indicate an American willingness to supply a fleet with carrier aircraft, to provide amphibious forces with access to U.S. facilities, and to provide general administrative support to British forces sent to the Pacific in 1944, though the Americans also made clear that a British carrier force had to be logistically self-supporting.[82]

This American line of reasoning and generosity were not shaped by altruism. In contemplating the Marianas offensive the American planners, faced by the calculation that seven U.S. fleet carriers might be opposed by six Japanese, could make a strong case to have three British carriers on station in order to provide cover for amphibious and oiler forces and thereby release American carrier formations for offensive purposes, and to serve as insurance against losses.[83] The limited operational role assigned a British carrier force in the Pacific in 1944 by American planners was thus not as generous as the administrative inducements offered in an attempt to ensure the presence of British carriers in the Pacific in mid-1944.

This offer of support, though tied to the Marianas operation, arose in the course of a series of discussions that had begun on 7 October with the American suggestion that the British should be assigned a holding role in Southeast Asia while their fleet went to the Pacific in order to maintain the schedule of the Twelve-Month Plan. But over the next three weeks the idea of British involvement in main force operations in the Pacific was developed alongside a second, alternative role. This was that British main force operations in Southeast Asia should precede and complement American operations in the Pacific, before both efforts came together in the enemy's Inner Defense Zone.

Thus the examination of the Formosa–Hokkaido alternatives ran in tandem with the development of the XYZ options. The X option called for British involvement in the invasion of Formosa in spring 1945 or for the invasion of northern Sumatra in spring or autumn 1945 if the proposed assault on Formosa was delayed for any reason, Y for the invasion of Singapore in late 1945 followed by British involvement in the assault on Formosa in the winter of 1945–46. The Z option again involved British participation in an assault on Formosa in the winter of 1945–46 but was preceded either in late 1944 or in 1945 by an invasion of northern Sumatra.[84] Naturally these planning discussions led to the consolidation of possibilities and the formulation of the Formosa spring 1945 and Hokkaido summer 1945 alternatives as the fourth of the WXYZ options.[85] No less natural was the fact that these same discussions raised logistical considerations that alarmed the British and lay behind the American assurances of late October. In their final form the WXYZ options called for British preparation of main bases at Vancouver and Ceylon and advance bases in Alaska and the Solomons,[86] but as early as the second week of October British planners in both Washington and London knew that resources could not be stretched to take on either an Australian or a Canadian commitment in addition to handling a residual Indian Ocean obligation.[87] The British planners were to experience considerable difficulty in convincing their opposite numbers that Britain could not prepare Australian, Canadian, and Indian Ocean bases simultaneously in anticipation of a decision that would render two of these efforts superfluous.[88] By 29 October the British planners in Washington were able to report both the American attempt to soothe British logistical fears[89] and a more sympathetic American reception of the argument that the British could not prepare bases in the northern Pacific, southwest Pacific, and Indian Ocean at one and the same time.[90] In this there was an obvious irony. In attempting to ensure a British presence in the Pacific the Americans were prepared to make light of administrative matters and very real and well-founded British concerns,[91] but what should have been equally real and well-founded logistical concerns had been notably absent when the British high command conducted its own evaluation of the Southeast Asia studies and settled its priorities in this theater.

* * *

After an examination of a process in 1943 that witnessed the Americans seeking British involvement in Ernie King's private war nothing should come as a surprise, but perhaps the most significant aspect of the WXYZ options, and one that is too easy to miss, is the fact that no fewer than three of these four options made provision for a CULVERIN variant. Of course the options were long-term, and the operations under discussion were, in October 1943, between one and two years hence, but even leaving aside the provisional British definition of national priorities on 16 September, the emergence of CULVERIN at the forefront of Allied deliberations, after having been discarded before QUADRANT and unfavorably reviewed immediately after that conference, was perhaps the least predictable development in what was by any standard a somewhat extravagant process—to which there was an inevitable rider. CULVERIN emerged from the studies that led to the WXYZ options as an operational possibility for late 1944 or 1945, but the planning discussions of September and October 1943 embraced both long-term possibilities and the more immediate demands of the coming season, and in these discussions CULVERIN presented itself as the operation most favored by the British high command for the 1943–44 season. And it did so despite being larger than BULLFROG, which was under threat at least in part because the force requirements for an assault on Akyab could not be met. When reality reasserted itself and in its turn a 1943–44 CULVERIN was abandoned, an assault on the Andamans, which like CULVERIN had been discounted before QUADRANT, took its place in the British scheme of things before it, too, was abandoned at the SEXTANT conference.

CULVERIN's resilience owed much to the fact that from the time of his return to London the prime minister sought to promote its cause and was prepared to override a series of objections in order to ensure its adoption. The route by which the British high command as a whole came to endorse CULVERIN, however, is obscure though marked by certain signposts, most notably the conferences of 28 September and 7 and 29 October. Moreover, the starting point of this route can be identified with Churchill's offer of a naval force for service in the Pacific and the BULLFROG study.

As recounted elsewhere, after his return from the United States Churchill allowed his Pacific option to lapse after Admiralty representations over the sanctity of its refitting program. There was, however, another factor in the prime minister's calculations. On his return to London he found the question of BULLFROG allocations demanding immediate attention,[92] and as early as the twenty-third the Chiefs of Staff were tackled on the issue of future amphibious operations in Southeast Asia.[93] By the twenty-seventh Churchill's coolness toward BULLFROG had transformed itself into a very marked interest in FIRST CULVERIN,[94] and it was on this day that Churchill effectively abandoned his Pacific offer. In a minute in which he conceded the Admiralty's arguments, the prime minister noted that there would be no opportunity to send a squadron to serve in the Pacific if British naval forces were to be gathered at Ceylon by mid-January in readiness for a FIRST CULVERIN in March. Churchill's line of argument was not inconsistent with the post-QUADRANT study options, which had considered a FIRST CULVERIN for May 1944. But the prime minister developed this argument with the observation that if British naval forces were to be concentrated in the Indian Ocean in the course of 1944, then he wanted to see a second amphibious operation that year and that he was determined to secure Akyab and Ramree as the prerequisites for an assault on Rangoon.[95]

This minute was not unaccompanied: Churchill also prepared papers on the possible uses to which the Italian fleet could be put and the employment of British naval forces in the Pacific. It was this minute, described by Brooke to his diary as "wild," that dominated three Chiefs of Staff meetings, two of which were with Churchill, which occupied some six exhausting hours of the evening of the twenty-eighth and early hours of the twenty-ninth.[96] These proceedings were confused, in part because the study paper needed for any reasoned discussion of FIRST CULVERIN had not been finalized.[97] But the other factor that made for confusion lay in the fact that Churchill's minute touched upon the crucial issue of procedure, established by Brooke in his guidance to the Directors of Plans on 16 September, that planning should proceed on the basis of fitting into an overall strategic scheme operations that were complete in their own right. In his minute Churchill stated what those operations were to be, in effect FIRST CULVERIN in 1943–44 and ANAKIM in 1944–45, but as one paper discussed on the twenty-eighth by the Chiefs of Staff in Churchill's absence noted:

> It is highly desirable that decisions as to what we should do in southeast Asia in the spring of 1944 should await the policy which might emerge from [the Twelve-Month Plan]. Obviously if we really think that there is a short cut to the defeat of Japan it might have a profound effect on our own action from the west. We may . . . have to deploy the bulk of our naval strength in the Pacific and assault the mainland of Japan or go straight for Formosa from Truk. Until we see the plan being prepared we cannot say whether it is best to put our main effort into Burma or Malaya.[98]

Given the fact that at the Chiefs of Staff meeting of the twenty-seventh Brooke had made a similar observation to the effect that there was a need to define whether Burma or Malaya was Britain's priority in Southeast Asia,[99] this paper suggests, the Pacific caveat notwithstanding, that not only Churchill but the service chiefs believed that the proper area of British interest and operations should be Southeast Asia.[100] The problem herein was that though most of the QUADRANT studies remained incomplete, the passing of time had not seen the prospects of any of the projected operations improve.

By the end of September none of the operations under consideration seemed any more promising than in mid-month, and indeed every week that passed without Germany's timely collapse rendered an already problematical CUL-VERIN in the second quarter of 1944 ever more so. BULLFROG retained its doubtful status because the lift required for the 50,000 men that India Command considered necessary for this operation was not available,[101] and the fact that BULLFROG was scheduled paradoxically made it ever less likely to be executed. As the Chiefs of Staff conceded when pressed on the matter by Churchill, the need for swift decisions on BULLFROG and the impossibility of meeting its overheads rendered the operation liable to cancellation in order to buy time for a later alternative.[102] Having been sanctioned, however, BULLFROG appears to have owed whatever life it still retained to the reality that cancellation threatened obvious problems with the Americans, particularly if it was to be abandoned with no credible alternative in its place. To add to this problem, the difficulties that would attend any attempt to reconquer Burma by an overland offensive from India remained at TRIUMPHANT's heels. More immediately, the form of an offensive into Upper Burma in the next campaigning season remained unresolved. SCEPTRE had been all but withdrawn from the lists on account of the Kra's difficult coastline and the perceived need first to secure the Andamans. CULVERIN remained, as ever, beset by India's limitations as a base of operations and the inescapable reality presented by Germany's willful refusal to be defeated. These rather somber conclusions were considered by the Chiefs of Staff when they met with the Directors of Plans between their meetings with Churchill on the twenty-eighth, the service chiefs being reminded that QUADRANT had limited amphibious operations in the Indian Ocean to the scale envisaged for BULLFROG and LYNCHPIN in order to release assault shipping for Europe. By extension, this consideration was the strongest possible argument against FIRST CULVERIN because this operation could be executed only at the expense of OVERLORD and the Mediterranean theater or, as was noted at this meeting, with very substantial American help. Apart from BULLFROG and LYNCHPIN, and with ANAKIM subjected to the same considerations that undermined CULVERIN, the proposal to land in the Andamans was the only option that could be executed within the force limitations imposed by QUADRANT. But with no good air base available in the Andamans, the value of BUCCANEER was somewhat limited.[103] With the Chiefs of Staff no doubt sustained through this meeting with their Directors by the prospect of immediately continuing their exchanges with Churchill, it is hard to resist the conclusion that this particular staff conference could not have been an auspicious occasion.

With the state of planning unable to recommend any single course of action but capable of raising well-nigh unanswerable objections to every option under consideration, Churchill's meetings with the Chiefs of Staff could never be anything other than inconclusive. In this situation Churchill fell back on his wish to raise "an amphibious circus" for service in the Indian Ocean and to carry out a British FIRST CULVERIN in spring 1944, his view being that as planned CULVERIN was excessive in its overheads and clearly outside the range of what was possible in March 1944.[104] This was the theme to which the prime minister returned at the second Chiefs of Staff meeting of 1 October which, attended by Mountbatten and his chief of staff, took the form of an official farewell to the new Supreme Allied Commander in Southeast Asia. From its minutes the meeting appears to have been a long monologue by Churchill, interrupted only by Mountbatten's sycophancy in seeking to fan Churchill's ardor for CULVERIN, which the prime minister modestly described as a "masterstroke."[105] Brooke less flatteringly described proceedings as a typical ploy in that Churchill, having secured the creation of a new command, was trying to seize "a chance . . . to get his pet operation started."[106] In fact Brooke seems to have disputed Churchill's claims and assertions at this meeting. Given the Chiefs' of Staff agreement to oppose the CULVERIN option at their earlier meeting on the first,[107] Brooke's opposition to Churchill's attempt to define policy could have been expected if only on the basis that failure to register dissent could have been taken by the prime minister to imply *qui tacit consensit*. According to one account of this meeting, Brooke's main argument against Churchill's demand for the raising of an amphibious force of two divisions in the Indian Ocean was that the idea was most unsound because such a force could only be raised at the expense of OVERLORD and the Mediterranean theater and that he, Brooke, was unprepared to see the latter weakened.[108] An observation of some significance in light of its implications, Brooke's comment may have been phrased for the benefit of his immediate audience rather than the historical record.

Unpromising though these meetings of 28 September and 1 October undoubtedly were, the basis of a compromise emerged at this time, though whether the terms of this compromise were realistic and in Britain's best interests was another matter. Despite Churchill's expressing on 1 October his intention to await Mountbatten's recommendations before settling policy, events could not wait upon so leisurely a timetable, and on the previous day, after discussing the FIRST CULVERIN study with the Directors, the Chiefs of Staff ordered the preparation of a paper that set out the factors involved in calculating the needs of FIRST CULVERIN and its anticipated problems. At the same time they were informed that BUCCANEER was a distinct possibility.[109] On the surface this appeared to be no real progress over what had previously been considered, but for two reasons this was not the case. First, with the American liaison officers in London no less skeptical about BULLFROG than their British hosts,[110] as a result of the Andamans study BUCCANEER emerged as an alternative to BULLFROG. Indeed, granted that other options could be discounted from serious consideration because of the limitations imposed at QUADRANT upon the scale of operations in Southeast Asia, BUCCANEER presented itself as the only alternative to BULLFROG.[111] BUCCANEER, therefore, emerged as the possible answer to the 1943–44 requirement.

Second, in the course of September various CULVERIN arguments were thoroughly rehearsed. But while Brooke might state the need to decide between Burma and Malaya as Britain's priority in Southeast Asia, the decision was perhaps given in the course of a CULVERIN argument that, at the level of the Chiefs of Staff, concerned itself with points of detail. At least some of the planners believed that the main effort against Japan had to be delivered from the Pacific and that no major amphibious operation in Southeast Asia was necessary,[112] but at the senior level, either from conviction or because of a desire to massage Churchill's strategic ego, the Chiefs of Staff allowed CULVERIN to emerge from the September deliberations as the operation likely to contribute more than other British efforts to the Allied cause. FIRST CULVERIN thus emerged as the operation that Britain would like to execute in the coming campaigning season, but BUCCANEER as the operation that was, or, more accurately, seemed to be, within its means.

This conclusion formed the basis of the Joint Planning Staff's recommendations in the reports that were finalized on 6 October.[113] But in setting out the BUCCANEER–FIRST CULVERIN formula as the basis of negotiations with the Americans, the Joint Planning Staff turned around its argument that FIRST CULVERIN could not proceed without American involvement. While not contradicting Churchill's insistence that FIRST CULVERIN should be a British rather than an Allied operation, and quite possibly as a deliberate means of bringing home to Churchill that this operation could not be mounted without American participation, the planners' final recommendation for the 1943–44 season was that the Americans should be approached with BUCCANEER and the suggestion that if American resources could be made available then FIRST CULVERIN would be put in its place. The following day, when the planners' reports received their preliminary examination in committee, the Chiefs of Staff, perhaps in an attempt to forestall a hostile reaction from Churchill, reversed this order of presentation.[114] It is clear that from this time, and specifically after their report to Churchill on the nineteenth, the Chiefs of Staff regarded the substance and the form of the British recommendations for the 1943–44 season to have been settled. Over the next three weeks, in the course of which the Chiefs of Staff had to frustrate the prime minister's insistence that a decision was not urgent and that Mountbatten be consulted,[115] the various studies were examined in detail.[116] This process produced nothing new, and it was on the twenty-ninth, but only after hesitations caused by the realization that problems with the Americans were certain to arise because their recommendation would necessarily involve BULLFROG's cancellation,[117] that the Chiefs of Staff formally adopted the FIRST CULVERIN–BUCCANEER formula[118] and the Joint Staff Mission so informed.[119] But it is equally clear that at the upper levels of the British high command the potentially disastrous implications of this recommendation went quite unsuspected.

With a British record that gives only a tantalizingly incomplete account of events, it is difficult to decide whether the recommendation itself or the timing of its presentation to the Americans was the more baleful aspect of the FIRST CULVERIN–BUCCANEER proposal. There were, in fact, three aspects of the proposal that could virtually guarantee its receiving a very hostile reception in Washington. First, the terms of the British statement of intention were tantamount to a gratuitous if unintended insult to the Americans. By placing FIRST CULVERIN before BUCCANEER the implication of the British proposal was that the Americans were expected to comply with British wishes with respect to an operation in a secondary theater about which they had not been consulted. The alternative was for the British to renege on BULLFROG and go their own way with BUCCANEER. This was not the way in which the British high command had intended its presentation, but this conclusion was too easy to draw from its form and wording, as at least one of the British planners belatedly recognized. In a memorandum that his superior declined to bring to Brooke's attention, one military planner referred to the need "to lessen the shock" of the FIRST CULVERIN proposal, not least because under the terms of the plan the Americans were to play the predominant role in this operation. The method of presentation was important, and, as this note stated, the best course open to the British in dealing with the Americans was to play up BUCCANEER and its expected results and then to allow the Americans to glimpse the greater prize.[120] There can be little doubt that in potentially troublesome negotiations with the Americans this was what the British should have done.

The second aspect of the FIRST CULVERIN–BUCCANEER formula likely to give offense to the Americans was the handling of BULLFROG. Through their liaison officers, who had been in London until 8 October,[121] the American planning staffs were aware of British thinking on BULLFROG. But if this operation was to be mounted in early February, the LSTs that were needed had to sail from the Mediterranean on or before 10 October.[122] Thereafter, every day that passed with neither sailings nor cancellation could only heighten American suspicions, if only because of current events in the eastern Mediterranean. Although Dill warned London to be open with the Americans on these matters,[123] the failure to consult the Americans over BULLFROG left British actions open to the interpretation of ensuring the cancellation of an agreed operation by default in order to then present an alternative that amounted to a *de facto* abandonment of the Burma theater. Even if the Americans took a tolerant view of proceedings, there was no getting around the fact that the FIRST CULVERIN–BUCCANEER proposal resurrected the Burma problem, on which the Americans retained very definite views.

But even this matter was of small significance when set alongside the third aspect of potential offense. By the end of October, the American planners had been some two months in the preparation of the Twelve-Month Plan, the draft of which had been forwarded to London on 7 October.[124] For three weeks and perhaps for six, the American planners had entertained the idea of a British naval role in the Pacific and the XYZ/WXYZ options had been passed to London between the eighteenth and twenty-fourth.[125] In this month, despite the fact that the option of a British amphibious role in Southeast Asia remained under consideration, a British involvement in the advance across the Pacific was at the forefront of American consideration in dealing with their ally. Having made a not-ungenerous offer to the British, the Americans could hardly be expected to take kindly to a FIRST CULVERIN proposal that was at best wholly irrelevant, at worst an indication that London either could not grasp the implications of the Twelve-Month Plan or had turned its back on it. Within the Joint Staff Mission the view that the FIRST CULVERIN–BUCCANEER formula did indeed demonstrate London's lack of understanding of the Twelve-Month Plan was expressed,[126] and London was warned that to present its proposals was to invite trouble with the Americans.[127] In fact the situation was much worse than this bare record would suggest. The full measure of London's lack of realism on these and related matters was demonstrated by its providing the Joint Staff Mission with no more than the final FIRST CULVERIN–BUCCANEER statement for presentation to the Americans. When the Joint Staff Mission vehemently protested that the reasoning behind the proposals had to be made available both to itself and the Americans,[128] London's initial reaction was that the Joint Staff Mission was not entitled to access to the QUADRANT studies but could receive them on condition they were not passed to the Americans.[129]

Leaving aside the obvious implications that such an attitude displayed, the Joint Staff Mission did receive the papers that it had demanded, plus a consolidated reasoning and proposal, in a Combined Chiefs of Staff paper on 7 November.[130] This paper was made available to and discussed with the Americans on the eighth,[131] but if the American reaction to the FIRST CULVERIN–BUCCANEER proposal can be imagined, the odd feature of this episode, and one thoroughly in keeping with so many of the transactions between QUADRANT and SEXTANT, is that the American answer to this proposal was given on 2 November, that is, six days before the British proposal was set before the American high command.[132]

Events unfolded in this reverse order because more than one set of discussions were in hand at this time. The process whereby the Americans provided a preemptive answer to the British proposal arose from the British attempt on the twenty-eighth to nail down the strategic argument about the Pacific. After the formal presentation of the Twelve-Month Plan three days earlier,[133] the British put four questions to the American high command.[134] Of these the second,

> Is it agreed that, to stand a reasonable chance of capturing either [Formosa or Hokkaido] in spring or summer 1945, the British fleet and amphibious effort is required in the Pacific for both the operations themselves and the 1944 Pacific operations?

was all-important: in fact it was the acid test of weeks of consultation. On 2 November, with the Joint Staff Mission adding the observation that "whilst admitting need for British naval assistance in the Pacific 1944–1945 U.S still hope against hope that they might be able to bring off decisive fleet action alone," the U.S. reply was sent to London. The answer to the second question was

> The U.S. planners do not consider that even the small portion of the British fleet and amphibious forces available in 1944 can be logistically supported in the Central and North Pacific areas. It is believed that the greatest contribution by the British naval and amphibious forces to the overall effort . . . would be to undertake continuing offensive operations in the southeast Asia areas.[135]

This was not a case, as Hayes has asserted, of the Americans reminding the British of their place.[136] In two sentences the American high command repudiated one of the main premises of their post-QUADRANT planning and, *en passant,* provided its answer to a FIRST CULVERIN–BUCCANEER proposal: American forces would not find themselves involved in a second-string operation in the Indian Ocean in March 1944.

The least that can be said about these various exchanges is that the different parts of the story do not hang together very well: indeed, some of the inconsistencies would seem to be extraordinary. After the revelation of the American need for British naval forces to operate in the Pacific, the American volte-face of 2 November is as extraordinary as the British decision to persist with the FIRST CULVERIN–BUCCANEER proposal despite being aware of what was being considered in Washington. Superficially at least, the apparent failure by the British to challenge the Americans on this change of course between 28 October and 2 November seems no less incredible, and perhaps one of the more surprising aspects of these exchanges is that they do not seem to have ended in mutual recriminations and accusations of bad faith. But, of course, the American definition of the British role was not inconsistent with the British proposal and paradoxically this definition strengthened the case for FIRST CULVERIN even as the Americans declined to be involved in this operation. For its part the British high command could not dispute the American refusal of a central Pacific option after it had pronounced itself in favor of options in Southeast Asia. Very oddly, the somewhat disingenuous British statement that the Americans should, with respect to British intentions in Southeast Asia, "signify their final agreement in the same way as we give our final agreement to their Pacific operations"[137] was realistic and the basis whereby both sides could leave matters to stand as they did, at least until the next Allied conference, which was less than three weeks hence.

Between these exchanges and the start of the SEXTANT conference little of importance occurred as planners on both sides of the Atlantic prepared for the fourth and last of the great Anglo-American gatherings of this conference-strewn year. But the account of events between QUADRANT and SEXTANT cannot be ended without some attempt to answer certain obvious questions: first, whether British participation in the Pacific war in 1944 was a realistic proposition; second, why the British persisted with the FIRST CULVERIN–BUCCANEER formula even after mid-October when both India and South East Asia Commands emphatically told London there was no prospect of mounting FIRST CULVERIN in March 1944;[138] third, what transpired within the British high command that resulted in the 28 October–2 November denouement; fourth, why the Americans reversed themselves between 28 October and 2 November; and, fifth and perhaps most difficult of all, whether the U.S. Navy's overtures to the British on the Pacific issue were genuine.

The first of these questions can be answered simply. Although not known at the time, the force levels that were the basis of negotiations were unrealistic: with the carrier refits proving much more difficult and protracted than anticipated, the British could not have operated in the Pacific in mid-1944 on the scale that the Americans envisaged.[139] The second question presents a more difficult problem of interpretation. With little in the record to serve as the basis of an authoritative conclusion, it may be that in the second half of October the FIRST CULVERIN–BUCCANEER formula had acquired a momentum that made it very difficult for the British high command to draw back as various staff studies and planning came together.[140] But persistence with this formula after mid-October, and particularly after 2 November when the American hand was shown, could do no other than ensure BUCCANEER's endorsement, or perhaps more accurately FIRST CULVERIN's rejection, and herein may be the explanation of events. It is clear that by early October the British military establishment was aware, first, that FIRST CULVERIN was problematical even as the FIRST CULVERIN–BUCCANEER formula was devised, and, second, that BULLFROG was destined to fall by the wayside. It is also clear that these facts of life were acceptable, perhaps even welcome, to the British military, and herein is perhaps the reason why this formula was retained into November: it was certain to end in the abandonment of BULLFROG and FIRST CULVERIN and thereby end Churchill's fixation with the latter.

Beyond this, however, is the wider point of how and why the British high command seemingly allowed the American offer to support a British carrier force in the central Pacific to pass by default. Two possible explanations exist, either of which might explain what would seem to be a most curious lapse on the part of the British leadership. The first is the obvious: at this time the British high command and the planners were so deeply immersed in other issues that the import of the American offer was not appreciated. Certainly by the end of October the British high command was so overwhelmed by a host of immediate problems—the Aegean, OVERLORD, Italy, South East Asia Command, and the forthcoming conference with the Americans—that the American offer may well have been squeezed in terms of time and attention. Moreover, if various planning papers that were completed in the first week of November serve as an accurate guide to the previous ten days' preparations, it would seem that the planning staffs at this critical time were caught in a basic dilemma with respect to the Japanese war. With CULVERIN options being studied both with a spring 1944 deadline and under the terms of the WXYZ program, and with other options in Southeast Asia also under consideration, the planners were trapped in a perennial planning problem: to determine whether policy decided administration or administration policy. At issue was the fundamental problem of whether what was sought or what was possible should form the basis of strategic priorities. The confusion within the British high command on this issue was very real, indeed it had dominated proceedings since QUADRANT. It may be, therefore, that distraction in terms of other, more pressing issues served to divert attention from the more important issue explicit in the American offer at the critical moment.

Such an explanation, however, is hard to reconcile with two immediate and obvious facts of life: the British leadership, and particularly the planners, were very sensitive to American thinking and this offer most definitely was not of the "nickel and dime" order. Distracted as it might have been, the planning staff could hardly have been unaware of the implications of the American offer, not least because the Joint Staff Mission was making the very point in its signals to Whitehall. The alternative explanation is that the exchange of signals at the end of October represented a stalling on the part of British planners who recognized these implications but also the problems that they presented for the British high command and war effort. If an awareness that a mid-1944 schedule was likely to be beyond British means did shape the planners' calculations, certain matters may fall into place, and most definitely there was no good reason to refuse the American offer or admit at this stage of proceedings the limitations of British naval capacity. If this was the British planners' calculation the events of 28 October–2 November may be explicable in terms of the Americans, who might well have worked out the calculation for themselves as a result of their work on the *Indomitable*, had to allow their offer to lapse because of the demands of their own planning schedules. The problem presented by these two—mutually exclusive—explanations is self-evident: neither can be developed beyond the realms of speculation. In either case, and specifically the latter, it is very unlikely that anything would be committed to paper, still less retained: no explanation of these events can be definitive.

The American dimension to these events provide equally grave problems of interpretation. Cynicism suggests that the U.S. Navy never really had any intention of allowing the British a role in the Pacific but, in accordance with good staff practice, was prepared to offer the British a role that the latter would be obliged to decline in order to place the British at a psychological disadvantage when it came to negotiations on more important issues. If this was the case, the U.S. Navy's planners seem to have been both persistent and elaborate in their finesse, too much so for the balance of probability to favor this particular interpretation of events. What seems more likely is that after QUADRANT the American planners undertook a series of studies on the basis of "the inverted Micawber principle," waiting for things to turn down, the approach to the British being but one possibility and study, though by the nature of things one that must have been endorsed at the highest levels. By the end of October, when the time for decisions approached and with the British clearly hesitant about committing themselves to a Pacific strategy, this particular option was allowed to pass by default without any great regret, most certainly not on the part of King.

Support for this second interpretation of proceedings exists in the fact that though the conversations of 28 October appear to have passed off well,[141] relations between the American and British high commands in October, particularly by month's end, were somewhat fragile. The month began badly, and at the end of its first week, when Brooke railed in his dairy against yet "another day of Rhodes madness" and asserted that Churchill was "in a very dangerous condition, most unbalanced, and God knows how we shall finish this war if this goes on," the Chief of the Imperial General Staff noted, perhaps more objectively, that "the Americans are desperately suspicious of him."[142] By the end of a very trying month the Joint Staff Mission had made London aware that the U.S. Chiefs of Staff "were showing a degree of irritation," partly because of certain specific incidents but mainly because of "a general feeling that our intentions regarding OVERLORD are dishonorable."[143] Noble made much the same point, again with reference to OVERLORD, when he advised Brooke against presenting the FIRST CULVERIN–BUCCANEER proposal to the Americans.[144] It would seem, therefore, that events in October 1943 made the American high command very wary in its dealings with the British, and if indeed there was little goodwill in Washington for the British by the end of October, then the reversal of the American position over a British role in the Pacific falls into place. In the final analysis, the British showed themselves concerned with a theater that was of marginal importance to the United States, and the Royal Navy, whether in the Indian Ocean or the Pacific, fell into the "nice-to-have" rather than the "need-to-have" classification. The U.S. Navy, having spent more than two decades in which its raison d'être had been to fight and win a naval war against Japan, could not have been too concerned if, in the end, it had to deal with the Imperial Navy alone. Herein may lie the reason why the Americans reversed themselves between 29 October and 2 November on the question of a British role in the Pacific and were prepared to let the British proceed with BUCCANEER. In any event, with many other issues at hand, what were at this stage only studies and provisional proposals could await final decisions at the SEXTANT conference.

CHAPTER TWO

An Unreasonable Thing to Do

From SEXTANT to OCTAGON, January–February 1944

The wartime Anglo-American conferences have been subjected to intensive examination and analysis. These pages could add little if anything to what is already known of SEXTANT, and will concern themselves only with general issues and those decisions with specific implications for the evolution of British policy for the war against Japan.

Preceded by talks with Chiang Kai-shek and separated by the EUREKA talks at Tehran, the two sets of Anglo-American discussions that together made up the SEXTANT conference were the least organized and most confused of the wartime Anglo-American meetings. It was perhaps wholly appropriate that the most important single development to emerge from these proceedings was neither American nor British in origin. The revelation of the Soviet Union's intention to enter the war against Japan once Germany was defeated had obvious implications, but ones that drew no American response. The certainty of support from a power that could ensure Japan's defeat on the Asian mainland offered the Americans the means whereby they might escape the China quagmire since the need for China to shoulder the military burden of the war had ended. Moreover, the decision to stage the strategic air offensive against Japan from the islands of the central Pacific further diminished the importance of China to the Allied cause. But by the time of these developments the significance of China in American calculations, always political and long-term rather than military and immediate, was too well established for there to be a recasting of American policy. By extension, therefore, Burma obstinately retained its previous status in Anglo-American calculations, though as events were to prove the Americans and British did not hold a monopoly on the power of decision in this theater of operations.

The Burma commitment thus survived SEXTANT: BUCCANEER, however, did not. Although endorsed at the meeting with Chiang, BUCCANEER did not survive the post-EUREKA discussions and the decision to make a winter attempt to break the deadlock in Italy by a landing at Anzio. Because this operation would involve the use of amphibious shipping needed for BUC-CANEER, the latter had to be abandoned, and Chiang, who had made Chinese involvement in a planned offensive into Upper Burma dependent upon BUCCANEER, availed himself of the opportunity to repudiate his undertaking. For their part the British, having seen both parts of their FIRST CUL-VERIN–BUCCANEER formula collapse in one month, were left only with PIGSTICK, the clearing of the Mayu peninsula, as an option in Southeast Asia, and this operation was to be canceled in the month after SEXTANT.

Exactly why PIGSTICK was canceled is not clear. FIRST ARAKAN had left the British high command less than enamored with the Mayu peninsula and Akyab, and past coolness perhaps eased a decision ostensibly made for reasons of timing. When the various administrative and training arrangements that were necessary if PIGSTICK was to proceed were not completed by final cutoff dates the operation had to be canceled, as it was on 4 January 1944,[1] with all other amphibious options in the Arakan abandoned on the thirtieth.[2] But it is legitimate to question whether timing was reason or rationalization for PIGSTICK's cancellation. An examination of the planning files of the various operations under consideration at this time—CUDGEL, HOOK, PIGSTICK, TARZAN et al.—reveals an apparent slowing of the tempo of planning. Questions of timing and means were immediate practical considerations in the planners' deliberations,[3] but as long as the British intelligence files remain closed perhaps a certain caution should be exercised in any examination of the circumstances of the cancellations of these operations. The final Japanese decision to undertake a preemptive offensive into northeast India was taken on 31 December 1943,[4] and one of those individuals whose writings contributed much to the generally held wisdom that warning of this offensive was provided by field intelligence no longer believes this to have been the case.[5] The Allied ability to read Japanese operational signals may well have provided warning of Japanese intentions and been a factor in the British drawing back from PIGSTICK and other options in the Arakan and Upper Burma in order to meet the "March on Delhi."

The continuing importance of China, the unchanged status of Burma, and the cancellation of BUCCANEER meant that SEXTANT was not the landmark in the formation of Allied policy for the war against Japan that TRIDENT and QUADRANT had been before it. Strategy for the Pacific war lay within the province of the Joint Chiefs of Staff, and increasingly the important decisions were to be taken in Washington and outside the major conferences. The next conference after SEXTANT did not take place until September 1944, but, as Hayes notes, January to May 1944 were, for the Pacific war, the "months of crucial decisions,"[6] and these decisions were American, not Allied. But SEX-TANT established the Twelve-Month Plan as the basis of Allied efforts, and while the British area of responsibility remained Southeast Asia, the door on the possibility of a British naval involvement in the Pacific remained open. A rather curious development in light of the American answers of 2 November, this issue had been brought to a head at a Combined Staff Planners' meeting on 28 November, notable, at least from the minutes, for the Americans' evasiveness on the crucial question, put directly by the British naval Directors of Plans, whether or not the Americans believed that they could operate in the central Pacific without British support. The American answer, that the Imperial Navy probably would not fight for Truk and was unlikely to give battle until the war neared the home islands, in effect precluded the British from a central Pacific role. Success at Rabaul and in the Gilberts, and the growing number of *Essex*-class fleet carriers entering service,[7] were clearly the basis of a growing American confidence that while losses might yet bestow upon the British a role in the central Pacific, American strength appeared adequate for the task in hand.

In response to a British suggestion, the American planners did not preclude a British involvement in the southwest Pacific, a theater tantamount in U.S. naval terms to a leper colony. The American planners also accepted the retention of British naval forces in the Indian Ocean for deception purposes and nuisance value. But while the Americans noted the possibility of the British playing "a most useful" role in the southwest Pacific, the British noted that the Allied priority had to be the central Pacific and that BUCCANEER would preclude their involvement in operations in the Pacific.[8] If the Americans thought that this seemed to be a problem of Britain's own making and wondered just what British priorities were at this stage, they were wise enough not to say so, but the final paper to emerge from the SEXTANT proceedings nevertheless retained a British option on the central Pacific offensive. Under its terms the British were to establish advanced bases in the Solomons and Bismarcks and operate in either the central or the southwest Pacific. With one amphibious division and its shipping left in the Indian Ocean, the British were to raise four divisions for the Pacific and to provide lift for three with no fewer than two of these divisions assigned an assault role. By June 1944 the British were to have in the Pacific a squadron consisting of the *Renown,* two fleet and seven or eight escort carriers, six light cruisers, and sixteen destroyers on station. Two more fleet carriers were to enter the Pacific in July, and in the last quarter of 1944 two fast battleships, two light fleet carriers, and a further nine escort carriers were to join company. The *Anson* and one light fleet carrier and the *Duke of York* and two light fleet carriers were to join the fleet in the first and second quarters of 1945 respectively.[9] When the Admiralty calculations were completed after SEXTANT, its planning envisaged two capital ships, one fleet and four escort carriers, five cruisers, one antiaircraft ship, and twenty destroyers remaining in the Indian Ocean throughout 1945, while a British build-up in the Pacific resulted in eight capital ships, five fleet, ten light fleet and twenty-one escort carriers, twenty-nine cruisers, five antiaircraft ships, eighty-seven destroyers, and ninety-one submarines being on station by year's end.[10]

The discussion of 28 November and these two papers would seem to suggest a number of conclusions, of which two may be raised in order that they may be dismissed from further consideration. First, even allowing for planning for the invasions of Hokkaido and Honshu involving upwards of 100 carriers of all types, just what this fleet was to achieve with such numbers, given the strength of the U.S. fast carrier force, is as hard to discern as the need for the 16,837 aircraft that the Combined Staff Planners envisaged being in the Pacific theater by October 1944. Second, with the *Richelieu*, the *Nelson* if modernized in time, and even the *Vanguard* included in the projected order of battle, there was never any possibility of the British planning targets being realized. But more pertinently, even if the 23 December 1943 program did not represent a settled decision or commitment, that the British military could in its dealings with the Americans cite such numbers and timings suggests something more than mere hope and intent. The implication of such programs would seem a commitment, or at least the intention to assume a commitment, in the Pacific. The Chiefs of Staff did not formally resolve upon such a commitment until 21 February 1944,[11] yet certain actions and calculations between SEXTANT and this date seem explicable only in terms of the decision to this effect having been taken well before this date, perhaps even at SEXTANT in some form of unofficial undertaking to the Joint Chiefs of Staff: King in January 1944 certainly believed that the British had promised to send a fleet to the Pacific in 1944.[12] If indeed this was the case, the prime minister's prolonged and vehement opposition to the sending of a fleet to the Pacific had not been anticipated. A British fleet was to enter the Pacific, but it would not sail from Sydney on its first operation until 18 March 1945, and then only after a bruising eight-month struggle within the British high command to determine national priorities and policy.

This struggle can be divided several ways into a number of different phases though the major events that were to loom like mountain ranges in a desert of strategic sterility obviously remain constant, irrespective of how the whole is divided. A not unreasonable arrangement of events would involve a threefold division, the shared lines of demarcation being provided by the months of March and June 1944. The problem inherent in this and any other division of this eight-month affair into phases, however, is that the basic issue that was in dispute remained, for the most part, unchanged throughout the duration of this struggle. Moreover, the arguments that were used by the contending factions took time to be developed in full, and at different times focused upon different matters of detail. They were subjected to changes of emphasis as events that came to hand were rationalized in support of predetermined arguments. But in this initial phase, the parties to this struggle gathered their conflicting arguments as the issue—in what form and in which theater an expanded British contribution to the war against Japan should be made—was joined and the main lines of the dispute that was to last until September were laid down.

The main lines of argument expounded in the course of this eight-month struggle can be defined with relative ease. For Churchill the national priority was that Britain had to win its own victories over Japan and had to avenge its previous defeats in order to recover its lost possessions and prestige in Southeast Asia.[13] Thus the prime minister was determined that the British effort against Japan had to be made not in the Pacific, where a British fleet would be no more than an appendage to an American power already sufficient to ensure Japan's defeat,[14] but in Southeast Asia within an existing British area of responsibility.[15] Not unnaturally, this was a strategic perspective supported by Mountbatten,[16] and because the latter shared Churchill's antipathy toward any major commitment in Burma he fanned the prime minister's insistence that the future British effort in Southeast Asia be amphibious.[17] For the Chiefs of Staff, however, the Burma commitment that Churchill sought to evade was inescapable,[18] and the national priority was not the recovery of colonies that would be repossessed with Japan's defeat[19] but the earliest possible end to the war in order to avoid the manpower crisis that threatened to paralyze Britain's military efforts if hostilities dragged into 1946.[20] As the weeks passed, this latter consideration emerged as one of the most important single calculations of Chiefs of Staff aware that one of the strongest arguments in favor of a naval commitment in the Pacific was manpower considerations. For the Chiefs of Staff the manpower demands of the economy and postwar occupation duties in Europe threatened to be so heavy that any significant redeployment of ground forces to the Far East was unlikely,[21] whereas the dispatch of "a far from insignificant fleet"[22] was not dependent, or at least not so dependent, upon manpower and European considerations.[23]

The latter arguments of the Chiefs of Staff provide a key to understanding why the struggle within the British high command was so protracted and divisive. Leaving aside the constitutional proprieties whereby the Chiefs of Staff in effect claimed to be the better judges of national interest than the head of government and refused to allow military policy to be determined by political considerations,[24] as 1944 wore on it became apparent that far from being the first of the services that would arrive in the Far East from Europe, the Royal Navy emerged as the only service likely to arrive in any significant strength for the final stages of the war against Japan, with all that implied in political and psychological terms. The fleet was the last British card in a hand that had been five years in the playing, and the question of its deployment was a matter of immense significance which brought to a head political and strategic issues involving Britain's role, both immediate and postwar, in the world, most obviously in terms of Britain's relations with the Empire and the United States.

The imperial dimension was secondary but complicated because it involved a reversal of the customary relationship between Britain and its Empire. In a series of wars Britain had looked to its Dominions, colonies, and India to supplement national power, but by 1944 Britain was forced to recognize that India and the Dominions primarily involved in the Japanese war looked to Britain to make good the exhaustion brought about by their earlier endeavors.[25] This was to present formidable problems because without an expansion of imperial facilities British forces could not be sent in any numbers to the Far East. This, however, was one aspect of the strategic debate between January and August 1944 that lent itself to rationalization rather than providing reasons. Imperial resources, indeed imperial views and expectations, were of concern to the British high command, but mostly for their value in supporting given lines of argument. The American dimension was very different, and infinitely more important.

Underlying the various arguments used between January and August 1944 was an ambivalent British attitude toward the United States. The need to settle policy brought into focus anti- and pro-American sentiments within the British high command. Churchill was well aware of Britain's dependence upon the United States. But just as he resented this dependence and the manner in which the power of decision rested in Washington, so he feared the ends to which American power would be put in the shaping of the postwar world.[26] Very conscious of American hostility to French rule in Indo-China,[27] the prime minister sought to ensure that when the war ended Britain was not dependent upon American largess for the return of lost colonies.[28] To the Chiefs of Staff, however, the United States was an ally that had to be supported to the full extent of available power, not a state against which provision had to be made. The service heads believed that Britain's best interests in the shaping of the postwar order were to be served by fighting alongside, but clearly subordinate to, the United States in the Pacific rather than by indulging in a secondary, peripheral theater of operations.[29] The problem herein was that the quickening of the American drives across the Pacific during 1944 weakened this Chiefs of Staff argument because, as Churchill noted, American success deprived the British of a real role in the Pacific.[30] No less seriously, this development came in a year when the prospects of victory over Germany receded into 1945 and when an estimated eighteen months might be necessary to complete the movement of British forces to the Far East.[31] American policy and success in the course of 1944 thus presented the British high command with a series of worsening practical difficulties and unenviable choices as it set about the task of ordering national priorities.

After SEXTANT the British high command was obliged to gather together the various matters left unresolved at Cairo, the most immediate being the fate of PIGSTICK. As noted elsewhere, this operation was canceled in the first ten days of January after a period of uncertainty and confusion.[32] But more substantially there were under consideration three questions which, though lacking the immediacy of PIGSTICK, provided the main themes of dispute over the next eight months. These questions involved Britain's relations with its Empire, the raising and manning of naval and amphibious forces for service in the Far East, and, central to the whole dispute, the conflicting claims of alternative Indian Ocean and Pacific strategies. The first and second of these questions were to cling to the third over the next eight months for the very obvious reason that policy could not be settled without consideration of means, but from the outset Churchill refused to consult the Dominions (i.e., Australia) before British policy was settled.[33] By this decision Churchill created obvious problems because policy would be partly determined by and dependent upon imperial considerations and could not be settled without imperial consultation. Moreover, as Cunningham noted, it was intolerable that Commonwealth governments be denied the right of consultation but informed by their own military of British intentions and requirements.[34] By this time, however, the question of procurement and manning had begun to infringe upon British deliberations in that not only had it been calculated that on the basis of existing Australian resources a British force sent to the Pacific would be limited to just two fleet carriers,[35] but the planners were also on the point of acknowledging that the amphibious goals set down at SEXTANT could not be realized. British long-term planning had envisaged the raising of three amphibious divisions: the addition of a fourth at Cairo presented impossible problems.[36] But more immediately a timetable that set OVERLORD and ANVIL for May 1944 precluded the dispatch of landing craft to the Far East before September and landing ships before November. The result was that the 1944 target figures, admittedly only provisional ones, could not be met either by time or by numbers.[37] At the very best, spring 1945 might see lift for three British divisions concentrated in the Far East, and provision for a fourth might be possible thereafter.[38] But by the time that these calculations were committed to paper, the Chiefs of Staff had been told by Churchill that he "was increasingly resolved" upon a post-monsoon FIRST CULVERIN.[39] Apparently based upon South East Asia Command papers that had set out FIRST CULVERIN in either October or November as the first of either two or three operations that this command might execute with forces en route to the Pacific,[40] Churchill's declaration of intention was wholly unrealistic. Not only was it very unlikely that the lift needed for FIRST CULVERIN could be assembled in time for this schedule, but if it was, then what might be gathered would be concentrated in the wrong theater, given the terms of the SEXTANT program.

In setting out his view Churchill brought the strategic argument back to the unreality of the WXYZ options of October 1943, but he was not alone. Even as late as mid-December the planners had shown themselves trapped by the same confusion in setting down the conclusion,

It is possible that if operations in the Pacific fail it will at a later date become necessary to resort to major amphibious operations in southeast Asia on an initial scale equivalent to that envisaged in FIRST CULVERIN. So far as they do not in any way conflict with [preparations for the implementation of a Pacific strategy,] base facilities should be prepared in India to enable this eventuality to be met.[41]

But herein lay the rub. Although in mid-December it would seem that the idea of simultaneous preparations in two oceans still held sway in London despite what had been said to the Americans since October, by mid-January the Chiefs of Staff were feeling their way to the conclusions that "preparations . . . could be made either in the Indian Ocean or the Pacific, but not simultaneously in both," and that, therefore, there could be no CULVERIN if a Pacific strategy was adopted.[42]

This, in essence, was the strategic reality on which British deliberations between January and August 1944 foundered. Churchill's endorsement of FIRST CULVERIN, plus the Chiefs' of Staff recognition that efforts in the Indian Ocean and the Pacific were mutually exclusive, marked the point when the struggle within the British high command was joined. In fact, though preceded by the somewhat notorious memorandum by Churchill that referred to a golden age, the martial races, and the need for "a continuous reduction in the vast number of low-grade troops now maintained under arms" in an India no longer under threat,[43] the start of this dispute can be dated precisely as 19 January 1944. Having returned to London on the previous day after an extended vacation and then treating the Chiefs of Staff to a rambling 75-minute monologue about strategic policy,[44] on the nineteenth Churchill presided over a War Cabinet meeting where, apparently for the first time, the small print of the SEXTANT program was placed before the prime minister. In response to the proposal to send a fleet to the Pacific, the prime minister agreed that British naval forces would be sent there if their presence was required by the Americans, but he also noted that the SEXTANT program involved British inactivity for the next fifteen months. By this Churchill meant that there would be no major amphibious endeavor in the Indian Ocean in the next fifteen months, but "nothing that had been said had convinced him that FIRST CULVERIN should be abandoned."[45] According to the official historian, it was on the nineteenth that Churchill repudiated the SEXTANT agreement on the grounds that he could not recall having initialed the final documents,[46] but while this does not appear to have been put into writing until 1 February the attitude of the prime minister on and after 19 January did indeed amount to a unilateral abrogation of the SEXTANT program. Moreover, after less than two days back in London his behavior had reduced the intemperate Brooke to confide to his diary that he did

not think [he] could stand much more of it. . . . We waffle about with all the usual criticism, all the usual optimist's plans, no long term vision, and we settle nothing. In all his plans he lives from hand to mouth, he can never grip a whole plan. . . . His method is entirely opportunistic, gathering one flower here and another there. . . . Being a born gambler he is always too ready to let fate look after the future provided he had what he wanted in the present.[47]

Unfortunately for the decisionmaking process, Churchill thereafter proceeded to provide proof of this damning assessment of his strategic acumen and methods of conducting the affairs of state. Within a week Churchill had produced a paper that noted that

> no plan of war . . . could be considered satisfactory which provides no outlet in 1944–1945 before Hitler is defeated for the very large air and military forces we have standing in India and around the Bay of Bengal.

The prime minister then stated that the only means of employing these forces effectively was FIRST CULVERIN, the operation being the means of either drawing Japanese forces upon itself or securing bases from which to strike "equally at Singapore, at Bangkok, in the Malacca Straits, and along the Japanese lines of communication with Burma." Leaving aside the point that Churchill could logically justify FIRST CULVERIN on one or other of these grounds but hardly both at one and the same time, Churchill proposed to get around the problem of lack of available lift by "making it clear to the Americans that if we help them in the Pacific . . . we shall expect them to assist us with a proper supply of landing craft [for FIRST] CULVERIN in October, November or December."[48]

With this last statement Churchill's arguments entered the realm of the incredible because the Americans had not asked and were very unlikely to ask for British help in the Pacific, and most certainly would not provide assistance on the scale that would be needed if FIRST CULVERIN was to proceed. Just what might be involved in this operation had been revealed in November when British studies had indicated the need for the Americans to supply 155 landing ships and 205 landing craft between 1 April and 1 November 1944 for operations in the Indian Ocean.[49] In December the Joint Staff Mission had warned London that the Americans would not provide assault shipping for the Indian Ocean. Moreover, if in the last resort the Americans had been willing to allow BUCCANEER and PIGSTICK to fall by the wayside rather than provide the means whereby they could be executed, there was no prospect of their involving themselves in a much larger FIRST CULVERIN. This fact of life was made in a paper that appeared over Cunningham's signature on 24 January, and which can be said to mark the point when battle within the British high command was joined. This paper anticipated a Chiefs' of Staff call for a point-by-point rebuttal of Churchill's arguments when the prime minister's memorandum was discussed in committee on the twenty-sixth,[50] and its contents were a statement of the obvious: that the assault shipping needed for CULVERIN could only be made available if Germany collapsed before OVERLORD or the Americans proved willing to recast their Pacific plans in order to accommodate this operation.

With obvious understatement, Cunningham's bleak conclusion was that neither eventuality was likely to occur.[51]

Despite overwhelming military logic and the realities of power stacked against it, FIRST CULVERIN remained at the forefront of British deliberations for a full month after the 24 January papers, and it was not until early April that it faded from the scene. It owed its prominence throughout February to the fact that in his paper Churchill had stated his willingness to await the arrival of a mission from South East Asia Command before settling policy, his intentions being made clear with instructions that the Chiefs of Staff and planners were not to discuss policy and planning matters with South East Asia Command before the mission presented itself.[52] Clearly Churchill, aware that South East Asia Command had to support his insistence upon large-scale amphibious operations in the Indian Ocean for reasons of its own credibility,[53] sought to preserve the AXIOM Mission from corrupting influences, but it is equally obvious that in seeking to ensure a constancy of purpose on the part of AXIOM the prime minister misjudged the situation badly. With respect to CULVERIN the Chiefs' of Staff argument was negative but pinned to the Pacific option. It was not until the second week of March, by which time AXIOM was in Washington and presenting its CULVERIN case to a distinctly unsympathetic American high command, that Churchill secured from Roosevelt acknowledgment that no American-planned operation in the Pacific was conditional on British participation.[54] Without this admission, the prime minister could not turn an insistence upon a Pacific strategy against itself and thereby weaken one of the strongest anti-CULVERIN arguments. More immediately, the technical objections to an Indian Ocean strategy that formed the small print of the Chiefs' of Staff objections to CULVERIN could not but impress themselves upon the AXIOM military, and whatever hope Churchill placed in AXIOM was belied by the fact that AXIOM lacked cohesion. It was to bring various CULVERIN options to London and these were not wholly compatible. Its proposal for a landing in Malaya in order to avoid a FIRST CULVERIN that would sacrifice surprise and present impossible maintenance problems between campaigning seasons[55] cut across its separate proposal, not to mention the prime minister's hopes, for a landing in northern Sumatra.[56] No less important, its CULVERIN proposal did not enjoy the unreserved support of two of the theater's commanders-in-chief.[57] Moreover, the AXIOM Mission brought to London one non-CULVERIN proposal, to bypass Malaya with landings in southern Sumatra and western Java,[58] that further weakened the unity of its cause, and in any case AXIOM could not but be uneasily aware that an Indian Ocean strategy left unresolved the problem of Burma, a fact noted immediately by the planners[59] and which was certain to arouse the suspicions of the American high command. Thus in discussions that were crucial in the sense that the resistance of the British service chiefs had to be broken if an amphibious strategy in the Indian Ocean was to have any chance of being accepted by the Joint

Chiefs of Staff, the AXIOM Mission lacked the unity, simplicity of aim, and singleness of purpose of the British Chiefs of Staff and their planners. As it was, a wholly unforeseen development, which served to weaken the CULVERIN cause even before AXIOM proceeded to Washington, coincided with the AXIOM talks in London.

The main arguments used by Churchill and AXIOM were those propounded by the prime minister during January and in the paper of 1 February in which he formally repudiated the terms of the SEXTANT agreement.[60] Likewise, the main arguments used by the Chiefs of Staff in the AXIOM discussion were those developed during January as justification for a Pacific commitment and then set down in response to Churchill's paper of the twenty-fourth.[61] The basis of the service chiefs' anti-CULVERIN case was fourfold. First, the Chiefs of Staff, in continuing to refer to a Pacific strategy that had been agreed at SEXTANT, reaffirmed their assertion that operations in the central Pacific would do more to speed the defeat of Japan than operations in any other theater. They also stressed the political advantage to Britain in terms of Australasian and Canadian opinion that would follow an adoption of a Pacific strategy.[62] Second, after noting that for amphibious operations in the Indian Ocean "very large land and naval forces would be required with completely separate naval forces for their support since no naval support could be provided from fleets operating in the Pacific,"[63] the Chiefs of Staff argued that CULVERIN was very unlikely to draw off important Japanese naval forces from other theaters but would involve committing "formidable naval forces to a comparatively idle role simply for deterrent and insurance purposes [and such forces would] seldom, if ever engage Japanese naval forces."[64] In fact the Joint Planning Staff had summarized this particular argument succinctly in its observations that "it is certain that on balance [CULVERIN] will draw off from the Pacific more of our forces . . . than those of the enemy, and for a much longer period." Its supporting argument, to the effect that under existing arrangements British amphibious forces would enter the Pacific in 1944 whereas CULVERIN would prevent their doing so until ten months after the end of the European war,[65] would seem neither to have had little basis in reality nor to have been used in the course of the AXIOM discussions. But undoubtedly the main thrust of the planners' argument was correct, and ironically so. CULVERIN was indeed unlikely to tie down more enemy forces than were presently committed to the theater and would mean "no appreciable build-up in the Pacific . . . until spring 1945,"[66] but there was to be no appreciable British buildup in the Pacific until the spring of 1945 even without CULVERIN.

Related military considerations formed the basis of the third and fourth arguments of the anti-CULVERIN lobby. Problems of resources and administrative overheads, in the form of the timetable for the European war, the nonavailability of American resources, and the inadequacy of India as a base for amphibious operations, formed the third line of argument deployed against the CULVERIN cause, and the rejection of the various AXIOM plans on points of operational detail, most obviously over required force levels, formed the fourth and last of these arguments.[67] If, however, these arguments demand synthesis in order to identify a single statement of the anti-CULVERIN case then it was provided in the statement that there could be no CULVERIN in November 1944 without American help and that two facts flowed from this reality: that CULVERIN in 1945 would be of little strategic consequence if the Americans were obliged to support an operation nominally intended to assist their offensives in the Pacific, and unless Germany was defeated in 1944 there could be no CULVERIN before autumn 1945.

These four arguments complemented one another neatly and together provided the Chiefs of Staff with a powerful, comprehensive but negative case. In very sharp contrast, the arguments of the pro-CULVERIN lobby were fragmented and could not evade the remorseless military logic involving deadlines, training and maintenance schedules, and force levels that undermined CULVERIN at every turn. In the absence of a convincing military case for CULVERIN the main argument that had to be developed on its behalf was political, but this involved one obvious problem. Political justification for CULVERIN existed at two separate levels, in terms of British strategic interests and of command raison d'être. But partly because AXIOM was headed by an American and partly because Washington had to be consulted, the national argument could not be fully marshalled. Probably the most effective statement of the specifically British interest in CULVERIN was provided in the so-called Dening paper in which Mountbatten's political adviser, after asserting that Allied strategy was being formed by MacArthur and Nimitz in the Pacific and increasingly by Stilwell in Burma, argued that

> [the] British role is merely contributory and . . . there is no place for an essentially British effort. . . . For South East Asia Command there appears to be no role at all, except to cover . . . Stilwell's supply route, and to deploy British forces at maximum disadvantage to themselves with minimum effect upon the enemy. . . . [And it is now] proposed to contribute to the Nimitz-MacArthur strategy the British fleet and a number of British divisions.

From this not inaccurate analysis of events and the Chiefs' of Staff strategic preferences, Dening proceeded to argue that Britain stood in need of success that would atone for previous defeats in Southeast Asia and that

> the British Commonwealth will be an essential factor in the maintenance of [the] peace [of] southeast Asia in the . . . years [to come]. To fulfil that role . . . British participation [in the war against Japan] should be a principal and not a subsidiary one.[68]

Although Foreign Secretary Eden endorsed the call for a distinctively British effort and Dening's arguments accorded with Churchill's own views, such a narrow definition of national interest, with its anti-American overtones, could hardly be used in talks with the U.S. high command as justification for CULVERIN.[69]

But if the national argument was one that had to be handled with great care, the alternative, the command argument, was no less difficult because South East Asia Command had to argue its case in terms of a directive that gave it the task of maintaining and broadening "contacts with China, both by the air route and by establishing direct contact through northern Burma [and] to engage the Japanese so as best to achieve attrition and diversion of their forces from the Pacific." In order to justify CULVERIN, therefore, South East Asia Command had either to secure revised terms of reference or to argue that CULVERIN fulfilled the requirements of its directive. The latter, of course, would require a certain measure of deviousness on the part of AXIOM and guilelessness on the part of the Joint Chiefs of Staff. Predictably, while one commodity was present in abundance the other was not. South East Asia Command was to develop various arguments in its attempt to secure for itself an amphibious role but none, in the final analysis, could evade the fact that endorsement of an amphibious strategy in the Indian Ocean would necessarily involve closing down the Burma theater. Indeed, in trying to argue that operations in Burma could neither hasten the tempo of the American advances across the Pacific nor be developed as "an alternative major thrust against Japan" as reasons for the adoption of CULVERIN, Mountbatten conceded this point.[70] The somewhat esoteric claims that "the course of action which best achieves attrition and the diversion of enemy forces is a breaching of the Malay-NEI barrier and an advance up the South China Sea"[71] could never be maintained in the face of a double American suspicion: that an amphibious strategy could only be effected at the expense of the resources needed for the Burma campaign,[72] and that adoption of an amphibious strategy could well involve closing down the Burma commitment in order to prepare for operations that might never be executed.[73] Even during the AXIOM discussions in London the Joint Chiefs of Staff made clear its displeasure with the attention being paid to CULVERIN,[74] and Roosevelt warned Churchill,

> I fail to see how an operation against Sumatra and Malaya requiring tremendous resources and forces can be mounted until the conclusion of the war in Europe. . . . There appears much more to be gained by employing all the resources we now have available in an all-out drive into Upper Burma. . . . I most urgently hope [for] a vigorous and immediate campaign in Upper Burma.[75]

In the context of alliance phraseology the American point was so clear as to be opaque, but very oddly Churchill, for all his insistence upon CULVERIN, his professed willingness to close down the Burma theater, and his attempt to portray the alternative to CULVERIN as doing nothing in South East Asia Command,[76] had glimpsed the weakness of his own argument even without American prompting. As the AXIOM discussions revealed the November 1944 schedule for CULVERIN for what it was, so Churchill asked the Chiefs of Staff, "Surely . . . there is no question of holding up operations in North Burma before the monsoon for the sake of CULVERIN, which cannot take place until the end of November and possibly April of the following year."[77]

Mountbatten might indicate a willingness to wait upon events and for a CULVERIN in March 1945,[78] but the political considerations that could provide justification for CULVERIN equally would not allow so casual a treatment of the Burma problem and so leisurely a timetable. Burma presented problems for the Chiefs of Staff and the anti-CULVERIN cause, but their "minimum necessary" solution to the Burma problem,[79] though it threatened to involve trouble with the American high command, could never involve problems of the kind that would be provoked by adoption of an amphibious strategy in the Indian Ocean as the basis of the national contribution to the war against Japan. The Pacific strategy, based upon the fleet, was not incompatible with the Burma commitment and indeed left that commitment intact and capable of further development. A CULVERIN-based strategy, conversely, was, or at least threatened to be, an alternative to that commitment and thus was unacceptable to Washington.

The problem of Burma, though it obviously affected both sides of the CULVERIN argument, thus served to strengthen the anti-CULVERIN cause, while further weakening the already brittle cohesion of the pro-CULVERIN case. But in a dispute between political imperatives and military necessities, the AXIOM discussion produced a dialogue of the deaf in which neither side could prevail. Despite the estimate on 15 February that the question of policy was likely to be settled within a week,[80] the AXIOM discussions settled down to staff studies and a wearisome exchange of memoranda after the first of the AXIOM conferences on 14 February.[81] Thus while the main discussions ranged over a variety of related matters, such as the administrative problems of northeast India, the air lift, and the Stilwell-Chennault dispute about air power and China, the CULVERIN question was examined at two levels. At the planning level the detailed examination of AXIOM's proposals, despite the Chiefs' of Staff instruction to reduce CULVERIN by 30 to 50 percent in order to bring it within the realms of the realistic,[82] produced accusations of mendaciousness on the part of South East Asia Command in the preparation of its estimates[83] and the inevitable conclusion that CULVERIN could not be executed on the basis of projected resources.[84] Moreover, the military planners noted that BUCCANEER, despite its cancellation at SEXTANT, remained an alternative to CULVERIN,[85] and that India's capacity to handle a major amphibious effort was limited, particularly in comparison to Australia.[86] The latter assertion, which was wrong, represented a complication of the anti-CULVERIN argument, the strength of which lay in the weakness of the argument for this operation and not in a comparison with a Pacific alternative. But because of the prime minister's strategic preferences and his patronage of the AXIOM cause, this complication was unavoidable, and though the choice between theaters was the province of the Combined Chiefs of Staff and not a single command, the Chiefs of Staff asked AXIOM to make a comparison[87] to the obvious irritation of the planning staff.[88] As a result the AXIOM Mission questioned the Chiefs' of Staff assumption that British participation was necessary to maintain the speed of the anticipated advances across the Pacific, and it asserted that the adoption of a Pacific commitment, involving as it would the castration of South East Asia Command, was a "serious step" and one that should not be undertaken unless "the employment of major British forces in the Pacific is strategically necessary and logistically feasible."[89] For their part the Chiefs of Staff stuck to views formed before these discussions, asserting that nothing new had emerged from the AXIOM arguments, that CULVERIN would involve an unjustified diversion of resources,[90] and that if political considerations were to be invoked in these discussions as justification for CULVERIN, then "they considered it only right that the views of Australia and New Zealand should be obtained."[91] The basic tactic of the Chiefs of Staff in these discussions had been revealed by Brooke to his long-suffering diary with the observation that at the meeting on the fourteenth "after much work I began to make him see that we must have an overall plan for the defeat of Japan and then fit in the details,"[92] but it was at the Chiefs of Staff meeting of the twenty-first that the various pieces in the anti-CULVERIN jigsaw were fitted together. At this meeting the service chiefs formally resolved upon the Pacific strategy, Brooke summarizing the occasion with the diary entry:

> Long COS meeting with planners discussing Pacific strategy and deciding on plan of action to tackle the P.M. with view to convincing him that we cannot take the tip of Sumatra for him. We shall have very serious trouble with him over this. But we have definitely decided that our strategy should be to operate from Australia with the Americans and not from India through the Malacca Straits.[93]

But by the time that the Chiefs of Staff put their names to the paper that gave notice that they were convinced of the correctness of the Pacific strategy,[94] the AXIOM discussions had been overtaken by a crisis, little known and short-lived, that both compounded the CULVERIN deadlock and revealed the extent of the unreality of the CULVERIN options because it demonstrated British naval weakness in Southeast Asia even as the high command discussed plans involving hundreds of British naval units.

On 17 and 18 February 1944 the American fast carrier force raided the Japanese base at Truk in the Carolines, and in the weeks that followed ran amok in the southern Marianas, western Carolines, and the Palaus.[95] Although great damage was wrought in the course of this rampage, the American carriers failed to account for any major enemy unit. The Japanese, suspecting an attack that they knew they could not parry, withdrew their main force units from Truk before the American blows fell. In so doing they intruded upon the AXIOM process because many of the fleet units withdrawn from the central Pacific made their way to Singapore.

The report of the Japanese move was passed to the Chiefs of Staff on the twenty-third. The service chiefs' response was to order the Joint Planning Staff to set out detailed proposals for countering an enemy redeployment that clearly threatened to upset the existing balance of weakness in the eastern Indian Ocean.[96] The reported move of two fast and five slow battleships, four heavy cruisers, some two dozen destroyers, and the fleet carriers *Shokaku* and *Zuikaku* brought to the Indian Ocean an enemy task force of a size and strength unequaled since the raids of April 1942. The British in February 1944, however, were no better placed to deal with such a force than they had been nearly two years earlier. Based on Ceylon were three squadrons of Hurricane day-fighters; one Beaufighter squadron of night-fighters; two squadrons of Beauforts that were supposed to operate as torpedo-bombers but which were assigned to antisubmarine patrols; and one Liberator and four Catalina squadrons earmarked for long-range reconnaissance and escort duties.[97] With the Eastern Fleet were the modernized battleships *Queen Elizabeth* and *Valiant*, the battlecruiser *Renown*, the fleet carrier *Illustrious*, plus an assortment of cruisers, destroyers, escorts, and minesweepers, most of which were engaged on convoy duties. An obvious numerical weakness was exacerbated by the fact that the main force units had only arrived at Ceylon at the end of January, the *Illustrious* being unready for main force action. Indeed, at this time she was taking part in Operation SLEUTH, a sweep to the south of the Cocos Islands, as part of her working-up.[98] The overall British position was a far cry from the three battleships, six carriers, and thirty-nine tactical air squadrons that were just part of the CULVERIN requirement that was under discussion in London at this time.[99]

The planners and Admiralty reacted swiftly to their orders, and before the day was out Somerville, Commander-in-Chief Eastern Fleet, was informed that two escort carriers were to ferry extra carrier squadrons to Ceylon. He was also told that he could retain the escort carriers after their arrival.[100] This, however, was but one part of a larger program that the planners had put together by the twenty-fourth. This envisaged the dispatch to Ceylon of a battleship, two cruisers, some fast escorts in order to release destroyers for fleet duties, and additional submarines. More air squadrons were to be sent to Ceylon, and minelaying and submarine patrols in the Malacca Strait were to be intensified. At the same time the Americans were to be asked to increase their submarine patrols in the Lesser Sundas, through which Japanese carriers had entered the Indian Ocean in 1942.[101] It was realized, however, that these measures would require weeks to become effective, and in the meantime "the Eastern Fleet was likely to be . . . in a dangerous position of inferiority."[102] But there was nothing that could be done about this, and as events were to prove, the British could not provide carrier and battleship reinforcement of the Eastern Fleet.

Britain's carrier problem was that, with the exception of the *Illustrious,* all of its modern fleet carriers were being refitted or completed in February 1944. With the *Indomitable,* almost lost off Sicily the previous July, being refitted at Norfolk, the British had taken advantage of the dual neutralization of enemy battle forces in Europe to dock both the *Formidable* and *Victorious.* The return of the *Victorious* from service in the southwest Pacific in September 1943 had coincided with the crippling of the *Tirpitz* and the surrender of the Italian fleet, and she had been docked at Liverpool in the expectation that she would recommission in mid-January.[103] The *Formidable* was docked at Belfast in mid-December, and with the dispatch of the *Illustrious* at the turn of the year the Americans had sent the *Ranger* to serve alongside the old *Furious* with the Home Fleet. In accordance with its SEXTANT planning, the Admiralty had intended to have the *Renown, Illustrious,* and *Victorious* with the Eastern Fleet by March 1944 in readiness for the move to the Pacific in mid-year,[104] but the refits proved more extensive than anticipated and timetables had slipped.[105] By February the Admiralty calculated that the *Victorious* would not be ready to sail until April, the *Formidable* and *Indomitable* not before June. The *Indefatigable* was expected to enter service in late May and would then relieve the *Furious,* and in her turn she would be released from service with the Home Fleet when the *Implacable* was commissioned.[106] Thus in February 1944 the Admiralty had no fleet carriers in service with which to reinforce the Eastern Fleet and would not be able to do so for several months.

Such a situation presented obvious problems. Replying to the Admiralty's signal, Somerville indicated his intention to use the additional escort carriers to provide fighter cover for the fleet and to use the air groups of the *Illustrious* and *Victorious* [*sic*] offensively,[107] an attempted marriage between thoroughbred and carthorse that had not worked well in other theaters and which he employed but once in June 1944. But long before naval intelligence indicated that the fleet carrier *Taiho* was probably with the *Shokaku* and *Zuikaku* and that six converted carriers might be in company if only in a ferrying role at this time,[108] the thoughts of the British planners, not surprisingly, had turned to the possibility of securing the loan of the *Ranger* for service with the Eastern Fleet.[109]

The British battleship position was no less difficult. In February 1944 the *King George V* and *Howe* were undergoing refit, leaving the *Anson* and *Duke of York* as the only modern battleships in service. When the first two completed their refits the second couple were to begin theirs, and with the *King George V* and *Howe* then nearing the end of their time in dockyard hands the *Anson* and *Duke of York* would barely have time to arrive in their untropicalized state at Ceylon before having to return to Britain. Despite the danger of interfering with tightly scheduled programs, the Admiralty's first choice was to send the *Anson* to the Far East. A poor third choice was to send both battleships, but the second choice included the battleship that enabled the Admiralty to escape from its problems. This choice was to send the *Anson* and *Richelieu* to the Eastern Fleet.[110]

At another time the Japanese redeployment would have caused few ripples, a passing anxiety, some hastily arranged precautionary measures, and then the turning of attention to more important matters. The service chiefs and staffs clearly thus regarded this episode, but it occurred at the time of and had obvious implications for the AXIOM discussions. The Japanese redeployment obliquely raised question marks against both sets of strategic proposals under discussion in London, and the need to use an American carrier and French battleship to support a British fleet in a British area of responsibility clearly raised very sensitive political issues. The *Richelieu* at this time was serving with the Home Fleet and had attracted favorable comment for her seakeeping and steaming qualities, her heavy tertiary armament, and good operational performances. But it was a mark of the Admiralty's reservations about the ship and her company that her file remains closed,[111] and her redeployment to the Far East necessarily raised the thorny problem of Indo-China and a Free French role in the Far East.[112] The British high command was not unsympathetic to the Free French, but on the question of their involvement in the Japanese war Churchill felt obliged to adopt an attitude of studied, if not negative, ambiguity.[113] But the fact of the matter was that in February 1944 the *Richelieu* was in service and could be sent to the Indian Ocean, if the Americans agreed. But to have to approach the Americans first for one of their carriers and then, of all things, a French battleship as reinforcements for the Eastern Fleet no doubt would have been cause for national mortification had this been known outside a very restricted circle. It is perhaps not surprising, therefore, that while the possibility of sending the *Richelieu* to the Eastern Fleet was raised by Cunningham on 25 February, eight days were to elapse before the Joint Staff Mission was instructed to approach the Americans with the request for their agreement to release the *Richelieu* for duty in the Indian Ocean until relieved by the *Howe* in or about July.[114]

At the routine Chiefs of Staff meeting of the twenty-fifth Cunningham reported to his colleagues that the Admiralty had already put in hand most of the measures that the planners had proposed, and certainly at least one of the aircraft transports detailed to move air squadrons to Ceylon began recalling her libertymen the previous day.[115] In fact at this meeting Cunningham almost seemed to welcome the prospect of an enemy move against Ceylon, and the Chiefs of Staff seem to have taken a fairly relaxed view of events. They had before them two papers, one the planners' proposals and the other a Joint Intelligence Committee appreciation of enemy intentions. The latter attached no great significance to the Japanese move, which it defined as defensive and caused by the need to avoid battle with the Americans but leave the fleet near sources of oil and rice.[116] The Chiefs of Staff clearly accepted the gist of this analysis,[117] and ordered the secretariat to forward this paper to the prime minister.[118] The apparent lack of concern on the part of the service chiefs had been reflected in Brooke's diary. Of the previous day's events Brooke had noted "a short COS for a change with no difficult problems," but, he added, "tomorrow promises badly as we then discuss the Pacific strategy with the P.M. and he will wish to fasten onto the tip of Sumatra like a limpet."[119] With the last of the AXIOM meetings scheduled for the twenty-fifth, before the Mission tried to peddle its wares in Washington, Brooke was correct in his assessment, but how "badly" was probably the one aspect of proceedings that not even he could have imagined.

After their own conference the Chiefs of Staff met Churchill at 1200. The conference began with Churchill in a towering rage because he had only just been informed of the Japanese move, and the meeting never recovered from this disastrous opening. It quickly degenerated into chaos as the alleged implications of the Japanese move became hopelessly entangled with the strategic issues involved in the CULVERIN versus Pacific dispute, seemingly to the confusion of all present. For nearly two hours the argument continued, with Churchill, after slighting references to American operations in the Marshalls, insisting that the enemy move to Singapore was proof of the need to concentrate in rather than abandon the Indian Ocean. He sought a "fleet-in-being" strategy that would tie down the Japanese in the same way as the *Tirpitz* had tied down the Royal Navy. For the Chiefs of Staff, however, the Japanese presence at Singapore was reason enough to be in the Pacific. With Cunningham arguing that he was "reasonably confident" that an attack on Ceylon could be frustrated but noting that the Americans would have to be asked for a carrier and that the *Richelieu* was available to go to Ceylon, Brooke sought approval for the development of bases in Australia. Obviously using SEXTANT's provisions for the concentration of amphibious forces in the southwest Pacific, Brooke stated that he wished British forces to be involved in MacArthur's planned advance to Borneo. This was obviously a sweetener: Churchill previously had indicated his preference for British involvement in operations in South West Pacific Command's theater rather than in Nimitz's Pacific Ocean Areas.[120] But the real sugar was provided in Brooke's suggestion that after Borneo there would be an option on a Malayan operation and, if this program was sanctioned, Australia and at least part of South West Pacific Command could be turned into a British area of responsibility.[121] Clearly, things were beginning to become complicated.

This midday meeting was followed by another that began at 1500 and lasted until 1730, and it seems to have been even more confused than its predecessor. Brooke's jaundiced assessment was that, for this meeting,

[Churchill] had packed the house against us. . . . Thank goodness I [now have] Andrew Cunningham to support me. It just makes all the difference from the days of poor old Dudley Pound. [The meeting was] very heated at times, especially when Eden chipped in knowing nothing about Pacific strategy. Winston pretended that this was all a frame-up against his pet Sumatra operation and almost took it personally. Furthermore, his dislike of Curtin and the Australians at once affected any discussion of cooperation with

> Australian forces through New Guinea to the Philippines. . . . It was a desperate meeting with no opportunity of discussing strategy on its merits.

The last comment, however, would seem to have been an overstatement because in what was obviously a very tempestuous exchange there appears to have been a very significant difference between this and the midday meeting. The latter meeting took the form of a last review of strategic issues with AXIOM before the Mission left for Washington. If, as a result, it witnessed a repetition of familiar, predictable issues, then it was largely spared the complications that arose from the Japanese redeployment of naval forces to Singapore. In fact, this matter provided an area of limited agreement between the pro- and anti-CULVERIN factions. Churchill conceded that CULVERIN could not be staged as long as the Japanese fleet was concentrated at Singapore: Brooke, more pointedly, noted that future planning would have to allow for the presence of a Japanese fleet at Singapore. But because Churchill's CULVERIN was perhaps fourteen months into the future, this was of small account. As Churchill himself noted, the British high command had to decide between Indian Ocean and Pacific alternatives, and, perhaps surprisingly, it was the prime minister, in an attempt to summarize the anti-CULVERIN argument, who provided the clearest exposition of its case. He noted, for example, that CULVERIN was too large an operation to be undertaken on the basis of available resources; that the presence of a Japanese fleet at Singapore told against it; and that it was opposed by his chief military advisers. Moreover, AXIOM's leader, Wedemeyer, also provided solid anti-CULVERIN arguments, if only indirectly. By noting CULVERIN's dependence upon Germany's timely defeat, Wedemeyer came close to conceding that CULVERIN was a nonrunner, and his emphasis on the need for large naval forces, particular escort carriers for a landing that had to be executed beyond the range of land-based air cover, could not but point to CULVERIN's weaknesses rather than its strength. But it was Wedemeyer who also claimed that India could meet the requirements of an amphibious strategy in the Indian Ocean whereas Australia could not provide the basis of a Pacific strategy, and in this attempt to keep CULVERIN alive he was supported by Dening's political forays. Arguing that Indian morale would suffer if no British effort was made in the Indian Ocean, Dening tried to counter Brooke's assertion that Australia and New Zealand had to be consulted with the assertion that they would want a British effort rather than a support for American operations in the Pacific. With Churchill arguing that as long as a Japanese fleet was at Singapore a British fleet in the Pacific was superfluous, Brooke contended that the Pacific axis represented a line of advance superior to any in the Indian Ocean, though after his suggestion at the midday meeting the minutes do not make clear to which axis he referred. With this reassertion of mutually exclusive arguments the deadlock of previous meetings remained unbroken, and it is perhaps surprising to note that

Churchill closed this conference by telling Wedemeyer that a British decision could be expected within a fortnight.[122]

Incredibly, this meeting was followed by another between Churchill and the Chiefs of Staff that began at 2200 and lasted until midnight. No less incredibly Brooke recorded that at this last meeting of the day Churchill was "in a much more reasonable mood, and I think a great deal of what we have been doing has soaked in."[123] If this was indeed the case, and whatever soaked in soaked away very quickly, then the cause of this reasonableness was not hard to find. It was on this day that Roosevelt had chosen to deliver his homily about CULVERIN, and after the events of this day Churchill knew exactly how to deal with this intrusion into British deliberations. At the midafternoon meeting Churchill asked Wedemeyer to assure his compatriots that there was no question of stinting the Upper Burma commitment in order to provide for CULVERIN. But he also asked that British reservations about the Ledo Road project be made clear to the American high command. In his reply to Roosevelt the prime minister elaborated on both matters. Claiming that the present American concern about the Ledo Road project arose from gross misrepresentation of the British position by Stilwell, Churchill noted that in light of the Japanese naval redeployment the British needed to secure their lines of communication in the Indian Ocean but that new opportunities presented themselves to the Americans in the central Pacific.[124] Clearly, not all of the Chiefs' of Staff efforts of this day had been wasted, if only with respect to trans-Atlantic signals.

The crisis provoked by the Japanese naval move lingered for a week or so, but after the twenty-fifth it amounted to little more than attention to points of detail. By the twenty-ninth Cunningham was able to report that the Americans had refused to release the *Ranger*, for which the U.S. Navy never had any great regard, but had detailed the *Saratoga*, "our best carrier,"[125] to serve with the Eastern Fleet.[126] The American high command had also agreed to the transfer of a Liberator squadron from West Africa and a Beaufighter squadron from the Mediterranean,[127] while on Ceylon one spare Corsair squadron from the *Illustrious* was made available for local defense and a previously planned reequipment of the Hurricane squadrons with Spitfires was put in hand. In addition, a detachment of Wellingtons and a squadron of Sunderlands had been made available to fill the gap caused by the reassignment of the Beauforts to antishipping duties.[128] More important, on 3 March twelve carrier squadrons, eight of which had been awaiting the recommissioning of the *Formidable* and *Indomitable,* left the Clyde in the escort carriers *Atheling* and *Begum* and the aircraft transports *Athene* and *Engadine* in the company of Convoy KMF 29A.[129] These reached Colombo on 4 April, one day after the *Richelieu*.[130] For her part the *Saratoga* sailed from Majuro on 4 March, the day that the British Admiralty Delegation sought confirmation that the U.S. Navy would maintain and repair units from the carrier force that the Admiralty still asserted would be sent to the Pacific later in the year.[131] After calling at Espiritu Santo, Hobart, and Fremantle, the *Saratoga* and her escorts effected a rendezvous with a task group from the Eastern Fleet some 1,700 miles south of Colombo on 27 March.[132] Thus for the second time in less than a year the *Saratoga* found herself as the American "half" of an Anglo-American carrier task group, and even without detailed knowledge of recent transactions in London the irony of her band striking up "Rule, Britannia" when she joined company was not lost upon Somerville.[133]

The story of this obscure episode can be concluded quickly. Although Somerville took his fleet west of the Maldives when the news of the Japanese move to Singapore was received[134] and was prepared to withdraw to Mombasa rather than accept battle with superior enemy fleet in the Bay of Bengal,[135] the only enemy move into the Indian Ocean was one staged by three heavy cruisers which accounted for but a solitary merchantman, the *Behar,* before returning to base.[136] Rather than meeting the enemy at sea, therefore, the *Saratoga* had to be content with raids on Sabang and Soerabaja,[137] both specifically requested by King, before returning on 18 May for a refit at Bremerton. Perhaps the only noteworthy feature of her time with the Eastern Fleet was that as part of a force of twenty-seven warships drawn from six nations, in the attack on Sabang the *Saratoga* was involved in perhaps the most cosmopolitan naval operation of the war.[138] But what might have proved perhaps the war's most esoteric naval operation never materialized. On 12 March the Admiralty's Director of Plans presented his Army and Air Force opposite numbers with a proposal for a carrier raid on the Japanese fleet at Singapore, but as planning led to the discounting of the use of Avenger aircraft staging through the Cocos Islands, the final proposal was to use twenty-five Mosquitos, each armed with two 950-pound HIGHBALL mines and launched from carriers, for this attack, the loss of all returning aircraft in water landings being accepted. HIGHBALL was the naval version of UPKEEP, with which 617 Squadron RAF had breached certain German dams in May 1943, UPKEEP having been a development from the idea for a weapon with which to attack the *Tirpitz* within her antitorpedo nets. But though the idea had thus come full circle, a satisfactory release mechanism for HIGHBALL could not be developed,[139] and the Japanese fleet was fated to fight and die off the Marianas and the Philippines rather than succumb to an unorthodox British attack at Singapore. But perhaps even more galling for the Eastern Fleet than its inability to attack the Japanese units gathered at Singapore was the fact that its operations along the Malay Barrier never drew a Japanese response in the three months the Japanese fleet remained at Singapore.

Japanese passivity in the face of British attacks was evidence that these operations were too small and directed against targets of too little importance to warrant response. This marginalization of the British effort in the Indian Ocean in the first half of 1944 nevertheless provides the convenient means to return to the deliberations of the British high command because it was on 26 February, at yet another of the interminable and inconclusive meetings between Churchill and the Chiefs of Staff, that the prime minister anticipated this reality. By noting that the Japanese fleet would probably return to the Pacific before the British could make a move in the Indian Ocean,[140] Churchill in effect recognized that the Eastern Fleet could not effect a "fleet-in-being" strategy. By the twenty-ninth, however, he had reversed himself on this matter. On this day he was to claim that by concentrating naval forces in the Indian Ocean the Eastern Fleet could tie down the enemy at Singapore and that "no greater service could be rendered an ally," an assertion that, had it been known to Washington, would have infuriated an American high command that had been obliged to send the *Saratoga* to the Indian Ocean because the Eastern Fleet could not look after itself, still less render such a service.

The staff meeting of the twenty-sixth[141] and the paper of the twenty-ninth[142] were ominous because they revealed that the basis of agreement within the British high command did not exist. Even worse, they revealed that the terms of reference of the debate about strategic policy were becoming dangerously blurred as Churchill and the Chiefs of Staff moved away from rather than toward a decision. At this stage of proceedings speed of decision was becoming increasingly important, yet on the twenty-sixth when Cunningham repeated his demand for a decision between the Indian Ocean and Pacific alternatives, Churchill suggested that a fleet be concentrated at Ceylon, "a half-way house," pending a decision, and on the twenty-ninth he argued that, because present plans envisaged the war against Japan lasting until 1947,[143] the most sensible course was to prepare for the next eighteen months and to use existing resources rather than make decisions "for the sake of a scheme . . . mapped out on paper, for three or four years ahead. I deprecate . . . a hasty decision to abandon the Indian theater and the prospect of amphibious operations across the Bay of Bengal."

Churchill conceded that the price of CULVERIN had been "made much too high," but he nevertheless displayed his attachment to the operation even as he paraded BUCCANEER as better than nothing. To his War Cabinet colleagues Churchill stressed that a Pacific strategy could not make use of the facilities that existed throughout the Middle East and in the Indian subcontinent, and to the service chiefs he made clear his view of CULVERIN as "a kind of Anzio," a singularly unwise and unfortunate analogy. Together, these observations indicated a determination to accept a reduced CULVERIN as the means of keeping the Indian Ocean option alive. This clearly threatened to delay still further a decision on policy, but in fact Brooke had not helped matters on this score. His suggestion that missions be sent to Australia to examine the base facilities of that country could hardly speed a decision, and his raising of the southwest Pacific and the question of command arrangements could only complicate matters when the greatest strength of the Pacific argument lay in simplicity.

Herein, perhaps, lay the most important single aspect of the policy debate within the British high command at the end of February 1944. However much the Chiefs of Staff might protest at the lack of a decision and Churchill might bewail the fact that FIRST CULVERIN had been proposed "on the assumption that no considerable detachment would be made from the Japanese main fleet" ("this was, of course, pure assumption based on what it was reasonable for the enemy to do, and there could never be any guarantee that the enemy would not do unreasonable things" such as deploying forces where they might prove effective), the argument within the British high command involved relatively simple issues until the end of February 1944. But even in this month, and with the deadlock of the first two months of 1944, there was a widening of argument, as issues became confused by the concentration of attention upon individual operations rather than plans of campaign. But however complicated and confused were the proceedings of January and February 1944, they were to be simplicity itself compared to the proceedings of the next four months.

CHAPTER THREE

Alice-in-Wonderland

From SEXTANT to OCTAGON, March–May 1944

*A*s February 1944 gave way to March with the revelation of a division between Churchill and the Chiefs of Staff that permitted no agreement, the basic simplicity of the issue confronting the British high command in settling national policy for the war against Japan became increasingly confused and obscured. The issue itself, whether a future expansion of the effort against Japan should be directed to the Indian Ocean or to the Pacific, remained unchanged, but its cohesion and form were all but lost as a result of its becoming increasingly entangled with related matters concerning means and the policymaking process itself.

In the opening weeks of this second phase the immediate problem facing the British high command remained the Indian Ocean option in the form of CULVERIN. With no credible amphibious alternative in the Indian Ocean to CULVERIN, by March 1944 the Indian Ocean strategy and CULVERIN had become, in effect, inseparable. In part this explains why CULVERIN was not canceled at this time despite the fact that the AXIOM discussions of February had shown that there was little if any prospect of this operation being staged in the 1944–45 season. By March 1944 it was clear that Churchill would not abandon his support for CULVERIN because to do so would necessarily involve the end of the Indian Ocean option. To avoid this eventuality Churchill insisted upon a revision of the CULVERIN plans and a search for a CULVERIN mutation, any CULVERIN mutation, simply in order to keep the Indian Ocean option in play. With the ill-considered plan to seize Simalur thus emerging as the CULVERIN alternative, March 1944 found the British high command concerned with an Indian Ocean option that was increasingly unrealistic on two counts. March 1944 brought home to the British high command a constancy of American opposition to CULVERIN in the course of the AXIOM discussions in Washington, and because the cutoff date for a CULVERIN in the 1944–45 season was 15 April, every day that passed without a decision in favor of CULVERIN was another day nearer its abandonment, tacit or otherwise. The fact of the matter was that Churchill's search in March 1944 for an amphibious strategy in the Indian Ocean was a search wasted, if not because of American resistance to any British effort outside the Burma theater then because, realistically, there could be no decision in favor of CULVERIN until the outcome of NEPTUNE and the progress of OVERLORD had become clear. It was only after the AXIOM Mission returned to London in early April, and the constancy of American hostility to CULVERIN could not be ignored, that reality began to assert itself and CULVERIN, in its many forms, began to fade from the forefront of British deliberations.

By the time this happened, however, the CULVERIN argument had been overtaken by wider administrative issues that took two quite separate forms. First, the question of the facilities available to meet the needs of an expanded British effort in the Far East increasingly intruded upon deliberations. The resources of Australia and India, and the fitness of these two countries to serve as the bases of the rival strategies under discussion, had concerned the British high command before March 1944, but in this month such matters became ever more pressing for obvious reasons, but to no positive effect. As the British planning staffs considered India's parlous condition and came to the realization that they knew little of the extent, or otherwise, of Australia's resources, so they became aware of the likelihood that imperial weakness and exhaustion were impartial in threatening Indian Ocean and Pacific strategies alike. In March 1944, as a result of the studies at hand, the planning staffs became conscious that, irrespective of the commitment adopted, the administrative margins on which British forces would have to operate would be desperately slender.

The second issue concerned the fact that by the third month of 1944 the planners were becoming uncomfortably aware that earlier assumptions regarding the resources that could be directed to the Far East for the final phase of the war against Japan were increasingly unrealistic. These assumptions covered every single aspect of the future British effort in the Far East— military, naval, amphibious, air, and logistical. In March 1944 the planners for the first time questioned not simply the British ability to raise the number of amphibious formations in the Far East that had been set down at SEXTANT but Britain's ability to raise any amphibious formations in the Far East. And with this came the parallel awareness that because the demands of the economy and of postwar occupation duties in Europe were likely to prove heavier than had been anticipated, the question of the dispatch of forces to the Far East during the final stages and after the end of the war in Europe had been rendered problematical. There had been an earlier awareness that schedules would be difficult, but during and after March 1944 there was an awareness that schedules might prove impossible. Moreover, at the same time the question of the logistical support for amphibious and naval forces took on an increasingly acute form because it was realized, belatedly, that after NEP-TUNE increasing demands on shipping necessitated an immediate choice between providing a train for the fleet and a train for amphibious forces because national resources could not provide both.

During and after March 1944, therefore, the British high command faced a narrowing of military options as a result of national weaknesses and exhaustion. Predictably these difficulties chose to manifest themselves in turn, with the result that as the British high command was driven from one position by the logic of unfolding events, so it found itself beset by lurking, unsuspected problems even as it sought to establish itself in a new one. At every position, therefore, the British high command found its deliberations plagued, and its intentions set at nought, by problems that were further aggravated by two changes of schedule. Because of lead-on periods and the timings of campaigning seasons in the Far East, the postponement of NEP-TUNE from May to June 1944 carried implications for any Far Eastern commitment that extended beyond a single month. Moreover, the prospects of rapid American success in breaking into the western Pacific in effect squeezed the British decisionmaking process by presenting it with the acceleration of the projected end of the Japanese war, if not into 1945 then into 1946, at a time when the British would need perhaps eighteen months to complete the transfer of forces to the Far East after the end of the war in Europe. This latter problem, quite separate from that of finding the forces to send to the Far East, took on its most urgent form after June 1944, but its reality was glimpsed by a British high command that in its second phase of deliberations became increasingly conscious of the complexity of the issues that beset any attempt to expand the national war effort in the Far East.

Time, therefore, was an increasingly important factor in British deliberations, but at this stage of proceedings time also imparted a political dimension of its own to the unfolding of events. The passing of first weeks, then months, without a decision clearly made the search for a strategy within the British high command an increasingly desperate affair, if only because of American and imperial aspects of alliance diplomacy. But such were the problems created by this lack of a decision and by the increasing unlikelihood that any decision could be reached, that in March the Directors of Plans bluntly advised the Chiefs of Staff that the present impasse could only be broken by the settling of British priorities in discussions with Roosevelt and the Joint Chiefs of Staff. In the event, however, the attempt to break the stalemate was made at the medium and junior levels of the planning staffs in London.

The available record does not permit a precise account of the search for alternative proposals that might break the deadlock at the highest levels of command. It is clear, however, that in the course of March 1944 the planners' previous preference, the Upper Burma–Pacific combination, was reaffirmed as the basis of policy even as the staffs examined the possibility of an offensive into the Lesser Sundas. It is equally clear that by April, even as the planners moved to the conclusion that such an offensive could not be undertaken, this proposal acquired a certain momentum as it seemed to offer the basis of a compromise that could be set before the imperial conference to be held in London in May. Thus while the Chiefs of Staff worked through April and May on the basis of the Lesser Sundas option, called the Middle Strategy, the planners worked on an alternative that, despite being called the Modified Middle Strategy, was effectively the Pacific commitment. When, in June, the Middle Strategy proposal collapsed after having served as the basis of imperial consultation in May, the planners then presented the Modified Middle Strategy in its place. The result was that Churchill repudiated all options other than a full-fledged Indian Ocean commitment, thereby leaving deliberations at the point from which they had started. In so doing, Churchill ushered in the third and final phase of British deliberations in which, with the OCTAGON conference in the immediate offing, an ambiguous and unworkable compromise was agreed in August, two months after a British fleet should have been in the Pacific.

The fact that so many individual questions had become entangled by the end of February ensured that CULVERIN continued to figure heavily in British deliberations even after the AXIOM Mission left for Washington and the "Japanese-fleet-to-Singapore" crisis passed from the scene. But if CULVERIN remained so, for the most part also did the unchanging arguments of the previous two months: the passing of time merely saw these honed rather than developed. Accordingly, the final items of business dealing with the reinforcement of the Eastern Fleet were accompanied by exchanges of memoranda between Churchill and the Chiefs of Staff that repeated known arguments in readiness for a War Cabinet conference on 8 March, which, given the deadline of 15 March,[1] clearly all regarded as critical. Thus even though the Chiefs of Staff in their paper of 1 March mixed the argument in favor of involvement in operations in the western Pacific with an emphasis upon a commitment in the southwest Pacific that previously had been absent,[2] the substance of argument differed but little from that contained in the paper of 5 February. Likewise, Churchill's responses of both 5 and 7 March covered very familiar ground.[3] Both papers sought to justify CULVERIN and an Indian Ocean strategy in political rather than military terms. Brooke's dismissive comment on the second paper was that "he has produced the worst paper I have seen him write yet. Trying to make out a case for an attack on the top of the island of Sumatra!"[4]

But with the planners simultaneously setting down as the basis of policy the consideration of military operations in terms of military merit before their being examined in terms of political acceptability or otherwise,[5] the meeting of the eighth proved predictably indecisive and bad-tempered. It confirmed the validity of the warning given two days earlier to the Chiefs of

Staff by the Directors of Plans that no amount of discussion and memoranda would break the impasse.[6]

The Chiefs' of Staff argument in this meeting was based upon the contents of two papers discussed in committee before this gathering with the War Cabinet.[7] The argument had three main provisions: a naval role in the southwest Pacific under American command; a logistical commitment to Australia rather than India; and an acceptance that northeast India could not be expected to shoulder the burdens that would be imposed by an amphibious commitment in the Indian Ocean. The military and technical weakness of this argument was that a lack of information about Australia precluded telling comparisons between India and Australia as the bases for the strategies under discussion, and in a War Cabinet meeting in which Brooke noted that Churchill was "in a hopeless mood, incapable of taking any real decision [and] Portal as usual not too anxious to argue against the PM, and dear old Cunningham so wild with rage that he hardly dared to let himself speak,"[8] this weakness was the point on which CULVERIN's immediate survival was ensured. The outcome of the meeting was that arrangements for CULVERIN and the planned buildup of forces in India were to proceed pending a decision on policy that would be reached after a mission had gone to Australia and reported upon its ability to receive the forces that would be sent to that country as part of a Pacific strategy.[9]

These arrangements in effect sealed CULVERIN's fate, and in this fact is the basis of the suspicion that the Australian issue was contrived. The cutoff date for a March 1945 CULVERIN was 15 April 1944,[10] and the delay of the choice between the Indian Ocean and the Pacific pending the report on Australia pushed back a decision until such a time that CULVERIN would be lost by default.[11] Given the fact that reports on the subject of national resources had been submitted by the Australian government in June and December 1943,[12] the basis for a decision between Australia and India would seem to have been available to the British high command in March 1944. Moreover, this mission seems not to have affected the final decision in favor of a Pacific strategy one way or another since that decision was made despite this mission's reports that indicated that Australia's condition was worse than expected. But if indeed the Chiefs of Staff and their planners were stalling a decision in order to eliminate CULVERIN from consideration,[13] they ran the danger of having the arguments reversed.[14] There could be little positive advantage in arguing a case for a Pacific strategy when, on the Chiefs' of Staff own admission, the logistical basis for such an undertaking was unknown. In any event, the meeting of 8 March threw up questions not simply about India and its administrative margins, as the Chiefs of Staff clearly intended, but about Australia, the fleet train, and amphibious forces, and on these matters the Pacific argument was decidedly weak. Moreover, the Chiefs' of Staff finesse could not but be short-lived, and it was on the twelfth, after the Chiefs of Staff ordered a complete review of CULVERIN,[15] that Churchill took the step of ordering a member of the AXIOM Mission in London to join the planning staff in order to produce a new CULVERIN variant by the twentieth. Completely in accord with the instructions that he had issued to AXIOM before it had arrived in London, Churchill tried to insist that the new CULVERIN planning be under his own direction and not that of the Chiefs of Staff.[16] At this same time Churchill told Dill that he wished to see an advance across the Bay of Bengal to the islands and Malaya, and that planning was to proceed for BUCCANEER and CULVERIN for late 1944 or, more realistically, for early 1945.[17] With Ismay also writing to Mountbatten's chief of staff that CULVERIN enjoyed heavyweight political support and was likely to prevail,[18] clearly the events of 8 March stirred Churchill into a frantic effort to ensure the adoption of an Indian Ocean commitment very literally before time ran out for CULVERIN.[19]

This effort, which gave rise to a Simalur variant of CULVERIN that even AXIOM was loathe to accept, was to founder, even before the Mission's return to London. It was to founder for several reasons as a number of issues came together, but long before it did so, other related matters had come to the fore and of these the most immediate concerned India. The reason for this was obvious. India would have to serve as the base for an Indian Ocean strategy but, as the Chiefs of Staff appreciated, question marks had to be placed against its ability to even sustain, still less expand, its war effort as the struggle against the Axis powers entered its sixth year.[20] By 1944 the Indian Army deployed the equivalent of thirty-two divisions and 2,688,000 troops,[21] but after the disastrous Bengal famine, which between July and December 1943 claimed 1,500,000 lives from starvation, cholera, smallpox, and malaria,[22] India's economic stability was threatened by an inability to secure more than half of its required imported foodstuffs, an increasingly serious shortage of raw materials for industry,[23] and an inadequate rail system that forced it to try to meet subcontinental responsibilities with fewer locomotives than the largest single British company.[24] The inevitable side-effect of these and other weaknesses was a gathering inflation that was deemed to threaten the country's financial stability[25] and which certainly affected the morale of the Indian Army, the soldiers of which were only too conscious of the plight of their dependents and villages.[26]

The military aspects of these problems took several forms. Most obviously, India lacked the administrative infrastructure necessary to maintain the naval, amphibious, and support forces needed to mount an amphibious strategy in the Indian Ocean. Moreover, with east coast ports out of bounds, the port facilities, handling amenities and rail system of India limited the flow of reinforcements passing through Bombay to 50,000 service personnel in a twenty-one-day cycle,[27] and Bombay was nine days from Calcutta by high-priority troop train and as long as a month by ordinary nonpriority train.[28] Bombay, however, was India's main commercial port, and its working arrangements were not helped by the disastrous accident of 14 April when two docks, fifty godowns, and some twenty warships and merchant-men were destroyed when the ammunition ship *Fort Stikene* exploded.[29] Bombay's limited processing facilities posed specific problems in that any major redeployment of forces to India could only be at the expense of the normal flow of replacements to and rotation of formations and units already in India.[30] Moreover, with twelve-month lead times for any con-struction of facilities in India,[31] and eighteen months for the provision of heavy port machinery,[32] the delay of British decisions represented a crip-pling liability for administrative and operational planning. And to add to these problems, incredible though this may seem, by 1944 southern India and Ceylon, where the greater part of facilities needed for a CULVERIN strategy would have to be built, were short of manpower, and the African labor supply was also exhausted.[33] In short, by 1944 India was taxed to the limits by the demands already placed upon it. This was known to Chiefs of Staff only too aware that India had no administrative margin with which to protect itself against the cyclones, floods, famines, and epidemics that periodically inflicted themselves upon it.[34]

At the time of the 8 March conference not all these details were known to the Chiefs of Staff and the planners, and indeed such incidents as the destruction of the *Fort Stikene* remained for the future. But many of these details were no more than the dotting of *i*s and crossing of *t*s: enough was known of India's increasingly desperate straits for the Chiefs of Staff to dis-count any possibility of adding to its problems. But Australia was another matter, and in setting out a preference for Australia over India as the base of future British operations in the Far East the Chiefs of Staff on 8 March were influenced by climatic and racial considerations. But as the Chiefs of Staff soon came to appreciate, Australia presented problems of its own, and these proved just as intractable as those of India.

The most obvious of Australia's problems was manpower exhaustion. By the end of 1943 half of the male population between 18 and 40 years of age had volunteered for the armed forces[35] and of the entire male pop-ulation of 2,850,000 over the age of 14 only 300,000 were not involved either in the services or in direct war work.[36] But such was the strain on its manpower reserves that the end of 1943 found Australia forced to consid-er reduction of its services in order to free manpower for industry and food production.[37] Moreover, Australia stood in desperate need of capital invest-ment programs that could be undertaken only by measures that would fur-ther reduce its already declining influence with its allies.[38] The Australian government was well aware that what little status it commanded was relat-ed directly to the military forces it could provide for operations, not to the less obvious contribution Australia made in terms of food production for Britain and India and the provision of facilities for U.S. forces in the country.[39]

In March 1944, however, the Chiefs of Staff focused immediate atten-tion upon two other Australian matters. First, however slender the dockyard facilities of India and Ceylon, they were nevertheless more substantial than those of Australia. The latter possessed just one graving dock that could take a capital ship, one floating and five graving docks for cruisers, and six graving docks for destroyers and escorts.[40] Under the circumstances, that Australia built and overhauled 13,815,000 tons of merchant shipping in 1943 was as remarkable an achievement as any registered by its armed forces.[41] But the implication for a British fleet entering the Pacific was clear enough. Second, a Pacific strategy based upon Australia necessarily involved a somewhat fragile Anglo-Australian relationship in which mutual antipathy and suspicions were well to the fore.

Reference has been made to the fact that Churchill after SEXTANT refused any suggestion that the British high command settle policy issues in consultation with Australia, and with the start of this second phase of post-SEXTANT deliberations within the British high command he reconfirmed this refusal.[42] There is little doubt that this high-handed treatment of Australia stemmed from an antipathy toward Australians in general and Curtin in particular,[43] and that this may well have been the legacy of the events of February 1942. But it had obvious implications for the formulation of British policy not least because policy could not divorce itself from Australian realities. The fact of the matter was that Australian realities at one and the same time both supported and weakened the Pacific argument. The Australians, having carried the burden of the imperial effort in the Pacific, sought a British commitment to their country in order to provide a distinctly British contribution to this war,[44] to prevent their own relegation to a secondary role in the Pacific,[45] and to counter an increasing American hegemony in the Antipodes.[46] But Curtin, having set great political and personal store upon a direct relationship with MacArthur, refused to consider the change of command arrangement that was one of the most important single considerations for the British high command as it deliberated upon a Pacific commitment,[47] and this despite the increasingly casual attitude displayed to Australia by the Americans in general and MacArthur in particular. As it was, the British high command collectively had little regard for Curtin, whom it saw as being MacArthur's creature,[48] and it was aware of Curtin's isolation in these matters because of the utter contempt of the Australian military for the U.S. Army in general and for South West Pacific Command and MacArthur in particular.[49] The Australian dimension, therefore, provided no easy options for the British high command as it set about trying to settle national policy, and other imperial considerations were not sufficient to influence matters one way or another. South Africa barely entered British considerations though it was known that its service personnel were not welcome in the Indian subcontinent.[50] Canada appears to have been discounted from British considerations long before it formally indicated that in Pacific matters it preferred to consider itself North American rather than imperial,[51] and New Zealand was as exhausted as Australia and most certainly could not make good any of its neighbor's weaknesses.[52] Whether or not the British high command fully appreciated the fact, in the spring of 1944 Britain was involved in a redefinition of its past relationship with its Dominions and Empire: whereas Britain had looked to the Empire as the means of supplementing national power, from this time India and the Dominions looked to Britain to make good their own individual and collective weaknesses.[53]

But from the start of this second phase of post-SEXTANT deliberations, the British high command was made increasingly aware that Britain could not make good imperial weaknesses and expectations. It was well aware that imperial ties had been loosened under the impact of war,[54] and Churchill was not alone within the British high command in fearing the ends to which American power could be put in the postwar world.[55] But March 1944 saw the start of the process whereby the British high command was brought to the realization that the resources needed for the expansion of the national effort in the Far East would not necessarily be available.

By definition, this realization dawned slowly, but in the first half of March the basic outline of the problems that the British high command faced in raising the means for an expanded national effort in the war against Japan began to come into focus. The question of the fleet train necessary for oceanic operations was the catalyst in this process, though in one sense this is hardly the correct way to describe a matter that had been raised in October 1943 and thereafter neglected. Be that as it may, in March 1944 the question presented itself in urgent form for one reason. The British navy was short-haul. In January 1944 it had a fleet train of 560 purpose-built and requisitioned auxiliaries, of which 114 were colliers and 165 had been decommissioned. Hulks, colliers, coasters, small tankers, accommodation and amenities ships accounted for much of a fleet train that had evolved either to provide temporary facilities or to supplement existing shore bases.[56] Of the 2,250,000 tons of merchant shipping under direct Admiralty control, 44 percent was under charter for single voyages only and 22 percent was committed to operational support that could not be curtailed. Only 111 ships of the train were suitable for oceanic work in the Pacific, and many of these would have to be refitted before they could move to the Far East.[57] With the European naval war approaching its climax in the first half of 1944, the fleet train problem was crucial because the nature and scale of the effort that would be made in the Far East would be determined by the size of the fleet train that could be mustered for its support.[58] But in its turn, the scale of this support had to be determined by what was available from national shipping resources once two higher priorities, namely the import requirements of the United Kingdom and the demands of OVERLORD, had been met. Britain needed 28 million tons of imports a year in order to sustain its population and war effort, but in 1944 the British high command was faced, on the basis of existing and projected shipping resources, by the prospect of shortfalls of 4 million tons for both 1944 and 1945. Because existing stockpiles were sufficient to cover a seven-week deficit in one year but not a three-month deficit accumulated over two years, the British high command in 1944 knew that the 136 ships needed for a fleet train in 1945[59] would have to be found from a merchant marine that was unable to meet minimum national requirements.[60]

This, however, was but one of two aspects of the fleet train problem, and the second was the more important because of its wider implications. The British high command realized that the demand on shipping would increase with the invasion of northwest Europe, but in 1944 it belatedly acknowledged that this demand would increase with the end of the war in Europe. The need to repatriate servicemen and ex-prisoners, to return Commonwealth personnel to their countries of origin, and to redeploy forces, both American and British, from Europe to the Far East could only add to the demands on shipping resources already inadequate to meet national needs.[61] And to this had to be added the need to maintain forces of occupation in Europe. March 1944 saw, with discussion of the implications of the Soviet demand for the division of postwar Austria into zones of occupation, the start of the erosion of earlier assumptions about the force levels needed to meet occupation duties. The Chiefs of Staff concluded that the Soviets would make the same demand over Hungary and Bulgaria and that "lack of adequate forces in southeast Europe after the last war precluded [Britain] from having an effective voice in the final settlement in that part of the world."[62] The full implications of this took time to reveal themselves, but the fact that in April 1945 the British Army in Europe numbered seventeen divisions serves as the yardstick by which the final calculation that 14.3 divisions were needed for postwar occupation duties[63] can be assessed. Thus in the spring of 1944 the British high command was forced to acknowledge that the divisions needed for any amphibious commitment in the Far East were unlikely to be available. This acknowledgment came alongside the realization that Britain did not have the assault shipping, the naval manpower, and the support shipping needed to mount an amphibious strategy, whether in the Indian Ocean or the Pacific.[64]

The lack of support shipping for an amphibious force followed naturally from the problems that surrounded the raising of a train for the fleet. The simple fact was that if national resources would not stretch to the provision of one train, they would most certainly not stretch to the provision of two.[65] No less intractable was the fact that as the British manpower shortage worsened, the navy would not be able to simultaneously cut manpower, maintain force levels in Europe, and provide both a fleet and an amphibious force in the Far East,[66] and, indeed, the navy was painfully aware that its manpower needs in 1944, which were the least of the services, could not be met by the whole of the available military class of that year.[67] In very simple terms, to raise a corps-sized amphibious force in the southwest Pacific involved the provision of 126,943 sailors to meet the base, loading, and manning requirements of such a force.[68] Such numbers were well beyond the navy and nation in 1944–45. But what focused the point of argument in March 1944 was the fact that whereas the United States had intended to build some 450 landing ships in 1944, Britain, which would need to build some 120 landing ships for various Far East options, would not complete more than half of its projected total of 80. Output could not be increased unless naval and merchant priorities were downgraded, and this was not possible.[69] But what was equally not possible was to seek American help for operations outside the Pacific. American planning involved the raising of a lift for twelve divisions and the accelerated Pacific timetable was taking on an air of permanence at this time, and as the British planners considered matters, the whole idea of any amphibious strategy assumed grotesque proportions: even the raising of two amphibious divisions on the NEPTUNE scale of establishment was impossible.[70]

According to the account of a naval staff officer, based in London and working on the transfer of assault shipping to the Far East, 11 May 1944 witnessed his reporting to the First Sea Lord that existing planning was unrealistic. Cunningham's alleged response was wholehearted agreement: thereafter planning continued even though its futility was recognized.[71] Not surprisingly, there is nothing in the records to substantiate this account. But the general course of events would seem to suggest that such an exchange could well have taken place: perhaps its only questionable aspect is why such an exchange did not take place long before May. It is clear that after SEXTANT there was a downward revision of British amphibious capacity in the Far East by the planning staffs, a revision that ran ahead of the discussions at the Chiefs' of Staff level.[72] But what is equally clear is that after the War Cabinet meeting of 8 March 1944 one other aspect of planning ran ahead of upper-level deliberations. Note has been taken that two days earlier the Chiefs of Staff had been warned by the Directors of Plans that no amount of discussion and memoranda would end the deadlock on policy. Their view was that this impasse could only be broken by Roosevelt and the Joint Chiefs of Staff within the context of the Combined Chiefs of Staff. This analysis could hardly have recommended itself to the Chiefs of Staff, and most certainly it would never have been entertained by Churchill for a moment, but another way of attempting to end the stalemate was at hand in the form of the Middle Strategy initiative. (See the map on p. 221.)

The pedigree of the Middle Strategy is impossible to establish. It may lie in the MacArthur Plan, drawn up some four months earlier as the basis of American operations in the southwest Pacific theater,[73] which Churchill professed to favor. It may lie either in those January signals from Mountbatten that sought to justify CULVERIN in terms of its being the first of several operations that would lead into other theaters,[74] or in the AXIOM exchanges, by which time Mountbatten's proposals had been formalized. Most certainly, there were similar elements between the Middle Strategy and the Sunda Strait option and between the Middle Strategy and Brooke's suggestion in late February 1944 for a movement against Singapore from the east. But an embryo Middle Strategy seems to have entered the lists for the first time in the form of a letter from Brigadier Ransome of the War Cabinet Office to Mallaby of the Joint Planning Staff, dated 6 March 1944, which stated,

> Even if sensibly pruned . . . CULVERIN can . . . not be met by the British until some months after the defeat of Germany. If this operation is undertaken it is very clear that we shall stand idle for many months . . . while the world waits for our blow to fall. Moreover, if Germany is not defeated as early as hoped, our effort against Japan is correspondingly delayed.

In making this point Ransome covered very familiar ground, but after noting that a Southeast Asia policy

> is therefore conditional upon the defeat of Germany and tied to that event in date [whereas] this is not true of our Pacific strategy,

Ransome noted that British and imperial forces would predominate in South West Pacific Command in 1945[75] and that

> British sub-commanders might be appointed to undertake . . . the following operations in 1945: Halmahera, northeast Celebes, northern Borneo, Formosa [the southern landing], Pescadores, Hong Kong–Ryukyus.

While certain of these operations, such as Formosa, had figured in Allied deliberations, others clearly either had not or had commanded but little consideration. Ransome, therefore, appears to have focused attention upon a British role in the central and eastern Indies for the first time even though the main axis of advance, through the Lesser Sunda into the East China Sea and a rendezvous with the Americans, in effect amounted to acceptance of a Pacific commitment. Indeed, Ransome was quite specific in this matter when he wrote, "Whether we like it or not the main thrust against Japan must be from the Pacific," and against this observation someone, perhaps Mallaby, noted in pencil in the margin, "and Anglo-American as far as possible."[76]

Herein may lie the origins of the Middle Strategy, but timing also provides one possible explanation of this option's beginnings. The formal terms of reference of a directive for an evaluation of the Middle Strategy was not issued to the planning staff until 1 April,[77] and on the previous day Dill reported an informal conversation that he and Noble had with Marshall and King after a Combined Chiefs of Staff meeting. In the course of this conversation the Americans suggested a British offensive along either the Java–Borneo–Saigon or the Java–Celebes–northern Borneo–Saigon/Canton axis.[78] It seems likely, therefore, that the Americans were at least the foster parents of this idea. As it was, the directive, in setting down the Timor–Celebes–Borneo–Saigon axis of advance and a timetable that involved landings on Amboina in either January or March 1945, on Timor in April, and a move against French Indo-China in either March/April or September/October 1945, shows obvious signs of preliminary, predirective study, and Churchill's signal to Roosevelt of 10 March, with its comments about operations based on northern Australia, can be interpreted to mean that planning for operations into the Indies was in hand in London, if only for the purposes of comparison.[79] But if there had been some form of preliminary planning, it was not enough to avoid the need to recast the Middle Strategy's terms of reference when the first staff paper was submitted on 12 April.[80]

By the time that this report was completed, however, its bleak conclusion that "the proposal has little to recommend it" had been overtaken by events. Obviously the cause of the Middle Strategy was not helped by the 10 April decision to strip the Indian Ocean of all its amphibious element in order to provide for ANVIL,[81] but, in fact, the study had been overtaken by events even before it had been authorized because of American planning changes. When Ransome put pen to paper, American planning was still governed by terms of reference supplied at SEXTANT, but in the course of March the British high command was made aware not simply of the American view that British involvement was not the sine qua non of Pacific operations but that these operations were to be accelerated. The first indication of the advancing of American schedules was made known to the British high command on 11 March[82] and the planning staffs made their first attempts to adjust to new American schedules in the form of the paper of the twenty-third.[83] But from the start the twin implications of the acceleration of the American schedules were obvious. First, an American advance into the western Pacific in 1945 robbed a CULVERIN in the 1944–45 season of what little military relevance it possessed.[84] This point was inescapable, as was the conclusion that the Americans would not be prepared to support an operation in the Indian Ocean at the very time that their own effort in the western Pacific materialized. As Dill noted, the "US intention [is] to break into [the outer] crust [of the Japanese defenses] at its weakest, in the Pacific, and by striking at the inner ring to leave [the] remainder of [the] crust to rot," and that, as a result, "it is clear that no American naval or amphibious resources will be available for other major operations such as CULVERIN."

But this military reality notwithstanding, the political logic behind CUL-VERIN remained undiminished:

It seems unlikely that British assistance will be required . . . in the approach to the inner ring [of Japanese defenses]. . . . It remains to be decided whether British help against the inner ring, and later against the Japanese mainland itself, will be necessary. . . . It may be that when Germany has been defeated the Americans will find themselves strong enough to strike the decisive blow singlehanded, and leave for us the task, which in any case must be ours, of picking the southeast Asia fruit, just as it ripens or rots.[85]

The proposed acceleration of the American timetable thus could be used as additional justification for an Indian Ocean strategy, just as Churchill had claimed, and despite Dill's argument in conversation with Marshall that "our [role] should be positive, important, and our own as opposed to something subsidiary to decisive American strokes."[86]

Second, the same logic, and particularly the military logic, applied to all British operations outside the Pacific, not just CULVERIN, and with an extra dimension when applied to the Middle Strategy. The staff paper of 12 April noted the obvious weakness of the Middle Strategy, namely how to exploit an offensive through the Lesser Sundas, remained unspecified. But no less important was that the fact that an advance through the Arafura and Banda Seas would be supported by American air power in western New Guinea. Thus the Middle Strategy would in no way support or help the Americans, and such support and help was the only military rationale for the Middle Strategy in the first place.[87] With this report conceding that a March 1945 schedule for an attack on Amboina was ambitious,[88] the logic of both the Middle Strategy and the Chiefs' of Staff argument in favor of a Pacific commitment was clearly undermined by developments in March 1944 in Washington. Indeed, Dill made this point in his signal of 31 March. Having previously informed London of American irritation with the lack of a British decision on Southeast Asia,[89] and despite his earlier assessment that "there are Americans who feel that British aid will be necessary . . . but the problem has not yet been worked out in detail," the signal of 31 March 1944 made it very clear that King, whom Cunningham noted "has become very difficult" in the time that the AXIOM Mission was in Washington,[90] did not envisage a British role beyond the New Guinea–Borneo–French Indo-China littoral.[91]

But the acceleration of the American timetable for Pacific operations was not the only development in Washington at this time: Dill's signals on this matter ran in company with reports on the fortunes of the AXIOM Mission. Despite and perhaps because of the fact that at the first formal AXIOM meeting in Washington on 3 March "controversial subjects were avoided,"[92] Dill's first AXIOM signal on 6 March indicated that Wedemeyer's initial report had gone well.[93] But at the same time London was warned that "the US Chiefs of Staff are not particularly interested at the moment in CULVERIN . . . and are content to let matters rest until they hear from our Chiefs."[94]

With the CULVERIN ball put firmly back in its court, the British high command was also warned that its American counterpart remained unconvinced about this operation and by AXIOM.[95] Thereafter the AXIOM discussions centered upon Upper Burma, and despite Dill's optimism[96] it very quickly became obvious that bad news was in the offing. Marshall's refusal to consider the removal of Stilwell,[97] American problems with Chiang Kai-shek,[98] and the American concern with the airlift to China proved to be the padding that surrounded the fact that by 15 March there had been no mention of CULVERIN.[99] Indeed, according to AXIOM's own record, its only discussions about CULVERIN in Washington were strictly off the record[100] and were notable, from the very first informal meetings of Wedemeyer with individual members of the Combined Chiefs of Staff on 1 March, for the utter lack of American enthusiasm for an operation that the Joint Chiefs of Staff defined as "projected and nebulous."[101] Long before the Joint Chiefs of Staff on 21 March provided the British with their revised timetable for the Pacific along with the information that they "cannot . . . at this time agree to support Operation CULVERIN or any similar operation involving [a] large amphibious commitment in South East Asia Command,"[102] the demise of CULVERIN, from neglect, had been foreshadowed.

It was against this background, therefore, that the Middle Strategy took shape and the CULVERIN variants ordered by Churchill were developed. Of the latter there were, in effect, two, namely CULVERIN *de novo* and the Simalur option. Despite a common name, the two were very different. The first, because of its pedigree, shared many features with CULVERIN plans that had been discarded already, and indeed the most obvious feature that it shared was a force requirement that made it wholly unrealistic. As developed, this new CULVERIN version involved the equivalent of five divisions[103] with 188,000 troops; a naval commitment, exclusive of the covering force, that included two fleet and 14 escort carriers, 15 cruisers, 45 destroyers, and 75 escorts; and assault and support shipping that totaled 108 landing ships, 853 landing craft, and 57 personnel and 122 store ships. Confined simply to the Sumatran aspect of CULVERIN, the new plan envisaged a four-phase operation. The first phase was preliminary landings against Tyalang, Meulabo, and Simalur which were to provide homes for nineteen fighter squadrons in readiness for the main force landings that were to take place two days after air cover was in position. The second phase was the seizing and consolidation of beachheads at Bireuen and Lho Seumawe, with troops airlifted into position and heavy bomber formations being deployed at Sigli and Lho Seumawe. Between D+5 and D+30 the third phase was to see armor used to secure Kota Raja while two long-range penetration groups secured the southern approaches to the beachheads: the fourth and final phase was to result in the reduction of Sabang.[104] With the final form of this plan involving the use of no fewer than three battleships, five fleet carriers, between 16 and 20 escort carriers, 73 destroyers, and lift for 114,000 troops,[105] it is difficult to see how this plan could do anything but reemphasize the impracticability of this operation. Indeed, an oblique acknowledgment to this effect was given in the planning treatment of the "artificial battlefield" concept: the idea of using five 3,600- by 240-foot air strips, each towed by ten Liberty ships to mooring positions off the Sumatra coast, was considered to be between eleven and nineteen times more expensive in terms of man-days than the preparation of five strips ashore. But an alternative explanation of this seemingly pointless staff examination might be found in the observation of a member of Churchill's staff that while CULVERIN should not be closed down because events might allow the operation to proceed, "the Prime Minister will react much more rationally to hard facts and figures if he feels that we here are really doing our best to make [CULVERIN] possible."[106] It may well be that such a calculation was behind the March 1944 reexamination of CULVERIN.

But if this reconsidered plan was unreal,[107] its alternative, the Simalur option, entered into the realm of the absurd. Simalur had no roads, and being so low-lying was all but indistinguishable from its surroundings in terms of water content. It had no capacity to operate an airfield, and had no anchorage.[108] The seizing of the island had been mooted in the Mountbatten–Wingate CULVERIN paper at QUADRANT, but it had never been seen, even in that frenetic document, as more than a minor extension of the main operation. But in his desire to secure any Indian Ocean commitment, and perhaps because the Simalur option seems to have been examined both as an operation complete in its own right and as a preliminary to a full-scale CULVERIN,[109] in March 1944 Churchill pronounced the Simalur sideshow as good as CULVERIN itself, besides being more economical in manpower. In this situation it was perhaps no surprise that Brooke was moved to express fears for the prime minister's sanity in "this ghastly Alice-in-Wonderland situation"[110] which was largely of Churchill's own making, and which prompted the Chiefs of Staff to decide on 21 March that they would resign together if the prime minister persisted in what amounted to "false statements, false documentation and defective strategic thinking."[111]

Confirmation that this was a genuine threat and not Brooke merely venting his frustrations to his diary was provided by the AXIOM Mission after its return to London: Wedemeyer's final report to Mountbatten noted that it was very likely that the British service chiefs would resign if Churchill tried to force an amphibious strategy in the Indian Ocean upon them.[112]

The return of the AXIOM Mission to London seems to mark the point when CULVERIN, in its many forms, was either killed or buried: the confusion of the planning process by this stage of proceedings in early April was such that it is impossible to provide a definitive comment other than to note that CULVERIN's ghost may well have stalked the corridors of Whitehall thereafter, but its mortal remains had been suitably interred.[113] What can be stated with some certainty about AXIOM and CULVERIN, however, is that the exchanges during this second session in London between 3 and 18 April, and particularly the staff conference of the fifth, were conducted very much with an eye on the historical record, if not by the British then certainly by Wedemeyer.

This Joint Planning Staff conference of the fifth was indeed a somewhat remarkable affair. It took the form of a final examination of the revised CUL-VERIN plan, and Wedemeyer raised three objections. He argued that the provision of both ground and air forces for this operation was inadequate, that the period between Phase 1 and Phase 2 was too short and should be lengthened to three months, and that an invasion force would have no protection against air attack from the Andamans and the Nicobars. As a practical point he suggested that a CULVERIN in March 1945 should be preceded in January by a division-sized assault on the Andamans, an option that the planning staff admitted had not been considered. The general agreement was that CUL-VERIN, in its present form, was underinvested, but when the chairman noted that South East Asia Command could not expect reinforcement until the end of the war in Europe Wedemeyer expressed considerable surprise and claimed that he had been led to expect that reinforcements were to be deployed to the Far East immediately after the breakout (i.e., in Normandy) occurred. Told very simply that the size of the German army rendered such a redeployment impossible, Wedemeyer brought the meeting to a close with the demand for written confirmation of what he had just been told.[114]

Given Wedemeyer's reputation as one of the most intelligent officers in the U.S. Army, and resisting the obvious comment and allowing for the fact that this reputation owes not a little to Wedemeyer's own pronouncements on this subject, that Mountbatten's emissary should express himself thus on this most obvious of matters is incredible. Seemingly the only rational explanation of this extraordinary episode is that Wedemeyer sought to ensure that responsibility for the demise of CULVERIN would be fixed firmly on the British planners, though whether this was for the sake of South East Asia Command or the Joint Chiefs of Staff is a moot point. The British planners, however, seem to have had no qualms on the matter, and if Wedemeyer held any other illusions about the real world these must have been dispelled at a meeting with Churchill and the Chiefs of Staff on the seventeenth when strategic discussions waited upon the prime minister's "commenting at length on the fauna and flora" of Southeast Asia. Churchill's continued support for the Simalur option even at this stage must have seemed like the kiss of death to the project as far as Wedemeyer and his AXIOM colleagues were concerned, but Churchill and Wedemeyer nevertheless remained in agreement that only in Southeast Asia did Britain have a real role in the war against Japan. But while Wedemeyer, presumably as a result of his recent refamiliarization with the wishes of the Joint Chiefs of Staff, concluded in his report to Mountbatten that there was no possibility of an amphibious strategy being sanctioned before Burma was cleared,[115] Churchill at this meeting indicated that the Middle Strategy seemed an area of agreement between himself and the Chiefs of Staff. Wedemeyer cast doubts upon the feasibility and merits of the Middle Strategy,[116] but, of course, so too by 17 April had the Directors of Plans and the planning staffs.

In the paper that set out the planners' twin hesitations about the Middle

Strategy, which had prompted the conclusion that this option had little to recommend it—its lack of aim and its dependence upon, rather than support for, American operations—was the acknowledgment that British naval forces would be available for operations in the Far East in late 1944. Clearly the mid-1944 schedule had slipped in the face of the problems that surrounded the raising of the carrier force, but in itself this acknowledgment was not new. The March discussions had noted that an Indian Ocean strategy would necessarily involve the enforced idleness of the fleet, and indeed Churchill had made this point in the course of the September 1943 affair. But in the staff examination of the Middle Strategy in the first half of April 1944 this acknowledgment was turned by the planning staff to form the basis of a formula that would enable the British to be seen to play an active role in the more vigorous prosecution of the war against Japan. Noting that the Americans in all probability neither needed nor wanted British help except perhaps the support that a fleet might be able to offer, the planning memorandum that was presented to the naval Director of Plans on 16 April sought endorsement of a Pacific–Burma combination as Britain's "most promising option."[117] A paper dated the following day elaborated upon this in the form of a listing of the six options available to the British in the Far East. These were defined as the Pacific, CULVERIN, northern Australia and Borneo (i.e., the Middle Strategy), the southwest Pacific and Borneo, operations along the Malay Barrier, and Burma. The inclusion of the fourth of these options suggests that the planners were already considering some form of Middle Strategy tied to the MacArthur Plan and the revised timetable for American operations in the Pacific. But the conclusion drawn from the statement of available options was that the first and the sixth, Pacific and Burma, could be undertaken simultaneously. That, clearly, did not apply to any other combination and this Pacific–Burma formula was recommended as the basis of British policy.

This recommendation was perhaps no more than a more positive, more carefully argued version of the Chiefs' of Staff decision of 21 February. It was a recommendation that in its outline form flowed naturally from the various planning considerations that had been in hand since SEXTANT. But the planners' recommendation went much further than a simple definition of options, be they singular or in combination. The Burma option was defined in terms of the clearing of Upper Burma in 1944 and 1945 and an amphibious and airborne landing at Rangoon that would lead to the clearing of central Burma as a result of a battle of encirclement and annihilation.[118]

Such, by mid-April, after twelve weeks of argument in the wake of SEXTANT, was the "most promising option" that the planning staff sought. It is somewhat difficult to imagine a more unrealistic basis of policy than was proposed unless it was any of the ones that the prime minister sought to implement. Although the basis of calculation clearly was that the Burma commitment was inescapable and the Pacific commitment was desirable, what the planners proposed was nothing less than ANAKIM in association with a Pacific strategy. As the planners must have realized, if only because of the objections to CULVERIN that their own studies had raised, virtually the same technical and administrative problems that confounded CULVERIN applied equally to ANAKIM. Dependence upon the European timetable, the shortcomings of India, and the division of effort between two oceans were insoluble problems that ANAKIM and CULVERIN shared. And if ANAKIM was unlikely to secure the endorsement of a prime minister intent on bypassing Burma, it was also unlikely to obtain American approval for reasons that were all too obvious. At least in part, and particularly the sapper part, the resources needed to meet an ANAKIM commitment would necessarily be those that would be needed to meet the requirements of an Upper Burma effort, and if the latter was stinted in order to provide for an ANAKIM that, for reasons that were all too likely to occur, had to be canceled, then nothing would have been secured in the theater.[119] Given the state of planning at this time, and the known attitudes of both Churchill and the American high command, the planners' definition of priorities in the paper of 17 April[120] would seem to have no basis in reality—most certainly not under the terms of reference that the staff applied to its own deliberations.

The least that may be said about matters, though applied in a slightly different context, is that Somerville's comment that "there appears to be some extraordinary cross-currents at work in connection with the general strategical policy for the East and I feel this must delay preparations for a well thought-out final plan"[121] most certainly applied to this situation. But amid these confusing and illogical developments one matter is clear enough: the planning staff had discounted the Middle Strategy. But equally clear is the fact that by the time it did so, the Middle Strategy had acquired a certain momentum. As early as 5 April the Middle Strategy was discussed by Churchill, the Chiefs of Staff, and AXIOM,[122] and on the fourteenth, as the political imperatives generated by the forthcoming Dominions Prime Ministers' Conference pushed the Middle Strategy ever more to center stage, so Churchill advised Roosevelt that "we are working very hard to prepare plans for amphibious operations designed to support your left flank, and I hope soon to have definite proposals to make to your chiefs of staff."[123]

Certainly the Foreign Office, in a paper prepared for Churchill after an internal conference on 20 April,[124] came down in favor of the Middle Strategy after weeks of procrastination in which it seems its main concern was to be on the side that prevailed in the argument between the prime minister and Chiefs of Staff. March had opened with the Foreign Office concerned lest British forces become pawns in another argument, between MacArthur and Nimitz, that seemed likely to be the price of a Pacific commitment.[125] At this time Eden's department seemed either to follow or to anticipate Churchill's political reasoning, but one of its arguments was in a class of its own. The statement that one of the advantages of a Pacific commitment over an Indian Ocean strategy was that palpable defeat in the Pacific would have a lesser effect on British prestige than defeat in Southeast Asia invokes obvious comments about faith in one's forces and the absence of any need for enemies.[126] But April found the Foreign Office clearly giving more attention to the arguments in favor of the Pacific commitment that it had merely noted in the previous month, and in May the Foreign Office conceded that though the Bay of Bengal represented the area where, for political reasons, the British effort should be concentrated, matters of timing and logistical considerations limited Britain's real choice between the Pacific and the Lesser Sundas. Perhaps not altogether surprisingly, the Foreign Office hesitated between the two. It noted that it was for the British "our duty and to our interest to dovetail our plans with those of the U.S. with the object of inflicting total defeat on Japan at the earliest moment" and that the Pacific option presented "strong ground for offering to participate [because even if] we . . . have to play second fiddle . . . we shall at least be full members of the orchestra with a definite part to perform, and not simply be expected . . . to improvise when the woodwind are out of breath."

But this was not sufficient reason for an unequivocal support for the Pacific commitment, and in stressing both the political and military advantages that could be expected to follow from a campaign in the Lesser Sundas it was suggested that a British decision between the Pacific and the Lesser Sundas could be delayed for a year and left dependent upon American operational requirements.[127] This, clearly, could not be countenanced, and in any event one of three commentaries upon this view flatly asserted,

> [It] seems to weigh the political points rather too heavily in favor of the Middle Strategy [and that] it seems . . . almost indispensable to have both in the contemporary and [in the] historical record that a British fleet had participated . . . in the assault on Japan. . . . In any case, the danger that an effort would be swallowed up seems less than the corresponding danger that we should be represented . . . as not having taken part in the decisive actions.[128]

The contrast between these views, despite their disagreement and internal nature, and those used by Eden in the first phase of post-SEXTANT discussions is striking. No less striking is the fact that much of the Foreign Office argument, irrespective of final conclusion, was couched in military terms that were in line with the Chiefs' of Staff reasoning. But the latter was not uncritically accepted by the Foreign Office, and the weakness of their reasoning was exposed in the commentary on this view that posed the question of which option in the Far East met two criteria:

> as early as possible with the least manpower effort. When hostilities with Germany terminate, manpower is the consideration which will outweigh all others. We shall not be able to occupy Germany, keep the peace in southeast Europe and the Middle East (especially in Palestine where there is a first-class

civil war brewing) and wage war in the Far East on the scale that the Prime Minister [and] the Chiefs of Staff . . . would like.[129]

Herein the Foreign Office representative on the Joint Intelligence Committee touched upon the issues that figured so prominently in this second phase of deliberations. In March and April, as the Middle Strategy was considered, practical questions involving administrative overheads vied with political and military requirements as the argument over policy grappled with the problem of relating strategic intent to what was tactically and technically possible. The problem was that these could not be reconciled but for the fleet, which alone could be made available in late 1944, or, more accurately, at this stage was believed could be made available in late 1944.[130]

At this stage of proceedings several practical matters were under consideration, and perhaps the most notable, as the Cavendish-Bentinck commentary noted, was the manpower question, which was ultimately to prove so crucial in British calculations. But in terms of the continuing failure of the high command to settle policy, and, perhaps even more important, as a measure of the unreality of this argument, the fleet train issues were all-important as the Middle Strategy emerged in the aftermath of the second AXIOM visit to London.

The need to provide a train for the fleet, irrespective of where it served, figured prominently in deliberations for two reasons. First, the strategic choice could not be separated from means, and in effect this meant that the rival Indian Ocean and Pacific strategies had to be examined in terms of their relative demands. Second, the provision of a train involved interdepartmental arbitration by Churchill. After SEXTANT the prime minister had asked what a Pacific commitment would involve, and while the planners had pondered the same question at this conference,[131] their initial conclusion was that, operating on a more modest scale than the Americans, a British fleet in the Pacific would need fifty 7,550- to 10,000-ton and thirty 2,000- to 3,000-ton ships.[132] After the prime minister asked whether or not the fleet train issue had been raised with the Department of War Transport,[133] the Admiralty attempted to mark out the ground on which it would base its case by stating that the secretary of state had been consulted at SEXTANT and was of the view that administration had to conform to policy as set down by the Combined Chiefs of Staff.[134] Noting that consultations with the Americans on this matter were in hand, the Admiralty stated the need to begin the process of conversion and refitting of units in order to switch resources to the Far East immediately after the end of the European war and thereby avoid the enforced idleness of the fleet.[135] Churchill's reply, that a fleet should go to the Pacific in mid-year if the Americans so required but that Pacific matters were to be so arranged that CULVERIN was not rendered impossible, had marked out an area of future conflict within the British high command.[136]

February 1944 seems to have passed quietly as far as the fleet train issue was concerned. The Admiralty, in one paper, did note its difficulties with King on the issue, and it acknowledged that manpower shortages dictated that shore-based support for a Pacific strategy would have to be pared to the bone,[137] but while routine planning clearly proceeded during this month it was not until March that the British high command addressed the implications of the prime minister's warning that the needs of a Far East fleet train were not to be met at the expense of OVERLORD and national import requirements.[138] But on 3 March the issue was joined in the form of a paper from the shadowy Cherwell that questioned why the navy, with 560 ships of 2,250,000 tons, should now require another 136 ships of 1,250,000 tons in order to provide Indian Ocean and Pacific trains. With the postmaster-general arguing that the navy, given the reduction of its commitments with the end of the European war, should meet its needs from its existing resources,[139] Ismay attempted to remind Churchill that policy had to be settled before the fleet train and amphibious issues were tackled.[140] By this stage of proceedings this was impossible, and with the additional complication of a contemporaneous Chiefs of Staff paper stating that the lack of an adequate train would prevent the raising of an assault force either in the Indian Ocean or the Pacific,[141] the Admiralty and Cherwell were drawn into a battle of statistics that Churchill attempted to resolve at the conference of 3 April: his solution was that fleet train needs should be met equally by the Admiralty and the Ministry of War Transport. Although this can be subjected to hostile interpretation on the grounds that Churchill had to make some such compromise in order to safeguard a faltering CULVERIN, his formula seems a genuine, if short-sighted, attempt to resolve the problem, though one that was doomed to failure. The fact of the matter was that the needs of an oceanic fleet train could only be met with oceanic shipping, and the Admiralty could only secure its requirements at the expense of Ministry of War Transport resources that this meeting of 3 April acknowledged were inadequate to meet minimum national import needs in 1944.[142]

To this was added the problem that the Admiralty's needs were immediate: if the fleet was to go to the Pacific, or indeed to the Indian Ocean, then its bases would have to be prestocked, and the shipping needed for this task would have to be refitted in order to prepare them for this duty. What this meant in practical terms for just one type of auxiliary was explained in the First Sea Lord's paper that noted that a Far East commitment in 1945 would involve four accommodation ships, of which two would have to leave for the Far East in July, one in September, and one in November. With six months needed to refit these ships, and all the different types of ships needed for a fleet train subject to similar timetables, the paper's date of 1 April possessed self-obvious significance: even with an immediate decision, and a decision that was evidently long overdue, in effect a fleet train could not be assembled before March or April 1945.[143]

Such calculations rendered all but ridiculous any and all strategic deliberations, most obviously the planners' Upper Burma–ANAKIM–Pacific formula of 16–18 April, and where these left the staff discussions with the Americans about the arrival of a fleet in the Pacific is somewhat hard to discern. The cause of clarity was not helped, however, by subsequent developments. As April progressed, further staff studies revealed that far from the 2,500,000 tons of shipping that would be needed to support a fleet in the Far East at the outset, ultimately some 5,000,000 tons would be needed, and that of the total national lift of 381,000 men some 100,000 would be unavailable but that, given disparity of distances and logistics support, a lift of 230,000 men in the Bay of Bengal would be equal to a lift of 180,000 in the Pacific. By the same token, the Indian Ocean commitment would involve the use of 89 tankers as opposed to the 184 needed for a Pacific strategy.[144] But given the need for speed of decision, not to mention the argument that matters had to be put in hand to prevent any delay in taking up the slack in the Far East after the end of the war in Germany, the observation of the planners and Chiefs of Staff that "the selection of our strategy, therefore, need not be governed by shipping considerations"[145] was somewhat mysterious. Indeed, as Cunningham seemed to indicate at the time, the Admiralty's acceptance of Churchill's formula of 3 April was nothing other than patently insincere.[146] Indeed, the whole question of shipping resources and the Pacific strategy is one with which the planners seem to have been deliberately mendacious at this time. The calculation that a Pacific commitment was possible only if there was a complete halt on all personnel movements in every other theater in the first half of 1945[147] clearly had implications for all strategic options under consideration, but it was a calculation seemingly withheld from superiors unsympathetic to the Pacific option.

Such was the context of the Middle Strategy, and yet by the time that the Dominions Prime Ministers' Conference opened, the Middle Strategy had been superseded by the Modified Middle Strategy, seemingly for one obvious reason. The planners' lack of enthusiasm for the Middle Strategy as revealed in the paper of 12 April was accompanied by a chart that at a glance provided every justification for such reticence. With the projected axes of advance marked on this chart, alternative dates of May 1945/September 1945 were marked against Mendano, July 1945/November 1945 against Jesselton, and late 1945/early 1946 against the arrows that led into the South China Sea. To the north Mindanao, shaded, was marked November 1944.[148] Even with an initial operation with one division against Amboina set for March 1945, the whole concept of the Middle Strategy, on grounds of timing alone, was nonsense, and quite clearly no real improvement over any of the CULVERIN options to which it was an alternative.

But despite this, as late as 16 May, two weeks into the Dominions Prime Ministers' Conference, the Chiefs of Staff reaffirmed their support for the Middle Strategy because "the point was being reached at which it might be better to adopt a less than satisfactory strategy rather than continue to have no strategy at all" and that the island targets of the Middle Strategy were within British means.[149] It would seem, however, that allowing for the fact that means were not available and time told against the Middle Strategy, the real reason for the Chiefs' of Staff support for this option at this time was as much political and concerned with the imperial gathering as with the means of denying Churchill a free run with his Indian Ocean options. There would seem to be no other obvious explanation of these developments, but whatever the reasoning behind these obscure episodes, and perhaps as an oblique confirmation of the accuracy of this analysis, on the following day the Directors of Plans provided the service chiefs with a memorandum that stated, "For naval reasons it is of prime importance to establish our bases in the right area, that is to say Australia. The details of the strategy that will eventually be adopted can be decided later."

After this interesting reversal of the argument that policy had to be settled first, the Directors of Plans noted that the only possible policy in Southeast Asia was to clear Burma and the only theater where naval forces might provide an important contribution was the Pacific.[150] The precise meaning of the latter was defined at the next day's meeting of the Directors and the Chiefs of Staff and consideration of CAESAREAN: the plan for the invasion of Hokkaido envisaged the use of 28 fleet, 13 light fleet, and 116 escort carriers, and of these 157 carriers the Royal Navy was to provide 50.[151] Seemingly the irony of this was lost upon the Chiefs of Staff: if the British were to be involved on such a scale in the assault on the Japanese home islands, the Middle Strategy was neither here nor there.

It seems clear, therefore, that by mid-May the significance of the Middle Strategy in British deliberations was political. Although the various strands of policy were but little developed from the conclusions that had been gathered between 16 and 18 April, a greater precision had been provided and for an obvious reason. In the aftermath of AXIOM and CULVERIN's falling by the wayside, there was a need to redraft the directive with which South East Asia Command had begun its existence in October.[152] This re-presented the problem of the previous autumn, and Churchill's insistence in March and April that the Simalur option be retained in order to provide Mountbatten's command with an amphibious alternative[153] was therefore predictable and not unreasonable, though under the circumstances perhaps unwise and certainly of dubious practical relevance. Indeed, Churchill's continued insistence, even after the Dominions Prime Ministers' Conference had opened, that Simalur's capture would have effects out of all proportions to the effort involved[154] was both misguided and thoroughly mendacious.[155] But this did not prevent the Chiefs of Staff from accepting and defining the Burma commitment. The Chiefs of Staff meeting of 25 April had noted that northeast India lacked the administrative base to handle the airlift to China, the Burma commitment, and the needs of an Indian Ocean strategy simultaneously. By stating that the conflicting claims of the airlift and an amphibious commitment had to be resolved, the Chiefs of Staff tacitly accepted that the Burma commitment was unavoidable.[156] But in a staff paper prepared on 5 May the planners noted that Mountbatten, as part of the redefinition of his command's role, had ruled out any attempt to reconquer Burma from the north: the very limit of South East Asia Command's ambitions was to secure Myitkyina.[157] This accorded with London's thinking that limited the Upper Burma commitment to no more than an advance to the Chindwin,[158] and indeed the realization that Burma could be reconquered from the north was to await 1945.[159] With the battles in front of Kohima and Imphal at this time slowly but remorselessly being decided in Britain's favor, the basis of a Burma policy was thus resolved, at least within British terms of reference.

The Pacific commitment had been too long established within the planning scheme to have been discarded voluntarily at this stage even though it was realized that its overheads were considerable and likely to prove beyond Britain's resources.[160] But the imperial dimension, and in particular the Australia dimension, was clearly crucial in bringing various matters together as the British military realized that for the war against Japan the Dominions and Britain might be able to pool their resources and thus disguise the extent of individual weaknesses. In short, awareness that the Australian contribution to the war would be reduced by three field divisions[161] and that the British contribution, despite planning that envisaged the dispatch to Australia of 675,000 service and civilian personnel,[162] effectively narrowed to the fleet, naturally led to the idea of Australasian involvement in British operations, both for self-evident military reasons and for the purposes of avoiding the Dominions being casually discarded as the war receded ever further from their shores.[163] The possibility of a pooling of resources apparently was first discussed, informally, by the British and Australian military in meetings on 10 and 11 May.[164]

The obvious problem herein was the lack of any realistic objective for an imperial effort in the Pacific other than the Japanese home islands. Having shouldered much of the burden of the land fighting in New Guinea, this was not to Australia's liking, but in 1944 there was but little that it could do other than agree to become a party to the Middle Strategy. The process by which it did so in the course of the Dominions Prime Ministers' Conference was a somewhat difficult one, notable for all the subtlety and finesse of Anglo-Australian exchanges.

Australian endorsement of the Middle Strategy was provided on 26 May after a meeting notable for Churchill's behavior, which clearly embarrassed Brooke and Eden.[165] In preparation for this meeting the Chiefs of Staff advised that a sanitized version of British deliberations be provided the Australian representatives,[166] but Churchill, in response to Ismay's request for direction, ordered that the full account be provided but only at a time when it was too late for the Australians to have read it before the meeting.[167] Perhaps not altogether surprisingly, the meeting began somewhat abrasively, but by its end the Australians had been convinced and seemingly with some ease: the prime minister's pettiness was probably quite unnecessary. But, of course, there was a catch, and the catch was that the Middle Strategy was placed before the Australians and, separately, the New Zealanders, on a provisional basis only and not as settled British policy.[168]

This formula had been devised by the Chiefs of Staff on the eighteenth,[169] and by the twentieth the Middle Strategy had been given an Australian dimension by the planners.[170] Churchill, however, had continued in his efforts to keep some form of Indian Ocean commitment in being at least until the twenty-first when he sent a signal to Somerville expressing the desire to secure reconnaissance reports of Simalur, northern Sumatra, Java, and the Sunda Straits:[171] indeed, even at the meeting with the Australians on the twenty-sixth he made clear his own preference for an Indian Ocean commitment even as he presented the Middle Strategy as the basis of discussion.[172] On the twenty-second, however, Brooke noted that the prime minister seemed to be coming around to an acceptance of the Lesser Sundas option.[173] On the twenty-third, after representations by Ismay,[174] a Chiefs of Staff paper noted that Churchill appeared attracted to the Middle Strategy.[175] This attraction was perhaps the result of a seemingly friendly and useful meeting among Churchill, Curtin, Cherwell, and Leathers at Chequers on the twenty-first when the balance of Australia's future war effort was discussed,[176] but in the absence of any firm indication of prior assent it seems more than likely that Churchill agreed to the Middle Strategy as the basis of Anglo-Australian negotiations only on the twenty-fifth, which was, literally, at the moment of truth. Certainly the implication of Mallaby's noting Dominion disappointment at the seemingly endless delays in the settling of policy on the twenty-fourth,[177] and of an observation made on the same day that the Middle Strategy had not been resolved,[178] is that by that date the Middle Strategy had not been presented formally to the Australians because the prime minister had not abandoned his Bay of Bengal schemes.[179] But by the time that the British and Australian leaders met on the twenty-sixth to discuss cooperation on the basis of the Middle Strategy, the planners had concluded a number of studies that in effect spelled its end.

This development, along with the Directors' memorandum of the seventeenth, presents obvious problems of interpretation. The problems that the studies raised were obvious enough: the Middle Strategy would involve forces that were unlikely to be available,[180] and would be directed against objectives such as Bangkok and Saigon, which was unrealistic because of the lack of troops for riverine operations.[181] In the context of May 1944, however, it is hard to avoid the conclusion that such matters provide rationalizations rather than reasons for dispensing with a Middle Strategy already discounted by the planners for reasons of timing. As early as 17 April the planners had put forward, as an alternative to the Middle Strategy, the idea of moving against targets in the Indies via northern New

Guinea and bases already secured by the Americans.[182] This idea became known as the Modified Middle Strategy, but it was not developed and formalized until the end of May, by which time it had assumed its own distinct form and the Middle Strategy had correspondingly declined. Therefore, an obvious inconsistency presents itself for consideration. If the premise of the Middle Strategy was its military significance as part of an overall strategic plan, and if one of the major objections to the Middle Strategy was that it would not assist American operations in the Pacific unless those operations were long delayed, the Modified Middle Strategy was open to exactly the same objections as the Middle Strategy. In fact, because the Modified Middle Strategy was dependent upon the Americans first clearing New Guinea in order to provide bases for a British move to the west, it would seem that militarily and in terms of timing the Modified Middle Strategy was even less relevant than the Middle Strategy. And the argument in favor of the former on the grounds that it could be put into effect more rapidly than the latter[183] seems irrelevant when set against the inescapable fact that neither could be implemented for want of necessary resources.

Clearly, these events of late May 1944 present problems of interpretation. There are two possible explanations, one military and the other political, and which one, if not both, provides the basis of an understanding of the events could be answered by the Middle Strategy file that is open to public inspection but for the fact that this file has been gutted. The file's docket and contents do not accord with one another. The file's contents seem wholly unrelated to the Middle Strategy, and most of the items listed in the docket have evaded the attentions of this writer. Some 124 references, culled from no fewer than 25 other files, throw little light upon proceedings.[184] Thus one is forced to deal with these events without that abundance of evidence that is a characteristic of the British planning effort, but in dealing with the military interpretation of events one matter does seem clear. Throughout the argument over policy the Chiefs of Staff and planners were adamant in their refusal to allow anything but strategic factors and consideration of timing to be the basis of policy, and they were insistent that British strategic choices had to be measured by strategic criteria. The planners' work was based not on political but military considerations, and, indeed, the planners made exactly this point in the argument that the capture of northern Borneo could not be justified in terms of time and effort.[185] But clearly neither the original Middle Strategy proposal nor, at the end of May, the new proposal, the Modified Middle Strategy, accord with military yardsticks, and certainly not those yardsticks that the planners used in dealing with Indian Ocean options. Moreover, though the available record is very far from complete, there would seem to have been no substantial military consideration that manifested itself between early April and late May that could explain the shift from the Middle to the Modified Middle strategy.

If, however, military criteria seem to offer no plausible explanation of developments, then consideration must turn to the political field to provide an alternative explanation of events. Here two possible interpretations present themselves for examination. The first, and perhaps obvious, is that the Middle Strategy was, as its very name suggests, an attempt to resolve the dispute between Churchill and the Chiefs of Staff by a splitting of the differences. Although the prime minister did try to deny this with the claim that the Middle Strategy was complete in its own right, this was undoubtedly so. In this case, the shift by the planners from the Middle to the Modified Middle Strategy could be explained in terms of an initial resistance to the Middle Strategy slowly, over several weeks, being rationalized in the normal process of staff work to the point when, in a manner of which von Schlieffen would have approved, the nettle, in the form of the Modified Middle Strategy, was grasped. Such an interpretation of developments could explain the widening difference between the higher and lower levels of command, that the political imperatives that bore most heavily upon Churchill and the Chiefs of Staff ensured a certain momentum to the Middle Strategy even as the staff, working with matters of detail, turned against it. These same political imperatives can explain why the initial reluctance of the planners was set aside. The comment, "How difficult it is for people to argue with enthusiasm about an operation which in their bones they feel is not the right strategy,"[186] could only have been applied to the original Middle Strategy proposal and would seem to indicate that the need to break the impasse at the highest level prevailed over every other consideration, and exactly the same consideration applied at the time of the emergence of the Modified Middle Strategy.[187]

But within the terms of reference supplied by a political interpretation of events there exists a parallel explanation, and one that would suggest that either from the outset or from very early in proceedings the Middle Strategy was seen by the planners as no more than the means whereby a commitment to "the right area," as defined by the Directors of Plans on 17 May, could be secured. If the Middle Strategy was devised in order to evade deadlock between Churchill and the Chiefs of Staff, and there is little doubt that this was the case, it does not seem too much to assume that it was concerned, primarily, with "the right area" for the planners. Given the fact that the Modified Middle Strategy could only be staged from eastern Australia, the link between it and a Pacific commitment assumes an obvious significance.

This explanation of events would suggest that the planners were capable of consistent deviousness over weeks, months indeed, and were successful in shielding their intentions from their superiors. That the planners were quite capable of sustained deviousness cannot be seriously disputed. In considering Churchill's demand that the new directive include a Simalur option, Sugden was prepared to concede this on the grounds that Simalur was the best (i.e., least damaging) of the CULVERIN options and that it could be left to Mountbatten and the inescapable commitment to Burma to take care of this demand. His view was that a minor inconvenience for South East Asia Command was not important as long as the fleet "is properly placed."[188] But there is, however, evidence that the whole of the Middle Strategy proposal was indeed devised by the planners not as the means of ending deadlock but as the means of breaking the prime minister's attachment to the Indian Ocean option and that the planners mounted a sustained effort, involving consistent deviousness over many weeks and some form of conspiracy in keeping the truth from the senior levels of command, in order to secure an Australian commitment. A draft prepared for a planners' meeting on 30 April noted that the change from the Middle Strategy was a bit abrupt,[189] but, as had been noted by one of the junior planners earlier, the Middle Strategy had to be destroyed because "the papers have already served its [*sic*] nefarious purpose."

"The right course" was the Australia base and the use of small-scale operations until such time as British forces could involve themselves in major operations, such as those against Formosa and the home islands,[190] though the writer was to note that such operations could include the Ryukyus in 1946 but not Formosa in 1945.[191] These three documents, supported by a paper that stressed the need to avoid a Simalur operation because it would tie up the fleet,[192] seem incontrovertible proof that with the Middle Strategy the British planners were involved in selling a false bill of goods in order to secure an administrative decision in favor of western Australia that could then be transformed into the Pacific commitment. In this attempt the planners could rely upon the Chiefs of Staff for they shared the same strategic view: as Brooke noted on 18 May, "Another day of continuous work. First a long COS when we had a meeting with the planners in order to try and settle a final Pacific strategy to put up to P.M. The problem is full of difficulties, though the strategy is quite clear."[193]

The Chiefs of Staff wanted the Pacific commitment, but in their efforts to arrive at a decision they were to continue to parade the Middle Strategy as the basis of discussion after May: the New Zealanders were tackled on the question of their involvement in June.[194] By that time the planners were in possession of reports that clearly indicated that Australia could not handle a Middle Strategy commitment that the planners had never intended to be anything other than transient. The planners, clearly, were working to very different rules to those of their superiors, but they misjudged. Despite the evidence of the previous five months, the planners underestimated the tenacity of the prime minister's attachment to the Indian Ocean: more than two more months were to pass before this attachment was overcome.

AFTERWORD:
THE BRITISH MISSION TO AUSTRALIA

In this chapter note was taken of the fact that the question of the administrative and support facilities of Australia was critical to a Pacific commitment and prompted the decision to send a mission to that country at the beginning of March. Moreover, note was also taken that this decision provoked a dispute between the British and Australian authorities, and that by the third week of May the Australian government had yet to agree formally to receive this mission. Given the crucial importance of time at this stage of proceedings, this delay presented obvious difficulties for the British high command.

The delay was perhaps predictable. The Curtin government was distinctly unsympathetic to a British intention that implied incompetence on the part of its civil service and military, and it was not convinced that the information that the British high command sought could not be secured from either existing Australian reports or the British permanent mission in Australia.[195] There is little doubt that Dominion reluctance would have turned to outrage had it been known that the Chiefs of Staff were determined that the proposed mission would not be responsible in any way to the Australian government and would not present its report to its hosts,[196] an example of British high-handedness that indicates that a somewhat cavalier attitude toward the Australians was not confined solely to Churchill. But by mid-April, and despite successive cuts in the mission's size and the fact that its leader had been at Noumea for three weeks awaiting permission to proceed to Australia, the Australian government had made its acceptance of this mission dependent upon its own consultations in London in the course of the Dominions Prime Ministers' Conference.[197] Thereafter there seem to have been two developments: the mission's entry into Australia before the conference,[198] and, perhaps unknown in History, the British being informed of etiquette in such matters by Australians. In any event, the British high command conceded what in all reasonableness it could not deny, namely that the mission would be attached to, part of, and responsible to the Australian staffs and that the latter would prepare the report that would be submitted to London.[199] Terms of reference to this effect were placed before the Chiefs of Staff on 24 May.[200]

Clearly, therefore, with the head of the mission leaving New Caledonia on 28 April 1944, there seems to have been an Australian agreement to receive the mission before that date, and a preliminary form of agreement on its terms of reference sufficient to allow it to provide a preliminary report on 10 May.[201] But the fact that it was not until the third and fourth weeks of May that these matters came before the Chiefs of Staff provides grounds for assuming that the issue was not finally resolved until that time. When various arrangements were concluded has defied exact dating.

CHAPTER FOUR

The Original Purpose

From SEXTANT to OCTAGON, June–September 1944

*T*he third and final period of British post-SEXTANT strategic deliberations saw British priorities and policy for the war against Japan settled, at least for the most part. It was a period that fell into two phases, the division being between those events that took place before and in readiness for OCTAGON and the transactions of the second Quebec conference itself in September. At OCTAGON, however, certain decisions, being dependent upon the course of the campaign in northwest Europe, had to be left open, to be resolved by the march of events within a month of the end of the conference. The resolving of these decisions, in effect, form part of the Quebec deliberations, and, in any event, October 1944 proved the cutoff point for the British decisionmaking process: the long lead times involved in planning for the war in the Far East and the end of hostilities in August 1945 combined to ensure that, for all intents and purposes, British decisions not made before or during October 1944 had little bearing upon the course of events in the Greater East Asia War. In the interest of simplicity, therefore, these post-OCTAGON matters of September and October will be considered as part of the conference itself in order that the final British decisions for the war against Japan may be considered as one, before the concluding chapter measures decisions against results.

This final period of British deliberations possesses a wealth of contradiction, inconsistency, and paradox as events moved to their conclusion. It was a period that opened, or, perhaps more accurately, the Dominions Prime Ministers' Conference and May 1944 drew to a close, with the British high command seemingly in possession of a formula whereby national priorities and policy for the war against Japan could be settled. May 1944 saw the question of the new directive to Mountbatten settled: with its priorities set as the clearing of Upper Burma and the airlift, South East Asia Command,

and by extension the Indian Ocean theater, was denied its major amphibious ambitions. The Middle Strategy had emerged as a credible option, at least at the level above the junior planning staffs, and June 1944 was to find the British Chiefs of Staff engaged in the same task as it had ended the previous month, selling the Middle Strategy idea, but this time to their American opposite numbers. The Joint Chiefs of Staff journeyed to Britain, the only time in the war that they did so, in order to be on hand should OVERLORD demand any immediate decisions. In so doing they made clear their willingness to consider wider policy issues but refused to involve themselves in a full-scale Anglo-American conference.[1] But even under these restrictive terms of reference there arose new and ever more urgent dimensions to the difficulties the British high command faced in trying to settle national policy. Five whole months had elapsed since the end of the SEXTANT conference, nine since the end of QUADRANT, with the British high command no nearer a decision than it had been at Cairo. In those months the American advances across the Pacific had assumed such a pace that on 27 May, the anniversary of Tsu-shima, American forces came ashore at Biak off western New Guinea. Thus the British search for a strategy, which had been cast in terms of the need to settle policy both before a meeting with the Americans and while Britain still possessed some freedom of action in the Far East, stood in obvious danger of being overtaken by events. Throughout these protracted British discussions the fear that there would be no genuine national role in the Far East was a very real one, and as spring of 1944 gave way to summer this prospect began to assume the shape of reality.

Moreover, irrespective of both sides' intentions, in June 1944 any American consideration of policy for the war against Japan necessarily came close to a Joint Chiefs' of Staff arbitration of a dispute within the British high command, and with it a British dependence upon an American decision that could only be abject given the British high command's inability to settle policy for itself. But the consultations with the Joint Chiefs of Staff failed to resolve British priorities, and the examination of the Middle Strategy continued into mid-July before this option was discounted. And when it was discounted, after Churchill's refusal to accept any commitment that would prevent the adoption of CULVERIN, the battle lines between the prime minister and the Chiefs of Staff were redrawn, exactly as they had been before the Middle Strategy had arisen three months before. The alternative Indian Ocean and Pacific commitments thus once more vied directly with one another for adoption, and it was not until August, with OCTAGON almost upon the British high command, that a questionable compromise was agreed by Churchill and the Chiefs of Staff. Thereafter the latter, having secured the prime minister's agreement to a formula that did not include CULVERIN, were hard-pressed to prevent his repudiating this compromise even before it presented itself for consideration at Quebec. In the confident, almost casual, atmosphere of OCTAGON this compromise was afforded considerable indulgence, and it was not until the end of the month, and the realization that the German war was not going to end in the current campaigning season, that realism applied itself to an Upper Burma–ANAKIM–Pacific formula that, in all seriousness, should never have been afforded even fleeting consideration. As a result, the ANAKIM dimension of British intent was discarded as policy was decided more by events than by choice, along those very lines noted on 6 March 1944 by Ransome and subsequently confirmed by the planners as the only possible basis of British policy for the war against Japan.

May 1944 ended, and June 1944 opened, with Chiefs of Staff meetings that directed the attention of service heads to two Far Eastern matters. The 31 May meeting and the first of these matters demand only passing consideration. The question of the provision of naval aircraft for service in the Far East had little immediate bearing upon strategic deliberations but nonetheless was of some significance for an obvious reason. It brought into focus national reliance upon the United States and the attempt to lessen that dependence. The question was one provoked by a double concern, that the majority of the most up-to-date naval aircraft in British service were American-supplied but that recent American deliveries had been erratic in timing and indifferent in quality, many aircraft being of older marks for which the United States clearly had no further use. Concern to safeguard the postwar British aviation industry united Cunningham and Portal and ultimately led to the decision to adopt a mix of American and British aircraft for service in the Pacific. It was a decision that had singularly unfortunate consequences for the British carrier force that entered the Pacific in March 1945.[2]

The second matter, the question of the availability of military forces for service in the Far East after the end of the European war, clearly was a more substantial and pressing issue. It was also more significant, not simply in terms of its obvious strategic implications for British policy but because it represented, at the very outset of this final phase of British deliberations, the start of the process whereby various matters of military detail that had increasingly impinged upon the decisionmaking process in the second phase of consultations began to assume critical proportions as time, distance, and administrative margins worked against the British high command. Thus what presented itself for consideration at the Chiefs of Staff meetings of 1 and 3 June 1944 was a development from earlier calculations of postwar requirements, namely the conclusion that the competing claims of Southeast Asia and the Pacific would have to be balanced against available resources after the needs of a postwar garrison of eleven divisions in southeast Europe had been met. This conclusion was placed in context by a planning paper that stated that whereas in May 1944 the British had the equivalent of twenty divisions in northwest Europe compared to twenty-one American, by October the British order of battle would stand at 15.5 divisions because of anticipated losses that could not be covered. Because at this stage of the war, with Rome about to fall, there were just five British and three Indian divisions in Italy with 15th Army Group,[3] the calculation that twelve divisions might be available at the end of the European war had a significance that demanded no elaboration.[4]

But if the long-term implication of these calculations was that Britain was very unlikely to be able to raise military formations for service in the Far East in 1945, in the days immediately before the Normandy invasion the Chiefs of Staff had to draw together various threads of policy in order to accomplish two aims. The short-term requirements of a meeting with the Joint Chiefs of Staff had to be met, and the prime minister had to be either appeased or opposed, one or the other, but in a way that ended the argument. It was perhaps just as well that the Chiefs of Staff could not have known the consequences of the course on which they embarked on the attempt to meet these two requirements. But in that frenetic second half of May, in the midst of the Dominions Prime Ministers' Conference, the Chiefs of Staff and their Directors of Plans had decided upon two matters that now, in the first three days of June, moved to center stage to meet one need but not the other. The first of these matters was yet another reconsideration of amphibious options in Southeast Asia and the Pacific.[5] Exactly what happened to this review is not clear,[6] but on 27 May a new study, which was to be completed over the weekend and was to be prepared for the meetings with the Americans, was ordered.[7] This study, finalized on 31 May, set out, in detail and for the first time, the Modified Middle Strategy. After the exchanges of the fourth week of May and the pushing of the Middle Strategy idea even as the planners argued in favor of its stepsister, the modified version of the Indies venture was spelled out with considerable candor: Amboina might need to be taken, but Halmahera would have to be taken first, and Halmahera could best be secured by an advance from western New Guinea, which in turn would necessitate the fleet being deployed to eastern Australia. Rather brazenly, the paper stated that the planners had always intended that the fleet should go to eastern Australia, and that the new proposals would ensure that this intention would be realized. With its parallel recommendation that the question of command arrangements should be raised with the American chiefs of staff personally and not by papers and memoranda,[8] one is left with the unanswerable question of other intentions and issues that might not have been committed to paper in recent weeks.

Be that as it may, the Chiefs' of Staff meeting of 3 June saw the service chiefs consider the presently unnamed Modified Middle Strategy. What was proposed in the study paper under discussion was the securing of Amboina, after which western and northern alternatives would present themselves. This was wholly in accord with the Middle Strategy as provisionally accepted by Churchill and discussed with Australian representatives during the Dominions Prime Ministers' Conference. But what had been the planners' hidden agenda was brought into the open with the idea that MacArthur's command should execute the attack on Halmahera and that British naval forces should then be committed to operations against Luzon or Formosa, "the choice of the appropriate area for the application of the British effort" being shaped by the speed of the American advance across the western Pacific. With the scale and speed of the British redeployment stated to be dependent upon the duration of the German war and the demands of post-war occupation duties in Europe,[9] what in effect were proposed were three quite separate matters: a short-term definition of objectives in the Indies; a deferment of long-term policy decisions; and, in the meantime, a concentration of British resources in the southwest Pacific that would effectively decide policy before a final decision was made. With this formula set down as the basis of discussion with the Joint Chiefs of Staff,[10] the British service chiefs had the means of dealing with their American opposite numbers on the basis of a Pacific commitment while continuing to deal with the prime minister on the basis of the Middle Strategy. Leaving aside for the moment the differences between the planning papers of 31 May and 3 June, it was at this time that the second matter, decided upon by the Chiefs of Staff in consultation with their Directors of Plans, moved to center stage. At their meeting of 18 May, in the midst of the Dominions Prime Ministers' Conference and faced by the prime minister's refusal for political reasons to abandon the Indian Ocean option, the Chiefs of Staff decided to end their attempt to secure acceptance of a Pacific commitment by an examination of strategic policy in terms of military comparisons of theater claims. Instead, the Chiefs of Staff resolved to press the Pacific claim by a comparison of options in terms of time, admittedly an inferior criterion to those that should have been the basis of strategic calculations.[11] Clearly the service chiefs hoped that such an examination would cut through the rhetoric and confront Churchill with the reality that a strategy that included an attack on Amboina in early 1945 presented itself as the realistic possibility that CULVERIN, in any of its forms, could never be.

Given the situation in which the British policymaking process had found itself at that time, the Chiefs' of Staff decision was perhaps inevitable: in any event the decision was not unreasonable. Timing had to be a factor in British calculations, and, indeed, it had been used by the Chiefs of Staff in their various arguments. In all likelihood, the Chiefs' of Staff decision probably implied shades of emphasis rather than a major reorientation of argument. But whatever the Chiefs' of Staff intentions, their decision rebounded upon them, and their Pacific strategy, in the course of June and July, and which further complicated an already knotted decisionmaking process.

But if the Chiefs of Staff were involved in underhanded, not to mention very dangerous, measures in order to overcome Churchill's reluctance to confront reality, the unanswerable question noted earlier in proceedings presents itself in two forms at this point. First, according to Brooke, the

Chiefs' of Staff meeting of 1 June was a long one in which the search for a Pacific policy to present to the Americans meant that

> we have to steer clear between the rocks of Winston's ramblings on Sumatra, Curtin's subjugation to MacArthur, MacArthur's love of limelight, King's desire to wrap all the laurels around his head, and last but not least sound strategy. The latter may well get a bad position at the starting gate.

Brooke also recorded some rather strange views about the situation in Burma,[12] but the 31 May paper does not seem to have crossed the Chiefs' of Staff desks. Second, the Aide Memoire that did was significantly different. The 31 May paper implied involvement in an attack on Halmahera whereas the 1 June paper leaves the impression of operating against Amboina from an Halmahera already secured by the Americans. Whether the Chiefs of Staff, in presenting the Joint Chiefs of Staff with a Middle Strategy proposal that gave northwest Australia as the main base for operations into the Indies,[13] were knowingly the party to or unwittingly the victim of a deliberate deception is not clear. What is clear is that whatever was in hand worked, at least in terms of dealings with the Joint Chiefs of Staff. The latter arrived in Britain on 9 June and met with their British counterparts on 10, 11, 14, and 15 June. The main Pacific meetings were on the fourteenth and fifteenth, the latter being the day American forces came ashore on Saipan,[14] but the British service chiefs were aware from the eleventh that there would be no serious American objection to the Middle Strategy proposal. It was on the eleventh that King, after asking for "an outline of British ideas as to how they might best assist U.S. forces in the war against Japan in order to be able to examine to what degree the U.S. could lend a hand,"[15] declared that he was in favor of a Middle Strategy that defined Borneo as its ultimate objective.[16] Clearly, King was not prepared to give away more than was absolutely necessary, but on the fourteenth, when the Joint Chiefs of Staff indicated that they "were in agreement with a proposed strategy . . . directed through Amboina towards Borneo"[17] and when he conceded that the U.S. Navy had no real use for its facilities in eastern Australia, King suggested that the main objective of the Indies venture might be Soerabaja rather than Amboina.[18] It may be that King was quite prepared to accept a British involvement in MacArthur's theater and sought to direct a British effort in the Indies westward, away from the central Pacific, for his own reasons. But the fact of the matter was that by mid-June 1944 the Chiefs of Staff and their planners knew that the idea of a British amphibious commitment that was not based on India, indeed the idea of British naval and amphibious involvement in the southwest Pacific, would not provoke the automatic opposition of the Joint Chiefs of Staff.

The opposition of the prime minister, however, was quite another matter, and indeed agreement with the Joint Chiefs of Staff over the Middle

Strategy was not extended into other areas of the Japanese war: when the British service chiefs raised questions of command in Southeast Asia,[19] they found it quite useless to argue with Marshall and his colleagues as the Americans availed themselves of the opportunity to berate the British theater commanders in South East Asia Command as the means of countering questions of Stilwell's role and responsibilities.[20] But this was of small account compared to Churchill's reaction, which was slow in materializing. After having warned the Chiefs of Staff that in their discussion of the Middle Strategy with the Americans they were to stress that Britain "must not be committed to any policy as a settled conclusion,"[21] the prime minister was so involved in other matters, especially the breaking of the ANVIL crisis at this time, that the demands of the war against Japan commanded little of his attention. This situation had been anticipated by the planners: in April a planning paper had stated the need for a decision on the Far East war before the opening of the campaign in northwest Europe lest the proper consideration of the war in the Far East thereafter became impossible.[22] It was not until early July, therefore, that the war against Japan reoccupied a central position in the deliberations of the British high command, and by the time it did so there had been one noteworthy development. At the time of the Joint Chiefs' of Staff visit, the Foreign Office had announced itself in favor of the Middle Strategy or, more accurately, it all but committed itself to support whatever the Chiefs of Staff proposed.

The reasons why the Foreign Office so decided were perhaps more important than the decision itself: after all, the Foreign Office was but little regarded by Churchill and the Chiefs of Staff other than as lightweight support or irritant, depending on circumstance. But the Foreign Office's decision was based upon considerations that could not but sap the political imperatives that Churchill paraded as justification for an Indian Ocean strategy. The Foreign Office's main concern was American attitudes, the North American Desk being of the view that a Pacific commitment was in Britain's best interest in dealing with the question of war debts, the negotiation of future loans, and shipping allocations, and with an American public opinion that needed to be assured that Britain would play its full part in the Japanese war. Indeed, Halifax had already requested that British forces earmarked for service in the Far East be sent via the United States in order to provide visual proof that Britain was committed to the defeat of Japan. To senior Foreign Office officials a "very distressing" failure to be involved in the final attack on the Japanese home islands was likely to prove "a very grave handicap to us for years to come in all Anglo-American questions."[23] As if to confirm these fears, June brought the revelation that King, in a meeting with New Zealand representatives in Washington on 10 May, had stated that he was intent on excluding Australasian forces from the central Pacific lest Australia and New Zealand try to use their involvement as a means of ensuring their consultation on the question of the postwar disposal of the Japanese-mandated territories.[24] The fact of the matter was that the New Zealanders had no objection whatsoever to American acquisition of the Japanese mandates: this would provide an automatic guarantee of New Zealand's security.[25] Although the Foreign Office comforted itself with the conclusion that an American "hands-off" policy was not likely to be applied elsewhere in the Far East, there was a possibility that it might be, and there was very little the British high command could do about such high-handed behavior as long as British policy remained unresolved. As a consequence, the Foreign Office was not prepared to support New Zealand in any redress of grievance,[26] but the episode had one positive implication for the Middle Strategy. With Australia receiving much the same treatment from MacArthur as New Zealand had experienced from King, the case for the Middle Strategy, with its prospect of employment for Australasian ground and air forces, was strengthened politically and militarily: the certainty of exclusion from the central and western Pacific left Australia and New Zealand with no role in the Japanese war except as part of a British effort.[27]

Although the Foreign Office saw an attack on Amboina as "distinctly modest,"[28] its support for the Chiefs of Staff over the Middle Strategy was committed to paper on 12 June in a memorandum that stressed the need for an immediate decision. In order to overcome possible American objections,[29] Eden proposed that the Americans be asked what British efforts could best complement their own operations and that the Middle Strategy should be proposed as a complement to those of MacArthur's command. Perhaps to disarm an immediate obvious objection that Churchill was certain to raise, Eden stated that "the relegation of South East Asia Command to a secondary role . . . is unfortunate politically but inevitable."[30] The Chiefs of Staff sought another way to deal with the Americans, their belief being that the best course of action was to station forces in eastern Australia and to advise the Americans that such forces would be available to support their operations.[31] But while Cunningham might continue to press for an immediate policy decision in order to prepare base facilities in Australia, to begin the survey of seas off northern Australia, to cancel construction programs that would not be needed, and to start the process whereby landing craft could be moved to the Pacific,[32] the final Amboina proposal encountered Churchill's immediate opposition. Drawing together the various points raised in the discussions with the Americans and in Eden's memorandum, the Chiefs of Staff rejected Soerabaja as an objective; stated the desire to be involved in operations against either Luzon or Formosa; and set out the intention to "recommend that the Combined Chiefs of Staff should instruct the Combined Staff Planners to frame a directive to General MacArthur in the light of the details of the U.S. program and resources and [of] the availability of British resources."[33]

This statement of intention showed how little the Chiefs of Staff understood the political realities of command arrangements within the U.S. military establishment, but predictably this was not the main point seized upon by Churchill, though he did question the assumption that an Amboina operation could be conducted under British auspices. The prime minister's main objections were that Britain could not return to Southeast Asia on the backs of the Americans and that a Middle Strategy would involve the downgrading of South East Asia Command and its subordination to South West Pacific Command. Accordingly, Churchill stated that it was imperative that the British recover Rangoon and Singapore, and he protested, apparently not without good cause, that the Amboina project had never been properly explained. He insisted that he wanted a full statement of the advantages of Amboina over CULVERIN and landings on the Kra.[34] Thus was revealed the danger inherent in the decision of 18 May to use time as the basis of the examination of strategic options. By seeking to focus attention on what might and might not be possible in terms of time and by bringing Amboina forward as the operation that could be staged within the period under discussion, the Chiefs of Staff inadvertently reduced the argument to one of individual operations rather than one of strategies, of which these operations were mere parts.

The planners' reaction to this latest development was to mix the immediate operational and broader strategic arguments. Noting that at QUADRANT the prime minister himself had argued that recovery of Singapore was a British objective best achieved after the war because an operation to recover the island and city was "definitely divergent from the main line of advance," the planners noted that

> an exhaustive examination of CULVERIN had already been carried out in conjunction with S.E.A.C. planners in which it was concluded that this operation, far from assisting the main drive in the Pacific, would on balance hamper it as the diversion of resources badly needed in the Pacific would outweigh the diversionary value. Singapore could not be captured early enough to open a way to the South China Sea in time

to have any beneficial effect. But perhaps because at least some of this was at best debatable, the planners' view that

> the inadequacy of ports, beaches and communications, combined with the difficulties of weather, would make any advance quite impossible [not least because] the largest force that could be [put] ashore was unlikely to exceed three divisions [landed] at four different places spread over some 280 miles [of the Kra][35]

was the one that commanded the Chiefs' of Staff attention. At their meeting of the thirtieth the service chiefs decided to concentrate the argument upon Amboina and the Middle Strategy. The main lines of argument that were to be used were that fewer troops would be needed for an attack on Amboina than for CULVERIN and therefore could be staged the sooner; that an Amboina operation was not beset by problems of the monsoon that attended any Bay of Bengal venture; that Australian forces could be involved in this operation; and that a Middle Strategy was ultimately aimed at northern Borneo and lost British colonies. The planners' parallel argument, that an attack through the Indies and a strangling of Japanese lines of communication would weaken the Japanese throughout Southeast Asia and allow Mountbatten's command to move to victories even without reinforcement, was clearly no more than a sweetener.[36]

The Chiefs of Staff, therefore, decided to fight Churchill on his own terms, but before they could do so three developments bore directly upon British deliberations. First, on 24 June Lumsden, the British representative at South West Pacific Command, sent a signal to London asking about the availability of a British naval task force for service in this theater in the last quarter of 1944. With command planning in hand, the implication was obvious.[37] Second, on 4 July Curtin sent a long signal to London in which he stated that South West Pacific Command proposed a partial clearing of the Philippines and then the envelopment of Japanese positions along the line of the Malay Barrier from the north. With MacArthur claiming that the ground and air forces presently under his command were adequate for these tasks, the significance of Lumsden's earlier signal was as clear as Curtin's own observation, that the situation provided an "ideal opportunity" and the "only effective means for placing the Union Jack . . . alongside the Australian and American flags . . . but the pace of events here demands immediate action in the form of the despatch and arrival in Australia of the fleet."[38]

South West Pacific Command and Curtin thus complemented the Foreign Office's time-factor argument: indeed, Curtin defined it as "the governing consideration." Moreover, between them the views and support of Curtin, Eden, and MacArthur represented a more than useful, not to mention timely, addition to the Chiefs' of Staff cause, whatever that might be.[39] As early as 29 May the planners had received clear, incontrovertible evidence that the Middle Strategy could not be implemented because of northwest Australia's inadequacies as a base of operations.[40] But it was at this time, 6 July, with the views of Curtin and MacArthur known and a southwest Pacific option opening for the British high command, that the Modified Middle Strategy was presented to the Chiefs of Staff by the Directors of Plans along with warnings of the tactical and administrative problems that would attend an Amboina operation. The claims of the Modified Middle Strategy were pressed by a comparison of the approach-to-contact phase, the 200 miles being compared favorably with a 580-mile advance, partially covered by enemy air power, through the Arafura and Banda Seas.

Perhaps because the Chiefs of Staff were scheduled to meet the War Cabinet later that day to discuss the Middle Strategy, the Chiefs' of Staff reaction was, or at least appears to have been, somewhat muted. Cunningham expressed the view that MacArthur's plans and timetable

seemed optimistic, but that there was little the British could do even to provide an advanced base from which to operate in the southwest Pacific.[41] But
there proved little that the Chiefs of Staff could do when it came to dealing with Churchill even on the Middle Strategy later on the sixth, in part,
it seems, because of the third development: the breaking of the full force of
the ANVIL argument. As if to anticipate the problems that the Chiefs of Staff
were to face on the sixth, the previous day Cunningham had confided to
his diary that "the trouble is the P.M. can never give way gracefully. He must
always be right and if forced to give way gets vindictive and tries by almost
any means to get his own back."[42] It hardly augured well, and if what transpired at the meeting with the War Cabinet was a disappointment, then it
could not have come as any great surprise.

In Brooke's words, the "frightful" four-hour meeting of the War Cabinet
on either side of midnight of 6/7 July proved

> quite the worst we have had with him. . . . He [Churchill] was in a maudlin,
> bad-tempered, drunken mood, ready to take offence at anything, suspicious
> of everybody, and in a highly vindictive mood against the Americans. In fact
> so vindictive that his whole outlook on strategy was warped. . . . It was not
> until after midnight that we got onto the subject we had come to discuss—
> the war in the Far East [and] here we came up against all the old arguments
> that we have had put up by him over and over again.

As Brooke implied, the lines of argument developed, or not developed, at
this meeting were all too familiar, but there were, nonetheless, two points of
difference from previous proceedings. Leaving aside the fact that at this
meeting the usually passive Portal abandoned his habitual crab-like avoidance of issues and confrontations with the prime minister, the Chiefs of
Staff very obliquely brought into play the Modified Middle Strategy and
Churchill found his political support falling away as "Attlee, Eden and
Lyttleton . . . fortunately . . . at last [sided with the Chiefs of Staff] against
him [and this] infuriated him even more."[43]

With the rest of the War Cabinet and the Chiefs of Staff ranged against
him, Churchill avoided any decision by adjourning the meeting until the tenth,
announcing that he remained in favor of an operation to secure Simalur in
November, a move against northern Sumatra in January 1945, and then, with
forces in Burma assuming the defensive, an attack on Singapore.[44]

At the resumed meeting on the tenth, in Brooke's predictably jaundiced
view, under the leadership of "a complete amateur . . . we wandered like a
swarm of bees from flower to flower, but never remained long enough at
any . . . to admit to . . . honey being produced."[45] But the various flowers
on which Brooke would have lingered did not include that most delicate of
blooms, *De Rebus Orientalibus:* other matters intervened to ensure that consideration of this wilting plant was deferred until the fourteenth.[46] The main
issues that dominated proceedings on the tenth concerned the European

and Mediterranean theaters, but there was a proliferation of problems at this time of which two had dimensions that concerned the Japanese war. First was the problem created as a result of a request from King for the transfer of six LSI(L) from the United Kingdom to MacArthur's command by 15 August. The Admiralty could not meet this deadline if the ships were to be manned by naval personnel, but could more or less do so if such assault ships were sent from Oran and replaced from the United Kingdom.[47] The Chiefs of Staff, conscious of the "advantage to be gained by meeting this request,"[48] and that "a refusal to meet the American demand would probably have unfortunate results upon the amount of assistance which the U.S. Chiefs of Staff might be prepared to provide for future operations,"[49] were only too anxious to oblige King, but Churchill demanded to know what British operations would be affected by the transfer, and set about trying to trade the dispatch of the LSI(L) against British allocation of future American LST production.[50] The argument was still going on more than two weeks later as the dispute widened to include more general shipping questions.[51] The Chiefs of Staff were only too anxious to avoid such matters because, it appears, there had been some sleight of hand in current British allocations of American production that might be revealed if these questions were pursued.[52] The LSI(L) were sent, with suitable Admiralty apologies for delay in dispatch and with due acknowledgment on the part of King.[53]

Second, the Chiefs of Staff took the opportunity presented by the adjournment to the fourteenth to finalize one aspect of amphibious planning. On 5 June Cunningham had raised the question of a downward revision of planning targets from that set at SEXTANT. With the service chiefs aware that sweeping manpower cuts were unavoidable with the end of the European war,[54] Cunningham suggested that economy could begin with a saving of the 21,000 sailors needed to man one of the four assault divisions authorized at Cairo.[55] Given staff calculations, this proposal, at best, would seem to have been halting: the raising of three amphibious divisions in the Far East was every bit as unrealistic as the raising of four. Nevertheless, by 11 July, the Chief of Combined Operations was concerned with securing specialist shipping needed "to support our two-divisional assault lift during the summer of 1945,"[56] and the Chiefs' of Staff consideration passed to other, similarly related problems, and to preparations for the reopening of the Far Eastern question on the fourteenth.

The first matter put in hand by the Chiefs of Staff was to order the planning staff to prepare an outline plan for an attack on Amboina.[57] It seems extraordinary that such an instruction had not been issued and that the debate within the high command over the previous six weeks could have been conducted in the absence of such a plan. But the Chiefs' of Staff instruction had been anticipated by the Directors,[58] with the result that the plan was completed on the day demanded and presented at the Chiefs' of Staff meeting of the thirteenth. There it was discussed and finalized,[59] the main details of the twelve-page plan being the use of 31,000 troops, a naval force that included ten assault escort carriers, and eighteen air force squadrons in a four-brigade assault landing. As the plan itself admitted, meeting the required force levels would be tight, but the contrast with the plans that Churchill favored was obvious from the memorandum that had been sent by the planners on the eighth to the prime minister. This had set out the respective requirements of the Simalur, northern Sumatra, and Singapore operations as one, 5.3, and 10 divisions; 12, 26, and 12 escort carriers in the assault role; and 23, 40, and 71 air force squadrons.[60]

Thus provided, and with the warning that an immediate decision was needed if the arrangements for an attack on Amboina were to be put in hand in order to meet a January 1945 deadline, the Chiefs of Staff entered the meeting of 14 July clearly determined to press matters to a decision. In their quest they were to be assisted by Attlee and Eden, but not by Lyttleton: the latter suggested carrying out simultaneous attacks on Amboina and northern Sumatra, and noted that the recapture of Malaya would ease British rubber problems in 1945. This aside, political support for the Amboina operation was rationalized around the realization that there was no chance of mounting CULVERIN in the foreseeable future. This was lost upon Churchill. As a result the meeting was "treated to the same old monologue of how much better it was to take the tip of Sumatra and then the Malay peninsula and finally Singapore than it was to join with the Americans and fight Japan close at home in the Pacific."[61]

The meeting was brought to an end with Churchill's declaring, perhaps in response to an ultimatum that Brooke claimed to have delivered,[62] that he had heard nothing to shake his confidence in the correctness of his own views, that a final decision would be forthcoming in a week, and that he was recalling Mountbatten for consultations. The only point of note in what was obviously a sterile meeting bereft of any serious discussion of issues was the fact that the Chiefs of Staff used the Middle Strategy rather than the Modified Middle Strategy argument with which to push their case. It would seem, therefore, that either the Chiefs of Staff discounted the latter or feared the possible results of trying to introduce a fresh proposal, and one that might wreck the Pacific case, at this late stage of proceedings.[63]

After a weekend in which to ponder the significance of these developments, the Chiefs of Staff met on the following Monday, issued the executive order recalling Mountbatten, and instructed that the Joint Staff Mission be informed of what had happened. With the 15 July deadline now passed, the Chiefs of Staff, conscious that policy was their prerogative and not that of theater commanders, also resolved that the prime minister had to be told that a policy decision had to be forthcoming that week, and before Mountbatten's return.[64] But, of course, Churchill obviously decided upon the recall of Mountbatten in order to avoid giving a decision, and the Chiefs' of Staff demand would be ignored because any decision would clearly do away with the need for his recall. The Future Planning Section apparently recognized this the next day with an acknowledgment that the Bay of Bengal strategy was not dead.[65] The planners' meeting of that day, and it is hard to believe that this could have been a joyous occasion, considered a direct assault against either Penang or Port Sweetenham in what was clearly yet another CULVERIN/SECOND CULVERIN option.[66] But the cause of clarity and simplicity could not have been helped by the Chiefs of Staff. On the twentieth, after having been told by the prime minister that there would be no policy decision until after Mountbatten's return, the Chiefs of Staff recorded that "[though] in our opinion the choice of . . . strategy in the [war against Japan] must not be allowed to depend at all upon a comparison between two specific operations [which in any event are] only the means of achieving a strategic end," they were not necessarily convinced that either CULVERIN or the attack on Amboina could be put into effect.[67] It would seem, therefore, that all the discussions of the previous two weeks had been concerned not with the merits of strategic policies that could be put into effect but the demerits of operations that could not. It was, by any standard, a somewhat confusing state of affairs, at least to this historian.

Inevitably, at the time of Mountbatten's recall no agenda for consultations had been prepared, and what happened in the last two weeks of July, as this agenda was prepared and planning proposals from London and from Kandy came together, is obscure. On the nineteenth, and apparently as a result of a planners' meeting held that day,[68] the Strategical Planning Section was ordered to conduct two examinations, one of which, for a landing in Malaya that bypassed northern Sumatra, was withdrawn the following day[69] and replaced by a general examination of options in the Bay of Bengal.[70] Seemingly, these two studies were the main London-based ingredients for the consultations with Mountbatten with regard to amphibious operations in Southeast Asia, but two other matters emerged to combine with these to provide the framework of discussions that had to settle policy. First, and of lesser importance, in the second week of July the Joint Staff Mission advised London that the Joint Chiefs of Staff had decided that future planning for the war against Japan was to be based upon the need for an invasion of the home islands rather than on the basis that an invasion might prove necessary.[71] Perhaps not surprisingly, the Chiefs of Staff were not quite certain what this meant and why the Joint Chiefs of Staff had made this change. It took some days to clarify these matters,[72] but by the nineteenth one matter had become obvious: if there was to be an invasion of the Japanese home islands the planners had to consider how best British forces might participate.[73] Second, on 23 July the planners received four signals from South East Asia Command which set out an ANAKIM option in the form of the CHAMPI-ON–VANGUARD alternatives.[74] On the twenty-sixth the Chiefs of Staff were advised that Mountbatten was returning to London with an amphibious grab bag that included plans for operations against the Nicobars, against Sabang and northern Sumatra, against Sabang and northwest Sumatra, and against the Cocos Islands, in addition to CHAMPION and VANGUARD.[75] The process of consultation, it seems, meant different things to different people, as, quite clearly, did the meaning of South East Asia Command's directive of 3 June.

The planners' studies, the Kyushu question, and South East Asia Command's plans ushered in the final, confused period of British deliberations, from the outset of which Churchill sought to anticipate developments by ruling out Chiefs' of Staff proposals that made no reference to any amphibious operation in the Indian Ocean. The proposals to which Churchill took exception in his memorandum of 25 July have avoided attention, but the prime minister's intentions could neither be missed nor mistaken:

> Though I consider the finest strategical opportunities are being thrown away by the abandonment of CULVERIN and the further attack on the Kra Isthmus or south of it, I would be willing . . . to support VANGUARD as a second-best plan. I prefer VANGUARD . . . to Amboina. It might be possible to give a detachment from the Fleet for co-operation with General MacArthur's left flank and carry out VANGUARD at the same time . . . but I cannot foresee any circumstances [in] which I would be able to agree to CHAMPION.

In other words, VANGUARD, the proposal for a landing at Rangoon as the preliminary to the clearing of Burma,[76] was the prime minister's minimum demand, and VANGUARD, either alone or in company with an attack on Amboina, was infinitely preferable to CHAMPION, which was the proposed clearing of Upper Burma. Leaving aside the Amboina matter, this definition of priorities would have had something to commend it but for the fact that the prime minister added, "I have no intention whatsoever of giving way to the U.S. chiefs of staff in this matter. The troops are ours, and we have the direction of forces in this theatre."[77]

Whether or not the troops and theater were British was irrelevant: the troops needed for VANGUARD were not available and the direction of forces in Southeast Asia was not wholly Britain's to decide. Given these considerations, Churchill's declaration of intent at least had the virtue of consistency: in dropping his support for CULVERIN in favor of VANGUARD the prime minister exchanged one irrationality for another. It was hardly a good omen for the final settling of British policy for the war against Japan.

Given the prime minister's obvious temper, and with the London-based planners intent on avoiding an Indian Ocean commitment that South East Asia Command was no less intent on securing, there would seem to have been no possible basis of agreement among the prime minister, the Chiefs of Staff, and Mountbatten. Paradoxically, however, there was, as indeed there had to be. With the first full-scale conference with the Americans since SEXTANT in the offing, British policy had to be settled, the basis of agreement had to be found, simply because it was impossible for the British high command to proceed to Quebec without having settled its priorities.

Agreement was reached, and British priorities settled after a fashion, in the course of three Chiefs' of Staff meetings with Churchill on 8 August 1944 and two further meetings on the ninth.[78] Various loose ends remained thereafter, and the agreement and definition of priorities were subject to considerable strain in the five weeks that elapsed between these meetings and the opening of OCTAGON, but for the most part British policy and priorities were defined on this second Tuesday and Wednesday of August 1944. But while the available record provides a detailed account of the meetings at which an agreement was concluded, it does not provide much insight into the consultative process between 25 July and 7 August. Somewhat strangely, certain exchanges after 9 August, particularly some that took place en route to and in Quebec, fill in some of the gaps, but this does not alter the fact that a certain caution has to be exercised in relating and interpreting developments between 25 July and 7 August. It appears from any examination of the events of 8 August, however, that in the previous fifteen days three matters came together, with the catalyst provided by the OCTAGON imperative, to produce the basis of an agreement between Churchill and the Chiefs of Staff. It also appears, if this analysis is correct, that of these perhaps the most important was that part of the memorandum of 25 July which could be overlooked: whether deliberate or unintended and despite the caveat with which he preceded his comments, in this paper Churchill conceded the principle of a British naval role in the Pacific, albeit in the southwest Pacific.

Churchill's capacity to reverse or change arguments and positions presents obvious problems of interpretation: the prime minister's observation, after all, was only tentative and was not the first time that he had referred to the fleet, or part of the fleet, proceeding to the Pacific. But it was the first time since the exchanges of the opening phase of British post-SEXTANT deliberations, the first time in at least four months, that the prime minister gave any indication of an acceptance of a British naval role in the Far East outside the Indian Ocean. This would seem to be a vital consideration if only for reasons of timing. In the course of this long, wearisome, and often futile search for a naval strategy for the war against Japan which so preoccupied the British high command between August 1943 and August 1944, two events stand out, like islands in a sea of sterility. These are the Dominions Prime Ministers' Conference and OCTAGON, though more accurately the latter in August 1944 would only be emerging over the horizon. To mix metaphors, these were acid tests, when reality asserted itself, when the time for self-indulgence mercifully drew to a close. Churchill could try to insist that he have his own way and that Britain commit itself to policies that were beyond its reach for much of the time, but time was running out, quite literally.[79] The political imperatives on which he set such store and which he used in attempts to justify his opinions had to force him, in the final analysis, to recognize realities. These realities had to be faced in August 1944, however unwillingly, which would seem to be why the 25 July statement, hedged around with provisions though it was, would seem so important: it gave, or promised to give, the Chiefs of Staff what they had demanded since SEXTANT, namely the Pacific option.

Clearly, however, this development by itself would not have been enough to form the basis of agreement between the prime minister and the Chiefs of Staff: alone, the 25 July comment indeed threatened the two-ocean commitment that the Chiefs of Staff had insisted since Cairo was impossible. What was needed to complement the 25 July statement, therefore, was some formula that would destroy the Indian Ocean entanglement, and this was provided, in two separate but critically related ways, in the unlikely form of South East Asia Command's proposals. The second and third matters that paved the way to the agreement of 9 August, putting the cart before the horse as was common with so much of these deliberations, were South East Asia Command's conclusions that the presence of a fleet in the Indian Ocean was superfluous to its needs and that a Burma commitment was inescapable and indeed desirable. Both separately and together, these conclusions were not without ambiguity, and South East Asia Command, predictably, was not beyond trying to escape such restrictive terms of reference even though these were of its own conviction, but what seems to be critical about these conclusions is their timing. The prime minister clearly recalled Mountbatten in an attempt to end his isolation within the War Cabinet and play the last card that would win the Southeast Asia trick, but the play failed because the open hand would not support declarer's bid.[80]

The process by which South East Asia Command reached its conclusions is not clear[81] and in any event forms no part of this story: what is important is that, in the first week of August, if not before, it set down strategic priorities that more or less accorded with those of the Chiefs of Staff and thereby forced the prime minister to accept a formula with which he obviously disagreed and would repudiate if given the chance. The latter was of no immediate consequence: the critical point was that agreement was reached, and the agreement, despite its ambiguities and Churchill's subsequent antics, was just enough to see the British high command through OCTAGON.

In the preliminaries to the meeting scheduled for 8 August the Chiefs of Staff meetings of 4, 5, and 7 August were of obvious importance. After a meeting on the first in which the Chiefs of Staff decided to attempt to settle priorities in Southeast Asia and to ignore the issues raised for South East Asia Command by the American demand that Stilwell be placed in supreme command in China,[82] on the fourth the service chiefs met to consider the claims of CHAMPION and VANGUARD. Faced with a paper that depressingly acknowledged that no recommendation of relative worth could be made without first deciding the British role in the war with Japan,[83] the Chiefs of Staff noted the conclusions that both individually and together CHAMPION and VANGUARD were beyond British resources but that VANGUARD would be possible in March 1945 if American help could be enlisted. Both Brooke and Cunningham clearly had reservations about VANGUARD, but noted that it was not incompatible with a naval commitment in the Pacific. They also noted that CHAMPION could not be halted in Upper or central Burma but would involve an open-ended commitment to clear the whole of the country.[84] At the next day's meeting, however, Mountbatten, who had arrived in Britain with Wedemeyer on the fourth, explained to the Chiefs of Staff that both operations would involve a commitment to clear the whole of Burma.[85] Thus the reality that the capture of Myitkyina on the third irrevocably committed the Allies to a land campaign in Burma was brought home to the Chiefs of Staff. Whatever their personal feelings on the matter, the Chiefs of Staff realized that the initiative, so hard won in recent months, could not be ceded.[86] CHAMPION, therefore, recommended itself to the Chiefs of Staff, not least because VANGUARD need not be lost as a result of adopting CHAMPION.[87]

The Chiefs' of Staff calculations were not in accord with those of South East Asia Command, but at the same time a closeness between them allowed compromise. Mountbatten's views, set down in the main paper before the Chiefs of Staff on the seventh, were that, with the Americans scheduled to break into the inner defense zone of the enemy in March 1945, the rationale for CULVERIN was no more and that the best course would be to bypass northern Sumatra because "its capture would be an expensive operation which in itself would no longer pay an adequate dividend." In this way Mountbatten kept open a SECOND CULVERIN option, indeed a number of options in the Indian Ocean. But if this did not recommend itself to the Chiefs of Staff, the conclusion that Burma was South East Asia Command's priority and Rangoon was the key to Burma must have been more acceptable. Mountbatten's paper claimed that taking Rangoon would be in accordance with South East Asia Command's directive,[88] would fully utilize existing British superiority in the theater, secure a rice-surplus area, and prove the "most economical and sound method of ensuring the recapture of the whole of Burma . . . and would allow the timely release of large resources for employment elsewhere."[89]

The Chiefs of Staff made clear to Mountbatten that they did not agree with some of these views, Brooke noting that the Irrawaddy south of Rangoon represented a line of supply rather than an axis of advance. But Brooke, noting that CHAMPION would have to be authorized in September and that October presented itself as the very last month when either or both operations could be sanctioned, set down the formula of proceeding with CHAMPION and leaving a decision on VANGUARD, scheduled for March 1945, for later.[90]

With South East Asia Command also left with an amphibious Arakan option and the question of securing the Cocos Islands left open, the Brooke formula provided the basis of a reasoned policy that could meet both the Chiefs' of Staff and South East Asia Command's requirements. It is clear, however, that both Brooke and Cunningham continued to entertain doubts about VANGUARD. The First Sea Lord, clearly no admirer of Mountbatten, noted of him that

> there was no doubt that . . . in his desire to have something to do in his command [he] is inclined to underestimate the difficulties and attempt to carry out operations with insufficient forces. A case in point the advance upriver from the sea to Rangoon, which is just wishful thinking. He said that James Somerville agreed with the plan but I can't believe it.[91]

Brooke, clearly, did not expect the operation to be carried out in the coming season,[92] a conclusion not made known to Mountbatten and one that raises a self-obvious question of interpretation, but both Brooke and Cunningham noted the one critical point to emerge from this and the previous meetings to lie alongside CULVERIN's demise—that British naval and imperial ground forces would be free to proceed to the Pacific under a CHAMPION plus VANGUARD formula.[93] In a very roundabout way, therefore, the Chiefs of Staff had arrived back at the "Burma unavoidable–Pacific desirable" program set down by Ransome four months and one day before, and they did so with South East Asia Command's support.

The various conclusions drawn at the Chiefs' of Staff meeting of the seventh were consolidated in the inevitable staff paper prepared in readiness for the meeting with Churchill and the War Cabinet the following day.[94] As noted elsewhere, this meeting turned into three, and they were every bit as bad as the Chiefs of Staff at their most pessimistic could have feared.

Whether or not any or all of these meetings had a prescribed order of business is impossible to tell: all conformed to an earlier comment Brooke made to the effect that "nothing whatsoever was settled. He cannot give decisions and fails to grip the cabinet, just wanders on reminiscing,"[95] while Cunningham, no less apoplectic, summarized proceedings with the observation, "What a drag on the wheel of war this man is."[96] Both service chiefs noted that the meetings of the eighth bogged down with Churchill's resurrection of CULVERIN, but from the minutes of the first meeting it would appear that the meeting was in considerable trouble even before CULVERIN raised its head. The meeting appears to have opened with consideration of the Burma question and Brooke's statement that of the CHAMPION and VANGUARD alternatives he preferred VANGUARD. This was obviously a sop to Churchill's known antipathy to the prospect of any major overland campaign in Burma, but while he later likened CHAMPION to "eating a porcupine quill by quill," Brooke noted that VANGUARD could not be undertaken without reinforcement from Europe. With no decision on that particular problem possible before October, Brooke explained that he therefore favored CHAMPION, at least as a makeweight while preliminary administrative arrangements necessary for VANGUARD's later authorization were put in hand.

Perhaps surprisingly, this drew a very reasoned initial response from the prime minister who noted that VANGUARD would draw Japanese forces from Upper Burma whereas CULVERIN would not. He stated his preference for VANGUARD over CHAMPION and noted that British naval forces would be free to move to the Pacific because of Japanese weakness in the Indian Ocean. But Churchill then proceeded, first, to express his horror that VANGUARD was not scheduled until March 1945, and, second, to announce that he considered VANGUARD but the initial step in a series of moves against either Moulmein and then Bangkok or the Kra and then Malaya. With this disastrous turn of events, Mountbatten and Wedemeyer were admitted to the meeting, and Mountbatten proceeded to destroy the rationale for any effort in Burma. Mountbatten argued that the clearing of Upper Burma would permit the opening of an overland line of communication to China in February 1945 but not an all-weather road until July 1946. While the implication of this statement was obvious and would not have been disputed, he quoted Stilwell as the basis of the calculation that if five divisions had to be left in Upper Burma to guard the road to China these would have to be supplied to the full capacity of the road they were supposed to protect. Mountbatten noted, moreover, that VANGUARD was not so certain of establishing an overland line of communication to China as CHAMPION but would certainly draw Japanese forces from Upper Burma.

It may be that these arguments were intended to push the VANGUARD case: after the previous day's meeting VANGUARD was clearly the second-string operation. But they raised the prospect of double failure, that attempting both operations, in Churchill's words, "would result in the whole effort of British-Indian forces being bogged down in Burma." Accordingly, Churchill returned to the theme that he had expounded before Mountbatten's arrival, that Rangoon should be seized as a bridgehead and that the rest of Burma should be bypassed, though how this would not have led to the whole British effort in Burma becoming bogged down he did not explain. The prime minister claimed that he had not realized that VANGUARD was but the prelude to a full-scale campaign in Burma, but his attempts to evade this reality were frustrated by Brooke who stated that there was no alternative to clearing Burma. Mountbatten endorsed this, but in a back-handed way. His estimation that six months would be needed to clear Burma once Rangoon was secured could have been intended to mollify Churchill, but he noted that such a schedule would accord with the campaigning season in Southeast Asia. The clearing of Burma during the next monsoon season, therefore, would leave British forces available come the 1945–46 season, and if the administrative infrastructure of India could be developed, the availability of these forces would leave Britain free to engage in "large-scale amphibious operations in the eastern Indian Ocean" thereafter. There could be little doubt to what operations Mountbatten alluded, and with them the role that South East Asia Command and Mountbatten himself would play in them, but the prime minister responded to that suggestion in a reasoned and measured way. He noted that no decision had been reached on such operations, that in any event the American advances across the Pacific had ramifications for CULVERIN, and that such operations raised again the question of the deployment of the fleet to the Pacific. Somewhat strangely, Churchill noted that there could be no major amphibious operation in the Indian Ocean before November 1945, but he was certainly very accurate in noting that what the Chiefs of Staff now proposed was that Britain commit itself to a land campaign inside Burma and an amphibious assault on Rangoon, both of which had been rejected in the past. Brooke intervened to note that circumstances had changed from the time that these operations had been rejected, and stated that CHAMPION involved the large-scale commitment in South East Asia Command that was demanded of Britain at this time. Obviously the meeting hovered at this point on the brink of a rational settling of policy, but at 1330, and with luncheon presumably exercising its own influence upon strategy, Churchill adjourned the meeting, though ominously: the last words recorded in the minutes were that the landings at Rangoon would be the first stage "in the march to the east" and a drive on Singapore.[97]

The second of these meetings opened at 1800 with Churchill stating that he accepted the Burma commitment and now posing the question of what should be done with those resources not devoted to the Burma campaign. In this way the prime minister raised the question of the employment of the fleet. To Brooke's answer that, given that the Americans were presently considering the bypassing of Mindanao and aiming directly for either Formosa or Kyushu, the fleet should proceed to the southwest Pacific, Eden intervened with the observation, hard to dispute, that it "was difficult to visualize a role for the British . . . under MacArthur." But in elaborating upon this theme the foreign secretary parted company with previous departmental calculations by arguing that it was "preferable to recapture our own territories than to play a minor role in the Pacific," and he suggested that the Australians should be asked to involve themselves in VANGUARD and that British forces, dispatched from Europe with the end of the German war, could then be used for an attack on Singapore. Perhaps not surprisingly, Eden was promptly savaged by Brooke and Cunningham for his ill-judged sortie into the realms of strategy. While Brooke contented himself with the observation that the Australians were very unlikely to agree to a proposal that he dismissed contemptuously as irrelevant, Cunningham noted that it was hardly logical to propose sending the fleet to South West Pacific Command and at the same time request the removal of ground forces from that theater.

But in arguing that the problems that presently beset VANGUARD concerned not assault forces but specialist troops, equipment, transports, and shipping, Brooke started exchanges that a rather cursory and incomplete record suggests were very confused. Churchill's immediate reaction to Brooke's comment was to the effect that he had been advised that VANGUARD could be carried out on the basis of existing resources. To this assertion, which seems somewhat unlikely, Mountbatten replied a landing could indeed be carried out but consolidation and exploitation could not be attempted without reinforcements. Mountbatten also stated that if Wedemeyer, who was not present at this meeting, backed VANGUARD, the operation might prove saleable to the U.S. high command. Thereafter the meeting seems to have concerned itself with how VANGUARD might be presented to the Joint Chiefs of Staff before Brooke brought some order to proceedings with the observation that no policy decision had yet been made, but would have to be made and made immediately. But in what appears to have been an attempt to focus the argument, his observation that only CHAMPION was a practical alternative to VANGUARD seems to have miscarried. The prime minister replied that the alternative to a landing at Rangoon was northern Sumatra and Singapore, and given Cunningham's subsequent observation that "the ugly head of CULVERIN reared itself up and we got no further. Lots of useless discussions,"[98] it would seem that this was the point at which any theme to this meeting was lost. Certainly, Mountbatten was obliged to raise tactical objections to CULVERIN and to argue that it might be possible to thin CHAMPION forces for VANGUARD but not for CULVERIN in an attempt to scotch the northern Sumatra option. As it was, those at the meeting agreed that CULVERIN was not possible without American support but that such support was unlikely to be forthcoming. The other area of agreement—the conclusion that a central Pacific commitment was likely to be beyond British logistical means—was seemingly unrelated to any other part of the discussions. Exactly how and why this conclusion was reached cannot be traced, but it was already accepted by Cunningham and perhaps it lay behind Brooke's advocacy of a southwest Pacific commitment at this meeting. Given the importance stressed at various times upon an involvement in the final campaign in the central Pacific and against the Japanese home islands, the pushing of the southwest Pacific option by the Chiefs of Staff on 8 August seems somewhat odd and offers itself to two possible explanations. It may be that the Chiefs of Staff endorsed a southwest Pacific option for genuine reasons, that a central Pacific option could not be taken up and as a result a commitment in MacArthur's theater was the only possibility open to Britain. It may be, however, and subsequent developments can be interpreted to this effect, that fear of losing the Pacific commitment per se by presenting what was at best a dubious central Pacific option led the Chiefs of Staff to present the lesser option in the expectation that the exact nature of a Pacific commitment might resolve itself in light of later developments. Whatever the truth of the situation, Churchill adjourned this meeting at 2030 with no decision having been reached.[99]

The third and final meeting of this day began at 2230 and lasted until 0100 the following morning. From its minutes it seems that Attlee opened the meeting with a measured, reasoned summary of the issues in hand, stating that because there was no alternative but to proceed with CHAMPION and because the fleet had to go to the Pacific, the meeting faced an unavoidable choice between VANGUARD and CULVERIN. Attlee explicitly rejected Churchill's assertions over Burma, and by arguing that Burma was not an island and the Japanese army there could not be left to wither on the vine in the manner in which Japanese-held islands in the Pacific could be bypassed and left isolated, the deputy prime minister made clear his support for VANGUARD. Unfortunately, such a business-like start to this meeting could not survive the interventions of Eden and Lyttleton. Eden indicated that he wished to see VANGUARD before the end of the European war but that of the various operations under consideration he would support the first that could be mounted. But his argument that Amboina should be attacked opened up a discussion of the Middle Strategy that drew from Cunningham the somewhat surprising statement, which was immediately passed over, that "unless some such [plan] were adopted, [it was hard to] see how we could employ the naval forces that we should not require in the Bay of Bengal," which could only mean that British naval forces had no role in the Pacific. After this distraction, Lyttleton proposed that Britain proceed with VANGUARD and with the preparation of base facilities in Australia in order to provide itself with a later choice between Bay of Bengal and southwest Pacific alternatives. From the minutes it would appear that this, mercifully, was Lyttleton's one and only contribution to proceedings.

Perhaps it was inevitable, and in one sense it was probably only right, that Churchill, with the sands in the Sumatra glass all but exhausted, should have made one last attempt to secure endorsement of CULVERIN. For more than seven months he, if not single-handedly then certainly single-mindedly, had kept the CULVERIN option alive, and if in the process he had displayed a willful and blind obstinacy that reflected ill upon his political and strategic judgment, then at least these had served his country well on another, more auspicious occasion. Now, with an effrontery and a selectivity that allowed him to gloss over his past actions, he claimed that the uncertainties that presently surrounded British intentions meant that "it had clearly been right not to divert resources to South East Asia Command at an earlier date," and that past delays had not resulted in the hampering of British operations in the Far East. Churchill stated that he was willing to back VANGUARD but wanted CULVERIN if there was an unexpectedly rapid German collapse and surrender. It was Brooke, predictably, who countered that suggestion, but in trying to support Brooke's comments, Mountbatten, by arguing that if VANGUARD was canceled there would be no loss to CULVERIN whereas the reverse was not the case, threatened to raise the CULVERIN issue in full because the prime minister immediately indicated that he would not accept VANGUARD if this operation involved any delay to CULVERIN. Mountbatten, no doubt aware of what Brooke and Cunningham must have been thinking at this turn of events, redeemed himself with the assertion that any delay to CULVERIN would be the result of European considerations and not VANGUARD, and then made the suggestion that policy could be settled by separating Burma from the Bay of Bengal and allowing decisions on the one to be taken immediately and on the other to be deferred. To this Churchill made no objection and indicated that he objected neither to VANGUARD nor to the fleet proceeding to the Pacific. With the suggestion that Britain should offer to be involved in operations against the Japanese home islands on the grounds that if the Americans refused "we should then [be proof against the accusation] of not fulfilling our part as an ally in Pacific operations," Churchill adjourned the meeting,[100] again without a decision, but, seemingly, for the first time with agreement in sight. It had been a long day, and an even longer haul from Cairo and SEXTANT.

The following morning the Chiefs of Staff met in committee in order to produce a policy paper that summarized the previous day's developments before meeting with the prime minister at 1230.[101] When they arrived for the latter, however, they found that Churchill had been similarly engaged, but to a very different end. Despite what had passed the previous day, Churchill now demanded that VANGUARD be executed before the end of 1944, irrespective of the situation in Europe, and that a final decision on VANGUARD should be so delayed that it would be possible to execute CULVERIN in its place. In addition, the prime minister insisted that measures be put in hand to allow the transfer of two British divisions in northwest Europe and four Indian divisions in the Mediterranean to the Far East with the end of the German war. With fifteen divisions thus available, attacks across the Bay of Bengal against "conquered British territories," namely Rangoon and Singapore, would then follow.

Even allowing for the incompleteness of minutes, it is hard to see how this program could be reconciled with the previous day's deliberations. In the event, however, there seems to have been no major argument between the prime minister and the Chiefs of Staff. The Chiefs of Staff could concede CULVERIN, given the caveats that made it very unlikely that it would ever be carried out, and in any case Brooke and Cunningham were obviously determined to force an agreement on the prime minister over certain specific and immediate points. The First Sea Lord's concern was the more practical: he insisted that a decision on the fleet was long overdue and had to be made. The chief of the Imperial General Staff, clearly acting as spokesman for his colleagues, insisted that a program with which to approach the Joint Chiefs of Staff had to be agreed, and he set down in five main points what that program should be. Brooke proposed the immediate authorization of CHAMPION; to set the VANGUARD proposal before the Americans; to start planning for an operation against Malaya; and to seek to deploy the fleet to the southwest Pacific with the proviso that it could operate in the central Pacific. With all other matters left open, Brooke also insisted that the Americans be approached with the proposal that South West Pacific Command should be brought under the Combined Chiefs of Staff, with executive powers vested in the Joint Chiefs of Staff, in accord with the arrangements of South East Asia Command relative to the British Chiefs of Staff. It would appear from this record,[102] therefore, that the two sides were as far apart as ever, but very strangely both Brooke and Cunningham noted the closeness between the Chiefs' of Staff and the prime minister's proposals.[103] After the meeting was adjourned, therefore, Brooke told Ismay to use the Chiefs' of Staff program and the prime minister's phraseology in a study paper that combined both sets of proposals.

According to Cunningham this paper was produced by 1600, but with the Chiefs of Staff scheduled to meet him at 2230, Churchill, perhaps recalling past practice, ordered Ismay "that he was not to circulate it to the Chiefs of Staff before the meeting. Thus we are governed!! I presume he himself has such a crooked mind that he is suspicious of the Chiefs of Staff," and, in fairness to Churchill, it may be said not without cause. But if the First Sea Lord was scathing on this matter, he was even more blistering about the agreement that was concluded at this meeting, and the methods of conducting the affairs of state that underpinned it, when he noted,

> We settled down and produced a paper of conclusions. The first four paragraphs directed to the subjects on which we were to approach the U.S. chiefs of staff and the way it was to be done and the fifth arranging to doublecross them. I often wonder how we expect the U.S. chiefs of staff to have any respect for us. We allow our opinions to be overridden and ourselves to be persuaded against our own common sense at every turn.[104]

For his part Brooke seems to have taken a less jaundiced, but hardly a more relaxed, view of proceedings. He noted

> After dinner another meeting with PM at 10.30 which lasted until 1.30 a.m. at which we finally arrived at a policy for southeast Asia. It was not what we set out for and not ideal, but it saves as much as it can out of the wreck, whilst also meeting the more rapid American advance, and the necessity [of] liquidating our Burma commitment by undertaking the capture of Rangoon. On the other hand, it still gives scope for the use of our naval forces in the Pacific and for the formation of a British task force in the Pacific.[105]

Clearly, therefore, the program that was agreed at this meeting was the least to which the Chiefs of Staff felt they could agree, and it was one that in its final form had nine provisions. The first four, to which Cunningham had not taken exception, were the acceptance of the commitment to a campaign in Upper Burma; to set in hand arrangements for VANGUARD; to plan for an eventual landing in Malaya; and to set in hand arrangements for the withdrawal of six divisions from Europe. The fifth provision, to which Cunningham had taken exception and which was clearly a concession to the prime minister, was to allow for a revision of plans in the event of a German collapse. The sixth and seventh covered the role of the fleet in the Pacific. The Americans were to be offered the services of a British fleet in operations against Formosa and the home islands, and in the event of this offer being declined, in the southwest Pacific. The eighth provision covered command arrangements, and the final one left open the question of further reinforcement of British forces in the Far East.[106] Set down thus, the program accepted by Churchill and the Chiefs of Staff seems both reasoned and reasonable, and in terms of the various influences at work in the shaping of policy decision perhaps it was. But what is remarkable about the agreement, and here it is hard to dispute Cunningham's view, is that the Chiefs of Staff were prepared to accept a program that, with nine provisions, involved a certain mental agility by the Chiefs of Staff on nine separate counts. The Upper Burma commitment was one against which the British high command had long since turned its collective face. VANGUARD, by the least exacting standard, was problematical. SECOND CULVERIN was at very best a highly dubious proposition, and even with Indian army divisions included in schedules the movement of six divisions from Europe to the Far East must have been known to be a dubious proposition. No comment needs to be passed upon the fifth provision. The meetings of the previous day had brought the admission that a British fleet could not operate in the central Pacific and this provision was clearly made with an eye to the historical record,[107] and equally clearly the prospect of British forces serving under MacArthur was not one that won the enthusiasm of the British high command. The intention to raise command questions with the Americans contradicted what had been told the Dominions, and the final provision, given British manpower problems, could only have been a dead letter. And once the agreement had been struck, there remained the small matter of selling it to the Joint Chiefs of Staff.

Three questions present themselves in any consideration of the agreement of 9 August 1944. The first, the most obvious, is why the Chiefs of Staffs agreed to this program, and one no-less-obvious answer commends itself: with OCTAGON one month hence, the Chiefs of Staff had to have something. Given the prime minister's obstinacy, the service chiefs may well have concluded that the terms of the agreement reached on this day were the best that could be obtained. To this may be added two other matters. For all its dubious contents, the agreement of 9 August 1944 did contain the

Upper Burma–Pacific formula, and this was clearly the Chiefs' of Staff main concern. Moreover, agreement was struck at a time when, with British and American armies breaking from the Normandy beachhead, the prospect of an end to the German war in 1944 was briefly glimpsed.[108] It may well be, therefore, that the Chiefs of Staff felt themselves able to accept what, after all, were provisional rather than binding arrangements, in the hope and expectation that the speedy end of the European war might indeed provide answers to at least some of the problems that presently defied solution.

But the reverse of this argument also presents itself as the basis of interpretation of the Chiefs' of Staff action. This would suggest that the question of the end of the German war was neither here nor there and that the Chiefs of Staff were prepared to agree to arrangements that they suspected they would never have to put in hand. Indeed, given the military's longstanding insistence that separate efforts in two oceans could not be undertaken,[109] there would seem to have been no good reason to have accepted VANGUARD except on the basis of there never being the least prospect of its being executed. But such an interpretation, with its overtones of paranoia and conspiracy, sits ill alongside abundant evidence of chaos and confusion throughout the British high command's deliberation upon Far Eastern questions. It is an interpretation best afforded proper consideration by an examination of the second and third questions that arise from the terms agreed on 9 August: how the agreement was to be presented to the American high command and what happened to the agreement at OCTAGON. And here the troubled waters of British deliberations become very murky indeed.

The Chiefs of Staff, true to routine, met on the morning of the tenth to consider the signal that would be sent to the Joint Chiefs of Staff outlining the program that had been agreed.[110] They also considered two papers dealing with the Middle Strategy and the capacity of Australia to serve as the base for this effort.[111] The conclusion of these papers, and one that was drawn with an evident lack of enthusiasm, was that the Middle Strategy could be mounted from northwest Australia. The basis of this conclusion is somewhat hard to discern in light of evidence that noted that Darwin could not dispatch two divisions in less than two weeks, that northwest Australia was without the major facilities needed by all three armed services for such an enterprise, and that January was a month noted for its bad weather. But what is perhaps significant about these papers was the fact that while the Middle Strategy, not the Modified Middle Strategy, had been discussed during the recent conferences, the first of these reports, prepared by the Joint Administrative Planning Staff, had been based upon information received from the Australians on 29 July.[112] The report had then been discussed by the Chiefs of Staff who on the thirty-first referred it to the Joint Planning Staff for comment in a process that was time-consuming and seems somewhat superfluous. Both the finalized and covering reports nevertheless had been available for the discussions of the eighth and ninth, but had not been used. In other words, papers that clearly cast doubts upon the Middle Strategy, and one that was unequivocal in stating that the fleet had to go to eastern rather than western Australia, were not made available to conferences that concerned themselves with the Amboina proposal and the claims of an Indian Ocean strategy. At very best, the timing of these developments gives rise to suspicion. Moreover, at this very same time, and in a quite separate development, Mallaby was advised that "the assumption that cargo shipping can be made available to move resources eastward for VANGUARD prior to the completion of the war in Europe would . . . be taking too much for granted."[113]

In other words, the Middle Strategy, in spite of an awareness that the proposal was flawed, was paraded as an alternative to a Bay of Bengal commitment until the time that CULVERIN was finally lost, and once VANGUARD was accepted, albeit provisionally, evidence that suggested that it too was flawed made itself available. It is difficult to believe that such evidence was not available, at least to the planning staffs, before this time, and in part it was. A memorandum of 19 April had noted that a Pacific commitment would involve a complete halt of all personnel movement in other theaters throughout the first half of 1945:[114] VANGUARD could have had no different an effect.

The signal to the Joint Chiefs of Staff was another matter, not least because it had to be couched in such a way as to elicit American support and avoid Churchill's objections.[115] As it was the draft prepared by the Chiefs of Staff on the morning of the tenth "came back . . . amended by the P.M. As usual, full of inaccuracies, hot air and political points [and] not the sort of business-like message we should send to our opposite numbers."[116]

In fact it was not until the twelfth that the final text, with VANGUARD given preference over CHAMPION, was agreed and the signal dispatched to the Joint Staff Mission,[117] but it is clear that from the time that the agreement was struck that VANGUARD was in trouble on a number of counts, most obviously concerning its projected force levels. Tasked with approaching the Joint Chiefs of Staff with the British program, the Joint Staff Mission expressed a polite skepticism. On the fourteenth it noted that the Burma proposals, while containing proposed force requirements as calculated by South East Asia Command, gave no indication whether or not the Chiefs of Staff accepted these figures; that no date was provided for VANGUARD; and that the program failed to show whether or not British ground, amphibious, and air forces were to proceed to the Pacific.[118] Also on the fourteenth, with Wedemeyer scheduled to proceed to Washington in order to sell VANGUARD to the Joint Chiefs of Staff (and which he attempted to do on the eighteenth),[119] the Chiefs of Staff met with Mountbatten and Wedemeyer to consider the relationship among CHAMPION, VANGUARD, and the European situation. It was recognized that CHAMPION might well consume the resources that would be needed for VANGUARD and that the European war might not end in so timely a way as to allow VANGUARD to proceed. It was at this meeting, with an acknowledgment that the ports of western India lacked the facilities to mount this operation, that Mountbatten suggested that British formations earmarked for the landings at Rangoon and the battle of encirclement and annihilation in central Burma could be dispatched direct from Liverpool.[120] Given such thinking, or lack of thinking, it was small wonder that VANGUARD was in difficulties.[121]

The planners, too, recognized the same problems, but despite what had transpired at the meeting with Mountbatten and Wedemeyer on the fourteenth Brooke recorded that, on the seventeenth,

> the J[oint] P[lanners] came to attend our COS meeting and we discussed all difficulties facing us if we are to stage a Rangoon attack by next March. The War Office has been raising just one series of difficulties and delays. Their examination proved that it would be impossible to do it by that date. I therefore had a two-hour meeting this afternoon to prove to them that it is possible and must be done.[122]

If this means anything other than Brooke trying to make light of problems in dealing with objections while concealing his own suspicion that such objections were correct, this must mean that Brooke and his colleagues were in earnest about VANGUARD. Brooke was prepared to admit, if only to his diary at this stage, that VANGUARD's future depended upon the release of the 6th Airborne Division by or on 1 October 1944, and that VANGUARD "is a gamble, but I believe one that is worth taking,"[123] but how projected force levels and the logistical overheads of VANGUARD were to be met was, at best, problematical. In fact, the Chiefs of Staff, their planners, and Mountbatten were already embarked upon a process that admitted as much. The VANGUARD proposal taken to the War Cabinet had envisaged the use of no fewer than nine divisions.[124] With Mountbatten insisting that VANGUARD had to be executed in March 1945 if there was to be any prospect of an attack on Malaya and Singapore later that year,[125] the fact that after VANGUARD was accepted Mountbatten recast plans in order to allow VANGUARD to proceed with only five divisions[126] and the Directors of Plans provided a seven-division estimate[127] strongly suggests that the Chiefs' of Staff support for VANGUARD was conditional on its being revised. But any attempt to reduce the operation's scale had to encounter a predictable and insoluble problem. VANGUARD could not be executed unless its scale was cut, but any downward revision of requirements to bring VANGUARD within what was administratively possible rendered the operation tactically impossible.

Such considerations, moreover, did not elude the Joint Chiefs of Staff, who had been presented with the proposed British program on the thirteenth.[128] In their meeting with Wedemeyer on the eighteenth the American service chiefs were sympathetic, but as the British chiefs of staff advised on that day, with deficiencies of six divisions, 42 LST, 60 LCI(L), 60 LCT,

752 transport aircraft, and 584 gliders,[129] VANGUARD's case was hardly self-evident. As it was, the Joint Chiefs of Staff rested their reservations on the obvious point: they would sanction CHAMPION and accept VANGUARD in March 1945 if circumstances allowed, but would not accept the amphibious operation if CHAMPION was in any way circumscribed as a result.[130] Although Wedemeyer noted that Marshall stated, not without ambiguity, that he "did not think that there would be any great difficulty in resolving this matter," the Americans would not consider sanctioning VANGUARD for fear that if VANGUARD was allowed to proceed with resources needed for CHAMPION but was then canceled, a stunted CHAMPION would fail. It must have been galling to the British to learn that the American leaders, in setting down this argument, acknowledged their debt to Stilwell's signal of the fourteenth making precisely this point.[131]

The British program of 9 August, therefore, was under some pressure from the time that it was settled, and the predictable reaction of the Americans in seeking to discover what level of logistical support the British proposed to send to the Pacific in support of their fleet[132] obviously did not augur well for the future. But by the twenty-third, when Noble reported to London that he had not raised this and the question of American support for British naval and amphibious operations with King,[133] the outline of how the British high command was to handle this and VANGUARD began to become clear with the specific instruction to the Joint Staff Mission that it was not to raise the question of VANGUARD's military requirements and deficit with the Americans.[134]

As Wedemeyer reported on the eighteenth, with his VANGUARD submission to and talks with the Joint Chiefs of Staff the informal avenues of consultation were closed and the VANGUARD issue had to await formal consideration by the Combined Chiefs of Staff and by OCTAGON.[135] Marshall, assured by the British of their commitment to CHAMPION,[136] reaffirmed the provisional American position on VANGUARD on the twenty-third,[137] but until the formal American reply to the VANGUARD proposal was received on 1 September[138] the operation was removed from center stage, to be merely one of many other issues that commanded the attention of the British and American high commands immediately before the start of OCTAGON. Two of what might have proved the more difficult of these, and obviously related to VANGUARD, concerned the definition of objectives in Upper Burma and the framing of yet another directive to South East Asia Command in order to take account of changing conditions and Allied aims in that theater of operations. In the event these took time but raised no real problems. The British high command was willing to accept an Upper Burma commitment and for their part the American Chiefs of Staff, with no overriding objection to VANGUARD, had no incentive to thwart a proposed redrafting of Mountbatten's directive to take account of this and other possibilities. But if, therefore, VANGUARD did not present itself as an immediate cause of Anglo-American dispute, and after 1 September it was clear that it would not, other areas of potential disagreement—such as the Pacific commitment—remained and VANGUARD itself nevertheless continued to present its own practical difficulties simply because the problems identified by the planners could not be overcome as a result of a pep-talk by Brooke. Even before the British high command embarked for Quebec in the *Queen Mary* two of VANGUARD's many problems that Brooke would have wished away had assumed some importance. Mountbatten's schedule for VANGUARD in March 1945 involved a cutoff date of 1 October 1944,[139] and with every day that passed this assumed, obviously, an ever more urgent significance. Moreover, the force levels required for VANGUARD became increasingly unrealistic in light of growing American demands upon transport aircraft and gliders[140] and as a result of South East Asia Command's plan to support a landing at Rangoon with air attacks on the Andamans and Nicobars. Because such attacks would involve a minimum of two fleet carriers,[141] VANGUARD could only threaten the proposed move of the fleet to the Pacific. This was precisely the danger against which Mallaby had warned the Directors of Plans on the very day when the Chiefs of Staff had gone before the War Cabinet with the VANGUARD proposal. On 8 August Mallaby had warned that while VANGUARD promised to be quicker than CHAMPION in clearing Burma, the latter was likely to be the more economical because it did not make any demand upon naval resources.[142] The warning had been not lessened in any way by being implicit, but by the first week of September, with the examination of post-VANGUARD operations in hand in London,[143] the dangers explicit in embracing a two-ocean formula must have been coming apparent to the members of the British high command who embarked for Canada on the fifth. In fact, a more immediate danger had become clear by this time, and this was that the prime minister

is still always set on capturing the tip of Sumatra. He has agreed to our . . . campaign in Burma but limits his sanction to the capture of Rangoon alone without the clearing of the rest of Burma . . . when the main idea of the . . . campaign was to reopen communications . . . to China. . . . This makes the expedition practically useless and . . . cannot appeal to the Americans.[144]

In fact the planning staffs were seeking a program that could meet the prime minister's demands and yet provide a means whereby the fleet could proceed to the Pacific. In the first days of September, with 21st Army Group advancing rapidly into central Belgium, the planners considered two possibilities. They allowed themselves the luxury of considering the withdrawal of three divisions for VANGUARD in the anticipation that current operations in northwest Europe would not be prejudiced as a result,[145] and they proposed an alternative timetable with a small-scale operation in the

Bay of Bengal in mid-1945, VANGUARD in December followed by attacks on Bangkok and other targets on the Kra, and an attack on Singapore in early 1946 from the South China Sea.[146] But neither proposal, and particularly the latter with an assault on Rangoon—Operation DRACULA[147]—staged from the Indian Ocean and a CULVERIN-scaled operation staged from the Pacific, could be the answer to British problems. In fact there was no answer because, as the Directors of Plans explained to the Chiefs of Staff on 5 September, "The original purpose was to have an added argument against the Istrian operation in that it conflicted with DRACULA which otherwise would be possible. The question therefore is whether in fact DRACULA is likely to be possible in March 1945," the consequences of DRACULA's being accepted apparently not having been anticipated. The Directors of Plans stated that the real choice facing the British high command was between a full-scale CAPITAL or closing this operation down in order to concentrate resources in the Pacific, and if the latter course was adopted the prospect of losing Mogaung and Myitkyina had to be accepted.[148] The latter, obviously, was never a practical proposition.

The Chiefs' of Staff reaction to this memorandum has to be left to the imagination: the available record, perhaps thankfully, gives no indication of what could hardly have been the most sanguine of pre-OCTAGON meetings of senior British officers. Whatever the reaction, and leaving aside what this memorandum must imply in terms of deception and long-term intentions of the planning staffs, it seems more than likely that fear of the prime minister and of the American high command focused the concentration of the British military at this stage of proceedings: the Chiefs of Staff and their senior staffs could not afford to dispute between themselves while sharing a ship to Quebec with the prime minister. If such considerations were indeed the reason why this paper was thus dated, then they were rewarded as a series of meetings aboard the *Queen Mary* hammered out the basis of British policy and, in so doing, put before the prime minister and Chiefs of Staff such calculations regarding DRACULA that even Churchill came to express the view that of the two operations he preferred CAPITAL.[149] But by the time that the prime minister so expressed himself it was too late for the British high command to drop DRACULA from its program: having presented the Joint Chiefs of Staff with proposals that included a Rangoon landing, the British high command could not open the OCTAGON exchanges with a repudiation of its own proposal.

The final form of the British program for the war against Japan, the problems of DRACULA included, was considered in seven of the conferences held by the British high command on the way to and in Quebec before the start of the OCTAGON conference. DRACULA's problems, well to the fore in no fewer than five of these conferences, presented themselves under several headings. The problems caused by the 1 October deadline and by dependence upon American agreement were recognized, as were the difficulties that were likely to arise because the engineering resources needed for DRAC-ULA had to be committed to first-phase CAPITAL, with all the implications that flowed from that fact. But the main concern of the British high command in dealing with DRACULA stemmed from an acknowledgment that shipping considerations presented a twofold problem. The movement of British forces to the Far East for DRACULA would mean that virtually the entire British trooping capacity would be thus committed for five months,[150] and the British contribution to the movement of American forces to Europe, 70,000 troops or two divisions a month, would have to be halted. Somewhat surprisingly, the Chiefs of Staff did not anticipate an unfavorable American reaction to this latter prospect.[151] The former, however, was another matter because it involved the withdrawal of British forces from northwest Europe during the current month and their immediate dispatch, without home leave, to India,[152] and the withdrawal of those British forces in the Mediterranean theater earmarked for this operation by December.[153] Leaving aside the obvious operational imponderables that such deadlines implied, these movements would involve the halting of the routine flow of reinforcements to and of the normal rotation of formations in India, and the negotiation of the bottlenecks presented by Bombay's port facilities and the Indian rail system.[154] In fact, India could not handle the movement of the 370,000 men and 24,000 vehicles that would have to be sent from northwest Europe and the Mediterranean for this operation, and given such numbers it was small wonder that Churchill noted, at the conference on the tenth, that the demands being made on the part of DRACULA would kill the operation.[155] It is somewhat hard to resist the idea that it might well have been in British interests if not to kill the operation then to have changed the balance of emphasis between it and CAPITAL at this time, but as a result of the argument that followed his observation, the prime minister acknowledged that DRACULA was indeed preferable to CAPITAL as the means of clearing Burma.[156] DRACULA, therefore, retained its position within the British program. In this the prime minister deferred to the Chiefs of Staff, just as he had the previous day when he had attempted to repudiate the commitment of British forces to South West Pacific Command.[157] In so handling Churchill on these matters, the Chiefs of Staff showed a deftness of touch that was certain to be needed in the discussions with the Americans. Not merely did the Chiefs of Staff prevail upon the prime minister on these matters on 9 and 10 September, but they did so by linking DRACULA to the Istria question. After stating that they disliked this latter operation and the Americans would like it even less, they tied the two proposed landings together with the request for political guidance on the merits of DRACULA while suggesting that it might be possible to redeploy formations from Europe for an operation that would end the lingering commitment in Upper Burma.[158]

The question of the Pacific commitment also exercised the attention of the British high command, but in a different manner. DRACULA involved an element of British choice, and as the Chiefs of Staff noted on 6 September, the question of cutting British forces in Europe in order to meet a widening commitment in the Far East did not have to be tackled immediately.[159] DRACULA, therefore, could wait upon events, and, given the unfolding of events in Europe, decisions on these matters could be deferred. The Pacific question similarly had to wait, but upon an American decision on the offer of a British contribution to the Pacific war. When this decision was forthcoming on 9 September,[160] the British high command had to deal immediately with its implications: these, clearly, could not wait on events. It was the receipt of the American decision, with its statement that a British imperial task force would be welcomed in MacArthur's theater of operations, which made Churchill's attempt to repudiate such a commitment so ill-judged. The prime minister was brought, apparently not without some difficulty,[161] to the realization that promises given to the Australians and New Zealanders in May could not be lightly discounted.[162] More to the point, the British high command was in no position to repudiate what was an American decision between alternative courses of action that the British themselves had proposed and presented for a decision, or, more accurately, the British high command could not repudiate the American decision openly.

From the subsequent British decision that when the matter was considered at OCTAGON the Chiefs of Staff were to raise the questions of the central Pacific alternative and the command arrangements of South West Pacific Command, it is evident that the American pronouncement was not to the Chiefs' of Staff liking.[163] Having come so far in defense of a Pacific commitment, the Chiefs of Staff clearly had no intention of being relegated to a strategic backwater, and evidently those political considerations demanding British involvement in the central Pacific offensive that had been raised in the course of the August meetings played their part in the Chiefs' of Staff decision to request a formal statement of the American position.[164] Clearly, the Chiefs of Staff kept an eye on the historical record, but they must have known, at the staff conference on the twelfth as they listened to Churchill say that he was willing to take up the central Pacific issue with the Americans,[165] that a British fleet would indeed find itself involved in the final operations against the Japanese home islands. At the end of a long and exhausting process the Chiefs of Staff could rely on the prime minister, if convinced that the American selection of the southwest Pacific option was intended as a slight, to use his powers of persuasion to good effect.[166]

In fact, there proved no need to unleash the prime minister upon the American high command. Brooke, who had expressed his reservations about OCTAGON even as he embarked for the conference, noted at its end that while the Americans had a low regard for Churchill as a strategist and regarded him with the deepest suspicion, they "have shown a wonderful spirit of co-operation"[167] that was apparent from the conference's first plenary session on 13 September. At that meeting Churchill, with some gall, noted that "certain elements inimical to good Anglo-American relations" had referred to an alleged British dragging of feet when it came to the Pacific war, and that accordingly he was offering the services of a British fleet in the central Pacific as proof of national intent: the offer was thus elevated to a status of national honor and Britain's faithfulness as an ally. Roosevelt's comment that the offer was no sooner made than accepted spelled the end to the whole issue,[168] King's notorious behavior at the infamous meeting of 14 September notwithstanding.[169] In fact King would have been far better advised not to have opposed Roosevelt's decision, to find himself isolated within the Joint Chiefs of Staff as a result, but to have impaled the proposal upon the "balanced and self-supporting" proviso to which the British were bound. Be that as it may, the central Pacific strategy was accepted, incorporated in the final American program, and, once approved by the Chiefs of Staff, formed the basis of the final OCTAGON agreement. With the landings at Rangoon scheduled for either March or December 1945, Burma was to be cleared in its entirety; the assault on Malaya and an air offensive against Bangkok were to be conducted in the winter of 1945–46; a British bomber force was to proceed to the central Pacific, and so was the fleet.[170] There remained, therefore, only the task of ensuring that DRACULA was not stillborn.

DRACULA, however, presented no serious problem at OCTAGON. In the confident atmosphere of Quebec, and with the basic Burma problem not giving rise to Anglo-American friction,[171] the Combined Chiefs of Staff were prepared to wait a matter of two weeks in order to see if events in northwest Europe would allow the operation to proceed. In an attempt to ensure that it did so, Churchill tried to ensure a reduction of DRACULA by 170,000 men, but because this was accompanied by a demand that the operation be brought forward two months,[172] this was no more than a palliative and, indeed, was largely besides the point. The fact of the matter was that the British, for any number of good reasons that have long detained us, could not stage this operation. It was against the background of this reality that the British made the request, on 22 September and after the American high command had accepted the principle of DRACULA at OCTAGON, that American combat formations be made available for this operation.[173]

Of all the episodes in the British search for a naval strategy for the war against Japan this request is one of the strangest, the least easy to interpret. To ask for American ground troops in Southeast Asia while British naval forces moved to the Pacific was not as illogical as it may seem. It nevertheless remains somewhat incongruous, particularly in light of the fact that South East Asia Command was one in which the British high command attempted to maintain and preserve whatever freedom of action remained to it as the imbalance of American and British resources tipped the power of decision ever more in favor of the United States. This was a theater that provided clear evidence of British resentment of American influence,[174] yet it was a theater where, with this request, the British sought a major role for American combat troops in retaking the capital of a lost colony. By any standard, and particularly by the standards employed in the arguments within the British high command on Indian Ocean questions, the British request made little sense, and it is one that made even less sense in light of the fact that at the second and closing plenary session at OCTAGON the prime minister noted that no U.S. divisions would be employed in Burma.[175]

It seems that the British request did not meet with an immediate rejection, though Marshall's immediate response that all available divisions were earmarked and that "a change in allocation does not appear advisable" pointed to its likely fate.[176] The U.S. planners, by noting that American help might be made available if the European situation resolved itself, were more forthcoming, but with MARKET GARDEN faltering at this time London was advised that the Americans might be more receptive to the idea of their sending two extra divisions to Italy in order to release Indian divisions for service in Southeast Asia.[177] On the twenty-third this suggestion was put to Marshall after he had indicated his reluctance to commit U.S. divisions to Burma.[178] Marshall's reticence was apparently based on a desire not to be involved in a British theater and to avoid British command of American troops, and the need to send more forces to Europe in order to ensure that those already there could be released at the end of the war.[179] The issue went to the Joint Chiefs of Staff on the twenty-sixth, and London was advised that the Americans had agreed to the release of one division from Italy and would probably agree to the release of a second: the question of American divisions being sent to Burma was to be referred to Roosevelt.[180] What was not said in this signal seems important: either the Americans did not undertake to cover British formations moved from Italy or the question of their doing so was not put. In either case, with the 1 October deadline at hand and MARKET GARDEN in its death throes, the American answer made no difference: for the British and Americans alike, the failure to cross the Rhine and take the war into the enemy heartland spelled the end of DRACULA. On 2 October—ironically on the very day when the headlines of the *New York Herald Tribune* announced "British Crush Major Nazi Drive in Holland" and a single-paragraph item noted that Eisenhower's headquarters had broadcast a warning to Austrians to "prepare for the arrival of the Allies"—Churchill and the Chiefs of Staff acknowledged the inevitable with the prime minister indicating that DRACULA should be postponed until after the 1945 monsoon season and that CAPITAL should be pursued with utmost vigor.[181] DRACULA seems to have been canceled with not too many tears shed on its behalf,[182] and even if there was remorse it was sufficiently controlled to allow the British high command to piece together a masterly signal to the Joint Chiefs of Staff announcing the cancellation of the operation without actually stating the fact.[183] It was a mark of the efficiency of British staff work that the search for an interim operation began long before 13 October when the Joint Staff Mission recommended an Andamans attack as the means of demonstrating British commitment:[184] BUCCANEER had been dusted down on the third,[185] reexamined, and the Arakan cited as its alternative.[186] Be that as it may, the long British search for a naval strategy for the war against Japan was over, though probably no one realized it at the time.[187] With Japan's surrender some ten months in the future and the German war certain to last into 1945, DRACULA's deadline was one for Britain as a whole. No major decision that the British high command took after that date could be implemented before the Japanese surrender.

There remain many loose ends at the end of this story of how the British high command came to its decisions, all of them of considerable importance and each worthy of detailed consideration in its own right. The relationship with the Dominions, shipping considerations, the implementation of the Pacific decision, and the continuing search for amphibious options in Southeast Asia between October 1944 and March 1944 are just four such post-OCTAGON subjects that quite reasonably could command rigorous investigation, but not here. Rather, one matter commands attention, though in the end no conclusion may be drawn from it. The record is incomplete, but from what is available it seems that the idea of asking the Americans for divisions for DRACULA was broached during the OCTAGON conference, but in London, by the staffs that remained holding the shop,[188] and it seems that the crucial first signals on this matter were between London and the Joint Staff Mission. With senior officers away, it may be that the impetus for this last effort on the part of DRACULA was made by the junior staff, from which so many of the initiatives over the last months had come. But throughout those months the junior staff had demonstrated a tenacious support for the Upper Burma–Pacific combination, and with so much evidence of subterfuge and deviousness at hand it is legitimate to pose the question if this last ploy on the part of DRACULA was not a straw man, indeed not just the DRACULA proposal from the time that the Joint Staff Mission was instructed not to discuss force levels for DRACULA with the Americans, but the whole of the DRACULA proposal from the time it was accepted as the basis of policy, was not superbly calculated. A check had been issued in the expectation that it would never be presented,[189] and an American dimension added in the anticipation that if the United States accepted the obligation all would be well and if it did not then nothing of substance would be lost—most certainly not the Pacific commitment. Perhaps, and perhaps not. In any case, it did not matter: Britain had its policy. Britain's search for a naval strategy for the war against Japan was at its end.

AFTERWORD: ROOSEVELT'S STATEMENT OF 13 SEPTEMBER 1944

Although the decline of the influence of Harry Hopkins and Cordell Hull by this stage of proceedings, plus Roosevelt's deviousness and casual working habits, make it difficult to assess Roosevelt's reasons in welcoming the British offer of a fleet for service in the central Pacific, it is equally difficult to resist the conclusion that the president's action was not unrelated to certain exchanges within the administration which had involved Hopkins and Hull in the two weeks before OCTAGON. On 1 September the ambassador in London, Winant, signaled Hopkins that

> if we allow the British to limit their active participation to recapturing areas that are to their selfish interest alone and not participate in smashing Japan . . . we will create in the United States a hatred for Great Britain that will make for schism in the post-war years.[190]

In his reply of the fourth Hopkins noted that "we simply must find a way to have Great Britain take her full and proper place in the war against Japan."[191] Hull, in one of at least three memoranda that he sent to Roosevelt on the eighth, noted

> that one of the most important objectives of U.S. policy must be to bring the British into the war . . . in the Far East to the greatest possible extent. The advantages of such a course are obvious. . . . The disadvantages of the failure of the British to participate to the full [are an] immediate and hostile public reaction in the United States.[192]

Hull clearly saw Britain having a major role in the preservation of the postwar order, both in Europe and the Far East, and because this was also Roosevelt's view it may be that the president was anxious to see British involvement in the central Pacific in order to ensure postwar British cooperation in the Far East.[193] These statements are of value not simply because they suggest that the support forthcoming from Roosevelt and the State Department for the Chiefs' of Staff position was based on exactly the same considerations as those that guided the British service chiefs. Paradoxically, however, these were arguments that the British could not have used in dealing with the Americans and which the latter, in their turn, could not openly acknowledge in their dealings with the British.

CHAPTER FIVE

The End of Strife

Such is the story of the British search between QUADRANT and OCTAGON for a naval strategy for the war against Japan. The story is neither complete nor particularly edifying: the inadequacies of the record account for the former, the attitudes and actions of the *dramatis personae* explain the latter. The tangled events that together made up this search reflect little credit upon any of the individuals caught in their march, and the most charitable comment that can be made about the prime minister in this sorry tale is that Churchill, clearly, was not at his best. Overall, the British attempt to settle strategic priorities in the Far East reflected both the strengths and weaknesses of the "war-by-committee" system: the ability to check misdirected or irresponsible intention was matched by an inability to come to decisions other than those imposed, more or less, by events. In the final analysis, arguments that reflected conflicting political, strategic, and military perspectives counted for little in the shadow cast by American power, and British decisions were those rendered inevitable by immutable factors of time, distance, and national frailty as Britain faced the prospect of the war continuing into its seventh year.

The British search for a naval strategy for the war against Japan raised many issues, but because the final phase of the Greater East Asia War witnessed an expansion of the British effort the conflicting arguments that were used in the course of British deliberations can be measured, at least in part, against what was achieved. And what was achieved in the period of these deliberations was suitably unimpressive: what was achieved thereafter was somewhat different and perversely so. After January 1945 the expansion of the British effort in the Far East took the form of separate naval and amphibious efforts in different oceans, though the latter was not on the scale of CULVERIN or VANGUARD, a form of ANAKIM and what amounted to the reconquest of Burma by an overland offensive from northeast India. Together these represented a rather strange outcome in light of the various arguments used in the committee rooms of Whitehall between January and August 1944.

For the Royal Navy the Indian Ocean in 1944 proved almost as sterile and unrewarding as the discussions of the high command. The Royal Navy came to exercise an ever-growing superiority in the Indian Ocean in the course of 1944 but the buildup of the Eastern Fleet, from a strength of one unmodernized battleship, one escort carrier, one heavy and seven light cruisers, and eleven destroyers assigned to fleet duties at the start of 1944 to an order of battle that included four capital ships, three fleet, one light fleet, and five escort carriers, three heavy and five light cruisers, twenty-five destroyers, twenty submarines, and ninety-three assorted units with escort formations on 12 November,[1] was not accompanied by any significant strategic achievement: indeed many of the operations executed by the Eastern Fleet in 1944 as it slowly added to its strength only served to demonstrate the inadequacies of British carrier forces and technique as the Royal Navy prepared for its anticipated Pacific role. Thus Operation COCK-PIT resulted in British carrier aircraft missing many targets of opportunity at Sabang as well as a "Battle of the Pips" when Force 70 engaged false radar targets.[2] Operation BANQUET revealed that the *Victorious* was unable to spot more than twenty-two aircraft in readiness for a strike mission,[3] and Operation LIGHT saw the *Indomitable* need forty minutes and two separate deckloads to dispatch just eighteen aircraft.[4] There were commendable achievements. During Operation PEDAL the *Illustrious* became the first British carrier to operate fifty aircraft at any one time,[5] and in Operation MILLET the Royal Navy employed a two-phase attack plan with its carrier aircraft for the first time in the war.[6] Moreover, between July and October 1944 the Eastern Fleet carried out four offensive operations involving more than one fleet carrier, all but doubling the number of such operations executed by the Royal Navy since September 1939.[7] There were other points of interest, the most obvious being that in Operation CRIMSON the *Queen Elizabeth* engaged an enemy with her main armament for the first time since 1915 when she had fought off Gallipoli, no mean achievement for a battle-ship built to fight the Kaiser's navy in the North Sea.[8] But overall there was no escaping the fact that by the time that it was dissolved and its units divided between the East Indies and British Pacific Fleets, the Eastern Fleet's record of underachievement belied a recent supremacy that was not disputed but which could not be applied to any real effect.

It was against so undistinguished a background, therefore, that the British Pacific Fleet was raised,[9] and for a force on which so many hopes rested, its career began inauspiciously. At OCTAGON the British promised to send a fleet of four fleet and two light fleet carriers, two fast battleships, eight cruisers, twenty-four destroyers, and sixty escorts to the Pacific by the end of the year, but 22 November 1944, the date when it was formed, found the British Pacific Fleet unable to proceed from Ceylon, well below its planned establishment, and with no prospect of being brought to full strength. A series of infuriating delays in reequipping the carrier air groups with Avengers, and Sydney's inability to receive it, condemned the British Pacific Fleet to an extended stay in the Indian Ocean, but this at least provided additional time in which it could be worked up to full operational efficiency. As Operation LIGHT had shown, such time was needed, and more was provided as a result of the American request that the British Pacific Fleet attack the Palembang refineries in December.[10] Because of meteorological considerations, the British put back an attack on Palembang until January 1945 and instituted the OUTFLANK option, three operations of increasing size and importance against oil targets in Sumatra that culminated with the attack on Palembang by the fleet en route for Australia and the Pacific.

The first two attacks were executed on 20 December 1944 and 4 January 1945 by aircraft from the *Illustrious* and *Indomitable* and from the *Indefatigable, Indomitable,* and *Victorious* respectively. The third operation, MERIDIAN, was against Palembang,[11] and was the first occasion on which the Royal Navy employed four fleet carriers offensively. Palembang was struck on 24 and 29 January, and though British aircraft losses were heavy, the damage inflicted on the refineries was such as to draw from the Royal Navy's official historian the observation that the attack was the British Pacific Fleet's "greatest contribution to final victory over Japan."[12] This is a comment which, if true, leaves obvious question marks against the importance and value of the British Pacific Fleet's subsequent operations off Okinawa and the Japanese home islands.

The British Pacific Fleet arrived at Sydney on 10 February, and eighteen days later sailed for Manus, arriving on 7 March. It sailed without the *Illustrious,* which had been docked and did not rejoin until the fifteenth, one day after the British Pacific Fleet received its operational orders for ICEBERG. On the eighteenth it sailed for Ulithi, arriving on the twentieth, and three days later it sailed for the first phase of the Okinawan campaign with four fleet carriers, two fast battleships, five light cruisers, and eleven destroyers under command. It arrived on station on the twenty-fifth, and between the following day and 20 April it conducted offensive operations on twelve days against enemy air bases in the Sakishima Gunto. Throughout this phase of operations, which included an attack on Shinchiku in Formosa on 12 April, the British Pacific Fleet deployed four carriers, though on 14 April the *Formidable* replaced the *Illustrious* in the order of battle. After this phase of operations the fleet retired to Leyte, from whence it sailed on 1 May for the second phase of ICEBERG. Between 4 and 22 May the British Pacific Fleet conducted offensive operations on ten days with all four carriers, three of which were damaged by *kamikaze* attack. Partly as a result of such damage and partly as a result of losses sustained in a hangar fire on the eighteenth, the *Formidable* was detached on the twenty-second and missed the final two days of operations before the fleet withdrew via Manus to Brisbane and Sydney.

When the carriers reached Sydney the *Indomitable* was docked. Her place with the fleet was taken by the *Implacable*, which had arrived on station in early May and which was then at Manus. While the other carriers remained at Sydney, the *Implacable*, an escort carrier, four cruisers, and five destroyers conducted Operation INMATE, a series of strikes against Truk between 13 and 15 June.[13] Suitably blooded, the *Implacable* sailed with the *Formidable* and *Victorious*, one battleship, six cruisers, and fifteen destroyers from Manus on 6 July for operations in the company of Task Force (TF) 38 against the home islands. The three carriers conducted strike operations on two days before being joined on the twentieth by the *Indefatigable*, and between 24 July and 12 August the four carriers conducted offensive operations on six more days. On the latter date the British Pacific Fleet divided, the bulk of the fleet returning to Sydney because it was short of fuel and could no longer delay putting in hand a refitting program that was essential if the fleet carriers were to be on station in October for the invasion of Kyushu.[14] The *Indefatigable, King George V,* two cruisers, and ten destroyers remained on station as Task Group (TG) 37.3 and conducted one more full day of offensive operations before the end of hostilities on 15 August. The latter event, of course, rendered the invasion of Kyushu unnecessary, just as it rendered superfluous the raising three days earlier of a second British carrier formation at Sydney. This formation, TG 111.2, consisted of the *Indomitable* and three newly arrived light fleet carriers, but four of the latter were at Manus by the time that the instrument of Japan's surrender was signed in the *Missouri* on 2 September. Thus their first encounters with the Japanese were to take place under conditions that were very different from those that had been anticipated. The *Colossus* was to proceed to Shanghai as part of the Allied occupation force committed to this most westernized of Chinese cities. The *Venerable*, in the company of the *Indomitable,* was to be involved in the reoccupation of Hong Kong, and was to be joined in this task by the *Vengeance* after the latter's part in the liberation of Singapore was canceled. The last of the arrivals, the *Glory*, was to accept the surrender of enemy forces at Rabaul. Thereafter the light fleet carriers were engaged in repatriation duties, and formed the backbone of British naval power in the Far East after the fleet carriers returned to Britain.[15]

Such is the bare outline of the British Pacific Fleet's career in the Indian and Pacific Oceans, and with a total of 140 carrier-strike days between December 1944 and August 1945 its record, by American standards, was not very impressive. The fleet was the equivalent of a weak U.S. carrier task group which it was unable to match in scale, duration, and intensity of operations.[16] In combat its relative losses were much heavier than those incurred by the Americans,[17] and while in the final phase of operations off Japan relative successes may have been more evenly shared than was the case during ICEBERG,[18] the Americans undoubtedly accounted for a disproportionately high share of the losses inflicted upon the enemy.[19] By comparison with the Americans, British rates of aircraft serviceability were low despite British carriers having larger maintenance parties than those available to U.S. carrier air groups.[20] Such shortcomings were symptomatic of a general British technical inferiority to the Americans in, and a lack of experience of, carrier warfare, which was more readily acknowledged at the time than it has been in most postwar British accounts of operations. Less well known, however, are the reasons for these shortcomings.

Part of the answer lies in the fact that the inability of the British high command to settle priorities and policy between January and August 1944 imposed handicaps on the British Pacific Fleet that could not be overcome, at least not in full, in the course of its operations. It was a measure of the lateness of British decisions, for example, that 90 percent of requested aircraft stores had not arrived in Australia by the time that the British Pacific Fleet sailed from Manus for ICEBERG. Moreover, the improvisation that had to be adopted at that time was reflected in the fact that air logistics, the lack of which "came closer to causing a complete breakdown of operations than any other single factor,"[21] was the province of four separate organizations,[22] while the task of reconciling their activities and the needs of the fleet was handled by a staff of one, a lieutenant-commander from the engineering branch. A complete collapse of supply was averted only by the arrival at Manus of the aircraft repair ship *Unicorn* and by her officers' assuming the necessary staff duties in addition to the routine running of their ship. It was not until the second quarter of 1945 that the first attempts were made to bring order to the whole muddled area of air logistics, and it was not until June that matters were resolved with the creation of, and the issue of formal directives to, an air train staff that was to number hundreds and be headed by a commodore.[23] By that time, however, the hitherto-desperate supply position had begun to ease with the arrival in the advance base areas of the aircraft maintenance ship *Pioneer*, the component repair ship *Deer Sound*, and the first of the MONABS,[24] but predictably the improvements that were brought about were felt primarily in shore bases rather than with the fleet at sea.[25]

That at least some aspects of logistical administration improved in the course of operations points to the fact that the delay of decisions between January and September 1944 was a major factor in the difficulties of the British Pacific Fleet. Yet the improvements that took place in the course of 1945 are evenhanded in their implications. Clearly, other factors were at work, most obviously that national weakness in terms of securing the means to stock Australian bases and to provide an adequate fleet train that had so concerned the Chiefs of Staff in spring 1944. But national weakness was exacerbated by a lack of knowledge of what was logistically involved in carrier warfare, which stemmed from the fact that until this time British fleet carriers had been employed on operations that involved their use rather than carrier operations per se. Small-scale and fragmented operations, which very seldom involved the use of more than one carrier, had been poor preparation for the type of warfare that the British Pacific Fleet was called upon to wage in the Far East in 1944 and 1945. This lack of experience was reflected in administrative arrangements and practices that drew a great deal of adverse comment in the various staff reports penned at the end of the war. No doubt many of these observations were overharsh and reflected the exhaustion and frustration of individuals, not just the weaknesses of the system within which they had worked, but a random sample of their strictures provides some insight into the unpreparedness of the British Pacific Fleet for an operational role and into the difficulties under which it labored.

Prior to the British Pacific Fleet's beginning operations, its logistical needs, in the words of one report, were "considered solely in terms of oil, ammunition and aircraft."[26] One officer, in his report to the Admiralty, stated that the latter's provisions appeared to have been "governed either by childlike faith or ostrich-like escapism,"[27] and there is no doubt that staff organization and establishment were totally inadequate to deal with operational needs in March 1945. Although the munitions branch of the Royal Australian Navy was considered by the Admiralty to be one of the very few RAN staff sections competent enough to be entrusted with arrangements for the British Pacific Fleet,[28] none of the staff of the ammunition stores office other than its head and one officer arrived in Sydney before the fleet left Manus for ICEBERG.[29] At the turn of the year the fleet train engineering staff consisted of five officers, with one room and a single chair.[30] One U.S. liaison officer was amazed to find that no section of the staff dealt solely with fleet oil requirements and that certain staff officers were expected to deal with oil matters in addition to their other responsibilities.[31] Such examples can be multiplied many times but to no useful purpose; suffice it to note that by the end of the war the fleet as a whole was not unlike its radars, "trembling on the edge of unserviceability."[32] The fact was that after more than five years of war in which the main British naval commitment was to trade defense in the eastern Atlantic, navy and nation were ill-placed to meet the demands imposed by changes of role and theater. In any event, certain problems that the British Pacific Fleet faced could never have been anticipated and others flowed from technical decisions made long before the Pacific commitment was endorsed and which were irreversible. These owed little if anything to the delay of decisions by the British high command between January and August 1944.

The most obvious of these was an underestimation of losses as a result of the attempt to cater for a monthly loss of 20 percent of initial air establishment. This figure was derived from American sources and experience,[33] but it was one that proved a poor planning guide despite the fact that an average monthly attrition rate of 23.4 percent between March and August 1945 confirmed its general accuracy.[34] The 20 percent figure proved misleading for three reasons. First, the air establishment of the American fast carrier force formed a much smaller part of the American naval air establishment in the Pacific than did the British carrier air groups with respect to the British Pacific Fleet area: in March 1945, for example, the fleet carriers accounted for 71 percent of the total British air establishment in the Pacific. Second, the heaviest losses of American carrier air groups were invariably sustained in short but intense periods of combat, and by the time that the British fleet entered the fray these periods were becoming compressed as the pace of the Pacific war quickened. Third, British carrier groups were much smaller than those of the Americans and their losses in action were relatively higher. Thus while the scale of American air resources in the Pacific allowed the U.S. Navy to absorb its carrier group losses within the very large operational and administrative margins available to it, the British found that their losses, which by the nature of things were concentrated at the point of contact by the formations least able to sustain them, could not be balanced within the overall air establishment, though the problem did ease somewhat as the latter increased with the passing of months.

In the first phase of ICEBERG the British Pacific Fleet lost one-third of its carrier air establishment, and in the course of operations in May, its worst single month, the British Pacific Fleet lost 42 percent of its original strength—and 79 percent of its Corsair establishment—in just three weeks. During ICEBERG as a whole, involving twenty-four strike-days within a total of forty-six days on station, the British Pacific Fleet lost 81 percent of the establishment with which it began operations on 25 March. In July and August, in operations against the home islands, British carriers lost 39 percent of their overall establishment, that is, original strength plus replacements. Had these operations been conducted with the same intensity of those in May, their losses would have accounted for well over half of their overall strength.[35] In the attacks of 24 and 25 July alone, the *Implacable* lost 28 percent of her aircraft, and on 10 August, the last occasion when she conducted offensive operations, her losses almost touched the 20 percent mark.[36]

With the Admiralty having attempted to provide for 25 percent losses within an eight-day strike cycle,[37] the experience of combat clearly presented the British Pacific Fleet with problems that perhaps not even the sanctioning of air groups 130 percent above initial establishment would have solved.[38] But the difficulties created by unexpectedly heavy losses were only one part of the British problem. The severity of British air losses was in part the result of British carrier air groups lacking the numbers that allowed the saturation of target areas, and British aircraft lacked the electronic countermeasures, standoff weapons, and fragmentation bombs that gave the Americans some measure of immunity when attacking heavily defended airfields and port installations. In relative terms, British losses in strike operations were 48 percent above those incurred by the Americans despite the latter's policy of attacking the more heavily defended targets themselves.[39] The relative smallness of British carrier air groups was the result of the prewar decision to build carriers with armored hangars, but three subclasses of carriers with different hangar heights served with the British Pacific Fleet, and as a result five different types of combat aircraft were embarked. Lack of standardization imposed operational problems involving the reconciliation of the performances of very diverse aircraft, but it also meant that the carriers could not necessarily service aircraft other than their own. Moreover, the British practice was to modify American-supplied aircraft, but subsequent enforced dependence upon directly supplied (and unmodified) American aircraft left the British Pacific Fleet with aircraft that it could not maintain. To complicate these problems still further, the British fleet carriers were dependent upon American-built escort carriers for the ferrying of replacement aircraft to the fleet at sea. Leaving aside the fact that five different types of combat aircraft presented the planning staffs with an impossible problem of anticipating losses and loading the ferries accordingly,[40] the escort carriers, because they could not use their catapults to launch British aircraft,[41] could only embark twenty-four aircraft rather than a full load of forty.[42] But despite reduced loads, their manpower shortages meant that they could not maintain even those aircraft they carried and could not undertake their own routine self-maintenance. With only four escort carriers available to bring aircraft forward from Manus in August, the end of hostilities could not have come too soon for the units of the 30th Aircraft Carrier Squadron, and the same was true for the oilers on which the British Pacific Fleet was dependent.

If, as was alleged, inadequacies of air logistics came closer to curtailing the operations of the British Pacific Fleet before August 1945 than any other single cause, then there is little doubt that the weaknesses of the oiler force committed to the support of the British Pacific Fleet would have acquired this dubious distinction had the war lasted beyond that time. As early as June 1945 the fleet train staff was of the view that even if only one oiler had been lost or forced to withdraw from service during ICEBERG the operations of the fleet would have been, if not jeopardized, then seriously imperiled, and it was well aware by July of the intractability of oil problems in trying to prepare for Operation OLYMPIC.[43] For the invasion of Kyushu the Americans intended to operate two carrier fleets, the 5th, under Spruance, in the close-support role, and the 3rd, under Halsey, in the general-support role. It was the British intention, prompted by political considerations, to deploy the full strength of the British Pacific Fleet with Halsey's force.[44] It was to contribute four fleet and four light fleet carriers, four battleships, nine cruisers, and upwards of thirty destroyers divided between two task groups, but the staff calculations showed that refueling such numbers, in the short hours of daylight available off Kyushu in the autumn months, would require no fewer than thirty large, fast oilers. These would have to operate in five groups of six on a two-day replenishment cycle with five days between cycles. In August 1945 there was one such oiler on station, and there was no prospect of there being thirty available even in January 1946. The staff calculation was that two full-strength groups could be refueled but once and thereafter only one group could have been maintained on station, the only alternative being to strike the battleships and a complete destroyer flotilla from the order of battle and operate two much reduced groups.[45] Which way the choice would have gone but for the enemy's surrender is not clear, but what does seem clear is that had the invasion of Kyushu gone ahead the British Pacific Fleet would have been seen to falter in full view of Britain's allies and the Commonwealth. Fraser's final report to the Admiralty, by stating that the manner and speed with which the war ended resolved an impossible logistical problem with respect to OLYMPIC,[46] admitted as much.

Such, then, were some of the many problems that confronted the British Pacific Fleet in the first British experience of large-scale protracted carrier warfare. Among the many comments that have been made in the last forty years about the performance of the fleet, two, both made soon after the end of the war, are of particular interest and relevance. The confidential Naval Staff History noted, "The fact that the British Pacific Fleet played its part in the Pacific war was justification for the trials it underwent."[47] On the other hand, the Director of Stores at the Admiralty, commenting upon the fleet commander's report covering operations between November 1944 and July 1945, noted,

> It is impossible to escape the obvious conclusion, so forcefully now brought before us, that even in time of war the resources of the British Empire were incapable of providing the ships, bases and facilities necessary to maintain adequately the Pacific Fleet, operating as it was under exceptional circumstances at great distances from the main base.[48]

The two observations are not mutually exclusive, and in their different ways both are correct. The Director of Stores was undoubtedly correct in noting the Empire's inability to sustain a carrier fleet in the Pacific. By noting an inability to engage effectively in arguably the most important of the three dimensions of naval warfare he clearly pointed to the problems that the Royal Navy was to encounter in trying to maintain a capability across the whole spectrum of naval warfare in a postwar era dominated by stringent financial and manpower restrictions. But the fact was that the British Pacific Fleet did justify its existence. For all its shortcomings, its enforced dependence upon the Americans to keep it in action, and the precarious administrative margins by which potential disasters were avoided, the British Pacific Fleet was proof to the Americans that they would not be left to deal with the last of the Axis powers alone. No doubt many Americans, not just King, would have been more than content to have been left to finish their private war with Japan without the encumbrance of dependent allies. But off Okinawa in late March, and again in April, when TF 58 fell from its peak strength of February 1945 to levels below that of June 1944 when it fought and won the battle of the Philippine Sea, the British Pacific Fleet undoubtedly fell into the "nice-to-have" category. There is no reason to suppose that the Americans would not have prevailed over, off, and on Okinawa if the British Pacific Fleet had not been on station. If anything, the evidence would seem to suggest that neither off Okinawa nor in subsequent operations in July or August was the British Pacific Fleet essential to success: the fleet was not the difference between victory and defeat. But even if the fleet never fell into the "need-to-have" classification, the capture of Okinawa involved the services of no fewer than sixty fleet, light fleet, and escort carriers spread over a three-month period. By being on station the fleet enabled Britain and its Empire to escape the accusation of not pulling their weight in the main theater of operations when the war in Europe was over and the U.S. Navy was engaged in perhaps its most grueling campaign of the Pacific war. It is not idle to speculate on the likely American reaction, and not simply in the Hearst press, if the British had not been on station to share the risks and contribute to the common cause to the best of their ability. Senior American officers expressed their appreciation of British efforts which, because and in spite of the difficulties under which the British Pacific Fleet labored, reflected very creditably on the Royal Navy. Herein, perhaps, lies the real value of the British Pacific Fleet and a contribution to Japan's defeat that far outweighed anything that was achieved at Palembang in January 1945. The British Pacific Fleet was useful and, within limits, it was effective, but the psychological significance of its just being there was probably more important to the Empire and the Americans alike than anything it achieved in battle.

Although the British Pacific Fleet clearly did not realize all the hopes and claims made on its behalf in the 1944 discussions, it is somewhat difficult to resist the notion that its record nevertheless justified the time and effort that the Chiefs of Staff and planners spent in 1944 in ensuring the adoption of a Pacific commitment. The Pacific strategy worked, the British made a modest contribution to its success: the war was brought to an end in 1945. Britain thus avoided the manpower nightmare that would have been presented by the war continuing into 1946. But the other parts of the British naval contribution to final victory, the execution of DRACULA, present a more difficult problem of interpretation. DRACULA, of course, came as the climax to the clearing of Burma, but the campaign in Burma has figured only *en passant* in this account of the formulation of British policy for the Japanese war. An evaluation of DRACULA in the final pages of this book does not lend itself easily to an examination of the Burma campaign, but DRACULA cannot be considered without some consideration of this campaign. Sufficient to needs, however, is the recounting that between December 1944 and May 1945 Burma, apart from Tenasserim, was largely cleared of the Japanese, and the first overland convoys reached Kunming via Tengchung on 20 January and via Bhamo on 4 February. The Ledo Road was completed on 20 January at a cost of $148 million, but carried no more than 7.19 percent of all material supplied to China between February and October 1945.[49] But, as the British high command had suspected, with no effective Chinese Nationalist contribution to the war, the China hope proved an illusion, worse, a trap in which the Americans were ensnared and from which they proved unable to release themselves until 1972. The clearing of Burma, in the final analysis, contributed little if anything to victory over Japan: by the time Burma was reconquered, Japan's general defeat had acquired such proportions that the loss of an outlying sub-theater was of little consequence. But Burma had to be cleared if only because the American high command, in its confusion, ordained thus, and perhaps the clearing of Burma proved to be in Britain's own best interests. Just as the American liberation of the Philippines was of little strategic value but undoubtedly had the effect of ensuring the postwar rehabilitation of American power in the islands in a way that a bypass strategy could not have effected, so the clearing of Burma provided the Indian empire and army with a final victorious campaign, and undoubtedly helped the process whereby Britain reestablished itself in its Far Eastern colonies at the end of the war.

An examination of the reality of the Burma campaign in terms of the arguments that raged within the British high command between January and August 1944 provokes consideration of obvious ironies. Throughout the 1944 deliberations the notion that Burma could be reconquered by an overland offensive from northeast India was given no serious consideration, and in 1944 the basic terms of reference of the argument within the British high command rested on the premise that the Indian Ocean and the Pacific strategies were mutually exclusive. Yet the reconquest of Burma was achieved by the combination of an overland offensive from northeast India and a series of amphibious operations in the Arakan that culminated in May 1945 with DRACULA at the time when the British Pacific Fleet was en route for Okinawa and Operation ICEBERG. What had been considered to be two impossibilities, therefore, were brought about, and in any consideration of this paradox three matters would seem to demand some examination.

First, histories of the Burma campaign invariably have told the story of the reconquest of Burma in 1945 in terms of air power, and for good and obvious reasons. Air power, in the shape of the Douglas Dakota, alone freed ground forces from dependence upon overland lines of communication and sustained the various British advances into Upper and central Burma that were primarily responsible for the clearing of these areas of the enemy. But the question that presents itself for consideration is whether or not air power could have sustained the offensives from northeast India had it not been for the fact that the XV Army, the cutting edge of the Burma Area Army, had been broken before British forces entered Burma. Even allowing for the actions that were fought around Mandalay and Meiktila, the offensive of XIV Army that cleared Burma took the form of maneuver and pursuit rather than a running fight or set-piece action on the Imphal-Kohima scale. Had XIV Army been obliged to fight its main battle of attrition or annihilation inside Upper or central Burma, the demands that would have been placed upon its airborne lines of communication would have been considerably more substantial than was the case, and even if the transport aircraft supporting XIV Army's advances operated at less than capacity, whether any increase of supply would have been sufficient to meet this extra demand is problematical.

Second, mention of the battles fought around Mandalay and Meiktila raises the question of what factors shaped the British plan of campaign. The British offensive through Upper Burma was made on three fronts that resulted in bridgeheads being thrown across the Irrawaddy at Thabeikkyin and Kyaukmyaung on 11 January, on either side of Ngazun between 13 and 21 February, and at Nyaungu on 14 February. The XIV Army's intention was to hold the attention of Burma Area Army around Mandalay while striking through Nyaungu against Meiktila, thereby severing Japanese lines of communication between Lower and central Burma and trapping the bulk of the XV and XXXIII Armies in the general area of Mandalay. Thus there developed two quite separate battles, around Mandalay between 20 February and 21 March, and around Meiktila between 21 February and 28 March. Meiktila was taken by the XIV Army on 4 March, and it was not until mid-month that the Japanese, belatedly aware of the danger presented by the British possession of the town, concentrated against this thrust, only to abandon the fight on the twenty-eighth. Thereafter the XV and XXXIII Armies sought safety by withdrawals through the Karen Hills and to the east of the Sittang, but the XXVIII Army, in the Arakan, found itself trapped west of this river by the combination of British operations in the Arakan that secured possession of Akyab, Ramree, and Taungup and the converging attacks that on 6 May brought the British to Hlegu. The latter was secured by the advance of the 17th Indian Division, IV Corps, southwards from Meiktila, and the advance northwards of 26th Indian Division, XV Corps, from Rangoon, which had been secured by amphibious assault on 2 May.

DRACULA, therefore, was executed, and at short notice,[50] and this fact forms the third matter that commands examination. It does so because, in common with the landings in the Arakan and the thrust through Nyaungu to Meiktila, it raises the question of the extent to which the British plan of campaign was based upon an exact knowledge of Japanese intentions. Histories of this campaign have noted that DRACULA found Rangoon undefended, but have not questioned whether this operation was mounted because it was known that Rangoon was or would be undefended. Similarly, the selection of the Nyaungu-Meiktila axis as the main direction of the British effort accords with the fact that the Japanese plan of campaign, as devised by Lt. Gen. Kimura Hyotaro in October 1944, accepted the risk of an open left flank in order to make the main defensive effort of Burma Area Army in the Mandalay region.[51] Again, histories of this campaign have not posed the question whether this particular axis of attack was selected because it was known that the Nyuangu-Meiktila sector was but lightly covered. Likewise, the landings in the Arakan were notable for the fact that all nine were accelerated improvisations that encountered little or no immediate resistance as the XXVIII Army pulled back the bulk of its forces in order to conform to the events to the east.[52] The comment applied to the previous two matters does not improve with repetition. Whether or not there was more than mere coincidence to the fact that each of these various British efforts was directed against weakly held or undefended sectors cannot be answered definitively as long as the relevant intelligence files remain closed. The evidence available in the public domain is inconclusive: Lewin and Winterbotham leave the indelible impression that there was no coincidence.[53] Allen is ambiguous, but contradictorily and unconvincingly so. His assertion that the British could not have known of Kimura's decision to abandon Rangoon because Burma Area Army's staff did not know of it[54] is not merely difficult to accept but impossible to reconcile with the fact that the relevant staff history states that between 27 April and 2 May Operation GABLE was mounted by three destroyers of Force 62 against shipping known to be evacuating Japanese forces from Rangoon.[55] It is difficult to believe that it was mere coincidence that the DRACULA directive was issued on the same day, 22 April, as the Japanese began their evacuation of Rangoon. Given what is now known of the extent of Allied penetration of Japanese codes and ciphers and knowledge of Japanese intentions in the Pacific theater, to assume a lack of detailed knowledge of Japanese intentions in southeast Asia would seem to stretch the limits of credulity. Moreover, to assume that the British in Burma did not enjoy the advantages that were available to the Allies in the Pacific would sit uneasily alongside the fact that one of the first ships to enter Rangoon after it was retaken was the *Ulster Queen*. The commander-in-chief of the East Indies Fleet spent 11 to 14 May aboard her, and did so in order to have the results of signals intelligence to hand as consideration turned to the question of whether the next amphibious effort should be directed against the Andamans, the Nicobars, or the Kra Isthmus,[56] and Power was in the same ship when the hunt for the *Haguro* reached its climax. The signals that were sent to British formations in the Bay of Bengal during these days, and specifically to submarines with reference to their search areas, would seem to be incomprehensible unless one assumes detailed access to Japanese naval signals, and it is difficult to believe that if this was indeed the case there was not a parallel penetration of enemy military traffic, on which the plan of campaign for the reconquest of Burma was based at least in part.[57]

The *Ulster Queen*, her guests, and her business form the basis of legitimate historical suspicion, but no more. For this work, what is important is DRACULA because, conveniently, this operation was appropriate comment on British deliberations and policy. It was executed, not with the seven divisions that had been deemed necessary, but with seven battalions, and it was directed not against the enemy main base in Burma but an undefended city. Better than any other operation or aspect of the war against Japan, DRACULA illustrates the gap between British aspirations and capabilities in the Far East war, between what would and what could be achieved. Such differences, the clearing of Upper and central Burma and the operations of the British Pacific Fleet, serve notice of the extent to which whatever success British arms commanded in the Far East in 1945 was divorced from the 1944 decisionmaking process. Although a certain care needs to be exercised with respect to the fleet's role and operations, none of these successes was anticipated and actively pursued in 1944 and in effect success arose from the unfolding of events rather than as a result of decisions taken in London. The fleet's record, moreover, was significant in that its weaknesses and problems were structural and long-term and but little related to the vagaries of the decisionmaking process in 1944: the administrative margins that formed the difference between success and failure would always have been slender irrespective of the timeliness, or otherwise, of British decisions in 1943 and 1944. In overall terms, the best that may be said about the British Pacific Fleet is the obvious, that its record was confirmation that in naval warfare the margin of superiority can never be too great given immutable factors of time, distance, and human frailty and the remorseless erosion of available national power at the point of contact with the enemy.

The unfolding of events in 1945 pose various questions, most obviously that of the extent to which the assumptions and calculations of the British high command in 1944 were substantiated. No easy or simple answer presents itself in dealing with such intangible and transitory matters as perceptions of national prestige and standing, but it may be noted that in an area where nationalist and revolutionary forces provided the main impetus to subsequent events, after 1945 British power was rehabilitated, successfully and without the campaigns of reconquest that Churchill deemed indispensable to the process. But the policy debate of 1944 clearly reveals, most obviously in Churchill's arguments and calculations but also implicitly in those of the service chiefs, the truth of the dictum that allies are not necessarily friends and that those divergent interests held in check by common need assume ever greater substance and significance as that need weakens. Obvious enough in Europe in 1945 with respect to the anti-German partnership, this phenomenon lay at the heart of British difficulties in settling national objectives in 1944 for the war in the Far East. The arguments within the British high command that brought to the fore the ambiguity of pro- and anti-American sentiments reflected a changing national role, acceptance of which must have been both difficult and painful for a prime minister (and First Sea Lord) whose commission had been that of Queen Victoria. Britain, after all, in 1944 remained in terms of global responsibilities second only to the United States, and perhaps it was not altogether surprising that the process of adjustment to change and reduced national circumstances gave ample evidence of Churchill's conforming to "the narcissism of petty differences." The prime minister's conduct in the course of the 1944 policy debate nevertheless was obstructive, willful, and altogether lacking realism and vision. Indeed, it is hard to resist the conclusion that in this debate the Chiefs of Staff and their planners together proved the better, more perceptive judge of national interest than the head of government, and doubtless part of the confusion of the decisionmaking process stemmed from this.

In the end, however, the strength of the British system was revealed, albeit at a cost of time that Britain could ill afford, in the form of decisions that gave positive proof that "all government is founded upon compromise."[58] The compromise of 1944 was between past realities and present intentions. The realignment of realities and policies is invariably a confused and difficult process, and the confusion and difficulties of the 1944 process were so marked, partly because of the speed with which events unfolded and partly, but more important, because of the seriousness of the issues and their consequences for the state. This process was one from which certain reputations emerge the lesser but which nevertheless reflected well upon the staffs and the system within which they worked. Doubtless there was on occasion a certain unevenness of performance on the part of the staffs, most obviously in autumn 1943 over the XYZ/WXYZ options, but any serious and detailed consideration of the various episodes and issues that littered the decisionmaking process prompts the conclusion that decisions, though belated, nevertheless were reasoned and reasonable and represented good as opposed to strong government. This work has set out these episodes and issues, and in so doing has provided insights into matters that have been as neglected as they are important to an understanding of the evolution of British policy. The XYZ/WXYZ options and Anglo-American negotiations of autumn 1943, the February 1944 affair involving the *Richelieu* and *Saratoga*, the Middle/Modified Middle Strategy, and the tangled purpose of DRACULA have received but scant attention over the last four decades. If one of *Grave of a Dozen Schemes*'s main claims to originality of evidence and interpretation lies in its detailed recounting and placing in context of these and other episodes, it is altogether appropriate that its final comments should be concerned with them, specifically with DRACULA. When this operation was executed, plans were in hand for further amphibious landings involving British forces, but in the event DRACULA proved the last British amphibious operation of the Second World War. And it was surely only right and proper that this last endeavor should have been directed against a city the name of which is an anglicized corruption of *Yan Gon*, which in Burmese means "The End of Strife."

The raison d'être of the British Pacific Fleet: the surrender ceremony aboard the U.S. battleship *Missouri*, 2 September 1945. The commander in chief of the British Pacific Fleet, Adm. Sir Bruce Fraser, signs the instrument of Japanese surrender on behalf of the United Kingdom. Fraser's seconds were Vice Adm. Sir Bernard Rawlings and Rear Adm. E.J.P. Brind. *(Fleet Air Arm Museum Pers/1962)*

Operation DIPLOMAT, Trincomalee, April 1944. *From left, Newcastle, Illustrious, Valiant* (moored in the distance), *Renown*, and *Saratoga*. The *Renown* remained the fastest and most heavily armed capital ship in British service in 1945, but her age and light armor precluded her being sent to the Pacific. *(Imperial War Museum A.23475)*

Operation BANQUET in August 1944 marked the first time the British used a two-wave attack by two fleet carriers. For the attack on Padang airfield, Emmahaven's port facilities, and the Indaroeng works, the *Indomitable* (leading the *Howe*) embarked

twenty-two Barracudas and twenty Hellcats. The *Victorious* (bringing up the rear) carried two fighters on deck, fifteen Barracudas, and thirty-seven Corsairs. *(Fleet Air Arm Museum Cars.I/186)*

Riverine warfare in Burma on a tributary of the Kaladan, January 1945. *(Imperial War Museum IND.4222)*

The Cairo summit, November 1943. *Seated from left,* Chiang Kai-shek, Roosevelt, Churchill, and Madame Chiang. *(U.S. Naval Institute collection)*

Old rivals gather in the garden at 10 Downing Street, 7 May 1945. *Seated from left,* Marshal of the RAF Sir Charles Portal, Field Marshal Sir Alan Brooke, Churchill, and Admiral of the Fleet Sir Andrew Cunningham. *Standing,* Maj. Gen. Leslie Hollis and Gen. Sir Hastings Ismay. *(Imperial War Museum H.41834)*

The 1st Aircraft Carrier Squadron at Manus prior to Operation ICEBERG, mid-March 1945. *From front, Indomitable, Indefatigable,* the maintenance carrier *Unicorn, Illustrious, Victorious,* and an oiler, probably of the *Dale* class. *(Imperial War Museum ABS.1258)*

The *Formidable* moments after being struck by a kamikaze off Miyako during Operation ICEBERG, 9 May 1945. She had also been hit by Japanese suicide aircraft five days earlier. The structural damage done by the two attacks contributed to the accident on 18 May that resulted in the loss of thirty aircraft. She was the first British carrier to be laid up after the war. *(Imperial War Museum A.29717)*

The *Formidable* and *Indomitable* at Leyte, late April 1945. The light cruisers in the background are *(from left) Gambia, Uganda,* and *Argonaut. (Imperial War Museum ABS.1254)*

The fleet carriers *Implacable* and *Victorious* are seen beyond the Avengers and Corsairs of the *Formidable* on 10 July 1945. Having left Sydney on 28 June, the British carriers were on their way to join Task Force 38 and attack targets in the Japanese home islands. *(Imperial War Museum A.30193)*

British claims regarding the destruction of a Japanese carrier during operations on 24 July 1945 have long been disputed, primarily because the only carrier other than the *Unryu* that appeared to have been disabled was the *Kaiyo* in Beppu Bay, southwest Honshu. In fact, available records now indicate that British carrier aircraft from the *Formidable* broke the back of this escort carrier, the converted oiler *Shimane Maru*, off Takamatsu, Shikoku, on that date. *(Imperial War Museum A.30153)*

The East Indies Fleet and preparations for ZIPPER in Trincomalee, 29 August 1945. *From left,* first column, the stern of a destroyer, *Vigilant,* a Type II Hunt-class escort, *Volage,* and *Penn;* between columns, a tanker and an oiler, probably *Ennerdale,* with *Brecon* alongside; second column, an auxiliary, an escort carrier, *Pursuer, Woolwich, Scout,* and another auxiliary; third column, *Khedive* and *Stalker,* and beyond them *Searcher* in the main channel, *Empress* under tow, and *Richelieu* astern of *Sussex* off Round Point; fourth column, *Ontario,* a Red Cross ship, and *Royalist;* fifth column, *Cumberland, Shah* (with the

stores ship *Bushwood* alongside), and *Nigeria*. Beyond Plantain Point in China Bay is *Smiter*, two escort carriers, and *Phoebe*. In the middle distance are an auxiliary alongside No. 1 Oiling Berth, an LST alongside No. 2 Oiling Berth, an auxiliary between the two berths, and (beyond *Smiter*) a landing craft or lighter in the area of Railway Quay. The other carriers are *Ameer, Emperor*, and *Trumpeter*. The escort carrier *Begum* was also in Trincomalee, but she was moored on the Radar Buoy in the outer anchorage. *(Fleet Air Arm Museum Cars.A/324)*

Duke of York in Tokyo Bay, 2 September 1945. Below the flag of the commander in chief of the British Pacific Fleet fly the Soviet naval ensign and the national flags of France, China, and the United States. The foremast carries the colors of South Africa and Australia. *(Imperial War Museum ABS.951)*

The Eastern and East Indies Fleets

1 January 1944–15 August 1945

If the British XIV Army was "the forgotten army," the Eastern Fleet, and its successor in the Indian Ocean, the East Indies Fleet, rather than the British Pacific Fleet, were its naval equivalents. The two fleets have attracted little public attention in the five decades since the end of the Second World War, yet their story, and the unfolding of Allied operations in the Indian Ocean and adjoining seas, possess obvious importance in the formulation of British strategic policy for the war against Japan. Admittedly, the fleets and their operations were in a position of dependence upon events elsewhere, and rather than Indian Ocean policy being shaped by strategic choice, naval policy in the Indian Ocean theater was fashioned by necessities established by the timetable of other, more important priorities. While the pages of this book that remain are wholly insufficient to provide a proper account of these fleets and their operations, what follows is an explanation and operational chronology of events in theater, plus a separate and, for obvious reasons, shorter operational chronology of the British Pacific Fleet.

The last nineteen months of the war in the Indian Ocean saw the British and their associates undertake four related efforts: the defeat of the enemy attack upon shipping; the carrying of war to the enemy in the form of attacks upon shore installations and shipping; the raising of the British Pacific Fleet and its preparations for redeployment to the Pacific; and the conduct of a series of amphibious operations in support of XIV Army operations in Burma. Thereafter, with the end of the war, British naval operations in theater were directed to the liberation and policing of enemy-occupied territories and to the repatriation of Allied prisoners and internees and of Japanese military and civilian personnel. Given the confused state of Southeast Asia in the immediate aftermath of Japan's surrender, these various duties and responsibilities were certainly thankless and perhaps as important in terms of the shaping of the postwar world as anything that British fleets in the Indian Ocean achieved during the war.

The defeat of the enemy attack on shipping was all but fact as 1943 gave way to 1944, though this was not readily apparent at the time. Between March 1943 and March 1944 shipping losses in the Indian Ocean were greater than those incurred in all other theaters with the exception of the North Atlantic, and indeed the losses incurred in the Indian Ocean were greater even than those suffered in the North Atlantic if the returns of spring 1943 are deleted from consideration. But the loss of ninety-nine ships of 604,104 tons in the Indian Ocean between April 1943 and March 1944 was not the margin between defeat and victory, though it needs to be noted that in the context of this theater any loss was very difficult to absorb. The ships that were lost in the Indian Ocean tended to be larger—and, in the case of tanker traffic working the Gulf, more valuable—than those lost in the North Atlantic and, even more important, their loss could involve as long as an eighteen-month lead time in terms of cargo: industrial or heavy plant sunk in theater—such as the steamrollers lost when the unescorted *Daisy Moller* was sunk on 14 December 1943 by the *RO. 110*—could easily take that length of time to be replaced in terms of order, manufacture, and delivery.

What ensured that the enemy campaign against shipping in the Indian Ocean had all but run its course by the beginning of 1944 was the simple fact that neither the Germans nor the Japanese possessed the means to conduct sustained operations in this theater. At this time the Germans had five U-boats at Penang and the Japanese eight, but despite the dispatch of twenty-three U-boats from European waters for the Far East during 1944, circumstances conspired to ensure that the number on station could not be maintained, still less increased. No fewer than fourteen of the U-boats were lost on passage and four of the boats that were on station in January 1944 or arrived in the Far East during 1944 succumbed in the course of a year that saw the logic of the Pacific priority exert itself to ever greater effect in terms of the number of Japanese submarines that could be spared for service in the Indian Ocean. The demands of the defense of the Marianas in spring 1944 and thereafter the need to concentrate all available units for the protection of the Philippines and the home islands ensured that the Imperial Navy's long-range boats disappeared from the Indian Ocean after June 1944. U-boat numbers in Japanese bases in Southeast Asia peaked at eleven in September 1944 but if numbers thereafter declined as units were recalled to European waters, the reality of torpedo shortages and deterioration of batteries had already presented long-term maintenance and logistic problems that robbed the German effort of any chance of waging a sustained campaign in the Indian Ocean. Excluding operations conducted during the transit of the Indian Ocean, in the last seventeen months of the war operational patrols were conducted by just ten of the U-boats in Southeast Asia, and with seven boats contributing but single patrols the total of fourteen war patrols, and the loss of five boats in the process, represented a wholly inadequate effort for the task in hand. The fact of the matter was that with some twenty-one of the U-boats in or sent to the Far East after

January 1944 committed to returning to European waters as blockade-runners, the Penang squadron never possessed the numbers to put three or more units to sea at any one time after December 1943 other than in February/March 1944 and in December 1944, U-boats in transit excluded. Rather than British countermeasures, the German lack of an adequate operational core with which to conduct a campaign in the Indian Ocean, the absence of good intelligence, the loss of supply ships in early 1944, and the inability of the Axis navies to coordinate their efforts were the main factors at work in ensuring that the attack on Allied shipping in the Indian Ocean in 1944 was a failing one.

For a hard-pressed Eastern Fleet such matters were largely obscured in early 1944. In terms of numbers of escorts that might be "working" at any one time the Indian Ocean theater would be lucky to muster thirty, realistically twenty, and quality left much to be desired. For example, the twenty merchantmen of Convoy BA62 were afforded a single sloop as escort for the voyage from Bombay to Aden, while in February 1944 two tankers were sunk and another seriously damaged from a convoy (PA69) that had two escorts, one without a working radar and the other without a working asdic and no radar. Too often escorts had to be provided from what little was available and there was little or no opportunity for units to train together and to absorb the lessons that had been so painfully learned in the North Atlantic. Given the state of the escort forces in the Indian Ocean in early 1944, convoy necessarily involved very considerable risk, but there was little if anything that the Eastern Fleet, all but immobilized for want of destroyers, and the Admiralty could do about the situation. In this situation there was an obvious irony. Although escorts made their way to the Indian Ocean from January 1944 there could be no significant reinforcement of the Eastern Fleet before OVERLORD, by which time the need for reinforcement had passed. Moreover, by the time that British forces were able to move to the Indian Ocean in some strength, not merely had the Axis threat to shipping all but ended but Japanese shipping had all but disappeared from the theater. By 1944 Japanese shipping losses had become so serious that very little could be spared for the Indian Ocean, even for military duties. With Allied aerial mining directed to denying the Japanese the ability to move by sea rather than aimed at the destruction of shipping, most Japanese movement by sea in the Indian Ocean in 1944 was coastal and limited to very small—and militarily uneconomic—dhows or junks, and the opportunities presented to Allied submarines and warships in this theater became increasingly rare.

The Eastern Fleet was thus in a paradoxical position. For most of its existence, and certainly in early 1944, it had to deal with an enemy threat with resources that were wholly inadequate but it slowly acquired the numbers necessary for the proper discharge of its responsibilities at the very time when the threat had been reduced to minor irritant proportions and when there was no real opportunity to use its forces offensively to any real purpose. Moreover, what little success came the way of Allied ships and submarines, achieved in dangerous coastal waters and under conditions of enemy air supremacy, seldom entered the ledgers because the victims were usually too small to be properly accounted. For example, the *Thorough* in one patrol sank sixteen native boats and two junks totaling 910 tons, and if she also sank two small Japanese landing craft there is no disputing the general conclusion that such returns were "scarcely a full justification for the submarine effort being expended."[1] For the British submarine service the sadness of the situation was that this judgment also applied to the Pacific. By the time that British submarines arrived in strength in the Far East there was virtually no Japanese shipping on which to prey. In the last full calendar month of the war, when all causes accounted for the destruction of 68 Japanese warships of 218,161 tons and 141 ships of 319,577 tons, submarines accounted for just 12 warships and 12 ships. Perhaps even more relevantly, of the Japanese losses 59 warships of 199,306 tons and 139 ships of 317,491 tons were sunk in the Kuriles, home waters, and the East China Sea. In the period 1 April–15 August 1945, of the total of 477 Japanese naval, military, and civilian merchantmen of 966,106 tons lost to all causes, 413 ships of 825,163 tons were sunk in home waters. If such figures demonstrate the futility of British submarine operations along the line of the Malay Barrier in the final phase of the war, they also demonstrate, very graphically, the extent to which Japanese strategic mobility had been destroyed by August 1945: virtually nothing moved outside the Japanese inner defense zone—and at least one-third of what did move in this zone was sunk.

The offensive phase of operations in the Indian Ocean involved two quite separate efforts: the deployment and use of forces in readiness for the raising of the British Pacific Fleet and the series of operations, both coastal and blue water, that formed part of the reconquest of Burma. The first of these was more than a year in the making, involving as it did the often-forgotten training of the light fleet carriers in the Indian Ocean in 1945 after the fleet itself had left the theater. The second was somewhat mixed in its results. The series of amphibious landings in the Arakan and coastal operations conducted in the first four months of 1945 had virtually no real military value. None of the operations resulted in British forces being able to establish themselves across Japanese lines of communications and none of the landings ended, even in a local context, with battles of encirclement and annihilation. In every case the Japanese ceded no more than they were prepared to yield, and perhaps the most useful aspect of the British operations was not connected with the prosecution of the war against Japan but with the prevention of sectarian violence in such towns as Akyab in the aftermath of the Japanese withdrawal. Moreover, probably the most important single effort in this phase, the landings on Ramree, manifestly failed in its objective to secure an airfield from which British operations in the Irrawaddy Valley and an amphibious assault on Rangoon could be supported. Both the operations in the Irrawaddy Valley and Operation DRACULA were carried to successful conclusions before the Ramree airfield was brought into service.

Lest the point be missed or forgotten, however, it needs be stated that in 1945 the East Indies Fleet was working to two very different timetables. The Burma commitment was immediate and improvised. The sudden awareness of Japanese weakness in theater and the lateness of the decision to attempt to reconquer Burma by means of an overland offensive from northeast India meant that the Arakan campaign was extemporized, as the frequent changes of directives, priorities, and targets in January 1945 testified. But beyond the Burma commitment was the Kra, Malaya, and Sumatra, and like the British Pacific Fleet in terms of its Operation DOWN-FALL deadline of October 1945, British efforts in the Indian Ocean were directed increasingly to longer-term commitments. An assault of Malaya was planned for September 1945, and certainly the pattern of British naval operations in Southeast Asia in 1945 changed very significantly after mid-April. Between 21 February and 11 August 1945 the East Indies Fleet employed seven escort carriers, three battleships, four heavy and five light cruisers, and nineteen destroyers on a total of seventeen operations of which DUKEDOM, with a total of twenty-three warships, was by far the largest. What is very significant about the pattern of these operations is the numbers and size of warships committed to operations after SUNFISH in mid-April: before that time British operations were all but limited to destroyers but thereafter the escort carriers, capital ships, and cruisers entered the lists. Overall, the seventeen operations conducted in this final phase of the war involved 128 warship sailings of which 78 were by destroyers. Seven were by battleships, 26 were by the escort carriers, and 17 by cruisers, and all but two of this balance of these sailings came during and after SUN-FISH. Very clearly, the increasing tempo of operations by heavier units as the war came to an end pointed to what was to come in and after August 1945. Be that as it may, while much has been written along the lines that the use of atomic weapons in August 1945 did away with the need to assault the home islands, it should be noted that the raids of August 1945, the Soviet entry into the war, and Japan's surrender did away with the need for the British to mount an assault landing in Malaya that was scheduled for September (Operation ZIPPER). In the event some 53,544 troops were put ashore in Malaya, a very respectable effort though one lessened by the hopeless confusion that surrounded an improvised and somewhat chaotic endeavor. Not just American marines and soldiers earmarked for assault landings after August 1945 had cause to be grateful for the ending of the war as and when it did.

Overall, British naval operations in the Indian Ocean were of very small account: the issue of defeat and victory was resolved elsewhere and by other means and was never dependent upon events in the Indian Ocean: the thirty-eight Japanese warships and thirty-one military, naval, and civilian merchantmen sunk in theater or by submarines operating in Southeast Asian waters were of small account.[2] Nonetheless, military forces can only defeat what they face, and most certainly the victory that was won in the Indian Ocean was comprehensive. The victory may have been the product and not the cause of supremacy, and certainly the victory was the product of American supremacy in the Pacific, but both victory and supremacy in the Indian Ocean in 1945 were nevertheless very real.

Operational Chronologies

NOTES

1. For the purposes of the chronologies the Indian Ocean theater of operations is defined as the Indian Ocean, adjoining seas, and the Gulf of Siam: it also includes operations by British and Dutch submarines irrespective of whether they operated in the Indian Ocean or in the Pacific. In the chronologies all units not designated by type were submarines.

2. With the exception of X-craft operations in the Pacific theater and which were staged from Subic Bay or Brunei, operations in the Pacific by British and Commonwealth ships outside the British Pacific Fleet are not included in the chronologies. Thus the British, Commonwealth, or Allied involvement in the landings in Lingayan Gulf (January 1945), at Wewak (May 1945), at Tarakan (May–June 1945), at Labuan, Muara, and Brooketon, and at Sarawak and at Balikpapan (June 1945) are not included in the second chronology. Also excluded are the bombardments in the Solomons and operations by the *Ariadne* under the auspices of the 7th U.S. Fleet before 31 January 1945 when she was detached for service in British home waters.

3. Sinkings by British and Allied submarines, especially of merchantmen and small coastal vessels, in the last months of the war very often cannot be confirmed by Japanese records. Certain entries, therefore, represent claims that cannot be confirmed.

4. In the period of the Second World War, between 3 September 1939 and 15 August 1945, a total of 385 British, Allied, and neutral ships of 1,789,870 tons were lost in the Indian Ocean. Of these totals, and in the period in and after March 1942 it is estimated that submarines sank about 250 ships of 1,400,000 tons.

   For purposes of comparison, the twin peaks of losses in the Indian Ocean were March 1942 when sixty-five ships (of 68,539 tons) and April 1942 when 153,930 tons (31 ships) were lost. The peak of the enemy submarine campaign against shipping was in November 1942 when twenty-three ships of 131,071 tons were sunk. The highest monthly losses to submarines in 1943 was in July when seventeen ships of 97,214 tons were sunk.

157

5. The first British fleet unit to be released for service in the Far East as a result of Italy's surrender was the *Trident* which, anticipating events, sailed from Aden to Colombo on 4 August 1943 (i.e., before the Italian surrender). Conversely, the surrender of Italy led to the Japanese forming the XIII Air Fleet, as part of the South West Area Fleet, on 20 September 1943. Its task was to cover Malaya and Burma. At the same time the Japanese strengthened their local forces in order to cover the straits into the Java Sea.

THE INDIAN OCEAN
The Eastern and East Indies Fleets
1 January 1944–21 October 1945

JANUARY 1944

A renewal of U-boat activity in the Gulf of Aden led to the reintroduction of convoy in the general area and the institution of convoy between the Persian Gulf and Aden. Convoy arrangements had been eased in late 1943 in light of the decline of losses, the paucity of escorts, and the absence of any real possibility of significant reinforcement from the European theater.

7 Jan   First operation by British naval units in the Irrawaddy delta since 1942. Between October 1943 and March 1944 inshore flotillas drawn from the British and Indian navies conducted a series of operations along the Burmese coast, partly in direct support of XV Indian Corps during the Japanese offensive in the Arakan. In February and March bombardments were conducted as far to the south as Gwa. The most notable episodes were attacks on Ramree in January, an attack on Kyaukpyu harbor in February that was foiled by the boom, and the assault on Alethangyan airfield on 11–14 March. Because of the worsening sea conditions in advance of the monsoon, these operations were curtailed after 23 March.

7 Jan   First British aerial mining operation in theater.

11 Jan   The Japanese light cruiser *Kuma* was sunk by the *Tally-Ho* in 6.00N 99.00E off Penang.

15 Jan   The army transport *Ryuko Maru* was sunk by the *Tally-Ho* in 10.50N 93.00E off Little Andaman Island.

19 Jan   (−31) Operation THWART. An abortive search for the German supply ship *Charlotte Schliemann*, this operation was conducted by three forces and shore-based aircraft off Mauritius.

20 Jan   The merchantman *Seikai Maru* was sunk by shore-based aircraft off Mergui, Burma.

26 Jan   The Japanese light cruiser *Kitakami* was badly damaged by the *Templar* eleven miles from Penang.

28 Jan   (and 29) The carrier *Illustrious*, capital ships *Queen Elizabeth*, *Valiant*, and *Renown*, and their escorts arrived at Ceylon.

Shipping losses: eight ships of 56,213 tons.

FEBRUARY 1944

The returns of the Eastern Fleet of 4 February indicate seven sloops, five cutters, six frigates, fourteen corvettes, twenty-two minesweepers, and twenty-two destroyers on station and operational: another ten escorts and two destroyers were non-operational.

In February 1944 five German submarines were based on Penang and a sixth was en route from France: the Japanese 8th Submarine Flotilla had eight submarines, and in March another came on station.

The number of convoys in the Indian Ocean rose from 50 to 62 and independent sailings fell from 380 to 246 compared to the previous month. Of the convoys, 39 received air support compared to 26 in January and the number of aircraft sorties in support of convoy rose from 87 to 116.

2 Feb   The arrival of the light carrier *Unicorn* and escorts at Trincomalee.

11 Feb   In the course of an attack on Convoy CJ36 (Calcutta to Colombo) the *RO.110* was sunk by escorts in 17.35N 83.40E in the Bay of Bengal.

12 Feb   The destroyer *Relentless* sank the German supply ship *Charlotte Schliemann* in 23.23S 74.37E, some 500 miles south of Diego Garcia, in the course of Operation CANNED.

12 Feb   In the course of an attack on Convoy KR8 in which she sank the troopship *Khedive Ismail* with heavy loss of life, the Japanese submarine *I. 27* was sunk by escorts in 1.25N 72.22E in One-and-a-Half Degree Channel, the Maldives.

12 Feb   The netlayer *Choko Maru* was sunk by *Stonehenge* in 5.45N 99.52E northwest of Penang.

14 Feb   The German cargo submarine *U.It.23* was sunk by the *Tally-Ho* in 4.25N 100.09E off Penang.

22 Feb   (–3 Mar) Operation SLEUTH. A sweep to the south of the Cocos by Force 66, this operation was part of the *Illustrious'* working up her air group: she was escorted by three destroyers.

Shipping losses: ten ships of 64,169 tons.

MARCH 1944

The returns of the Eastern Fleet of 3 March indicate six sloops, five cutters, eight frigates, seventeen corvettes, twenty-three minesweepers, and twenty-two destroyers on station and operational: another fourteen escorts and two destroyers were nonoperational.

Sinkings by enemy submarines reached a 1944 peak of 65,932 tons sunk in March, after which time the enemy effort ebbed. In part the surge of enemy activity was the result of the Japanese conducting six patrols, five by long-range boats, in this month, but, given the fact that the scale of convoy protection that could be afforded was often no more than token and independent sailings common, what is perhaps most significant about this month's returns was the relative ineffectiveness of the enemy effort: only 15,329 of 1,946,000 tons of shipping that worked the gulfs of Aden and Oman in March were lost. The number of aircraft-hours flown in direct support of convoys was some 3,200 or roughly four times the January 1944 figure.

With the arrival of the first S-class submarines at Ceylon, March saw the start of minelaying by British submarines: the first mission was conducted by the *Taurus* in the Strait of Malacca.

2 Mar (−15) The conduct of a raid in the Indian Ocean by three Japanese cruisers that resulted in the sinking of the steamer *Behar* in 20.32S 87.10E on 9 March: most of the crew of the *Behar* were murdered in the *Tone.*

5 Mar (−22) Operation COVERED. The German supply ship *Brake* was sunk by the destroyer *Roebuck*, detached from Force 67, some 200 miles southeast of Mauritius on 12 March.

8 Mar (−12) Operation INITIAL. This was a sweep conducted in the Bay of Bengal by the carrier *Illustrious,* two capital ships, two cruisers, and eight destroyers.

8 Mar The naval transport *Shobu Maru* was sunk by the *Sea Rover* in 3.38N 99.22E in the Malacca Strait.

21 Mar (−31) Operation DIPLOMAT. Forces that numbered the carrier *Illustrious,* two battleships, three cruisers, and ten destroyers effected a rendezvous on 27 March with TG 58.5 (the U.S. carrier *Saratoga* and three destroyers) in 13.17S 85.42E some 1,700 miles south of Ceylon.

28 Mar The army transport *Yasujima Maru* was sunk by the *Truculent* in 3.38S 109.50E off western Sarawak.

Shipping losses: twelve ships of 75,498 tons.

APRIL 1944

The returns of the Eastern Fleet of 17 April indicate seven sloops, four cutters, eleven frigates, eighteen corvettes, twenty-six minesweepers, and twenty-three destroyers on station and operational: another sixteen escorts and a destroyer were nonoperational.

3 Apr The French battleship *Richelieu* arrived at Ceylon.

4 Apr The escort carriers *Atheling* and *Begum* arrived at Ceylon.

8 Apr With Rangoon already mined and Japanese traffic to the port restricted, Moulmein was mined for the first time.

14 Apr Explosion of the British-built Liberty ship *Fort Stikene* inside the #1 Victoria Dock at Bombay. It would appear that twenty warships and merchantmen were destroyed, destroyed by fire, swamped, or incurred such structural damage as to be beyond repair or salvage. Every building within 400 yards of the ship was destroyed and the resultant fires were not extinguished until 1 May. Damage was assessed at $1 billion.

15 Apr The minesweeper *W. 7* was sunk by the *Storm* in 11.34N 93.08E off Little Andaman Island.

16 Apr (–21) Operation COCKPIT, an attack on Sabang. Conducted with two forces that together consisted of two carriers, the *Illustrious* and *Saratoga*, four capital ships, six cruisers, and fifteen destroyers, this operation involved attacks on Sabang and the Lho Nga airfield on 19 April in the course of which the naval transport *Kunitsu Maru* was grounded and the army transport *Haruno Maru* was sunk off Sabang as a result of attack by carrier aircraft. Oil tanks were destroyed, as were three Japanese torpedo bombers that attempted to counterattack.

22 Apr The salvage vessel *Hokuan Maru* was sunk by the *Taurus* in 7.14N 99.14E off Malacca, Malaya.

No Allied and neutral ships were lost in theater.

MAY 1944

3 May The *U. 852* was sunk by British aircraft in 9.32N 50.59E, south of Cape Guardafui, Horn of Africa.

3 May The army transport *Amagi Maru* was sunk by the *Tantalus* in 11.42N 92.44 off Little Andaman Island.

6 May (–27) Operation TRANSOM, an attack on Soerabaja. Conducted as part of a number of attacks in support of the landings on Biak and, more generally, the next American moves in the central Pacific, the operation involved two forces and a total of two carriers (*Illustrious* and *Saratoga*), four capital ships, four cruisers, and fourteen destroyers, plus an oiler group (with two cruisers) and six submarines detailed for reconnaissance and rescue duties.

After refueling at Exmouth Gulf in northern Western Australia, the carrier force sailed on 15 May and conducted a single strike on 17 May, the *Saratoga* and her escorts parting company on the following day. The raid resulted in severe damage to the Wonokromo refinery, damage to the dockyard, and the destruction in the harbor of the minesweeper *Wa. 101*, submarine chaser *Cha. 108*, and naval freighter *Shinrei Maru*.

During the return to Ceylon the capital ships refueled the cruisers and escorts and arrived with no more than 18 percent of their fuel remaining and clearly unable to fight any form of action had one materialized. The shortage of oilers at Ceylon meant that the force took three days to refuel after it returned to base.

12 May The naval transport *Kasumi Maru* was sunk by a mine in 3.24N 99.29E in the Malacca Strait.

22 May The gunboat *Kosho Maru* was sunk by the *Sea Rover* in 4.52N 100.00E off Penang, Malaya.

28 May The steamer *Tyokai Maru* was sunk by the *Templar* in the Malacca Strait.

No Allied and neutral ships were lost in theater.

JUNE 1944

The returns of the Eastern Fleet of 2 June indicate eight sloops, four cutters, thirteen frigates, eighteen corvettes, twenty-six minesweepers, and twenty destroyers on station and operational: another fifteen escorts and four destroyers were nonoperational.

10 Jun (–13) Operation COUNCILLOR. Conducted with the carrier *Illustrious*, the escort carrier *Atheling*, and a screen, this operation was a deception directed against Sabang that was staged in support of the American assault on Saipan.

10 Jun The army transport *Hiyoshi Maru* was sunk by the *Tantalus* in 3.00N 99.50E off northeast Sumatra.

12 Jun The naval transport *Kainan Maru* was sunk by the *Stoic* off Phuket Island, Siam.

18 Jun The gunboat *Eiko Maru* was sunk by the *Stoic* in 5.59N 99.10E northwest of Penang.

19 Jun (–23 Jun). Operation PEDAL. Staged by the carrier *Illustrious*, two capital ships, three cruisers, and eight destroyers, this operation involved attacks on Pt. Blair and other targets in the Andamans on the twenty-first: damage inflicted on the enemy was slight. PEDAL was notable for being the last single-carrier operation and the first occasion when fifty aircraft were operated simultaneously from a British carrier: the danger implicit in not having a second flight deck was the lesson learned from this operation.

26 Jun The army transport *Harukiku Maru* was sunk by the *Truculent* in 3.15N 99.46 off Medan, Sumatra.

Shipping losses: three ships of 19,319 tons.

JULY 1944

2 Jul The American merchantman *Jean Nicolet* was sunk by the Japanese submarine *I. 8* and most of the survivors murdered.

5 Jul   The fleet carriers *Indomitable* and *Victorious* arrived at Colombo.

17 Jul   The Japanese submarine *I. 166* was sunk by the *Telemachus* in 1.10N 103.45E east of Singapore.

22 Jul   (–27) Operation CRIMSON. The first operation since 1942 when two British fleet carriers were involved in a single operation, CRIMSON was conducted by a force with the carriers *Illustrious* and *Victorious*, three capital ships, seven cruisers, and ten destroyers.

This operation involved the carriers' aircraft attacking the Sabang, Lho Nga, and Kota Raja airfields while surface units bombarded Sabang and the radio station on Pulo We. There was no follow-up air strike and whatever damage was inflicted appears to have been slight. Three warships were hit by Japanese counterfire.

27 Jul   The steamer *Kiso Maru* was sunk by the *Storm* off Mergui, Burma.

Shipping losses: five ships of 30,176 tons.

AUGUST 1944

The returns of the Eastern Fleet of 4 August indicate eight sloops, six cutters, eleven frigates, seventeen corvettes, twenty-five minesweepers, and twenty-one destroyers on station and operational: another twenty-four escorts and eleven destroyers were nonoperational.

3 Aug   The battleship *Howe* arrived at Colombo.

8 Aug   The battleship *Valiant* was severely damaged by the collapse of the floating dock in which she lay at Trincomalee.

10 Aug   First minelaying by B-29 Superfortresses of XX Bomber Command, followed on 17 August by the last minelaying by the 10th U.S. Air Force, in this theater.

12 Aug   The *U. 198* was sunk by warships from Force 66 in 3.45S 52.58E northwest of the Seychelles. (This was the only occasion when a submarine was sunk by a hunter-killer group in the Indian Ocean.)

19 Aug   (–27) Operation BANQUET. Conceived as part of the program of working up the fleet, this operation selected the Padang airfield, the port facilities at Emmahaven, and the Indaroeng cement works as the targets of aircraft from the carriers *Indomitable* and *Victorious*, which were supported by one fast battleship, two cruisers, and five destroyers. A two-wave attack on 20 August was employed but results appear to have been somewhat sparse and certain aspects of the operation—the smallness and composition of air groups, launch times, and heavy avgas and fuel consumption—attracted critical comment.

22 Aug   The army transport *Sugi Maru #5* was sunk by the *Statesman* off the Andaman Islands.

Shipping losses: nine ships of 57,732 tons.

September 1944

In September, when only three Japanese long-range boats remained at Penang, the slackening of the enemy attack on shipping resulted in the abandonment of convoy in the Indian Ocean other than for troop and certain specific shipping.

2 Sep The army transport *Toso Maru #1* was sunk by the *Strongbow* in 7.57N 98.49E south of Phuket Island.

9 Sep The submarine chasers *Cha. 8* and *Cha. 9* were sunk by mines in 3.54N 98.44E off northeast Sumatra: the next day the merchantman *Takekun Maru* was lost in the same minefield.

14 Sep (–20) Operation LIGHT. This operation was conceived as a two-part operation involving attacks on the Medan and Belawan airfields on 17 September and on the Sigli rail center on 18 September. Force 63, with the carriers *Indomitable* and *Victorious*, one fast battleship, two cruisers, and seven destroyers, was obliged to abandon the first attack because of bad weather.

18 Sep The army transport *Junyo Maru* was sunk by the *Tradewind* in 2.53N 101.11E off Kelang in the Malacca Strait.

23 Sep The German submarine *U. 859* was sunk by the *Trenchant* in 5.46N 100.04E off Penang.

Shipping losses: one ship of 5,670 tons.

October 1944

The returns of the Eastern Fleet of 16 October indicate fourteen sloops, five cutters, sixteen frigates, fifteen corvettes, twenty-six minesweepers, and twenty-four destroyers on station and operational: another twenty-seven escorts and sixteen destroyers were nonoperational. The total of a hundred operational escorts and destroyers represented the peak strength of the Eastern Fleet in 1944.

In order to take advantage of the long hours of darkness in northern latitudes during the final stage of their voyage, the German decision to abandon operations in the Far East resulted in the sailing of eight U-boats for home between October and mid-January 1945. The first of the boats to leave, the *U. 168*, was sunk by H.N.M. submarine *Zwaardvisch* off Java on 5 October.

October 1944 saw the first mining of Penang and also the last minelaying by the 14th U.S. Air Force in the outer zone. As a result of mining operations the Axis submarine flotillas at Penang were obliged to abandon their bases and were transferred to Batavia.

6 Oct The submarine chaser *Cha. 2* was sunk by the *Tally-Ho* in 4.20N 98.24E west of Penang.

7 Oct   The minelayer *Itsukushima* was sunk by the *Zwaardvish* in 5.26S 113.48E in the central Java Sea.

13 Oct   Renewal of the campaign by coastal units with the end of the monsoon. Between this time and May 1945 British, Indian, and South African units were to conduct a series of operations involving 340 motor launches, mostly in the *chaungs* of the Arakan and in direct support of landings.

15 Oct   (–21) Operation MILLET. Partly intended to serve as a distraction reference the Leyte landings and partly to convince the Japanese of the imminence of a British landing in the area, this operation involved the carriers *Indomitable* and *Victorious*, three battleships, seven cruisers, and ten destroyers.

   This operation involved air attacks and bombardments against Nancowry and other targets in the Nicobars on the seventeenth, when the naval freighter *Ishikari Maru* was sunk, and on the nineteenth: bad weather precluded all but minor bombardment on the eighteenth. On the nineteenth British aircraft engaged Japanese army aircraft.

28 Oct   The naval transport *Sumatra Maru* was sunk, and another ship badly damaged, by Charioteer saboteurs, operating from the *Trenchant*, inside Phuket harbor.

No Allied and neutral ships were lost in theater.

NOVEMBER 1944

The returns of the Eastern Fleet of 3 November indicate fourteen sloops, five cutters, sixteen frigates, fifteen corvettes, twenty-six minesweepers, and twenty-four destroyers on station and operational: another thirty escorts and twenty destroyers were nonoperational.

2 Nov   The army transport *Tateyama Maru #2* was sunk by shore-based aircraft in 13.16N 97.46E southwest of Tavoy, Burma.

2 Nov   The naval transport *Hachijan Maru* was sunk by the *Tantalus* in 0.50N 107.44E southeast of Singapore.

4 Nov   The minesweeper *W. 5* was sunk by the *Terrapin* in 3.44N 99.50E in the Malacca Strait.

12 Nov   The returns of the Eastern Fleet (Admiral Sir Bruce Fraser) show that at sea and on the various stations in the Indian Ocean the Eastern Fleet had under command two battleships, three fleet and six escort carriers, two heavy and five light cruisers, nineteen destroyers, twenty-four submarines and various auxiliaries. In addition, it had various escort formations in Indian, Arabian, and African waters.

19 Nov   The Eastern Fleet was dissolved and the East Indies Fleet was formed under the command of Vice Adm. Sir Arthur Power (flying his flag in the *Caradoc*). Power's deputy and FO Ceylon was Rear Adm. R.S.G. Nicholson (ashore in Colombo in the *Lanka*) while tactical command at sea was designated to Vice Adm. H.T.C. Walker, VA 3rd Battle Squadron. Rear Adm. C. Moody (ashore at Colombo Racecourse in the *Bherunda*) served as FO (Air) East Indies.

On formation, the East Indies Fleet had eight escort carriers, two battleships, eight cruisers, thirty-four destroyers, plus auxiliaries and local escort forces, under command.

The merchantman *Nichinan Maru* was sunk by the *Strategem* south of Malacca.

20 Nov The minelayer *Ma. 4* was sunk by the *Tally-Ho* off Great Nicobar Island.

22 Nov The British Pacific Fleet was formed under the command of Adm. Sir Bruce Fraser (ashore in Sydney but with the battleship *Howe* assigned as flagship).

At this time it was intended that the Fleet should proceed to Australia before the end of the year, and the Australian government had been so advised, but delays in the reequipment of the fleet carriers with Avenger strike aircraft and the unpreparedness of bases in Australia led to the decision to keep the Fleet in the Indian Ocean for the moment.

With the receipt of an American request that the Fleet should attack the oil refineries at Palembang the decision was taken to put in hand a program of carrier operations, given the code name OUTFLANK, that would form the major part of the naval contribution to the attempt to bring the production and distribution of oil from Sumatra to a halt. The Fleet was to proceed to Australia after its attack on Palembang, which was scheduled for January 1945.

22 Nov Loss of the submarine *Strategem* to a Japanese destroyer off Malacca.

30 Nov The netlayer *Kumano Maru* was sunk, probably by a mine, in the Malacca Strait.

Shipping losses: two ships of 14,025 tons.

DECEMBER 1944

10 Dec The carrier *Indefatigable* and escorts arrived at Colombo.

14 Dec Start of a general offensive in the Arakan and first supporting operations by destroyers and riverine craft.

14 Dec The minesweeper *Choun Maru #7* was sunk by a mine in 3.55N 98.50E off northeast Sumatra.

16 Dec The gunboat *Shoei Maru* was sunk by the *Stoic* in the Sunda Strait.

17 Dec (–23) Operation ROBSON, an attack on targets in northern Sumatra. Originally planned as a strike against the refineries and installations at Pangkalan Bradan, this operation was carried out by two fleet carriers, three light cruisers, and five destroyers. It was executed on the twentieth by aircraft from the carriers *Illustrious* and *Indomitable* from a position sixty miles north of Diamond Point.

    Bad weather over the target forced the attackers to switch their attention to targets at Belewan Deli and Koela Simpang. On the afternoon of the twentieth fighter strikes were flown by the carriers against military and civil targets at Sabang, Oleelhoe, and Kota Raja as the task force withdrew to Ceylon.

26 Dec The minesweeper *Reisui Maru* was sunk by the *Terrapin* in 3.19N 99.45E off northeast Sumatra.

31 Dec The merchantman *Unryu Maru* was sunk east of the Andaman Islands by the *Shakespeare* which, three days later, was so severely damaged in an action with another Japanese ship that she was stricken after her return to base.

31 Dec (–7 Jan 1945). Operation LENTIL, an attack on targets in northern Sumatra. Staged in order to make good the failure to attack Pangkalan Bradan during ROBSON, this operation was carried out by three fleet carriers, one heavy and three light cruisers, and eight destroyers. It was executed on 4 January by aircraft from the carriers *Indefatigable, Indomitable,* and *Victorious* from a position off Simalur.

    In the course of the attack oil targets and military installations at Belewan Deli, Pangkalan Soe Soe and Medan were attacked in addition to the refineries at Pangkalan Bradan. After the operation the task force withdrew to Ceylon.

No Allied and neutral ships were lost in theater.

JANUARY 1945

The returns of the East Indies Fleet of 5 January indicate the peak of escort and destroyer strength in the Indian Ocean with 148 units on station though 50 of the 114 escorts and 23 of the 34 destroyers were nonoperational.

    January 1945 saw a major mining effort by British aircraft along the Japanese-held continental mainland: American aircraft undertook the mining of Singapore and Saigon, both of which were first mined on the twenty-fifth. Because of the Japanese paucity of steel ships in theater, the month also saw the first use of acoustic mines during the campaign.

1 Jan The *Kyokko Maru* was sunk by a mine in 12.26N 98.38E off Mergui, Burma.

2 Jan (–3) Operation LIGHTNING. The occupation of Akyab on the third by seaborne landing conducted by two brigades, the Japanese having previously abandoned the town. Three cruisers and three destroyers constituted a support force that was not required during this operation. Thereafter sloops (usually from the R.I.N.) and motor launches conducted a series of operations in the rivers and *chaungs* to the south against Japanese artillery positions and lines of supply and withdrawal. These operations continued for several weeks and often involved sloops operating with less than a foot of water between themselves and a court martial: on at least one occasion sloops were lashed fore and aft to trees during bombardments.

9 Jan The naval transport *Shinko Maru* was sunk by the *O. 19* in 3.41S 111.54E off southern Borneo.

11 Jan (–19) Operation PASSPORT. The attempt to secure Myebon by an amphibious assault with a force that totaled four brigades encountered strong resistance though Myebon itself was occupied on the thirteenth. The build-up ashore continued until 9 February but as early as 16 January the decision was taken to sidestep enemy resistance with a landing at Kangaw.

The Myebon operation involved the only clash between units in the *chaungs* during the Arakan campaign. Four flotillas of motor launches were responsible for a number of blocks that accounted for nine Japanese supply vessels over three successive nights until 15/16 January when four Japanese motor gunboats sought to destroy one block, being defeated and losing one vessel and abandoning another in the attempt. Between 11 and 19 January British units accounted for four MGB and twenty supply vessels, plus an unknown number of sampans. Nearly every British motor launch was damaged by grounding or gunfire in these exchanges, but none were lost.

15 Jan The minesweeper *Kyo Maru #1* was sunk by a mine in 5.18N 100.20E off Penang.

16 Jan The loss of the *Porpoise* while on a minelaying mission of Penang.

16 Jan (–4 Feb) Operation MERIDIAN, an attack on the refineries and airfields in the Palembang area in southern Sumatra. This operation was conducted by four fleet carriers supported by one fast battleship, three light cruisers, and nine destroyers, and was executed by aircraft from the carriers *Illustrious, Indefatigable, Indomitable,* and *Victorious* in two phases. On the twenty-fourth a force of 133 aircraft attacked the refinery at Pladjoe and the airfields at Lembak, Palembang and Talangbetoetoe, and on the twenty-ninth a force of about 124 aircraft struck the airfields and refineries at Soengei Gerong. The airfield at Mana, on the west coast of Sumatra, off which both attacks were mounted, was attacked on both 24 and 29 January.

After recovering aircraft on the twenty-ninth the Fleet was

counterattacked by *kamikaze* aircraft. The *Illustrious, Indomitable,* and battleship *King George V* were the targets of attack, but were not damaged.

In the course of MERIDIAN the carriers lost a total of forty-one aircraft: sixteen in combat, eleven by ditching, and the remainder as a result of other operational causes. The Fleet arrived at Fremantle, Western Australia, on 4 February.

18 Jan (−22 Feb) Operation MATADOR. Initially concerned with securing northern Ramree for its airfield and the Kyaukpyu anchorage, this operation involved three brigades supported by a force that included one escort carrier, one battleship, one cruiser, five destroyers, and two sloops. The landing was conducted on 21 January but by the twenty-sixth British forces had been halted. On 26 January a naval party secured Searle Point on Cheduba (Operation SANKEY) and the village was secured on the twenty-eighth. Further landing operations were conducted at the Ramree Gates and at Kyauknimaw on 31 January and 4 February respectively before Ramree was taken on the ninth. What was left of the Japanese battalion on the island was evacuated after the eleventh, on which date one British destroyer, the *Pathfinder,* was damaged beyond repair by enemy bombing. The airfield was not operational until mid-May and after the occupation of Rangoon.

The initial landing operation was conducted by two LSI, which embarked thirty LCA between them, three LCT and twenty assorted landing craft. In the company of a headquarters ship, these were sailed from Akyab in the company of two corvettes, eight minesweepers, and twelve motor launches. A total of 23,091 men were landed on Ramree between 18 January and 12 February.

Blocking operations by coastal forces during the Ramree operations claimed to have accounted for about 600 enemy killed and the destruction of between thirty and forty "country craft," plus two Japanese landing craft damaged.

22 Jan (−17 Feb) Operation PUNGENT. In an attempt to cut off enemy forces around Myebon a brigade was landed near Kangaw on the twenty-third. It was not until the twenty-eighth, however, that a major attempt was made to take Kangaw and British forces were subjected to counterattack, 31 January/2 February. It was not until the twelfth that the Japanese were cleared from the Kangaw area.

The initial landing involved one LCT and thirty-eight assorted minor landing craft, supported by various minesweepers and motor launches.

23 Jan The merchantmen *Hozan Maru #1* and *Nikkaku Maru* were sunk by mines in 4.08N 98.15E off northeast Sumatra.

No Allied and neutral ships were lost in theater.

FEBRUARY 1945

11 Feb The merchantman *Nanshin Maru #19* was sunk by the *Tradewind* off eastern Malaya.

15 Feb (–25) After a series of diversionary attacks mostly directed against Tamandu, a two-battalion landing on the 16th resulted in the capture of Ru-ywa on the 17th. Japanese counter-attacks on the nights of the 19th/20th and 22nd/23rd were repulsed, but it was not until 4 March that Tamandu was taken: the area was not secured until the 13th.

The Ru-ywa operation was perhaps the most difficult of the Arakan landings, involving as it did a complicated, indirect approach through *chaungs* that were both very narrow and shallow: one motor launch grounded on 32 occasions in nine days during this operation, another twelve times in one night. After landing the equivalent of a division at Ru-ywa—15,802 men and 68 guns— landing craft were withdrawn on 4 March. The last bombardment by naval units was conducted on the 5th and on 7 March naval forces were withdrawn from operations.

21 Feb (–25) Operation SUFFICE. The bombardment of the radar station on Great Coco was executed on the 24th by the four destroyers of Force 68 operating from Trincomalee.

22 Feb (–7 Mar) Operation STACEY. Conducted by two escort carriers, one cruiser, three destroyers and three frigates, this operation involved photographic reconnaissance by aircraft of the Kra and northern Malaya between the 26th and 28th and of Sumatra and Penang on the 4th. The three Japanese aircraft shot down on 1 March represented the first enemy aircraft destroyed by British escort carrier aircraft in the Far East.

23 Feb The last sinking by an enemy submarine in theater: the steamer *Peter Silvester* was sunk by the *U. 862* in 34.19S 99.37E off southwest Australia.

27 Feb (–4 Mar) Operation TRAINING. The return passage of Force 68 from Akyab, this operation involved a sweep of the coast between Heanzay and Tavoy on the night of 1st/2nd and a bombardment of Pt. Blair on the 3rd.

Shipping losses: one ship of 7,176 tons.

MARCH 1945

The Japanese in effect abandoned the port of Bangkok as a result of mining, switching ships to Tachin: the latter was subjected to bombing and blockade by submarine before being mined in June.

4 Mar The submarine chaser *Ch. 8* was sunk by the *Terrapin* and *Trenchant* in 4.04N 100.35E south of Penang and the chaser *Kiku Maru* by the *Selene* off northwest Sumatra.

13 Mar Operation TURRET. The last of the amphibious operations in the Arakan, a landing at Letpan by a brigade from Ramree, was conducted with the aim of securing Taungup. Reached on 14 April, Taungup was not secured until the twenty-ninth.

The original assault force consisted of a headquarters ship, two LSI, five LCI, three LCT, and eighty-eight assorted landing craft, and was escorted from Kyaukpyu by ten minesweepers and sixteen motor launches: two destroyers and two sloops formed the support force. The last fire support missions were conducted on 4 and 5 April.

14 Mar (–20) Operation TRANSPORT. This was the first operation conducted following the decision (made after TRAINING) to intensify operations in the Bay of Bengal. Conducted by three destroyers, Force 70 bombarded enemy installations at Sigli in northern Sumatra on the seventeenth and at Pt. Blair and around Stewart Sound in the Andamans on the nineteenth. In the course of the latter, two of the destroyers were heavily damaged by Japanese batteries. (By coincidence, two of the ships, the *Saumarez* and *Volage*, were involved in the Corfu Incident of 22 October 1946.)

25 Mar (–29) Operation ONBOARD. Conducted by four destroyers from a reconstituted Force 70 operating from Trincomalee, this operation resulted in what was officially described as "this unsatisfactory action" on the twenty-sixth in which two naval transports, the *Risui Maru* and *Teshio Maru,* and their escorts, the submarine chasers *Ch. 34* and *Ch. 63,* were sunk in the area of 10.38N 94.42E east of Little Andaman Island. No fewer than eighteen torpedoes and 3,160 rounds were fired by the British ships and an RAF Liberator was obliged to deal with the *Risui Maru* and was lost in the process.

27 Mar The minelayer *Ma. 1* was sunk by a mine (laid by the *Porpoise*) off northeast Sumatra.

28 Mar The last sinking by a German submarine operating from the Far East: the tanker *Oklahoma* was sunk by the *U. 532* in 13.37N 41.43W some 800 miles northeast of the mouth of the Amazon.

30 Mar (–5th Apr) Operation PENZANCE. Conducted by four destroyers constituted as Force 62 operating from Trincomalee, this operation involved on successive days landing a reconnaissance party in the Nicobars, a sweep of the Burmese coast between Tavoy and Mergui and between the Moulmein and Heanzay, and a bombardment of the Great Coco radar station.

No Allied and neutral ships were lost in theater.

APRIL 1945

7 Apr (–13) Operation PASSBOOK. The return passage of Force 62 from

Akyab, this operation involved a sweep of the coast near Heanzay that resulted in the sinking of five small vessels on the ninth. On the eleventh the ships recovered sixty-two Japanese and six impressed Sumatrans in the area 8.57N 93.38E from two ships that had been sunk that day by Liberators from 222 Group. (The large number of Japanese that allowed themselves to be captured was attributed to the gathering of sharks in the area.)

8 Apr (−20) Operation SUNFISH. Conducted by three escort carriers, two battleships, two heavy cruisers, and five destroyers, this operation was the second of three reconnaissance missions staged in preparation for a landing in Malaya. The intention to scout the Kra and the Penang area was abandoned because of catapult problems in the *Emperor*, but on the eleventh Sabang and Oleelhoe were bombarded while thirteen sorties were flown over the Pt. Dickson and Pt. Swettenham areas. On 14 and 15 April the western coast of Sumatra was scouted and on the sixteenth installations at Emmahaven and Padang were subjected to air attack.

11 Apr The submarine chaser *Ch. 7* and netlayer *Agata Maru* were sunk by shore-based aircraft in 8.57N 93.38E off Car Nicobar Island.

12 Apr The minesweeper *Wa. 104* was sunk and the chaser *Cha. 104* damaged and driven ashore by the *Stygian* in 8.55S 115.15E southwest of Bali.

15 Apr The Japanese high command in Burma took the decision to abandon the Arakan as a result of the collapse of resistance in central Burma.

23 Apr The Japanese began their evacuation of Rangoon: completed during the night of 29/30 April.

23 Apr The *U. 183* became the last German submarine to be sunk in the Far East when she was torpedoed by the U.S. submarine *Besugo* in 4.57S 112.52E northwest of Brunei.

27 Apr The start of operations BISHOP, DRACULA, and GABLE.

DRACULA. The six assault forces carrying the 26th Indian Division bound for Rangoon sailed from Akyab and Ramree between 27 and 30 April. After airborne landings on 1 May, landings on both banks of the Irrawaddy below Rangoon were executed on the second and the undefended city occupied on the third. Contact with forces advancing overland from central Burma was made on the sixth when patrols of the 26th and 17th Indian divisions met west of Hlegu.

The assault force consisted of two headquarters ships, five LSI, and 165 assorted landing ships and craft, and was escorted by five sloops and twenty-two minesweepers.

Operation GABLE. The Rangoon landings were preceded by a sweep of the Gulf of Martaban on the night of 29/30 April by the

three destroyers of Force 62. Shortly after midnight contact was
established with perhaps a dozen small craft, carrying an estimated
thousand troops, bound for Moulmein: nine of the vessels are
claimed to have been sunk.

Operation BISHOP. Cover for DRACULA was provided by the
escort carriers *Empress* and *Shah*, two battleships, four cruisers, and
five destroyers. This operation involved bombardments of Car
Nicobar and Pt. Blair before Force 63 took station 120 miles south
of Rangoon on the second to cover the landings. Thereafter the
coast between Heanzay and Rangoon was swept and enemy
coastal installations and traffic attacked: on 5 May strikes were
mounted in the Mergui–Victoria Point area and on the seventh
Car Nicobar was subjected to air attack. On the sixth a detachment struck at Pt. Blair and Stewart Sound. The units committed
to this operation returned to Trincomalee on 8 and 9 May.

28 Apr The tanker *Takasago Maru #8* was sunk by the *Tradewind* off
Singora in the Gulf of Siam.

30 Apr By the end of April the Japanese had abandoned all their positions
in the Arakan and had begun to withdraw through the Yomas in
an attempt to avoid encirclement by enemy forces advancing down
the Irrawaddy valleys.

No Allied and neutral ships were lost in theater.

MAY 1945

The returns of the East Indies Fleet of 4 May indicate that 106 escorts and
destroyers were on station, though 47 of the 85 escorts and 5 of the 21
destroyers were nonoperational.

On 1 May 1945 the Royal Navy had at sea four fleet and five escort carriers
in the Pacific, six escort carriers in the Bay of Bengal, five escort carriers in
Norwegian or Arctic waters, four light fleet working up in home waters or
the Mediterranean as part of their preparation for joining the British Pacific
Fleet and one fleet and one escort carrier en route for the Far East. The
total of twenty-six carriers probably represented the highest number of
British carriers at sea on any single day of the Second World War.

4 May British occupation of Sandoway by overland advance.

7 May With the German surrender, control of the four U-boats in the Far
East was assumed by Japan.

9 May The start of a Japanese attempt both to resupply and to withdraw
some of the forces on the Andamans with the heavy cruiser *Haguro*
and destroyer *Kamikaze*. Alerted to this attempt, Force 63, with four
escort carriers, two battleships, three cruisers, and eight destroyers
sailed from Trincomalee on the tenth but was sighted by enemy

aircraft on the eleventh with the result that the two Japanese warships retired, the *Haguro* being missed by the *Subtle* on the twelfth. With more British warships committed to Operation DUKEDOM, the two Japanese ships evacuated 450 men from Car Nicobar on the fifteenth, on which date five British destroyers were detached to a sweep of Penang and the *Haguro* and *Kamikaze* again attempted to complete their mission. Shortly after midnight of 15/16 May contact was made between these groups and the *Haguro* was sunk in 5.00N 99.30E southwest of Penang.

9 May The last British loss of minor units in the Burma campaign: two motor launches were lost by stranding in the Sittang and being swamped by the bore while attempting to intercept Japanese escaping across the river.

15 May British occupation of Gwa by overland advance from Sandoway.

17 May The final naval action of the Burma campaign: four British motor launches destroyed three Japanese landing or riverine craft on the Bawle, some thirty miles from Rangoon.

25 May The minesweeper *Wa. 105* was sunk by the *Trenchant* in 6.21S 110.57E north of central Java.

25 May The merchantman *Nittei Maru* was sunk by the *Thorough* off Soerabaja, Java.

No Allied and neutral ships were lost in theater.

JUNE 1945

8 Jun The heavy cruiser *Ashigara* was sunk by the *Trenchant* in 1.59S 104.57E in the Banka Strait.

12 Jun The submarine chaser *Ch. 57* and guardship *Kushio Maru #2* were sunk by warships from Force 65 in 6.20N 95.45E northwest of Sabang Island (Operation IRREGULAR).

14 Jun (−21) Operation BALSAM. The final reconnaissance mission of southern Malaya conducted on 18, 19, and 20 June, this operation was staged by three escort carriers, two cruisers, and five destroyers.

No Allied and neutral ships were lost in theater.

JULY 1945

July 1945 saw the halting of all minelaying operations in theater, there being insufficient enemy shipping to justify further effort. The total number of mines laid by Allied aircraft in the S.E.A.C. area and Gulf of Siam was 4,474 of which 4,192 were magnetic, 246 acoustic, and 36 contact.

By the end of July an airstrip, prepared in the Cocos Islands from which operations against southern Sumatra could be conducted in support of landings in Malaya, was brought into service.

2 Jul (–13) Operation COLLIE. Planned as a strike and minesweeping mission off Car Nicobar, COLLIE was conducted by two escort carriers, one cruiser, three destroyers, and a minesweeping group. Between the fifth and tenth 167 mines were swept east of Car Nicobar and air strikes conducted on the first two days. Nancowry was attacked on the seventh, as were Kota Raja and Lho Nga on the eleventh.

19 Jul (–30) Operation LIVERY. Planned as a sweep of Phuket Island, LIVERY involved two escort carriers, one battleship, one cruiser, four destroyers and a minesweeping group constituted as Force 63. Operations were conducted between the twenty-fourth and twenty-sixth, fifteen locomotives being claimed in strikes in the Brandon-Dhungsong area. LIVERY witnessed the last loss of major units in the Second World War: two minesweepers were lost, one to mines and the other to *kamikaze* attack.

27 Jul Patrols in the area between latitudes 10.00 and 14.30N were discontinued.

31 Jul At Singapore the heavy cruiser *Takao* settled after having been attacked by midget submarines towed to the target area by the *Spark* and *Stygian* from their base in Brunei Bay.

No Allied and neutral ships were lost in theater.

AUGUST 1945

2 Aug Command boundary changes that resulted in Borneo, Celebes and Java passing into the South East Asia Command area of responsibility were instituted.

10 Aug (–15) Operation CARSON. Planned as an attack on Penang and Medan, this operation involved five escort carriers, one cruiser, and four destroyers but was abandoned on the eleventh with the realization of the imminence of the end of the war.

14 Aug In the last British submarine action of the war, the *Statesman* sank nine junks by gunfire in the Malacca Strait: in nine patrols she accounted for 49 vessels of about 10,000 tons.

15 Aug The Japanese announcement of acceptance of the terms of the Potsdam Declaration: the cessation of hostilities in theater.

No Allied and neutral ships were lost in theater.

27 Aug A task force from the East Indies Fleet, consisting of two escort carriers, one battleship, one cruiser, and three destroyers, sailed from Rangoon in order to arrange local surrenders in the CULVERIN area. All Japanese forces in Sumatra were surrendered on 31 August and Sabang was occupied on 2 September. The Penang garrison surrendered on the thirty-first and the town was occupied on 3 September (Operation JURIST).

28 Aug Representatives of the Japanese Southern Army Command and of local commands signed an instrument of surrender in the presence of the Chief of Staff to the Supreme Allied Commander, South East Asia Command, at Government House in Rangoon.

SEPTEMBER 1945

2 Sep The instrument of Japan's unconditional surrender was signed on board the USS *Missouri:* Adm. Sir Bruce Fraser, Commander-in-Chief British Pacific Fleet, signed the instrument on behalf of Britain.

3 Sep Operation TIDERACE. The first British naval units to serve at Singapore since February 1942 arrived on station. Japanese military and naval forces in Singapore and Johore formally surrendered on board the heavy cruiser *Sussex* and British and Indian formations were disembarked on the fourth.

3 Sep The *Trident,* the last British submarine to return from patrol, arrived at Trincomalee at the end of her thirty-fourth war patrol, the first having begun on 24 October 1939.

In the course of 1945 a total of 28 British and one Dutch submarines of the East Indies Fleet undertook patrols that totaled 1,336 days and sank or drove ashore 261 Japanese vessels and landed or withdrew agents on sixteen occasions. One submarine was lost and two damaged beyond repair in the course of operations.

8 Sep The surrender of the Japanese garrison at Balikpapan.

9 Sep The formal surrender of all Japanese forces in the Indies at Morotai.

9 Sep (−11) Operation ZIPPER was conducted with the landing of 53,544 troops in Malaya: the 25th Indian Division was landed south of Pt. Swettenham and the 23rd Indian Division north of Pt. Dickson.

10 Sep The surrender of the Japanese garrison at Labuan.

12 Sep Representatives of the Japanese Southern Army and the commands in the theater formally signed the instrument of surrender of all Japanese forces in Southeast Asia in the presence of the Supreme Allied Commander, South East Asia Command, Admiral Lord Mountbatten, in the Municipal Council Chamber, Singapore.

13 Sep The surrender of the Japanese garrison at Kuching.

15 Sep A British heavy cruiser and escorts, followed the next day by additional units that included a Dutch light cruiser, arrived at Batavia but such was the extent of disorder ashore that British military forces were not disembarked until the twenty-ninth. The first British formation (the 26th Indian Division) to land in Sumatra came ashore on 10 October, and after the twenty-fifth British formations were landed at Soerabaja.

26 Sep One R.I.N. sloop arrived in the Andamans and on the twenty-ninth the Japanese garrisons in the Andaman and Nicobar groups formally surrendered at Pt. Blair.

OCTOBER 1945

3 Oct The arrival of the first French military convoy at Saigon.

19 Oct Japanese naval formations and units remaining in Burma were surrendered formally to the Royal Navy at Mergui.

21 Oct Japanese military and naval representatives formally surrendered Sumatra to British forces at a ceremony at Pedang on the 140th anniversary of the Battle of Trafalgar.

THE BRITISH PACIFIC FLEET
14 September 1944–1 October 1945

SEPTEMBER 1944

At the OCTAGON conference in Quebec the British undertook to send a fleet consisting of four fleet and two light fleet carriers, two fast battleships, eight cruisers, twenty-four destroyers, and sixty escorts to the Pacific by the end of the year. The fleet was to operate under American command.

The ultimate British objective was the raising of a fleet of 4 fleet, 7 light and 18 escort carriers, 4 fast battleships, 12 cruisers, 60 destroyers, 100 escorts, 24 submarines, 900 carrier- and 300 land-based aircraft, and the provision of an amphibious lift for two divisions.

NOVEMBER 1944

12 Nov The returns of the Eastern Fleet (Adm. Sir Bruce Fraser) show that at sea and on the various stations in the Indian Ocean the Eastern Fleet had under command two battleships, three fleet and six escort carriers, two heavy and five light cruisers, nineteen destroyers, twenty-four submarines, and various auxiliaries. In addition, it had various escort formations in Indian, Arabian and African waters.

19 Nov The Eastern Fleet was dissolved and the East Indies Fleet was formed.

22 Nov The British Pacific Fleet was formed under the command of Adm. Sir Bruce Fraser (ashore in Sydney but with the battleship *Howe* assigned as flagship). Designated to command at sea was Fraser's deputy, Vice Adm. Sir Bernard Rawlings: Rear Adm. D. B. Fisher (in the *Montclare*) served as FO Fleet Train. Vice Adm. C. S. Daniel (ashore in Melbourne in the *Beaconsfield*) served as VA(Q) and Rear Adm. R. H. Portal (ashore in Sydney in the *Golden Hind*, which was commissioned into service this day) served as FO Naval Air Stations Australia.

At this time it was intended that the Fleet should proceed to Australia before the end of the year, and the Australian government had been so advised, but delays in the reequipment of the fleet carriers with Avenger strike aircraft and the unpreparedness of bases in Australia led to the decision to keep the Fleet in the Indian Ocean for the moment.

With the receipt of an American request that the Fleet should attack the oil refineries at Palembang the decision was taken to put in hand a program of carrier operations, given the code name OUT-FLANK, that would form the major part of the naval contribution to the attempt to bring the production and distribution of oil from Sumatra to a halt. The Fleet was to proceed to Australia after its attack on Palembang, which was scheduled for January 1945.

DECEMBER 1944

2 Dec   The departure of the first ships of the British Pacific Fleet, the battleship *Howe*, and three British and one Australian destroyer, from Trincomalee for Sydney.

10 Dec   The carrier *Indefatigable* and escorts arrived at Colombo.

17 Dec   (–23) Operation ROBSON, an attack on targets in northern Sumatra. Originally planned as a strike against the refineries and installations at Pangkalan Bradan, this operation was carried out by two fleet carriers, three light cruisers and five destroyers. It was executed on 20 December by aircraft from the carriers *Illustrious* and *Indomitable* from a position sixty miles north of Diamond Point.

Bad weather over the target forced the attackers to switch their attention to targets at Belewan Deli and Koela Simpang. On the afternoon of the twentieth fighter strikes were flown by the carriers against military and civil targets at Sabang, Oleelhoe, and Kota Raja as the task force withdrew to Ceylon.

31 Dec   (–5 Jan 1945) Operation LENTIL, an attack on targets in northern Sumatra. Staged in order to make good the failure to attack Pangkalan Bradan during ROBSON, this operation was carried out by three fleet carriers, one heavy and three light cruisers, and eight destroyers. It was executed on 4 January by aircraft from the *Indefatigable, Indomitable,* and *Victorious* from a position off Simalur.

In the course of the attack oil targets and military installations at Belewan Deli, Pangkalan Soe Soe, and Medan were attacked in addition to the refineries at Pangkalan Bradan. After the operation the task force withdrew to Ceylon.

JANUARY 1945

The returns of the British Pacific Fleet of 26 January show a total of four fleet carriers, two battleships, five cruisers, sixteen destroyers, eight escorts, and sixteen Australian minesweepers under command. The fleet train numbered the *Unicorn*, four escort carriers, eight oilers, and thirty-one other auxiliaries.

11 Jan In the South China Sea, the only occasion during the Second World War when a British submarine sighted and chased Japanese capital ships: the submarine, which was unable to conduct an attack, was the appropriately named *Tantalus* which reached Fremantle on the twenty-sixth after a patrol of 55 days and 11,690 knots.

16 Jan (–4 Feb) Operation MERIDIAN, an attack on the refineries and airfields in the Palembang area in southern Sumatra. This operation was conducted by four fleet carriers supported by one fast battleship, three light cruisers, and nine destroyers, and was executed by aircraft from the *Illustrious, Indefatigable, Indomitable,* and *Victorious* in two phases.

On the twenty-fourth a force of 133 aircraft attacked the refinery at Pladjoe and the airfields at Lembak, Palembang and Talangbetoetoe, and on the twenty-ninth a force of about 124 aircraft struck the airfields and refineries at Soengei Gerong. The airfield at Mana, on the west coast of Sumatra, off which both attacks were mounted, was attacked on both 24 and 29 January.

After recovering aircraft on the twenty-ninth the Fleet was counterattacked by *kamikaze* aircraft. The *Illustrious, Indomitable,* and battleship *King George V* were the targets of attack, but were not damaged.

In the course of MERIDIAN the carriers lost a total of forty-one aircraft: sixteen in combat, eleven by ditching and the remainder as a result of other operational causes.

The Fleet arrived at Fremantle, Western Australia, on 4 February.

19 Jan The leading formation of the British Pacific Fleet, the battleship *Howe*, light cruiser *Swiftsure* and three destroyers, arrived at Manus, the Admiralty Islands.

FEBRUARY 1945

10 Feb The British Pacific Fleet arrived at Sydney, New South Wales.

28 Feb The British Pacific Fleet, less the *Illustrious*, sailed from Sydney for Manus in the Admiralty Islands, arriving on 7 March.

MARCH 1945

1 Mar The *Illustrious* was docked at Sydney and her central propeller was removed. She was undocked on the fifth and sailed for Manus on the following day. She arrived at Manus and rejoined the Fleet on the fifteenth.

11 Mar The *Formidable* arrived at Sydney, having sailed from Britain for service with the British Pacific Fleet the previous September. Her arrival on station had been delayed by a major breakdown in the Mediterranean which had necessitated her spending three months in the Gibraltar dockyard.

14 Mar The British Pacific Fleet received its orders for ICEBERG.

16 Mar The first of the auxiliaries committed to supporting the fleet during Iceberg sailed from Manus, the oiler group that was to carry out the first replenishment sailing on the following day.

18 Mar The British Pacific Fleet sailed from Manus for Ulithi, in the western Carolines, arriving on 20 March.

19 Mar The Japanese Army took control of French Indo-China from the Vichy administration.

23 Mar The British Pacific Fleet sailed from Ulithi for Operation ICEBERG with four fleet carriers, two fast battleships, five light cruisers, and eleven destroyers under the command of Vice Adm. Sir Bernard Rawlings. The Fleet, designated TF 57 for operational purposes, refueled on the twenty-fifth preparatory to its going into action the following day.

26 Mar (–20 Apr) Operation ICEBERG. In this first phase of operations in support of the landings on Okinawa, TF 57 conducted offensive operations against airfields and other military installations in the Sakishima Gunto on 26, 27, and 31 March and on 1 and 2 April, as well as 6, 7, 16, 17, and 20 April. On the twelfth and thirteenth aircraft from TF 57 struck targets in northern Formosa.

Throughout this period of operations TF 57 always had four fleet carriers under command and operational. On 1 April, however, three were damaged. The *Indomitable* was machine-gunned along her flight deck, the *Victorious* was clipped by a *kamikaze* that crashed into the sea and exploded in her wake, and the *Indefatigable* was lightly damaged by a direct hit by a *kamikaze* on her flight deck. None of the carriers was forced to withdraw from the battle. The destroyer *Ulster,* however, was badly damaged by a *kamikaze* and had to be towed to Leyte.

On the sixth the *Illustrious* survived an attack by a *kamikaze* that exploded in the sea alongside. Initially it was thought that the carrier had been undamaged, and the Americans were informed accordingly, but she had been damaged below the waterline and was relieved on the fourteenth by the *Formidable.* The latter had sailed from Sydney on 24 March and had arrived at Manus on 30 March.

The *Illustrious* was detached on 14 April and arrived at Leyte two days later. There an examination revealed that the damage that she had incurred was both extensive and beyond local repair. She returned via Manus to Sydney, sailing for home on 24 May. She did not rejoin.

In this phase of operations TF 57 alternated on station with the escort carriers of TF 52.

APRIL 1945

23 Apr TF 57 arrived at Leyte for replenishment and reorganization. Repairs to the *Indefatigable* were completed in six days.

MAY 1945

On 1 May 1945 the Royal Navy had at sea four fleet and five escort carriers in the Pacific, six escort carriers in the Bay of Bengal, five escort carriers in Norwegian or Arctic waters, four light fleet working up in home waters or the Mediterranean as part of their preparation for joining the British Pacific Fleet and one fleet and one escort carrier en route for the Far East. The total of twenty-six carriers probably represented the highest number of British carriers at sea on any single day of the Second World War.

1 May TF 57 sailed from Leyte for the second phase of ICEBERG with four fleet carriers, two fast battleships, five light cruisers and fourteen destroyers under command. It refueled on the third in readiness for going into action the following day.

4 May (–25) Operation ICEBERG. In this the second phase of operations off the Sakishima Gunto. TF 57 conducted offensive operations on a regular "two-days-on, two-days-off" cycle, again alternating with the escort carriers of TF 52.

Offensive operations were conducted on 4 and 5, 8 and 9, 12 and 13, 16 and 17, 20 and 21, and 24 and 25 May. On the eighth, however, only offensive combat air patrols were flown before bad weather brought flying to a halt, and no strike missions were executed on this particular day.

On the fourth units from the screen carried out a bombardment of Miyakoshima, the *Formidable* and *Indomitable* being hit by *kamikazes* in their absence. Five days later, on the ninth, *kamikaze* aircraft struck the *Formidable* and *Victorious*. The damage incurred by the three carriers on these occasions was not sufficiently serious to cause any of them to be withdrawn from the battle, but the fact that the *Formidable* was unable to repair much of the damage she sustained was a major reason for the heaviness of the losses she incurred as a result of an accidental fire in her hangar on the eighteenth. On that occasion she lost thirty-two aircraft destroyed or damaged beyond repair. As a result of her damage and losses the

Formidable was detached on the twenty-second and thereby missed the last two days of operations conducted by TF 57 before it, too, withdrew. The *Formidable* reached Sydney on the thirty-first.

The destroyer *Quilliam* was badly damaged as a result of a collision in heavy fog with the *Indomitable* on the twentieth. She had to be towed clear of the battle area.

TF 57 withdrew from the battle after operations on the twenty-fifth and reached Manus on 30 May. Thereafter it dispersed because Sydney at that time could not accommodate the whole force.

29 May The *Implacable,* originally intended as relief for the *Illustrious,* arrived at Manus. She had arrived at Jervis Bay on the eighth, and had sailed for Manus on the twenty-fourth.

31 May The first three of the light fleet carriers earmarked for service with the British Pacific Fleet—the *Colossus, Venerable,* and *Vengeance*—concentrated and conducted joint exercises off Ceylon.

JUNE 1945

5 Jun The fleet carriers arrived at Sydney, the *Indomitable* being docked the following day for a short refit. She remained in dockyard hands until 18 July.

12 Jun (–17) Operation INMATE, an attack on Truk by TG 111.2. This formation consisted of the *Implacable,* the escort carrier *Ruler,* four light cruisers, and five destroyers. The operation was the last occasion on which the British employed the fleet carrier/escort carrier combination. The attack took the form of air and surface bombardments on 14 and 15 June, after which TG 111.2 returned to Manus.

29 Jun The British Pacific Fleet sailed for Manus from Sydney, arriving on 4 July.

JULY 1945

6 Jul The British Pacific Fleet, now designated TF 37, sailed for operations against the Japanese home islands with the fleet carriers *Formidable, Implacable,* and *Victorious,* one battleship, six light cruisers, and fifteen destroyers under command. The formation refueled on the sixteenth.

American carrier formations had opened proceedings with an attack on targets in the Tokyo area on the tenth, and on the fourteenth detached units had conducted the first surface bombardment of the Japanese home islands of the war.

This final phase of operations began with aircraft from TF 37 attacking targets in northern Honshu on 17 July and in the Tokyo area on 18 July. The *Indefatigable* and three destroyers joined company on the twentieth, and thereafter the four fleet carriers attacked targets in northeast Shikoku and in the Inland Sea on 24, 25, and 28 July. On the thirtieth targets on both coasts of southwest Honshu were struck, and on 9 and 10 August offensive missions were flown against targets in northern Honshu. In addition, British warships took part in surface bombardments of enemy installations in northern central Honshu on 17 July, in southern central Honshu on the twenty-ninth, and in northern Honshu on 9 August. The bombardment of the Hamamatsu factory on the night of 29/30 July was the last occasion when a British battleship fired her guns in anger.

In the course of these operations the Americans denied the British the opportunity to engage enemy main force units, the British being relegated to secondary targets during the main efforts of 24 and 28 July. On the twenty-fourth, however, aircraft from TF 37 crippled the escort carrier *Shimane Maru* off Takamatsu, Shikoku, and on 9 August an attack that left a Japanese escort, the *Amakusa*, sunk off Onagawa brought the Fleet Air Arm the only Victoria Cross (posthumously) awarded to a carrier pilot in the course of the Second World War.

On 11 August the decision was taken to withdraw the major part of TF 37 from operations because of a shortage of oil and the need to put in hand a short refitting program that was essential if British naval forces were to take part in operations in October.

31 Jul At Singapore the heavy cruiser *Takao* settled after having been attacked by midget submarines towed to the target area by the *Spark* and *Stygian* from their base in Brunei Bay: one midget submarine, towed to the target area off Cape St. Jacques by the *Spearhead*, cut the Saigon–Hong Kong and Saigon-Singapore submarine telegraph cables. Three days later another midget submarine, towed to the target area off Lamma Island by the *Selene*, unsuccessfully attempted to cut the Hong Kong–Singapore cable but nevertheless rendered it inoperative.

The *Trenchant* and the eight S-class submarines of the 8th Flotilla, operating from Subic Bay, conducted thirteen patrols, totaling 282 days, in the South China Sea in 1945 and accounted for two warships and forty-one vessels, mostly small coastal craft.

The 4th and 8th flotillas, operating from Fremantle and numbering twelve S-class, thirteen T-class, and four Dutch submarines, mounted forty-seven patrols with 1,544 days in the waters beyond the Malay Barrier: two enemy warships and eighty-five auxiliaries and other vessels of all descriptions and sizes were sunk. Six of S-class submarines of the 8th Flotilla that operated from Fremantle were transferred to Subic Bay.

AUGUST 1945

12 Aug   The British Pacific Fleet raised its second carrier task group in the shape of TG 111.2. This group was raised at Sydney with the flagship *Indomitable,* three light fleet carriers of the 11th Aircraft Carrier Squadron, and attached units under command. The first of the light fleet carriers, the *Venerable,* had arrived at Sydney on 22 July.

13 Aug   Aircraft from the *Indefatigable* conducted strike operations against targets in the Tokyo area in the last single-carrier strike of the war. On the following day the *Indefatigable* and her consorts were attached to TG 38.1.

15 Aug   The *Indomitable* sailed from Sydney for Manus.

As part of TG 38.1, the *Indefatigable* conducted offensive operations before the announcement by the Japanese of their willingness to surrender brought an end to hostilities. In the course of operations on this day British aircraft fought only their second aerial battle during this phase of operations, and a single Avenger bombed a factory in the Tokyo area. The *Indefatigable* was narrowly missed by a *kamikaze* after the announcement of the end of hostilities.

28 Aug   In the company of American forces, British units entered and anchored in Sagami Bay, and on the following day entered Tokyo Bay. On 29 and 30 August British forces participated in the occupation of the Yokohama Naval Base. The British units, constituted as TG 38.5, consisted of the fleet carrier *Indefatigable* and two battleships, two light cruisers, and eight destroyers: one New Zealand light cruiser and two Australian destroyers were included in the British formation.

30 Aug   TG 111.2, consisting of the *Indomitable* and light fleet carrier *Venerable,* two light cruisers, four destroyers, and the auxiliary antiaircraft ship *Prince Robert,* began the reoccupation of Hong Kong (Operation ARMOUR). The formal surrender of Japanese military and naval forces at Hong Kong was completed at Government House on 2 September.

TG 111.2 was joined on 5 September by the light fleet carrier *Vengeance* and units from TG 111.4, which had been formed originally as the formation that was to proceed to Singapore. In the event, however, the task of reoccupying Singapore and taking the surrender of Japanese forces both there and in the general area of Southeast Asia fell to South East Asia Command and the East Indies Fleet.

SEPTEMBER 1945

2 Sep   The instrument of Japan's unconditional surrender was signed on board the USS *Missouri.* Adm. Sir Bruce Fraser, Commander-in-Chief British Pacific Fleet, signed the instrument on behalf of Britain.

The British and Empire representation in Tokyo Bay was the battleships *Duke of York* and *King George V*, the fleet carrier *Indefatigable*, the escort carriers *Ruler* and *Speaker*, the light cruisers *Gambia* and *Newfoundland*, nine destroyers, four sloops, one frigate, four corvettes, and six units of the fleet train.

The official returns of the British Pacific Fleet show five fleet, four light fleet, and seven escort carriers, four fast battleships, eight light cruisers, twenty-eight destroyers, eight sloops, ten frigates, fifteen corvettes, one auxiliary antiaircraft ship, two fast minelayers, and twenty-two submarines under command and both operational and on station.

6 Sep TG 111.5, consisting of the light fleet carrier *Glory* and two sloops, in the company of four minesweepers and assorted units, arrived at Rabaul to take surrender of the Japanese South Eastern Army and associated naval forces and in the Bismarcks and Solomons: the local surrender of the Japanese XVII Army and VIII Fleet in the Solomons was completed off Cape Torokina on the eighth. The surrender of Japanese forces in New Ireland was formalized on the nineteenth.

9 Sep The escort carrier *Speaker* arrived at Nagasaki for the repatriation of British internees and Allied prisoners-of-war.

9 Sep The formal surrender of all Japanese forces in the Indies at Morotai.

10 Sep The surrender of the Japanese garrison on the islands off Wewak.

13 Sep The formal surrender of the Japanese 18th Army at Wewak.

14 Sep The surrender of the Japanese garrison on Nauru.

15 Sep A British heavy cruiser and escorts, followed the next day by additional units that included a Dutch light cruiser, arrived at Batavia but such was the extent of disorder ashore that British military forces were not disembarked until the twenty-ninth. The first British formation (the 26th Indian Division) to land in Sumatra came ashore on 10 October, and after the twenty-fifth British formations were landed at Soerabaja.

18 Sep After having called at Kiirun, Formosa, TG 111.3, consisting of the light fleet carrier *Colossus*, three light cruisers, and four destroyers, arrived off Shanghai in order to participate in the Allied reoccupation of the city. On the twenty-fourth the *Colossus* was ordered to proceed to Japan on repatriation duties.

OCTOBER 1945

1 Oct The surrender of the Japanese garrison on Ocean Island.

Orders of Battle

Notes

1. The fleet orders of battle are limited to units under command and both operational and on station: units that were nonoperational or not on station are listed separately.
2. The ships are listed by type and alphabetically other than flag or command ship: bases are grouped by command where appropriate. The definition of types as given in the Admiralty histories has been used in these orders of battle even though these may not be in accordance with normal usage.
3. (Aus) denotes warships of the Royal Australian Navy; (Can) denotes warships of the Royal Canadian Navy; (Ind) denotes warships of the Royal Indian Navy; (NZ) denotes warships of the Royal New Zealand Navy; (SA) denotes South African warships. Dutch, French and Italian warships are designated appropriately. * denotes unknown (or no) pennant number; naval (not military) hospital ships have been given their identification numbers.
4. The light cruiser *Achilles* was manned by New Zealanders: the destroyer *Nepal,* the three *Q*-class destroyers not listed as Australian, and the corvettes with the British Pacific Fleet were manned by Australians.
5. British, Commonwealth, and foreign warships whether in the Indian or Pacific Oceans that were not under Admiralty operational control or part of the British Pacific Fleet have not been included in these orders of battle. Thus the Dutch light cruiser *Tromp* (D.28), which had served with British forces in the Indian Ocean and which was at Manus on 13 August 1945, and five Dutch submarines based in Australia have been excluded from the orders of battle on account of their being under the direct operational control of the 7th U.S. Fleet: the greater part of the Royal Australian Navy likewise has not been included. Also, the orders of battle do not include a number of warships that were on station but had been paid off, for example, the five submarines in the Far East in August 1945 that were in various stages of disrepair and cannibalization.
6. For ships in the hands of dockyards the sequence is status, place, and estimated completion.

7. In the first section, dealing with the East Indies station, units were at Colombo or Trincomalee or at sea unless otherwise stated.

8. *The Pink List* was the name given to the roll call kept by the Admiralty of its warships, Royal Fleet Auxiliaries, and merchantmen of the fleet train. It was updated every two or three days, but obviously its accuracy was dependent upon timely and accurate reporting of movements by stations.

Warship movements were supposed to be reported to the Admiralty by radio. While certain stations (such as Sydney) were somewhat remiss in recording the movement of warships, the general accuracy of the warship record may be assumed. The Fleet Train returns, however, could be made by surface mail and therefore must be treated with some caution. The entries provided in these orders of battle are taken from *The Pink List* of 17 August 1945—the previous one being assembled on the fourteenth—despite its being known to be inaccurate in at least one case: the *City of Dieppe* is stated to have been in Sydney on 15 August but was either at an advance base or at sea on that date because she is known to have been with TG 38.5 in Tokyo Bay on 2 September 1945.

The last entry in these lists is perhaps the most important.

THE ORDER OF BATTLE OF THE EAST INDIES FLEET, 15 AUGUST 1945

SOURCES

The Pink List of 17 August 1945;
B.R. 619(2)(1944), Distinguishing Pendants and Signal Letters; Naval Staff History, *The Second World War: War with Japan.* Volume 6, *The Advance to Japan,* Appendix ZB, 287–93; and
J. D. Brown, Head of the Naval Historical Branch, Ministry of Defence.

THE EAST INDIES FLEET

3RD BATTLE SQUADRON
  Battleships
    28 *Nelson* (B.S.3) and F.S. 58 *Richelieu* (en route from Diego Suarez).

21ST AIRCRAFT CARRIER SQUADRON
  Light Cruiser
    89 *Royalist* (A.C.21)
  Assault Escort Carriers
    D.01 *Ameer,* D.02 *Attacker,* B.98 *Emperor,* D.42 *Empress,* D.80 *Hunter,* D.62 *Khedive,* D.73 *Pursuer,* D.40 *Searcher,* and D.91 *Stalker*
  General Purpose Escort Carriers
    D.21 *Shah,* D.55 *Smiter,* and D.09 *Trumpeter*

Ferrying Escort Carriers
D.94 *Activity* and D.38 *Begum*

5TH CRUISER SQUADRON
Heavy Cruisers
57 *Cumberland* (en route from Aden), 69 *London*, and 96 *Sussex*
Light Cruisers
60 *Nigeria* (C.S.5), 30 *Ceylon*, 33 *Cleopatra*, and 43 *Phoebe*
Fighter-Direction Ship
F.118 *Ulster Queen*
Destroyer Depot Ship
F.80 *Woolwich* (Comdre D)
Destroyer Tender
H.51 *Scout*
Destroyers
2ND DESTROYER FLOTILLA
R.06 *Myngs* (D.2)
10TH DESTROYER FLOTILLA, 19TH DIVISION
F.43 *Tartar* (D.10) and F.36 *Nubian*
10TH DESTROYER FLOTILLA, 20TH DIVISION
G.69 *Paladin*, G.77 *Penn*, and G.56 *Petard*
11TH DESTROYER FLOTILLA, 21ST DIVISION
H.09 *Rotherham* (D.11), H.11 *Racehorse*, H.15 *Raider*, and
H.41 *Redoubt* (Bombay)
11TH DESTROYER FLOTILLA, 22ND DIVISION
H.32 *Rapid*, H.85 *Relentless*, and H.92 *Rocket*
26TH DESTROYER FLOTILLA, 51ST DIVISION
G.12 *Saumarez* (D.26) (en route from Diego Suarez) and
R.28 *Verulam*
26TH DESTROYER FLOTILLA, 52ND DIVISION
R.93 *Vigilant* and R.41 *Volage*

2ND SUBMARINE FLOTILLA
Depot and Accommodation Ships
F.37 *Wolfe* (S/M 2) and F.30 *Wuchang*
Tender
H.I.M.S. *Eritrea*
Submarines
P.216 *Seadog*, P.237 *Scythian*, P.242 *Shalimar*, P.217 *Sibyl*, P.265 *Spur*, P.246 *Statesman*,
P.251 *Subtle*, N.37 *Thrasher*, N.79 *Torbay*, and N.52 *Trident*
Anti-Submarine Training Submarines
P.74 *Vigorous*, P.76 *Visigoth*, and P.77 *Vivid*

ESCORT FORCES

Unallocated Destroyer
F.S. H.02 *Le Triomphant*

Destroyer Escorts

18TH DESTROYER FLOTILLA

L.70 *Farndale* (D.18), L.43 *Blackmore,* L.50 *Bleasedale,* L.71 *Calpe,* and L.31 *Chiddingfold*

Frigates

EAST INDIES ESCORT FORCE

K.526 *Awe,* K.21 *Dart,* K.300 *Evenlode,* K.302 *Inver,* K. 235 *Jed,* K.241 *Kale,* K.609 *Loch Craggie,* K.619 *Loch Glendhu,* K.620 *Loch Gorm,* K.625 *Loch Katrine,* K.437 *Loch Lomond,* K.639 *Loch More,* K.434 *Loch Quoich,* K.645 *Loch Ruthven,* K.365 *Lochy* (Rangoon), K.303 *Lossie,* K.224 *Rother,* K.367 *Taff,* and K.222 *Tevoit*

For transfer to RIN

K.265 *Deveron,* K.392 *Nadder,* and K.239 *Test*

Anti-Aircraft Sloops

U.10 (Ind) *Cauvery,* U.52 (Ind) *Godavari,* U.46 (Ind) *Kistna,* U.40 (Ind) *Narbada,* and U.95 (Ind) *Sutlej* (Bombay)

General Purpose Sloops

L.34 *Falmouth,* and L.32 *Shoreham*

Corvettes

J.322 (Ind) *Assam,* and K.274 (Ind) *Sind* (Calcutta)

For transfer to RIN

K.395 *Charlock* (refit Pt. Elizabeth, undecided)

KILINDINI ESCORT FORCE

K.285 *Honesty*

Air-Sea Rescue

K.43 *Freesia* (left Kilindi 14 August), K.144 *Meadowsweet,* (Rangoon), K.207 *Monkshood* (Rangoon), K.51 *Rockrose,* K.286 *Rosebay* (Bombay), K.280 *Smilax* (Rangoon), K.211 *Snowflake* (Rangoon), K.210 *Thyme* (Bombay), K.29 *Tulip* (Calcutta), and K.35 *Violet*

Anti-Submarine Vessels

4.158 (Ind) *Kalavati,* and 4.206 (Ind) *Sonavati*

Cutters

Y.59 *Fishguard,* Y.92 *Gorleston,* Y.60 *Lulworth,* and Y.21 *Sennen*

Fleet Minesweepers

6TH MINESWEEPING FLOTILLA

J.398 (Ind) *Friendship,* J.287 (Ind) *Gozo,* J.276 (Ind) *Lennox,* J.288 (Ind) *Lightfoot,* J.289 (Ind) *Melita,* J.291 (Ind) *Pelorus,* J.347 (Ind) *Persian,* and J.296 (Ind) *Postillion,* and attached danlayers J.422 (Ind) *Imersay* and J.423 (Ind) *Lingay*

7TH MINESWEEPING FLOTILLA

J.293 (Ind) *Pickle* (arrived Mauritius 13 August), J.387 (Ind) *Chamelon* (arrived Mauritius 9 August), J.294 (Ind) *Pincher,* J.295 (Ind) *Plucky,* J.298 (Ind) *Recruit* and J.299 (Ind) *Rifleman,* and the attached danlayer J.425 *Scaravay* (Kilindini)

37TH MINESWEEPING FLOTILLA

J.182 (Ind) *Baluchistan*, J.243 (Ind) *Bengal*, J.247 (Ind) *Bihar*, J.249 (Ind) *Bombay*, J.199 (Ind) *Carnatic*, J.129 (Ind) *Deccan*, J.155 (Ind) *Kathiawar*, J.190 (Ind) *Khyber*, J.228 (Ind) *Konkan*, J.164 (Ind) *Kumaon*, J.200 (Ind) *Orissa*, J.245 (Ind) *Oudh*, J.239 (Ind) *Punjab*, J.197 (Ind) *Rajputana*, and J.180 (Ind) *Rohikhand* (Bombay)

BASES, BASE SHIPS, DEPOT SHIPS, AND FLEET TRAIN

Depot Ship
F.27 *Lucia*

Dockyard Ship
F.137 *Wayland*

Escort Depot Ship
D.60 *Caradoc*

Repair Ship
F.53 *Ausonia*

Escort Depot/Maintenance Ship
F.141 *Gombroon*

Escort Maintenance Ship
F.02 *Beachy Head*

Minesweeper Maintenance Ship
FY.1951 *Corbrae*

Motor Craft Maintenance Ship
F.26 *Mull of Galloway*

Survey Vessels
J.98 *Challenger*, J.430 *Nguva*, FY.031 *Virginia*, 4.02 *White Bear*, H.D.M.Ls. *1238*, *1288*, and *1376*

Aircraft Target Ship
H.I.M.S. *Carabiniere*

Controlled Minelayers
M.22 *Dabchick*, M.31 *Redshank*, and M.06 *Sandmartin*

Boom Carriers
Z.168 *Devon City* and Z.167 *Ethiopian* (Burma)

Deperming Ships
F.119 *Bushwood* and 4.94 *Springtide* (both Kilindi)

Rescue Tugs
W.113 *Aimwell*, W.142 *Assiduous*, W.114 *Bold* (Aden), W.115 *Destiny* (Bombay), W.116 *Eminent*, W.154 *Emphatic*, W.175 *Enigma*, W.151 *Flare* W.14 *Integrity*, W.117 *Oriana* (Kilindini), and W.73 *Prudent* (Durban)

Salvage Vessel
Ocean Salvor

ROYAL NAVAL BASES, BASE SHIPS, DEPOT SHIPS, AND ATTACHED TENDERS

Lanka (Colombo), *Highflyer* (Trincomalee), and *Maraga* (Addu Atoll). Y.56 *Landguard* (Kilindi), *Mayina* (Kilindi), and F.102 *Ying Chow* (Kilindi). *Tana* (Kilindi), *Ironclad* (Diego Suarez), *Sambur* (Mauritius), and *Sangdragon* (Seychelles). *Sheba* (Aden). *Jufair* (Bahrain), *Euphrates* (Persian Gulf), and *Oman* (Khor Kuwait)

ROYAL NAVAL BASES IN INDIA

Amazari (Vizagapatam), *Anderson* (Colombo), *Braganza* (Bombay), *Chilwa* (Calcutta), *Chinkara* (Cochin), *Pangkor* (Bombay), R.N. Base Madras, and *Tengra* (Mandapan)

ROYAL NAVAL AIR STATIONS

Bambara (Trincomalee), *Bherunda* (Colombo), *Garuda* (Coimbatore), *Kaluga* (Cochin), *Rajaliya* (Puttalam, Ceylon), *Ukussa* (Katukurunda, Ceylon), *Vairi* (Sular), and *Valluru* (Tambaram, Madras)

THE ROYAL INDIAN NAVY

ROYAL INDIAN NAVAL BASE AND DEPOT SHIPS AND ATTACHED TENDERS

Adyar (Madras), *Circars* (Vizagapatam), *Dalhousie* (Bombay), *Hoogli* (Calcutta), *Monze* (Karachi), T.300 (Ind) *Moti* (Bombay), *Patunga* (Chittagong), *Sita* (Ceylon), and *Venduruthi* (Cochin)

Sloop
L.79 (Ind) *Clive* (Bombay)

Anti-Submarine Vessels
L.83 (Ind) *Lawrence* (Karachi) and 4.111 (Ind) *Ramdas* (Bombay)

Survey Sloop
L.80 (Ind) *Hindustan* (Bombay)

Training Vessels
4.109 (Ind) *Dipavati* (Bombay), T.301 (Ind) *Hira* (Bombay), J.81 (Ind) *Investigator* (Karachi), T.299 (Ind) *Lal* (Bombay), and T.302 (Ind) *Nilam* (Karachi)

Radar Training Ship
J.237 (Ind) *Madras* (arrived Bombay 16 August)

COASTAL ANTI-SUBMARINE FORCE (WEST COAST GROUP)
Corvette
K.348 *Gondwana* (operating from Bombay)
Anti-Submarine Patrol Vessels
T.254 (Ind) *Agra* (from Cochin), T.249 (Ind) *Baroda* (from Bombay), T.287 (Ind)

Berar (from Bombay), T.262 (Ind) *Karachi* (from Karachi), T.253 (Ind) *Lahore* (from Cochin), T.258 (Ind) *Nasik* (from Bombay), T.255 (Ind) *Patna* (from Cochin), and T.260 (Ind) *Poona* (from Cochin)

COASTAL ANTI-SUBMARINE FORCE (EAST COAST GROUP)
Anti-Submarine Patrol Vessels

T.264 (Ind) *Ahmedabad* (operating from Madras), T.261 (Ind) *Amritsar* (from Madras), T.339 (Ind) *Calcutta* (from Calcutta), T.251 *Cuttack* (from Vizagapapatam), T.268 (Ind) *Madura* (from Vizagapapatam) T.250 (Ind) *Shillong* (from Calcutta), and T.312 (Ind) *Travancore* (from Calcutta)

FORCE W

L.S.H.(L)
F.82 *Bulolo* and F.43 *Largs*

L.S.H.(S)
K.215 *Nith* and K.248 *Waveney*

L.S.I.(L)
*Barpeta, 4.196 *Glengyle*, 4.256 *Glenroy*, (Ind) **Llanstephen Castle*, 4.422 *Persimmon*, F.184 *Rocksand*, F.183 *Sainfoin*, F.162 *Sansovino*, and F.123 *Sefton*

L.S.I.(M)
4.44 *Prinses Beatrix* and 4.180 *Queen Emma*

L.S.I.(S)
4.35 *Prins Albert*

L.S.C
*Empire Elaine

L.S.D
F.140 *Highway*

L.S.G
X.51 *Dewdale*, and X.73 *Ennerdale*

OTHER UNITS (1).

The following ships were assigned to the East Indies Fleet but were non-operational, not on station or on passage

Assault Escort Carrier
D.85 *Trouncer* (Home Fleet, for refit)

Ferrying Escort Carrier
D.48 *Campania* (in the Clyde)

Heavy Cruiser
78 *Norfolk* (refit Malta, 22 September)

Light Cruisers

    21 *Glasgow* (Portsmouth Command, Portsmouth), 44 *Jamaica* (Portsmouth Command, Plymouth), and H.N.M.S. D.20 *Jacob Van Heemskerck* (Amsterdam)

Monitors

    F.109 *Abercrombie* (left Suez 11 August) and F.40 *Roberts* (left Suez 15 August)

Gunboats

    T.57 *Aphis*, T.72 *Cockchafer*, and T.59 *Scarab* (all undergoing refit at Taranto, September),

Fighter-Direction Ships

    F.121 *Boxer* (left the Clyde 9 August), **F.D.T.13* (left the Clyde 11 August), and F.98 *Palomares* (Aden)

Destroyers

    2ND DESTROYER FLOTILLA, temporarily attached to Home Fleet

        R.66 *Zambesi* (Kristinsand), R.81 *Zebra* (Rosyth), and R.54 *Zodiac* (Flensburg). Nonoperational, R.39 *Zealous* (refit Portsmouth, 18 September), R.95 *Zenith* (Portland), R.19 *Zephyr* (refit Portsmouth, 1 September), and R.02 *Zest* (refit Leith, 17 November)

    11TH DESTROYER FLOTILLA

        H.95 *Roebuck* (refit Durban, undecided)

    19TH DESTROYER FLOTILLA

        F.75 *Eskimo* (arrived Durban 10 August)

    26TH DESTROYER FLOTILLA

        R.50 *Venus* (Simonstown) and R.75 *Virago* (Durban)

    Unallocated:

        H.N.M. Ships G.16 *Tjerk Hiddes* (refit Dundee, November) and G.84 *Van Galen* (Rotterdam)

Frigates

    K.256 *Bann* (refit Cape Town, 25 August), K.349 *Calder* (refit Belfast, 26 September), K.351 *Duckworth* (refit Belfast, 12 September), K.353 *Essington*, (refit Belfast, 30 August), K.432 (SA) *Good Hope* (refit Cape Town, August), K.417 Halladale (refit Cape Town, 4 September), K.426 *Loch Achray* (refit in the Clyde, August), K.433 *Loch Eck* (Avonmouth), K.429 *Loch Fyne* (arrived Gibraltar 15 August), K.433 *Loch Insh* (repairs Leith, 21 August), K.628 *Loch Killisport* (in the Clyde), K.648 *Loch Scavaig* (Suez), K.431 *Loch Tarbert* (arrived Pt. Said 15 August), K.403 (SA) *Natal* (Simonstown), K.219 *Ness* (on the Tyne), K.305 *Shiel* (refit Pt. Elizabeth, undecided), K.217 *Swale* (trials Cape Town), K.232 *Tay* (on the Tyne), K.602 (SA) *Transvaal* (Durban), and K.423 *Trent* (for refit at Cape Town)

Anti-Aircraft Sloop

    Anti-Aircraft, U.21 (Ind) *Jumna* (refit Massawa, 21 November)

Corvettes
>K.23 *Jasmine* (refit East London, 24 September) and K.19 *Nigella* (trials East
>>London)

Destroyer Escort
>L.08 *Exmoor* (arrived Malta 14 August)

Cutter
>Y.43 *Banff* (arrived Durban 13 August)

Minesweepers
>J.390 *Jewel* (refit Antwerp, undecided), J.354 *Serene* (Chatham), and the danlay-
>>er J.424 *Sandray* (refit Massawa, undecided)
>8TH MINESWEEPING FLOTILLA
>>J.350 *Coquette* (Messina), J.360 *Mary Rose*, J.329 *Moon*, J.325 *Providence*, J.384 *Rowena*,
>>J.333 *Seabear*, and J.302 *Thisbe* (formation off station at Malta)

Boom Carrier
>Z.243 *Laomedon* (left Ostend 29 July)

Anti-Boat Net Layer
>T.197 *Brittany* (refit Alloa, 25 August)

Salvage Vessel
>*Salviola* (left the Clyde 2 August)

Hull Repair Ship
>F.186 *Mullion Cove* (Malton)

Coastal Force Workshop Tender
>K.438 *Derby Haven* (arrived at Portland 7 August)

OTHER UNITS (2)

The following ships are recorded as having arrived at Trincomalee
and/or Colombo between 23 March and 15 August 1945 but do not
appear on the muster lists of either the East Indies Fleet or the British
Pacific Fleet: units known to have been inward-bound or to have been on
another station on 15 August 1945 have been excluded

Heavy Cruiser
>F.S. *Suffren*

Sloops
>L.43 *Bideford*, L.75 *Egret*, and U.35 F.S. *Dumont D'Urville*

Corvettes
>K.348 *Burnet*

Anti-Submarine Patrol Vessel
>T.16 *Hoxa*

Danlayer
>*Cyclone*

OTHER UNITS (3)

By the end of hostilities, the following had been nominated as reinforcements for the East Indies Fleet:

Destroyer Escorts

L.12 *Albrighton* (refit Humber), L.32 *Belvoir* (refit Sheerness, 8 October: to be French-manned), L.30 *Blankney* (refit Simonstown, 18 October), L.81 *Catterick* (arrived Gibraltar 15 August), L.62 *Croome* (Ferryville), L.88 *Lamerton* (arrived Freetown 1 August), L.95 *Lauderdale* (left Gibraltar 13 August), L.90 *Ledbury* (refit Gilbraltar, undecided), L.74 *Middleton* (refit Simonstown, 18 October), L.98 *Oakley* (Taranto), L.69 *Tanatside* (refit Taranto, mid-September), L.99 *Tetcott* (refit Gibraltar, mid-September), L.122 *Wheatland* (Plymouth), L.128 *Wilton* (arrived Freetown 1 August), and L.59 *Zetland* (refit Alexandria, 8 October)

L.S.D.

F.142 *Northway* (Home Fleet)

* * *

In addition, the heavy cruisers *Berwick* (Portsmouth Command, arrived Sydney 17 August) and *Devonshire* (Nore Command, left Fremantle on 12 August inward) and the light cruiser *Enterprise* (Portsmouth Command, arrived Colombo 13 August outward) were engaged in trooping to Australia. The heavy cruiser *Suffolk* was scheduled to leave for Sydney from Liverpool on 25 August.

THE ORDER OF BATTLE OF THE BRITISH PACIFIC FLEET, 15 AUGUST 1945

SOURCES

The Pink List of 17 August 1945;
B.R. *619(2)(1944), Distinguishing Pendants and Signal Letters;*
Naval Staff History, *The Second World War: War with Japan,*
Volume 6, The Advance to Japan, Appendix T, 277–78;
Appendix U, 279–80; Appendix ZC, 294–99; and
J. D. Brown, Head of the Naval Historical Branch, Ministry of Defence.

TASK FORCE 37 / TASK FORCE 113

1ST BATTLE SQUADRON
Battleship
41 *King George V* (V.A.B.P.F.)

1ST AIRCRAFT CARRIER SQUADRON
Fleet Carriers
67 *Formidable* (A.C.1), 86 *Implacable*, 10 *Indefatigable*, and 38 *Victorious*

4TH CRUISER SQUADRON
Light Cruisers
59 *Newfoundland* (C.S.4), 70 *Achilles*, 61 *Argonaut*, 81 *Black Prince*, 42 *Euryalus*, and 48 (NZ) *Gambia*

4TH DESTROYER FLOTILLA
G.11 *Quadrant*, G.62 *Quality*, G.70 *Queensborough*, G.81 (Aus) *Quiberon*, and G.92 (Aus) *Quickmatch*

7TH DESTROYER FLOTILLA
G.97 (Aus) *Napier* (D.7), G.25 *Nepal*, G.38 (Aus) *Nizam*, and G.49 (Aus) *Norman*

19TH DESTROYER FLOTILLA
R.80 *Barfleur* (R.A.D.B.P.F.)

24TH DESTROYER FLOTILLA
R.00 *Troubridge* (D.24), R.23 *Teazer*, R.45 *Tenacious*, R.89 *Termagant*, and R.33 *Terpsichord*

25TH DESTROYER FLOTILLA
R.97 *Grenville*, R.69 *Ulysses*, R.53 *Undaunted*, R.42 *Undine*, R.05 *Urania*, and R.99 *Urchin*

27TH DESTROYER FLOTILLA
R.59 *Wakeful*, and R.48 *Wrangler*

TASK GROUP 111.2

(Technically TG 111.2 did not become operational until 20 August 1945.)

Battleship
79 *Anson* (B.S.1)

11TH AIRCRAFT CARRIER SQUADRON
Fleet Carrier
92 *Indomitable* (C.T.G.111.2)
Light Fleet Carriers
15 *Colossus*, 04 *Venerable*, and 71 *Vengeance*

2ND CRUISER SQUADRON
Light Cruisers
52 *Bermuda* (C.S.2) and 08 *Swiftsure*

Auxiliary Anti-Aircraft Ship
F.56 (Can) *Prince Robert*

Destroyers
R.03 *Kampenfelt* (D.27), R.11 *Tumult*, R.56 *Tuscan*, R.67 *Tyrian*, R.22 *Ursa*, and R.87 *Whirlwind*

OTHER FORMATIONS AND UNITS ON STATION

Battleship
17 *Duke of York* (Manus)

Fast Minelayers
M.01 *Apollo,* and M.70 *Manxman* (both at Melbourne)

Destroyers
27TH DESTROYER FLOTILLA
R.98 *Wager,* and R.37 *Whelp* (both at sea for Manus)

4TH SUBMARINE FLOTILLA, at Fremantle or on patrol
Depot Ship
F.64 *Adamant* (S/M.4) (Fremantle)
Submarines
P.334 *Taciturn,* P.335 *Tapir,* P.339 *Taurus,* P.324 *Thorough,* P.325 *Thule,* P.332 *Tiptoe,* P.352 *Totem,* P.331 *Trenchant,* P.333 *Trump,* P.326 *Tudor,* and P.354 *Turpin*

8TH SUBMARINE FLOTILLA, at Subic Bay or on patrol
Depot Ship
F.44 *Maidstone* (S/M.8) (Subic Bay)
Submarines
P.253 *Sea Scout,* P.254 *Selene,* P.259 *Sidon,* P.261 *Sleuth,* P.262 *Solent,* P.236 *Spark,* P. 263 *Spearhead,* P.238 *Stubborn,* P.249 *Stygian,* and P.252 *Supreme*

14TH SUBMARINE FLOTILLA, at Brunei
Depot Ship
F.139 *Bonaventure* (S/M.14)

Anti-submarine Training Submarines
P.78 *Voracious* (Sydney) and P.73 *Vox* (Auckland)

Aircraft Target Ship
G.68 *Lewes* (Sydney)

Boom Carriers
Z.208 *Fernmoor,* and Z.197 *Leonian* (both at Brisbane)

Headquarters/Accommodation Ship
F.168 *Lothian* (Sydney)

TASK FORCE 112
THE FLEET TRAIN

(operating from Manus, July–August 1945)

(1). UNITS AT SEA, MANUS OR ADVANCED BASES IN THE PACIFIC

Base and Headquarters Ship
F.85 *Montclare* (R.A.F.T.)

Destroyer Depot Ship
F.37 *Tyne* (Eniwetok)

Escort Carriers, Replenishment
D.12 *Striker* (A.C.30), D.31 *Arbiter,* D.32 *Chaser,* D.72 *Ruler,* and D.90 *Speaker*

Frigates
> 32ND ESCORT FLOTILLA
>> K.289 *Barle*, K.257 *Derg*, K.356 *Odzani*, K.271 *Plym*, and K.295 *Usk*

Sloops
> 21ST MINESWEEPING FLOTILLA
>> J.184 *Ballarat*, J.187 *Bendigo* (Eniwetok), J.198 *Burnie*, J.167 *Goulburn* (Eniwetok),
>> J.195 *Maryborough*, J.157 *Toowoomba*, and J.153 *Whyalla*
> 22ND MINESWEEPING FLOTILLA
>> J.175 *Cessnock*, J.188 *Gawler*, J.178 *Geraldton*, J. 186 *Ipswich*, J.179 *Launceston*,
>> J.189 *Pirie*, and J.181 *Tamworth*
> 31ST ESCORT FLOTILLA
>> U.49 *Pheasant* (E.F.31), U.23 *Crane*, K.301 *Findhorn*, K.304 *Parret*, U.69 *Redpole*,
>> U.29 *Whimbrel*, and U.90 *Woodcock*

Aircraft Component Repair Ship
> F.99 *Deer Sound*

Aircraft Repair Ship
> I.72 *Unicorn*

Heavy Repair Ship
> F.28 *Artifex*

Radio Repair Ship
> K.403 (NZ) *Arbutus*

Aircraft Maintenance Ship
> D.76 *Pioneer*

Escort Maintenance Ship
> F.88 *Flamborough Head*

Minesweeper Maintenance Ship
> F.166 *Kelantan* (Eniwetok)

Accommodation Ships
> F.41 *Aorangi* and G.05 *Lancaster*

Transport
> 4.250 *Glenearn*

Boom Vessel
> Z.01 *Barbain*

Deperming Ship
> **Springdale*

Salvage Vessels
> W.176 *Salvestor* and W.190 *Salvictor* (both Milne Bay)

Tugs
> W.17 *Lariat* (Milne Bay) and W.120 *Weazel* (Eniwetok)

Fleet Tankers
Aese Maersk (Eniwetok), X.66 *Bishopdale* (Madang), *Carelia*, X.80 *Cedardale*, *Dingledale*, X.104 *Eaglesdale*, X.116 *Olna*, *San Adolfo*, *San Amado*, *San Ambrosio*, X.100 *Wave Emperor*, X.103 *Wave Governor*, and X.82 *Wave King*

Small Tankers
X.69 *Brown Ranger* (Eniwetok), *Darst Creek*, *Golden Meadow*, X.42 *Green Ranger*, *Iere*, *Loma Nova*, X.58 *Rapidol*, X.62 *Serbol*, and *Seven Sisters*

Air Stores Issuing Ships
Y1.15 *Fort Colville* and *Fort Langley*

Armament Stores Issuing Ships
Y2.101 *Corinda*, Y2.100 *Darvel*, Y2.104 *Hermelin*, *Kistna*, Y2.11 *Pacheco*, Y2.105 *Prince de Liege*, Y2.108 *Princess Maria Pia*, *Robert Maersk*, and *Thyra S*

Naval Stores Issuing/Distilling Ship
X.03 *Bacchus* (Eniwetok)

Victualling Stores Issuing Ships
Y1.20 *Fort Constantine* (Sydney), Y1.19 *Fort Dunvegan*, Y1.75 *Fort Edmonton*, *Fort Wrangell*, and *Glenartney*

Naval Stores Carriers
Jaarstroom (Subic) and *Marudu*

Hospital Ships
67 *Gerusalemme* and 42 (NZ) *Maunganui*

Colliers
W.41 *Atlas* and *Edna*

Floating Docks
AFD 18 and *AFD 20*

(2). OTHER FLEET TRAIN UNITS ON STATION

(Including units in or bound for Australian harbors, 15 August 1945)

Ferrying Escort Carrier
D.15 *Vindex* (at sea for Brisbane)
Replenishment Escort Carrier
D.26 *Slinger* (Sydney)

Frigates
21ST MINESWEEPING FLOTILLA
J.145 *Lismore* (Melbourne)
22ND MINESWEEPING FLOTILLA
J.172 *Wollongong* (at sea for Sydney)

Net Layer
T.89 *Guardian* (Sydney)

Heavy Repair Ships
  F.79 *Resource* (Sydney)

Fleet Tanker
  X.108 *Wave Monarch* (at sea for Manus)

Water Carriers
  *Empire Crest (Brisbane) and **Vacport* (Sydney)

Armament Stores Issuing Ships
  *Heron (at sea for Sydney), **Hickory Burn*, **Hickory Dale*, **Hickory Glen*, and **Hickory Stream*

Victualling Stores Issuing Ships
  Y1.61 *Fort Alabama* (Sydney), Y1.20 *Fort Constantine* (Sydney), and Y1.47 *Fort Providence* (Sydney)

Naval/Victualling Stores Issuing Ship
  Y1.08 *City of Dieppe* (Sydney)

Stores Carriers
  Y2.109 *Gudrun Maersk* (Sydney) and **Kola* (at sea for Sydney)

Naval Stores Carriers
  *Bosphorus, **San Andres*, and **Slesvig* (all at Sydney)

Hospital Ships
  3 *Tjitjalengka* (Samoa) and 4 *Vasna* (Wellington, 8 August)

BASE DEPOTS

Beaconsfield (Melbourne), *Furneaux* (Brisbane), *Golden Hind* (Sydney), *Pepys* (Manus), and *Wooloomooloo* (Sydney)

EN ROUTE FOR THE PACIFIC, 15 AUGUST 1945

Light Fleet Carrier
  62 *Glory* (left Colombo 3 August)

Ferrying Escort Carriers
  D.64 *Fencer* (arrived Cochin 16 August) and D.82 *Reaper* (left Norfolk, Va., 13 August)

Light Cruisers
  35 *Belfast* (left Colombo 7 August) and 53 (Can) *Ontario* (left Aden 14 August)

Destroyers
  R.07 *Caesar* (arrived Colombo 7 August), R.15 *Cavendish* (arrived Colombo 8 August), and R.72 *Wizard* (left Colombo 3 August)

Frigates
  K.630 *Cardigan Bay* (Gibraltar), K.634 *St. Austell Bay* (Malta), K.600 *St. Bride's Bay* (Malta), and K.615 *Widemouth Bay* (left Colombo 13 August)

Anti-Aircraft Sloops

U.60 *Alacrity* (left Suez 8 August), U.16 *Amethyst*, L.57 *Black Swan*, U.03 *Erne*, and U.58 *Hart* (all left Colombo 11 August), U.39 *Hind* (left Suez 8 August), U.82 *Magpie* (Malta), U.30 *Mermaid* (Malta), U.96 *Peacock* (en route for Malta), and L.86 *Pelican* (Malta)

Destroyer Escorts

L.06 *Avonvale* (Malta), L.34 *Bicester* (left Aden 15 August 1945), *Brecon* (arrived Bombay 13 August), L.79 *Brissenden* (Malta), L.52 *Cowdray,* and L.15 *Eggesford* (both left Colombo 11 August), and L.16 *Stevenstone* (Malta)

Submarines

P.266 *Sanguine,* and P.244 *Sea Devil* (both left Malta 15 August), P.258 *Scorcher* (arrived Trincomalee 8 August), and P.243 *Scotsman* (left Trincomalee 30 July)

Fast Minelayer

M.65 *Ariadne* (left Colombo 2 August)

Escort Command and Headquarters Ship

L.56 *Enchantress* (arrived Colombo 12 August)

Command Ship Logistic Supply Group

K.262 *Aire* (left Suez 8 August)

Aircraft Target Ship

G.77 *Penn* (at Trincomalee 15 August)

Auxiliary Repair Ship

F.173 *Assistance* (left Colombo 25 July)

Hull Repair Ship

F.185 *Dullisk Cove* (left Alexandria 8 August)

Escort Maintenance Ship

F.18 *Berry Head* (due Brisbane, 19 August)

Salvage Vessel

W.191 *King Salvor* (left Colombo 1 August)

Mine Issuing Ship

Y6.09 *Prome* (due on station August)

Hospital Ship

54 *Empire Clyde* (arrived Pt. Said 10 August)

OTHER UNITS

(1). The following ships were assigned to the British Pacific Fleet and the Fleet Train but were nonoperational, or not on station or not en route:

Battleship

32 *Howe* (Durban)

Fleet Carrier
    87 *Illustrious* (refit Rosyth, 27 October)

Light Cruiser
    66 (Can) *Uganda* (refit Esquimalt, 21 September)

Destroyers
    R.17 (Can) *Algonquin*, R.77 *Trafalgar* (Mediterranean Fleet working up), R.14
        Armada (Mediterranean Fleet working up), R.32 *Camperdown*
        (Mediterranean Fleet working up), R.74 *Hogue*, G.09 *Quilliam* (left
        San Diego, Calif., 14 August damaged), R.83 *Ulster* (Home Fleet refit
        Chatham, undecided), and R.78 *Wessex* (refit Auckland, 19 August)

Frigates
    31ST ESCORT FLOTILLA
        K.97 *Avon* (refit Brisbane, 1 September)
    32ND ESCORT FLOTILLA
        K.252 *Helford* (refit Brisbane, undecided)

Minesweepers
    10TH MINESWEEPING FLOTILLA
        J.369 *Felicity* (Harwich), J.349 *Courier* (S.O.) (repairs London, 31 August), J.389
            Hare (refit Cardiff, 5 September), J.391 *Liberty* (refit Antwerp, unde-
            cided), J.444 *Michael* (repairs Granton, 19 August), J.445 *Minstrel*
            (repairs Granton, undecided), J.385 *Wave* (repairs Milford Haven, 15
            September), and J.386 *Welcome* (refit Liverpool, 31 August)
    21ST MINESWEEPING FLOTILLA
        J.192 *Kalgoorlie* (refit Brisbane, undecided)
    22ND MINESWEEPING FLOTILLA
        J.183 *Cairns* (Fremantle)

Submarine
    P.223 *Seanymph* (Subic)

Anti-Submarine Training Submarine
    P.75 *Virtue* (Sydney)

Fleet Tanker
    *Arndale (Brisbane)

Armament Stores Issuing Ship
    Y2.36 *Kheti* (Sydney)

Distilling Ship
    *Stagpool (Sydney)

(2). Units nominated to serve as reinforcements for the British Pacific Fleet:

Frigates
    K.661 (Can) *Antigonish* (refit Pictou, 8 October), K.407 (Can) *Beacon Hill* (refit Liverpool
        NS, 15 September), K.606 *Bigbury Bay* (Portsmouth), K.685 (Can) *Buckingham*

(refit Liverpool NS, 20 August), K.663 (Can) *Cap de la Madelaine* (refit Quebec, undecided),K.350 (Can) *Cape Breton* (refit Vancouver, 15 October), K.409 (Can) *Capilano* (refit Shelburne NS, 15 September), K.664 (Can) *Carlplace* (refit St. John NB, 20 August), K.244 (Can) *Charlottetown* (refit Sydney CB, 30 September), K.388 (Can) *Dunver* (refit Vancouver, 30 September), (Can) K.670 (Can) *Fort Erie* (refit Pictou, 20 August), K. 518 (Can) *Grou* (refit Dartmouth NS, 20 August), K.667 (Can) *Inch Arran* (refit Sydney CB, 20 August), K.337 (Can) *Kirkland Lake* (refit Quebec, 30 September), K.668 (Can) *La Hulloise* (refit St. John NB, 15 September), K.400 (Can) *Levis* (refit Lunenburg NS, 15 September), K.319 (Can) *Montreal* (refit Shelburne NS, 20 August), K.321 (Can) *New Waterford* (refit Liverpool NS, undecided), K.448 (Can) *Orkney* (refit Lunenburg NS, 15 September), K.322 (Can) *Outremont* (repairs Sydney NS, uncertain), K.326 (Can) *Port Colborne* (repairs Liverpool NS, 20 August), K.675 (Can) *Poundmaker* (refit Lunenburg NS, 20 August), K.662 (Can) *Prestonian* (refit Halifax, 20 August), K.324 (Can) *Prince Rupert* (repairs Esquimalt, 30 September), K.677 (Can) *Royal Mount* (refit Sydney NS, 15 September), K.325 (Can) *St. Catherines* (refit St. John NB, undecided), K.456 (Can) *St. John* (refit St. John NB, undecided), K.680 (Can) *St. Pierre* (refit Quebec, 20 August), K.454 (Can) *St. Stephen* (repairs Halifax, 15 September), K.323 (Can) *Springhill* (refit Pictou, 15 September), K.327 (Can) *Stormont* (refit Shelburne NS, undecided), K.682 (Can) *Strathadam* (refit Liverpool NS, 20 August), K.683 (Can) *Sussex Vale* (refit Shelburne NS, 20 August), K.328 (Can) *Swansea* (left Trinidad 14 August), K.651 *Veryan Bay* (in the Clyde), K.684 (Can) *Victoriaville* (refit St. John NB, 20 August), K.330 (Can) *Waskesiu* (Refit Esqimalt, 30 September), K.331 (Can) *Wentworth* (refit Shelburne NS, 20 August), and K.633 *Whitesand Bay* (working up at Tobermory)

Frigates being refitted as Fighter Direction Ships
K.314 *Bentinck* (Belfast, 7 October), K.465 *Bentley* (Cardiff, 15 September), K.468 *Braithwaite* (Southampton, 30 September), K.510 *Cotton* (Liverpool, 2 October), and K.553 *Fitzroy* (Belfast, 30 September)

Anti-Aircraft Sloops
U.38 *Cygnet* (Leith), L.18 *Flamingo* (in reserve at Liverpool to refit), U.33 *Opossum* (Portsmouth), U.66 *Starling* (arrived Tobermory 10 August), L.81 *Stork* (Newport), U.45 *Wild Goose* (refit Leith, 17 September), and U.28 *Wren* (repairs Leith, 29 September)

Destroyers Escorts
L.14 *Beaufort* (refit Cardiff, 5 September), L.09 *Easton* (refit Southampton, 23 August), L.75 *Haydon* (Malta), L.73 *Melbreak* (refit Sheerness, undecided), and L.18 *Talybont* (refit Malta, 13 September)

Dan Layers
J.426 *Shillay* (repairs Pt. Dinorwic, 18 September) and J.431 *Trodday* (refit Belfast, undecided)

(3). Units nominated to serve in the Fleet Train:

Defence Vessel
    M.49 *Helvig* (in the Clyde, September)

Net Layer
    T.98 *Protector* (repairs Bombay, August)

Fast Fleet Tankers
    *Nordmark (conversion on the Tyne, September) and X.46 *Oleander* (completing March 1946)

Fleet Tankers
    X.68 *Broomdale* (due November) *Empire Herald (due December) **Empire Mars,* **Empire Neptune,* **Empire Protector,* **Empire Salisbury,* **Nacella,* **Naranio,* **San Cipriano,* **San Venancio,* *Tibia (all due November), and X.110 *Wave Regent* (due September)

Small Tankers
    X.16 *Celerol,* **Empire Tegados,* **Empire Tegamas,* **Empire Tegidad,* **Empire Tegincent,* **Empire Teguda,* **Tandora,* **Tannadice,* **Tanova,* and *Tantallon (due November)

Collier
    *Empire Boswell (due November)

Naval Stores Issuing Ships
    X. 142 *Fort Rosalie,* *Fort Sandusky (Montreal), and *Fort Wayne (Montreal)

Victualling Stores Issuing Ships
    *Fort Beauharnois (completing Vancouver, October), **Fort Charlotte,* and X. 141 *Fort Dusquesne* (both Vancouver)

Mine Issuing Ship
    *Empire Cheer (due September)

Naval Stores Carriers
    **Northern Master,* **Northern Traveller,* and *Northern Warrior (all due December)

Vegetable Carriers
    *Erin and *Eros (both due November)

Aircraft Engine Repair Ship
    F.187 *Beauly Firth* (Rosyth, November), F.62 *Moray Firth* (completing 22 September, November), and F.190 *Solway Firth* (January 1946)

Aircraft Component Repair Ships
    F.188 *Cullin Sound* (repairs Tyne 31 August, October) and F.189 *Holm Sound* (Tyne, October)

Auxiliary Repair Ships
    F.15 *Alaunia* (trials Plymouth, November), F.174 *Diligence,* and F.39 *Ranpura* (completing Portsmouth, January 1946)

Aircraft Maintenance Ship

    51 *Perseus* (completing August, October)

Armament Maintenance Ship

    *Portland Bill (due December) and **Selsey Bill* (due January 1946)

Escort Maintenance Ship

    F.34 *Rame Head* (October)

Motor Craft Maintenance Ship

    F.26 *Mull of Kintyre* (completing December)

Accommodation Ship

    *Southern Prince (refit, August)

Amenity Ship

    M.93 *Menestheus* (converting Vancouver, November)

TABULAR REPRESENTATION OF THE ORDERS OF BATTLE
OF THE EAST INDIES AND THE BRITISH PACIFIC FLEETS, 15 AUGUST 1945
(i). THE EAST INDIES FLEET

	1	2	3	4	5	6	7	Total
Battleships	2	-	-	-	-	-	-	2
Escort Carriers	14	-	-	-	-	2	-	16
Heavy Cruisers	3	-	-	-	-	1	-	4
Light Cruisers	5	-	-	-	-	3	-	8
Monitors	-	-	-	-	-	2	-	2
Gunboats	-	-	-	-	-	3	-	3
Destroyers	17	1	-	-	-	13	-	31
Submarines	13	-	-	-	-	-	-	13
Frigates	-	22	-	-	-	20	-	42
Sloops	-	9	-	1	-	1	-	11
Corvettes	-	14	-	1	-	2	-	17
Destroyer Escorts	-	6	-	-	-	-	15	21
Cutters	-	4	-	-	-	1	-	5
Escorts	-	2	-	2	-	-	-	4
Patrol Vessels	-	-	-	15	-	-	-	15
Minelayers	-	-	3	-	-	-	-	3
Minesweepers	-	29	-	-	-	10	-	39
Danlayers	-	3	-	-	-	-	-	3
F/D Ships	1	-	-	-	-	3	-	4
LSH all types	-	-	-	-	4	-	-	4
LSI all types	-	-	-	-	13	-	-	13
Other Landing Ships	-	-	-	-	4	-	1	5
Boom Carriers	-	-	2	-	-	1	-	3
Netlayer	-	-	-	-	-	1	-	1
Deperming Ship	-	-	2	-	-	-	-	2
Survey Ships	-	-	7	1	-	-	-	8
RIN Training Ships	-	-	-	6	-	-	-	6
Depot Ships	2	-	6	-	-	-	-	8
Tenders	2	-	-	-	-	1	-	3
Accommodation Ship	1	-	-	-	-	-	-	1
Target Ship	-	-	1	-	-	-	-	1
Repair Ship	-	-	-	-	-	1	-	1
Maintenance Ships	-	-	3	-	-	9	-	12
Salvage Ships	-	-	1	-	-	1	-	2
Rescue Tugs	-	-	11	-	-	-	-	11
Total	*60*	*90*	*36*	*26*	*21*	*75*	*16*	*324*

KEY
1. Units with the East Indies Fleet.
2. Units with escort formations.
3. Units with the fleet train and base and depot ships.
4. Units of the Royal Indian Navy.
5. Units with Force W.
6. Other units assigned to the East Indies Fleet but nonoperational, not on station or on passage.
7. Other units nominated as reinforcements for the East Indies Fleet.
NB: The totals given in this table are subject to amendment in light of the material provided in appendix D.

THE BRITISH PACIFIC FLEET

	1	2	3	4	5	6	7	8	Total
Battleships	1	1	1	-	-	-	1	-	4
Fleet Carriers	4	1	-	-	-	-	1	-	6
Light Carriers	-	3	-	-	-	1	-	-	4
Escort Carriers	-	-	-	5	2	2	-	-	9
Light Cruisers	6	2	-	-	-	2	1	-	11
AA Ship	-	1	-	-	-	-	-	-	1
Destroyers	23	6	2	-	-	3	8	-	42
Submarines	-	-	23	-	-	4	2	-	29
Frigates	-	-	-	19	2	4	-	39	64
Sloops	-	-	-	7	-	7	2	5	21
Destroyer Escorts	-	-	-	-	-	7	-	5	12
Minelayers	-	-	2	-	-	1	-	-	3
Minesweepers	-	-	-	-	-	-	10	-	10
Danlayers	-	-	-	-	-	-	-	2	2
F/D Ships	-	-	-	-	-	-	-	5	5
Headquarters Ships	-	-	1	1	-	2	-	-	4
Boom Carriers	-	-	2	1	-	-	-	-	3
Netlayers	-	-	-	-	1	-	-	1	2
Deperming Ship	-	-	-	1	-	-	-	-	1
Depot Ships	-	-	3	1	-	-	-	-	4
Accommodation Ships	-	-	1	2	-	-	-	1	4
Transport	-	-	-	1	-	-	-	-	1
Targets Ships	-	-	1	-	-	1	-	-	2
Repair Ships	-	-	-	4	1	2	-	3	10
Maintenance Ships	-	-	-	3	-	1	-	4	8
Salvage Ships	-	-	-	2	-	1	-	-	3
Rescue Tugs	-	-	-	2	-	-	-	-	2
Tankers, Large/Fast	-	-	-	13	1	-	1	14	29
Tankers, Small	-	-	-	9	-	-	-	10	19
Water Carriers	-	-	-	-	2	-	1	-	3
Colliers	-	-	-	2	-	-	-	1	3
Issuing Ships	-	-	-	16	9	1	1	3	30
Stores Ships	-	-	-	2	5	-	1	2	10
Hospital Ships	-	-	-	2	2	1	-	-	5
Floating Docks	-	-	-	2	-	-	-	-	2
Others	-	-	-	-	-	-	-	2	2
Total	*34*	*14*	*36*	*95*	*25*	*40*	*29*	*97*	*370*

KEY

1. Task Force 37/Task Force 113.
2. Task Group 111.2.
3. Other units on station.
4. Task Force 112. Units at sea, Manus or advanced bases in the Pacific.
5. Other fleet train units on station.
6. Units en route for the Pacific, 15 August 1945.
7. Other units assigned to the British Pacific Fleet and the fleet train but nonoperational, not on station or not on passage.
8. Units nominated to serve as reinforcements for the British Pacific Fleet or in the fleet train.

COMBINED ORDERS OF BATTLE OF THE EAST INDIES AND BRITISH PACIFIC FLEETS

| | East Indies Fleet | | | Pacific Fleet | | | |
	1	2	3	4	5	6	Total
Battleships	2	-	-	3	-	1	6
Fleet Carriers	-	-	-	5	-	1	6
Light Carriers	-	-	-	3	-	1	4
Escort Carriers	14	2	-	-	7	2	25
Heavy Cruisers	3	1	-	-	-	-	4
Light Cruisers	5	3	-	8	-	3	19
Monitors	-	2	-	-	-	-	2
Gunboats	-	3	-	-	-	-	3
AA Ship	-	-	-	1	-	-	1
Destroyers	18	13	-	31	-	11	73
Submarines	13	-	-	23	-	6	42
Frigates	22	20	-	-	21	43	106
Sloops	10	1	-	-	7	14	32
Corvettes	15	2	-	-	-	-	17
Destroyer Escorts	6	-	15	-	-	12	33
Cutters	4	1	-	-	-	-	5
Escorts	4	-	-	-	-	-	4
Patrol Vessels	15	-	-	-	-	-	15
Minelayers	3	-	-	2	-	1	6
Minesweepers	29	10	-	-	-	10	49
Danlayers	3	-	-	-	-	2	5
F/D Ships	1	3	-	-	-	5	9
Headquarters Ships	-	-	-	1	1	2	4
LSH all types	4	-	-	-	-	-	4
LSI all types	13	-	-	-	-	-	13
Other landing ships	4	-	1	-	-	-	5
Boom Carriers	2	1	-	2	1	-	6
Netlayers	-	1	-	-	1	1	3
Deperming Ships	2	-	-	-	1	-	3
Survey Ships	8	-	-	-	-	-	8
RIN Training Ships	6	-	-	-	-	-	6
Depot Ships	8	-	-	3	1	-	12
Tenders	2	1	-	-	-	-	3
Accommodation Ships	1	-	-	1	2	1	5
Transport	-	-	-	-	1	-	1
Target Ships	1	-	-	1	-	1	3
Repair Ships	-	1	-	-	5	5	11
Maintenance Ships	3	9	-	-	3	5	20
Salvage Ships	1	1	-	-	2	1	5
Rescue Tugs	11	-	-	-	2	-	13
Tankers	-	-	-	-	14	15	29
Tankers, Small	-	-	-	-	9	10	19
Water Carriers	-	-	-	-	2	1	3
Colliers	-	-	-	-	2	1	3
Issuing Ships	-	-	-	-	25	5	30
Stores Ships	-	-	-	-	7	3	10
Hospital Ships	-	-	-	-	4	1	5
Floating Docks	-	-	-	-	2	-	2
Others	-	-	-	-	-	2	2
Total	*233*	*75*	*16*	*84*	*120*	*166*	*694*

Key
1. Units with the East Indies Fleet, escort formations, the fleet train, the Royal Indian Navy, and Force W, and base and depot ships.
2. Other units assigned to the East Indies Fleet but nonoperational, not on station or on passage.
3. Units nominated as reinforcements for the East Indies Fleet at the end of hostilities.
4. Task Force 37/Task Force 113, Task Group 111.2, and other units on station.
5. Task Force 112. Units at sea, Manus, or advanced bases in the Pacific and other fleet train units on station.
6. Units assigned to the British Pacific Fleet and the fleet train but nonoperational, not on station or not on passage; units en route for the Pacific, 15 August 1945; and units nominated to serve as reinforcements for the British Pacific Fleet or in the fleet train.

*   *   *

The totals include one ship, the *Penn*, counted twice, first as a destroyer with the East Indies Fleet and subsequently designated as an aircraft target ship earmarked for service with the British Pacific Fleet. She was at Trincomalee on 15 August 1945 and never went to the Pacific.

The totals given in this table with reference to the East Indies Fleet are subject to amendment in light of the material provided in Appendix D.

*   *   *

Errors and Omissions Excepted

Operation ZIPPER and the British Pacific Fleet

The *leitmotif* of this work has been that the British high command in 1943–44 had to make a choice between the rival claims of an Indian Ocean amphibious strategy and a fleet commitment in the central Pacific. The main line of argument developed in the text has been that limited national resources, specifically shipping and manpower resources, precluded simultaneous efforts in two different oceans, and that the size of forces that were in the two oceans had to be determined by the scale of shipping support that was available after minimum national demands were met. This was the explicit instruction given by the prime minister in his minute of 9 April 1944 to the Admiralty. The difficulty of complying with this instruction, given that a decision between the Indian and Pacific Oceans was not made for another four months, and the lack of definition of what these commitments would entail forms one of the themes of this book. Another theme developed in these later pages is that the British Pacific Fleet labored under all but impossible conditions, and that its performance in light of the difficulties, especially the logistical handicaps, under which it was obliged to operate, was very respectable.

The research for this work was completed between 1983 and 1988 and the doctoral text was written in 1989–90: the defense of the thesis was conducted on the forty-ninth anniversary of the fall of Singapore. In setting out the terms of reference of the thesis, October 1944 was chosen as the cutoff date on the grounds that after that month there were no major decisions that affected policy and deployment before the end of the war in August 1945. Obviously decisions were made and deployments ordered after October 1944 that resulted in formations and units making their way to the Far East before the end of hostilities, and sometimes at very short notice and very quickly: some of the men who came ashore at Akyab in January 1945 had served at Walcheren the previous November. But clearly this month and the demise of DRACULA was, or to this writer at the time of writing seemed to be, the time and occasion after which the basic framework of ighter-direction ships, three minesweeping flotillas, and eighteen auxiliary minesweepers, which together total fifty-four fleet units plus the minesweepers. This same report also stated that the amphibious forces committed to the operation numbered 12 LSH/LSI, 42 LST, 311 landing craft of all descriptions, and 112 merchantmen. The size of this force, and particularly the number of merchantmen involved in this operation, are somewhat surprising. Certainly, the scale of Operation ZIPPER is difficult to deduce from material in the public domain. The *Pink Lists* do not list the merchantmen under military control in Indian ports, while one of the two relevant Naval Staff histories does not make any reference to the operation other than to note that it was conducted, and the other does not afford ZIPPER even that dignity.[2] The fifth volume of the official history of the war against Japan contains a number of appendices that provide outlines of the ZIPPER force levels but the absence of a statement of overall numbers and the implication of planning status detracts from the significance of its contents.[3]

From the operational orders and call signs that were issued, it appears that Operation ZIPPER was to have involved the battleships *Nelson* and *Richelieu*, the light cruisers *Ceylon, Cleopatra, London, Nigeria,* and *Royalist,* the escort carriers *Ameer, Attacker, Begum, Emperor, Empress, Hunter, Khedive, Smiter, Stalker,* and *Trumpeter,* the fighter-direction ships *Boxer, Palomares,* and *Ulster Queen,* and the tender *F.D.T.13,* all available destroyers, escorts, and minesweepers, plus assorted minor craft. There was to be a fleet train of seven units, mostly mother ships for inshore vessels. The ships allocated to Force W were as follows, the designations being taken from the operational orders list:

Appendix B to ZIP—ONE. Part 4
Code Numbers of Red Ensign Ships

"A" Personnel Ships

P.1 *Almanzora,* P.2 *Antenor,* P.3 *Arawa,* P.4 *Aronda,* P.5 *Boissevan,* P.6 *Cheshire,* P.7 *Chitral,* P.9 *Circassia,* P.21 *Cilicia,* P.10 *Derbyshire,* P.11 *Devonshire,* P.12 *Dilwara,* P.13 *Dunera,* P.14 *Egra,* P.15 *Ekma,* P.16 *Empire Pride,* P.17 *Esperance Bay,* P.18 F.S. *Felix Rousell,* P.20 *Highland Brigade,* P.19 *Highland Chieftain,* P.23 *Highland Monarch,* P.22 *Indrapoera,* P.24 *Largs Bay,* P.25 (NZ) *Monowai,* P.26 *Moreton Bay,* P.27 *Nea Hellas,* P.28 (Dut) *Nieuw Holland,* P.29 *Orduna,* P.30 *Ormonde,* P.31 *Rajula,* P.32 *Ranchi,* P.33 *Salween,* P.34 *Sobieski,* P.35 *Staffordshire,* P.36 *Takliwa,* P.37 *Talma,* P.38 *Tamaroa,* P.8 (Dut) *Tegelberg,* P.39 *Worcestershire.*

"B" M.T. Ships

M.59 *Ammla,* M.18 *Baharistan,* M.53 *Carlton,* M.36 *City of Auckland,* M.14 *Empire Beauty,* M.32 *Empire Canning,* M.43 *Empire Capulet,* M.30 *Empire General,* M. 34 *Empire Guinevere,* M.25 *Empire Miranda,* M.19 *Empire Niger,* M.78 *Empire Rabaul,* M.41 *Empire Rani,* M.57 *Eskbank,* M.21

British policy was in place and which was not altered in the lifetir
war. The Arakan campaign and the reincarnation of DR/
April–May 1945 did not really change this state of affairs.

Thus excluded here was any consideration of Operation ZI
landings conducted in Malaya in September 1945 after the Japa
render, not least for the very obvious reason that it was conductec
end of hostilities. In any event, this writer experienced some diffi
researching an operation which is barely mentioned in the official
In the process of conversion from doctoral thesis into book form
this book added to itself various appendices, namely the comm
the Eastern and East Indies Fleets, the operational chronologie
orders of battle, in order to provide an account of events in the Ir
Pacific Oceans in the last twenty months of the war and in the v
followed Japan's surrender. On 22 February 1995 and more than s
after the manuscript was lodged with Naval Institute Press, hor
Naval Historical Branch, Ministry of Defence, brought the auth
tion to a ZIPPER file held in its operational archives. Although rep
the archives, the contents of these files have never been listed a
to have been untouched for at least eighteen years.

The file divides into two, a series of reports written after the
and *No. 80L/22/1944. Force "W" Orders. Office of Flag Officer, Fc
August 1945,* which appears to have been issued four days later. 1
uments could not be fully analyzed and assessed before this boo
press, but certain points need to be noted in terms of the integ
argument presented in this book.

Preliminary planning for ZIPPER began with the Combined Chi
issuing of a new directive to South East Asia Command on 3 Febr
that set its tasks as clearing Burma, liberating Malaya, and openin;
of Malacca to shipping. It was not until 12 May, however, that the J
of Staff indicated approval of proposed landings in Malaya sub
condition that such an undertaking involved no reduction of prepa
operations against the Japanese home islands. Three days earlier !
Asia Command had instructed its planners to proceed with detailec
and on the thirtieth the date of 9 September was settled for ZIPPER.
ing was to be followed by an advance to Johore and an assault on
in January 1946 (Operation MAILFIST). Shipping gathered for ZIP
make its way to the central Pacific in order to provide for the Brit
al corps that was to be part of Operation CORONET, the assault o
At best, such a schedule would seem to be somewhat stringent, I
this aside the reports and order of battle for ZIPPER makes intere
ing. The covering and support formations were suitably modest
Flag Officer's report of the operation stated the involvement of
warships and listed (without naming) two battleships, three ligl
eight escort carriers, sixteen destroyers, twenty-two frigates and sl

Floristan, M.33 *Fort Aklavik,* M.28 *Fort Chesterfield,* M.48 *Fort Enterprise,* M.47 *Fort Finlay,* M.46 *Fort Frontenac,* M.45 *Fort Gaspereau,* M.70 *Fort Glenora,* M.80 *Fort Hall,* M.76 *Fort La Joie,* M.50 *Fort Turtle,* M.12 *Frederick Banting,* M.15 *Geologist,* M.26 *Glen Affric,* M.51 *Gorgistan,* M.44 *Harpalyce,* M.22 *Havildar,* M.40 *Ikauna,* M.39 *Itaura,* M.38 *Itola,* M.37 *Itria,* M.79 *Kohistan,* M.23 *Lossiebank,* M.16 *Mahadevi,* M.17 *Malika,* M.35 *Ocean Angel,* M.52 *Ocean Gypsy,* M.49 *Ocean Pilgrim,* M.24 *Ocean Vestal,* M.68 *Ocean Viscount,* M.42 *Risaldar,* M.29 *Rivercrest,* M.62 *Samana,* M.60 *Samchess,* M.71 *Samconstant,* M.65 *Samdaring,* M.66 *Samfairy,* M.74 *Samfaithful,* M.77 *Samfield,* M.61 *Samfinn,* M.55 *Samflora,* M.1 *Samgara,* M.2 *Samgaudie,* M.3 *Samhain,* M.58 *Samharle,* M.11 *Samholt,* M.4 *Samlea,* M.72 *Samlorain,* M.64 *Samnethy,* M.10 *Samothrace,* M.69 *Sampford,* M.6 *Samrich,* M.9 *Samskern,* M.8 *Samspelga,* M.81 *Samsteel,* M.7 *Samsturdy,* M.75 *Samthar,* M.63 *Samtray,* M.56 *Samtremt,* M.5 *Samtroy,* M.13 *Samtruth,* M.54 *Stancleeve,* M.27 *Tamela,* M.31 *Trevaylor,* M.20 *Tweedbank,* M.73 *Welsh Prince,* M.67 *Weybank.*

"C" STORESHIPS
S.6 *Empire Meteor,* S.7 *Empire Prome,* S.1 *Esang,* S.2 *Eskbank,* S.8 *Fort Cadotte,* S.3 *Ocean Trader,* S.4 *Wosang,* S.5 *Wingsang.*

"D" MULE CARRIERS
H.2 *Gazana,* H.1 *Naringa,* H.3 *Nawab.*

"E" PETROL CARRIERS
Z.6 *Brockley Moor,* Z.5 *Cerion,* Z.1 *Empire Irving,* Z.2 *Ocean Valour,* Z.3 *Samdee,* Z.4 *Samburgh,* Z.7 *Samovar,* Z.8 *Trevose.*

"F" HOSPITAL SHIPS
A.3 *Amarapoera,* A.4 *Dorsetshire,* A.2 *Karapara,* A.7 *Llandovery Castle,* A.8 *Ophir,* A.6 *Somersetshire,* A.5 *Tairea.*

"G" HEAVY LIFT SHIPS
Y.6 *Belnor,* Y.2 *Belpareil,* Y.4 *Belfray,* Y.3 *Empire Byng,* Y.8 *Empire Elaine,* Y.1 *Empire Newfoundland,* Y.5 *Empire Viceroy,* Y.7 *La Pampa.*

CODE NUMBERS OF WHITE ENSIGN SHIPS
F.1 *Bulolo,* E.1 *Dewdale,* E.2 *Ennerdale,* B.8 *Glengyle,* B.1 *Glenroy,* F.4 *Largs,* B.9 *Llanstephan Castle,* F.3 *Nith,* B.6 *Persimmon,* B.4 *Princess Beatrix,* B.11 *Prins Albert,* B.5 *Queen Emma,* B.2 *Rocksand,* B.10 *Sainfoin,* B.3 *Sansovino,* B.7 *Sefton,* F.2 *Waveney.*

NB: The last list is included in ZIP—ONE, PART 4.

All lists in the original document are given both alphabetically and numerically: in this appendix the numerical sequence has been deleted in the interest of simplicity. The individual totals are A: 39, B: 81, C: 8, D: 3, E: 8, F: 7 and G: 8.

Before any comment can be made about the size and composition of the forces involved in Operation ZIPPER a number of observations need be made. First, the operational orders list appears to have double-counted one ship—the *Eskbank*—and to have misnamed or misspelled at least four others.[4] It also appears that the orders list either missed a number of units or these units were added after the orders were issued: the fleet train members *Carpio, Empire Elaine, Maid Marion, Mull of Galloway, Palestinian Prince, Philomel,* and an unnamed R.F.A. tanker are not listed, nor are the *Barpeta, Barracuda, Empire Ensign,* and *Highway.* These ships were employed on ZIPPER, but it must be noted that a number of units that had been earmarked for this operation were absent: the naval LSI *Glengyle, Llanstephen Castle, Princess Beatrix,* and *Queen Emma,* eight LST, twenty-four LCI, the *Dewdale* (with fourteen LCM), and the *Smiter* were detached and served with the forces that proceeded to Hong Kong, Penang, and Singapore. There is very considerable difficulty in trying to reconcile orders, call signs, and report lists and to confirm the numbers involved in ZIPPER.

Second, the fleet train involved in ZIPPER was decidedly modest. The provision of a fleet train for the Indian Ocean was in accordance with Churchill's directive of 9 April 1944 and there was a fleet train in the Indian Ocean in 1944, witness the attack on Soerabaja. Moreover, it must be noted that the East Indies Fleet and its amphibious force needed a substantial tail: Trincomalee, for all its physical attractiveness, was abysmally provided. Third, the shipping allocated to Force W has to be considered in terms of eventual redeployment to the central Pacific. Fourth, it should be noted that not all the ships named in the orders list were on station: certainly there were two units in British home waters, one as late as 11 August, and it appears that a number of landing ships that were to take part in the operation were en route when the ZIPPER orders were issued.

But these caveats notwithstanding, what the order of battle would suggest is that the difficulties of the British Pacific Fleet were compounded by decisions that resulted in the concentration in the Indian Ocean of shipping that would have represented a margin of near-luxury for Fraser's command. The logistical difficulties of the British Pacific Fleet were fourfold— a lack of numbers of ocean-going units; often forgotten or overlooked, the diversity and lack of homogeneity of what ocean-going units were available; the lack of shipping to work the routes between Australia and the advance bases; and the lack of lighters in the advance bases. It must be noted that at least some of the ships in the Indian Ocean and used in ZIPPER could not have eased the problems of the British Pacific Fleet had they made their separate ways to the Pacific rather than gathered in the Indian Ocean: the transports and landing ships were of little or no account in this particular part of the equation. But what is notable about the Red Ensign shipping employed on ZIPPER is its scale in terms of the number of ships, the size and relative newness of many of the ships, and their relative homogeneity. It would appear from the operational orders that no fewer than thirty Sams, eleven Forts, and seven Oceans were involved in this operation and thus held in the Indian Ocean when the carrier force was off the Japanese home islands. These were American- and British-built Liberty ships, and certainly possessed a standardization that TF 112 lacked. Moreover, if not ideal many of the landing craft could have been pressed into service in the advance bases.

Very clearly a certain caution needs be exercised in any consideration of such numbers and types: obviously the Indian Ocean had legitimate requirements and the needs of the British Pacific Fleet were not absolute and all-embracing. But given the priority supposedly afforded the British Pacific Fleet, the basis of such an assembly of shipping in the Indian Ocean in 1945 is somewhat hard to discern, not least because it is difficult to believe that the military shipping assembled in the Indian Ocean for ZIPPER represented an irreducible minimum consistent with the Pacific Fleet priority. Indeed, raising an amphibious force of any significant size in the Indian Ocean begs an obvious question: the British Chiefs' of Staff decision to raise Force W for service in the Indian Ocean was taken in October 1944, a somewhat strange state of affairs given the cancellation of DRACULA though perhaps not inconsistent with the anticipated freeing of amphibious shipping from European waters and the state of the landing ships and craft in the Indian Ocean at this time. It is not that at least some of the shipping held in the Indian Ocean could not have been used to effect in the Pacific, especially if the American practice of converting Liberty ships to oilers had been followed. When one remembers the desperate state of the British Pacific Fleet and its fleet train by August 1945, one wonders about the process of logic whereby South East Asia Command was so indulged, though one would note that the men committed to ZIPPER were certainly not pampered: the conditions on many of the transports were deplorable and one Army unit sailed for Malaya with no medical supplies other than the contents of one haversack, and was not alone in being so appalling provided.

But the basic points that emerge from even a cursory examination of the ZIPPER figures nevertheless stand and must be recounted, even though on four separate counts they would appear not to be wholly consistent with the basic arguments carried in the pages of this work. First, it would seem that the East Indies Fleet and South East Asia Command were provided with shipping on a scale considerably greater than can be reconciled if not with operational need then certainly with the implications of the decisions of August–September 1944. Second, the decisions that so provided for the Indian Ocean must have been taken, indeed were taken, after DRACULA's cancellation in October 1944: it would appear that Churchill after October 1944 must have secured his way with regard to an Indian Ocean amphibious strategy in a way that contradicts the logic of the pre–October 1944 policy deliberations. Third, the British Chiefs' of Staff estimate of shipping requirements for ZIPPER was issued on 18 May and on 7 June South East Asia Command was advised by London that the merchantmen requirement could be met: on 11 July SEAC was informed that its LST requirement would be met, if only by the arrival of units on station during August. Given the lead times involved in planning, the issuing of orders, and deployment, it must follow that the decisions made with reference to merchantmen must have been taken in the period between February and early May. Fourth, and by extension, it would seem that if the Indian Ocean could have been so provided, then the same ships, with equal facility, could have been dispatched to the Pacific, and it would appear, therefore, that the British Pacific Fleet could have been better provided with support shipping than was the case. It would seem that the concentration of shipping for ZIPPER was achieved at the expense of the British Pacific Fleet and that the latter's problems were, in part at least, consciously inflicted and not simply the result of circumstance. Nevertheless, two cautionary notes need be lodged because these ZIPPER conclusions cannot be regarded as definitive. The basic argument of this book would not seem to be jeopardized by the ZIPPER figures: October 1944 did indeed represent the month after which decisions could not be effected before the end of the war, though this is primarily negative and borders on semantics. More substantially, even if the fleet train and support shipping in South East Asia Command had been concentrated in the Pacific, it is difficult, if not impossible, to see how the oiler problems of British carrier forces could have been eased. Whatever the number of ships that might have been used in the Pacific but for their commitment in the Indian Ocean, it seems unlikely that this number represented the margin of administrative security that Fraser's fleet lacked in summer 1945, and if this was the case then such numbers could not have represented the greater margin that would have been needed for the British Pacific Fleet off Kyushu come October 1945. What is clear, however, is that a very considerable pool of shipping was held in the Indian Ocean at a time when the British Pacific Fleet's operations were hampered for want of an adequate fleet train, and this concentration of shipping with South East Asia Command hardly seems to accord with the priority afforded the British Pacific Fleet in 1944 and with the terms of the Joint Chiefs of Staff caveat of 12 May 1945.

The author would acknowledge his gratitude to Naval Historical Branch, Ministry of Defense, and specifically to David Brown, for bringing the existence and contents of this file to his attention and in time to permit the inclusion of this appendix.

On a lighter note, one would conclude that en route for Malaya one ship had to return to port after reporting that she had hit an underwater object. The damage control party found, however, that the cause of distress appeared to have been that the order issued in port to load field guns had been taken literally and that the movement of the ship had induced an accidental discharge. When all ships were asked to report whether they had likewise transgressed, two denied having done so on the grounds that their Army officers had provided assurance that the Bofors had never been classified as a field gun.

Maps

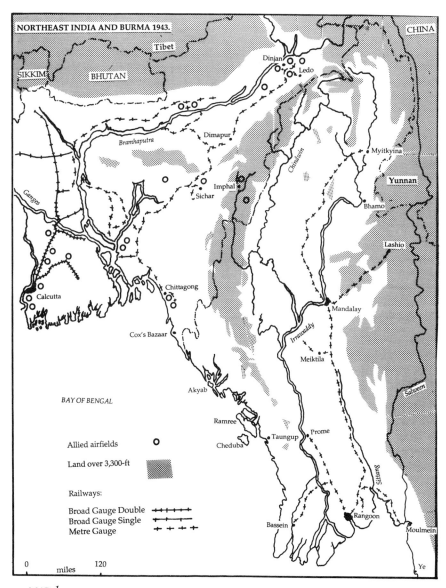

NORTHEAST INDIA AND BURMA 1943.

Tibet

CHINA

SIKKIM

BHUTAN

Dinjan

Ledo

Bramhaputra

Dimapur

Chindwin

Myitkyina

Yunnan

Ganges

Imphal

Sichar

Bhamo

Lashio

Chittagong

Mandalay

Cox's Bazaar

Irrawaddy

Meiktila

Akyab

BAY OF BENGAL

Saluween

Ramree

Allied airfields ⭕

Taungup

Prome

Cheduba

Land over 3,300-ft

Railways:

Broad Gauge Double ┼┼┼┼┼
Broad Gauge Single ┼──┼──┼
Metre Gauge ┼ ┼ ┼ ┼

Rangoon

Bassein

Moulmein

Sittang

0   120
  miles

Ye

MAP 1

219

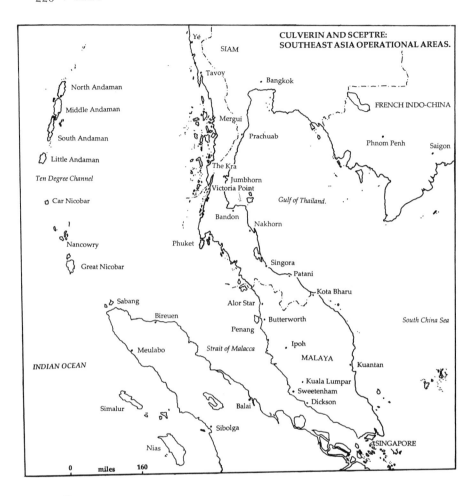

North Andaman

Middle Andaman

South Andaman

Little Andaman

Ten Degree Channel

Car Nicobar

Nancowry

Great Nicobar

Sabang

Bireuen

Meulabo

INDIAN OCEAN

Simalur

Nias

Sibolga

Balai

Strait of Malacca

Ye

SIAM

Tavoy

Bangkok

Mergui

Prachuab

The Kra

Jumbhorn

Victoria Point

Bandon

Gulf of Thailand.

Nakhorn

Phuket

Singora

Patani

Kota Bharu

Alor Star

Butterworth

Penang

Ipoh

MALAYA

Kuala Lumpar

Sweetenham

Dickson

Kuantan

CULVERIN AND SCEPTRE:
SOUTHEAST ASIA OPERATIONAL AREAS.

FRENCH INDO-CHINA

Phnom Penh

Saigon

South China Sea

SINGAPORE

0   miles   160

MAP 2

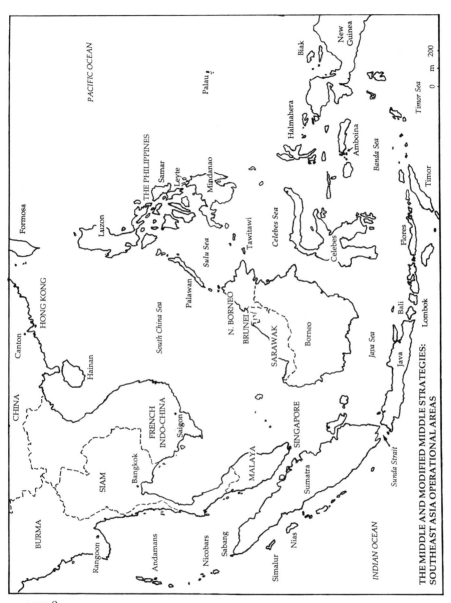

THE MIDDLE AND MODIFIED MIDDLE STRATEGIES:
SOUTHEAST ASIA OPERATIONAL AREAS

MAP 3

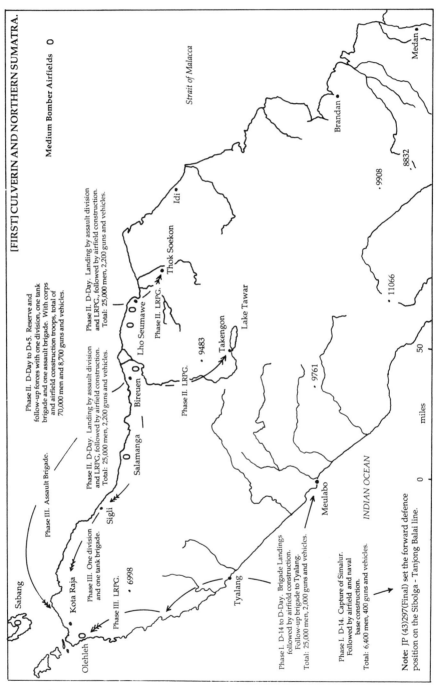

[FIRST] CULVERIN AND NORTHERN SUMATRA.

Medium Bomber Airfields O

Phase II. D-Day to D+5. Reserve and
follow-up forces with one division, one tank
brigade and one assault brigade. With corps
and airfield construction troops, total of
70,000 men and 8,700 guns and vehicles.

Phase III. Assault Brigade.

Phase II. D-Day. Landing by assault division
and LRPG, followed by airfield construction.
Total: 25,000 men, 2,200 guns and vehicles.

Phase II. D-Day. Landing by assault division
and LRPG., followed by airfield construction.
Total: 25,000 men, 2,200 guns and vehicles.

Phase III. One division
and one tank brigade.

Phase III. LRPG.

Phase II. LRPG.

Phase II. LRPG.

Phase I. D-14 to D-Day. Brigade Landings
followed by airfield construction.
Follow-up brigade to Tyalang.
Total: 25,000 men, 2,000 guns and vehicles.

Phase I. D-14. Capture of Simalur.
Followed by airfield and naval
base construction.
Total: 6,400 men, 400 guns and vehicles.

Note: JP (43)297(Final) set the forward defence
position on the Sibolga – Tanjong Balai line.

Sabang

Kota Raja

Olehleh

Sigli

Salamanga

Bireuen

Lho Seumawe

Thok Soekon

Idi

Takengon

Lake Tawar

Tyalang

Meulabo

Brandan

Medan

Strait of Malacca

INDIAN OCEAN

· 6998

· 9483

· 9761

· 11066

· 9908

· 8832

miles

0   50

0

MAP 4

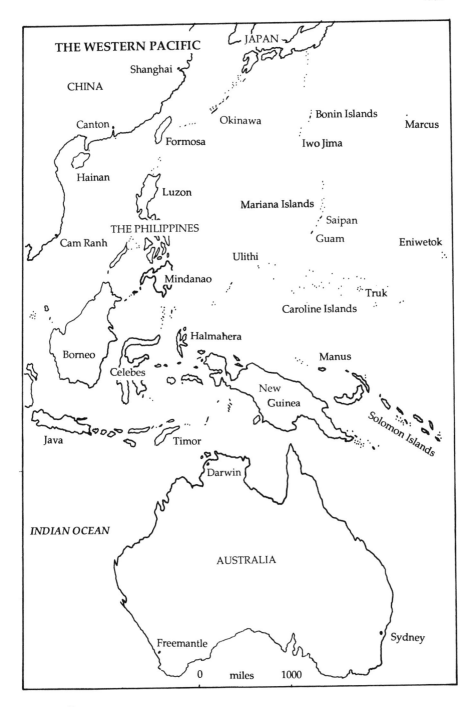

THE WESTERN PACIFIC

JAPAN

CHINA

Shanghai

Canton

Okinawa

Bonin Islands

Marcus

Formosa

Iwo Jima

Hainan

Luzon

Mariana Islands

THE PHILIPPINES

Saipan

Cam Ranh

Guam

Eniwetok

Ulithi

Mindanao

Truk

Caroline Islands

Halmahera

Borneo

Manus

Celebes

New
Guinea

Solomon Islands

Java

Timor

Darwin

INDIAN OCEAN

AUSTRALIA

Freemantle

Sydney

0   miles   1000

MAP 5

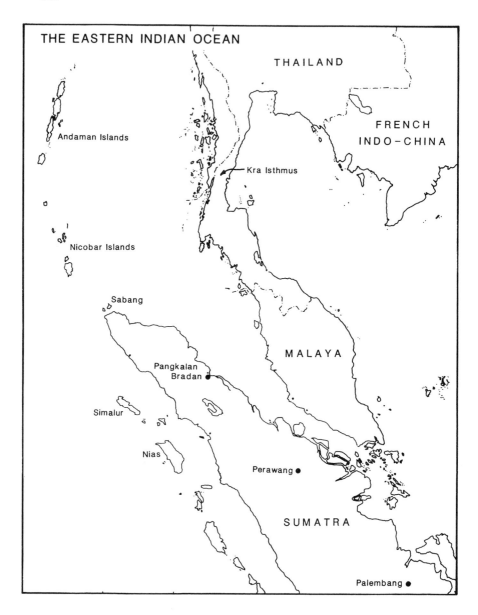

THE EASTERN INDIAN OCEAN

THAILAND

FRENCH
INDO–CHINA

Andaman Islands

Kra Isthmus

Nicobar Islands

Sabang

MALAYA

Pangkalan
Bradan •

Simalur

Nias

Perawang •

SUMATRA

Palembang •

MAP 6

Notes

INTRODUCTION

1. The others were the U.S. Congress and the U.S. State Department and, of course, Japan itself.

2. American engineering capacity confounded British calculations in the sense that the road was pushed through to Yunnan much faster than the British had calculated, but, ironically, the quickened pace of the American advances across the Pacific did not affect the basic correctness of the British argument.

3. It should be noted, however, that part of the problem was that these emerged in succession: there was never any single occasion when all issues could be seen and settled but the Anglo-American policymaking process took the form of a series of "encounter battles." Undoubtedly, this aspect of Anglo-American difficulties was very real in that successive difficulties bred mutual exasperation.

4. Preparations for amphibious operations in the Indian Ocean could only proceed if specialist troops were diverted from northeast India, and the Americans were always wary of endorsing any amphibious proposal for fear that a closing down of Upper Burma options in order to provide for an amphibious operation would be followed by the latter being abandoned at some stage or another with the result that no offensive operation at all would be staged in this theater.

5. For those unfamiliar with the game of cricket, the Bodyline Tour of 1932–33 was a series "played" in Australia between that country and England that retains a certain notoriety even after sixty years. England won.

CHAPTER ONE
A VERY DANGEROUS CONDITION

1. Grace Person Hayes, *History of the Joint Chiefs of Staff in World War II: The War against Japan* (Annapolis, Md.: Naval Institute Press, 1982), 433.

2. CAB 80.73.489: COS (43) 489 (0), 31 August 1943, QUADRANT, Part V, CCS 319/5, 24 August 1943, Report to the President and the Prime Minister of the final agreed Summary of Conclusions reached by the Combined Chiefs

of Staff. (The bombing plan was ordered under para. 44; the Twelve-Month Plan under para. 22; and the studies under paras. 37–41 and 43. The Moulmein operation was not named SCEPTRE until 30 September 1943. See CAB 119.21.13: Memorandum of 30 September 1943 from War Cabinet Office to Inter-Service Security Board.)

3. CAB 105.43.1144: Signal of 27 August 1944 from Joint Staff Mission to Chiefs of Staff London.

4. CAB 88.55: CPS 86/D, 26 August 1943, Preparation of Studies on the Defeat of Japan.

5. CAB 105.43.1184: Signal of 18 September 1943 from Joint Staff Mission to Chiefs of Staff London.

6. This paper was finalized on 10 September. See Wesley Frank Craven and James Lea Cate, eds., *The Army Air Force in World War II*, vol. 5, *The Pacific: MATTERHORN to Nagasaki, June 1944 to August 1945* (Chicago: University of Chicago Press, 1953), 19.

7. CAB 80.73.449: COS (43) 499 (0), 31 August 1943, The War against Japan.

8. CAB 122.1076.15: Signal of 25 August 1943 from QUADRANT to War Cabinet Office.

9. CAB 119.313.1: JP (43) 295 and JIC (43) 354 (0), 27 August 1943, Operations in South East Asia in 1943–1944.

10. CAB 88.55: JP (43) 295 (Revise) and JIC (43) 354 (Revise), 4 September 1943, Operations in South East Asia in 1943–1944.

11. Of the two LYNCHPIN was clearly the weak sister. It appears to have figured little in British deliberations because of operational considerations. It was limited to a March 1944 slot, which meant a 9 December 1943 deadline, and could not be exploited by a movement to the mainland before the onset of the monsoon. Planning anticipated occupation of northern Ramree alone, and this meant that the island's only airfield was outside the anticipated defensive perimeter. See W.O. 203.454: Executive Planning Section Paper, dated 7 December 1943, LYNCHPIN, Capture of Ramree.

12. CAB 84.56 and CAB 119.81.A.1: JP (43) 309 (Final), 3 September 1943, Operations in South East Asia, 1943–1944. This is a draft for the signal that was sent to India Command, the signal itself, No. 186, apparently not being present in the available files. The draft indicated that India Command by early October was to complete four operational studies, namely northern Sumatra in spring 1944, with offensive operations in Upper Burma beginning in February but with BULLFROG and LYNCHPIN canceled; northern Sumatra with BULLFROG or CULVERIN (i.e., Malaya); Moulmein or the Kra, with Upper Burma; and Malaya and Singapore, with Upper Burma and the Arakan.

Subsequently four Joint Planning Staff India papers, nos. 86 (25 August 1943, Recapture of the Andaman Islands), 93(A) (13 September 1943, Operations against Sumatra, Spring 1944), 100(A) (12 September 1943, Operations against Burma, 1944–1945), and 101(A) (12 September, Operations in the Moulmein area or Isthmus, Spring 1944) were taken to London and consolidated as JP (43)340. Dated 23 September 1943, the respective prospects of these operations were rated as good, unable to judge, recommended, and uninviting. See CAB 84.57.

These studies were obviously not those ordered, and a certain confusion was caused by the fact that whereas Delhi considered TRIUMPHANT in terms of an overland offensive only, London examined this operation with amphibious operations in the Arakan and an airborne landing at Rangoon added. India was thus ordered to conform to London's revised terms of reference. See CAB 119.22.6: Draft of signal for India Command, dated 21 September 1943 and prepared by A.E.M. and sent to Cornwall-Jones for consideration by Directors of Plans. CAB 119.1076.24: Signal of 23 September 1943 from War Cabinet Office to India Command.

13. This study must have been ordered under JP (43) 304 (TofR), which presumably was issued on 4 September 1943. Neither the originating document nor the final report is present in the PRO files, but reference to JP (43) 304 (Final) is made in JP (43) 322 (E) (TofR) and in JP (43) 322 (Final).

14. CAB 105.68.344: Signal of 16 September 1943 from Joint Planning Staff London to Joint Planning Staff Washington.

15. CAB 88.55: JP (43) 297 (E) (TofR), 4 September 1943, Operations against Northern Sumatra, FIRST CULVERIN.

16. CAB 88.55 and CAB 119.22.1: JP (43) 298 (0) (TofR), 4 September 1943, Operations Southward from Northern Burma; JP (43) 300 (0) (TofR), 4 September 1943, Operations for the Direct Capture of Singapore.

17. CAB 88.55 and CAB 119.22.4: JP (43) 299 (S) (TofR), 4 September 1943, Operations through Moulmein and the Kra Isthmus.

18. CAB 88.55: JP (43) 311 (S) (TofR), 4 September 1943, Operation CULVERIN.

19. CAB 88.55: JP (43) 313 (S) (TofR), 4 September 1943, Defeat of Japan, Twelve-Month Plan.

20. It must be noted, however, that during the summer and in the weeks immediately before QUADRANT the Navy had persuaded Arnold to side with it over the Marianas question. As a consequence the Army Air Force problem was not quite so severe as might first appear: the Navy was prepared to concede the AAF a strategic role after the Marianas were taken as the price of AAF support for this operation.

21. Winston S. Churchill, *The Second World War,* vol. 5, *Closing the Ring* (London: Cassell and Co., 1952), 108, 122–23, 128.

22. CAB 122.1075: Signal of 11 September 1943 from Planning Staff London to Joint Planning Staff Washington.

23. CAB 88.55: CPS 86/1, 13 September 1943, Studies on the Defeat of Japan, Interim Report by the Combined Staff Planners. (The copy of this report in the PRO file has the word "when" underlined and a question mark placed against it in the margin.)

24. CAB 105.71.327: Signal of 14 September 1943 from Joint Staff Mission to War Cabinet Office London.

25. CAB 122.1075: Signal of 14 September 1943 from Joint Planning Staff Washington to Joint Planning Staff London.

26. Hayes, *History of the Joint Chiefs of Staff,* 494.

27. Craven and Cate, eds., *The Army Air Force in World War II,* 5:19.

28. Hayes, *History of the Joint Chiefs of Staff,* 496.

29. Ibid., 494–95.

30. CAB 122.1074.12: Minutes of heads of delegation meeting (Joint Staff Mission) of 16 September 1943.

31. CAB 122.1074.14: Minutes of Combined Chiefs of Staff meeting of 17 September 1943.

32. CAB 122.1074.11: CPS 343, 16 September 1943, Studies for the Defeat of Japan. (This paper is also given in CAB 84.56 as JP (43) 329, 16 September 1943, Studies on the Defeat of Japan, Large-scale Development of the Air Route to China.)

33. There remain, however, other possible explanations of British behavior, of which two may be noted. First, at this time there were many issues dividing the American and British high commands, and it may be that British reticence on 17 September was simply a negotiating tactic, the air plan being for the British a minor matter in comparison to other issues that were at hand. Second, Anglo-American differences over the air plan were in part the result of the British not having access to the latest American aircraft production reports, which obviously formed the basis of American confidence that an air plan would indeed work. Given the informal contacts between members of the Joint Staff Mission and their opposite numbers it is possible that between the eleventh and seventeenth these reports were made available to the Joint Staff Mission.

34. BROOKE 3.A.IX: Brooke diary entry of 1 October 1943. F.O. 954.6.689: Letter of 1 October 1943 from Craigie to Eden.

35. See, for example, CAB 79.64.204, 217, and 219: Minutes of Chiefs of Staff meetings of 1, 16, and 17 September 1943 respectively.

36. A new study was ordered with JP (43) 337 (E) (TofR), 21 September 1943, Operations through Moulmein and the Kra Isthmus, and finalized as JP (43) 337 (Final), 6 October 1943, An Attack through Moulmein and the Kra Isthmus in the Direction of Bangkok, SCEPTRE. See CAB 84.56. At the same time, however, a SCEPTRE report was included as an appendix to JP (44) 298 (Final), 8 October 1943, Operations Southward from Northern Burma, TRI-UMPHANT. See CAB 84.56 and CAB 119.22.11.

37. CAB 84.56 and CAB 119.23.12: JP (43) 325 (0) (TofR), JIC (43) 384 (0), 16 September 1943, Operations for the Capture of the Andaman Islands. (The terms of reference of this directive initially covered the Andamans and the Nicobars but the latter was deleted before the directive was issued formally. See CAB 119.21.6: Memorandum of 20 September 1943 from Strategical Planning Section to Executive Planning Section.)

38. CAB 84.56: JP (43) 322 (E) (TofR), 11 September 1943, Re-organization of Command in India and South East Asia, Estimate of Naval Forces. (In fact, the conclusion of Admiralty planners was that not merely could FIRST CULVERIN in 1944 not proceed but that unless certain administrative measures were taken in hand immediately, no major operation could be undertaken even in 1945. See ELLIS, 3, Appendix 23: Minute of 10 September 1943, Future Allocation of LCT, and extract of memorandum of 14 September 1943 from DRO[CO] to ACNS[H].)

39. CAB 84.56: JP (43) 322 (Final), 16 September 1943, Re-organization of Command in India and South East Asia, Estimate of Naval Forces.

40. CAB 119.81.E.1: JP (43) 300 (Final), 4 September 1943, Operations for the Direct Capture of Singapore, on the Assumption that Northern Sumatra is Previously Captured.

41. CAB 119.21.10: Unsigned and undated memorandum: Operations through Moulmein and the Kra Isthmus, Differences between JIC India and JIC London. CAB 119.22.10: Unsigned and undated memorandum: Operations Southward from Northern Burma in November 1943, Differences between JIC India and JIC London. (The directive of 27 September 1943 that recalled the second of these two papers indicates that the memorandum was issued on the thirteenth.)

42. CAB 84.56: EPS (43) 455/JP (43) 297 (E) (Draft), 16 September 1943, Operation FIRST CULVERIN, Memorandum by the Executive Planning Staff.

43. CAB 119.18.26: JP (43) 326 (E), 16 September 1943, Operation FIRST CULVERIN. (Apart from the revised conclusion, this paper differed from the other by the inclusion of various annexes dealing with CULVERIN variants as examined at QUADRANT.)

44. CAB 84.56: JP (43) 318 (Final), 16 September 1943, Operations in Northern Burma, 1943–1944.

45. CAB 119.81.C.7: Summary of Directors of Plans meeting of 16 September with Chiefs of Staff.

46. CAB 119.38.17: Unsigned and undated memorandum: Summary of Planning. (From its contents this paper would seem to have been compiled on or about the fourteenth to serve as a briefing paper for the Directors of Plans, it being their practice to meet with the Joint Planning Staff before briefing the Chiefs of Staff.)

47. CAB 119.38.8: Signal of 6 September 1943 from GHQ India to War Cabinet Office.

48. CAB 122.1074.13: Signal of 16 September 1943 from Joint Planning Staff London to Joint Planning Staff Washington.

49. There is no indication in the record of this meeting that this statement of British views was presented.

50. CAB 79.64.217 and W.O. 106.4618a.56: Minutes of Chiefs of Staff meeting of 16 September 1943 and discussion of signal of 4 September 1943 from Commander-in-Chief India to War Cabinet Office.

51. CAB 84.6.5: Minutes of Joint Planning Staff meeting of 4 February 1943.

52. Such as the Andamans study, which was authorized this day as a result of this meeting. (This particular study was to be completed by the two officers sent to London by India Command. See AIR 9.485.3.)

53. CAB 105.68.344: Signal of 16 September 1943 from Joint Planning Staff London to Joint Planning Staff Washington.

54. CAB 84.56: JP (43) 327 (Final), 16 September 1943, Plans for the Defeat of Japan. (The British planners had first suggested biweekly summary papers and plans being exchanged by the American and British planners before being passed to respective Directors in JP [43] 306 [Final], 31 August 1943, Combined Planning. Seemingly nothing came of this proposal, which might have avoided the problems that now beset the British planning effort. See CAB 84.56.)

55. CAB 105.43.1191, CAB 105.43.1199, and CAB 105.44.1201: Signals of 18, 22, and 23 September respectively from Joint Staff Mission to War Cabinet Office.

56. CAB 105.44.1203: Signal of 25 September from Joint Staff Mission to War Cabinet Office.

57. The planners recognized this in JP (43) 339 (Final), 28 September 1943, Operations in Southeast Asia, Aide Memoire by the Joint Planning Staff, and asked for a decision on policy to be deferred until the terms of the Twelve-Month Plan were known. By the time they did so, however, it was too late. See CAB 84.56.

58. CAB 79.64.219: Minutes of Chiefs of Staff meeting of 17 September 1943. CAB 79.65.227: Minutes of Chiefs of Staff meeting of 27 September 1943, and discussion of JP (43) 328 (Final), 24 September 1943, Preparation of India as a Base. CAB 122.1074.35: Signal of 2 October 1943 from Joint Planning Staff London to Joint Planning Staff Washington.

59. BROOKE 3.A.IX: Brooke diary entry of 16 September 1943. (Brooke's diary contains just three references, two of which were *en passant*, to matters relating to the Japanese war in the whole of September 1943.)

60. Hayes, *History of the Joint Chiefs of Staff*, 483–84.

61. CAB 105.1075: Signal of 15 September 1943 from War Cabinet Officer to Joint Staff Mission.

62. PREM 3.167.7.47: Circular of 7 September 1943 from Churchill to members of the QUADRANT party.

63. CAB 88.3: Minutes of meeting held by the president and the prime minister with the Combined Chiefs of Staff, the White House, on 9 September 1943. CAB 105.43.1169: Signal of 10 September 1943 from Joint Staff Mission to Chiefs of Staff London. CAB 84.56: JP (43) 321 (S) (TofR), 10 September 1943, A Memorandum by the Prime Minister.

64. CAB 84.53: JP (43) 204 (S) (TofR), 2 June 1943, Defeat of Japan and Employment of British Naval Forces released from the Mediterranean when the Italian Fleet has been knocked out.

65. CAB 79.70.50, CAB 119.17.36, and CAB 122.1077.26: Minutes of Chiefs of Staff meeting of 17 February 1944 with Directors of Plans. CAB 119.79.108: JAP (44) 24 (Final), 15 April 1944, Potentialities of India as a Base.

66. PREM 3.163.7.32: Signal of 11 September 1943 from the Admiralty to QUADRANT.

67. PREM 3.163.7.27 and 25: Signals of 11 and 13 September 1943 respectively from QUADRANT to the Admiralty.

68. CAB 105.71.330: Signal of 18 September 1943 from Joint Planning Staff Washington to Joint Planning Staff London.

69. CAB 84.55: CPS 87, 9 September 1943, Review of the Strategic Situation in the Light of the Italian Collapse. Hayes, *History of the Joint Chiefs of Staff,* 472–73.

70. PREM 3.163.7.5: Minute of 3 October 1943 from Admiralty to Churchill. PREM 3.163.7.3: Minute of 4 October from Churchill to Admiralty.

71. CAB 105.68.354: Signal of 24 September 1943 from Joint Planning Staff London to Joint Planning Staff Washington.

72. CAB 105.71.343: Signal of 8 October 1943 from Joint Planning Staff Washington to Joint Planning Staff London. (The point was more or less the same as that made by the Combined Staff Planners on the day that Churchill made the offer. See CAB 88.55.87: Minutes of Combined Staff Planners meeting of 9 September 1943.)

73. CAB 122.1076.27: Minutes of Chiefs of Staff meeting 27 September 1943. CAB 69.5.65 and PREM 3.1.63.7.6: Minutes of Defence Committee meeting of 28 September 1943.

74. Maurice Matloff and Edwin M. Snell, *Strategic Planning for Coalition Warfare, 1943–1944* (Washington, D.C.: Department of the Army, 1959), 292.

75. CAB 105.71.343: Signal of 8 October 1943 from Joint Planning Staff Washington to Joint Planning Staff London. CAB 105.68.365: Signal of 11 October 1943 from Joint Planning Staff London to Joint Planning Staff Washington.

76. AIR 9.370.13, CAB 105.71.342, and CAB 122.1075: Signal of 7 October 1943 from Strategical Planning Section personnel (London) in Washington to Directors of Plans.

77. CAB 122.1075: Signal of 18 October 1943 from Joint Planning Staff Washington to Joint Planning Staff London.

78. CAB 105.71.361: Signal of 18 October 1943 from Joint Staff Mission to War Cabinet Office.

79. CAB 122.1075: Signal of 24 October 1943 from Joint Planning Staff Washington to Joint Planning Staff London.

80. CAB 88.55: CPS 86/2, 25 October 1943, Studies on the Defeat of Japan, The Defeat of Japan within Twelve Months after the Defeat of Germany, Interim Report by Combined Staff Planners.

81. CAB 122.1075: Signal of 23 October 1943 from Joint Planning Staff Washington to Joint Planning Staff London.

82. CAB 122.1075: Signal of 28 October 1943 from Joint Planning Staff Washington to Joint Planning Staff London: summary of Combined Staff Planners meeting held that day.

83. CAB 88.55: CPS 86/2, 25 October 1943, Studies on the Defeat of Japan, The Defeat of Japan within Twelve Months after the Defeat of Germany, Interim Report by Combined Staff Planners. (The outline calculations and planning of the Marianas operation are set out in the appendix of this report.)

84. CAB 105.71.361: Signal of 18 October 1943 from Joint Planning Staff Washington to Joint Planning Staff London.

85. CAB 105.71.370 and 373: Signals of 23 and 24 October 1943 from Joint Staff Mission to War Cabinet Office. (Formal submission of these options was made in CPS 86/2.)

86. CAB 122.1075: Enclosure to CPS 86/3 dated 8 November 1943.

87. CAB 105.68.371 and CAB 122.1075: Signals of 18 October 1943 from Joint Planning Staff London to Joint Planning Staff Washington. CAB 105.71.350: Signal of 18 October 1943 from Joint Planning Staff Washington to Joint Planning Staff London.

88. CAB 122.1075: Signal of 24 October 1943 from Joint Planning Staff Washington to Joint Planning Staff London.

89. CAB 122.1075: Summary of Combined Staff Planners meeting of 28 October 1943.

90. CAB 105.71.384: Signal of 29 October 1943 from Joint Planning Staff Washington to Joint Planning Staff London.

91. The American offer of support for a British carrier force that entered the Pacific by mid-1944 is surprising on several counts, not least because of the place in national demonology—both American and British—that the Royal Navy held in the Ernest J. King order of creation. It is also somewhat surprising in light of the fact that the American offer and the attendant discussions took place after the less than auspicious sojourn of the *Victorious* in the southwest Pacific in 1943.

The *Victorious* was detached from the Home Fleet for service in the Pacific in December 1942 in order to supplement an American carrier task force in the southwest Pacific severely weakened by its losses of that year. She arrived at Pearl Harbor in March 1943 but did not relieve the *Enterprise* on station at Noumea until May, having been delayed by the inevitable exercises off Hawaii but also by having to strip furnishing not fireproofed to American standards, by having to be twice refitted with stronger arrester gear, and by a fire. Her time in the southwest Pacific seems to have been less than happy, her service alongside the *Saratoga* being notable for the revelation of British inferiority to the Americans in terms of carrier aircraft and operational technique. Certainly many of the problems of operating American and British carriers together, and even of having a British task group in theater, must have become apparent in the time that the *Victorious* was in the southwest Pacific. Against such an unpropitious background the American offer to support a British carrier task group in the central Pacific seems somewhat curious: on the other hand, the experience of working with the *Victorious* may be the reason why the self-supporting provision was stressed and may provide partial explanation of why the offer was allowed to lapse.

92. CAB 79.64.221: Minutes of Chiefs of Staff meeting of 20 September 1943 and discussion of signal of 18 September 1943 from Commander-in-Chief India to War Cabinet Office.

93. CAB 79.64.224: Minutes of Chiefs of Staff meeting of 23 September 1943 with Directors of Plans.

94. CAB 79.65.227: Minutes of Chiefs of Staff meeting of 27 September 1943.

95. ADM 205.27 and PREM 3.163.7.15–19: Minute of 27 September 1943 from Churchill to VCNS Admiralty.

96. BROOKE 3.A.X: Brooke diary entry for 28 September 1943.

97. This was JP (43) 349 (Final), 1 October 1943, Operation FIRST CULVERIN. It appears that this was a reduced version of previous September plans and envisaged the employment of two assault divisions and two follow-up divisions. The conclusion of this report was that even with reduced overheads, FIRST CULVERIN could only be attempted by abandoning ANVIL and encroaching on OVERLORD, almost word for word the same as JP (43) 297 (Final), 29 September 1943, Operation FIRST CULVERIN. See CAB 84.57.

98. CAB 79.65.229: Minutes of Chiefs of Staff meeting of 28 September 1943 and discussion of JP (43) 339, 28 September 1943, Operations in South East Asia.

99. CAB.79.65.227: Minutes of Chiefs of Staff meeting of 27 September 1943.

100. The paper also implies that the question of British naval involvement in the drive through the central Pacific to Formosa or the Japanese home islands was discussed with the Americans before 7 October 1943. This was indeed one of the three options that were defined in a "state of planning" signal sent by the Joint Planning Staff in Washington to Strategical Planning Section in London on 11 September 1943, presumably as the basis of the latter's work on the Twelve-Month Plan. (See CAB 105.68.338.) The first draft of this plan was presented as CPS 86/1 on 13 September 1943 but contains no reference to this option (see CAB 88.55), but a signal sent on the fourteenth by the Joint Planning Staff in Washington on behalf of the American planners to London confirmed and elaborated upon the contents of the signal of the eleventh. (See CAB 122.1075.) Apart from these two references, the author could not find evidence of Anglo-American discussions on this subject before 7 October, but it seems unlikely that this subject could have been allowed to rest after 14 September and it may be that it was pursued independently in both London and Washington.

101. CAB 119.81.B.1: Signal of 18 September 1943 from GHQ India to War Cabinet Office. (This signal gave the lift then available in the Indian Ocean as sufficient for 27,000 men.) CAB 79.64.221: Minutes of Chiefs of Staff meeting of 20 September 1943. CAB 79.65.228: Minutes of first Chiefs of Staff

meeting of 28 September 1943, and discussion of JP (43) 335 (Final), 25 September 1943, Lift of Personnel for BULLFROG.

102. CAB 79.64.224: Minutes of Chiefs of Staff meeting of 23 September 1943 with Directors of Plans.

103. CAB 79.65.229: Minutes of Chiefs of Staff meeting of 28 September 1943 and discussion of JP (43) 339, 28 September 1943, Operations in South East Asia.

104. CAB 69.5.65: Minutes of Defence Committee meeting of 28 September 1943.

105. CAB 79.65.233: Minutes of Chiefs of Staff meeting of 1 October 1943.

106. BROOKE 3.A.X: Brooke diary entry of 1 October 1943.

107. CAB 79.65.232: Minutes of Chiefs of Staff conference of 1 October 1943 and discussion of JP (43) 349 (Final), 1 October 1943, Operation FIRST CULVERIN.

108. CAB 119.18.34: Summary of Chiefs of Staff conference of 1 October 1943.

109. CAB 79.65.231: Minutes of Chiefs of Staff meeting of 30 September 1943, and discussion of JP (43) 297, 29 September 1943, Operation FIRST CULVERIN. (Paper also given as CAB 84.55 and CAB 119.18.30.)

110. CAB 105.68.361: Signal of 1 October 1943 from Joint Planning Staff London to Joint Planning Staff Washington.

111. Despite its being slimmer than the pre-QUADRANT version, the new BUCCANEER nevertheless remained just beyond available British resources, hence the need for an American involvement in the operation. See CAB 84.56: JP (43) 325 (Final), 2 October 1943, Operation BUCCANEER.

112. W.O. 106.4618a.63: Memorandum of 19 September 1943 from M.O. 12 to M.O. 1. W.O. 106.4618a.88: Undated and unsigned memorandum attached to JP (43) 351 (Final) as a briefing paper for the Chiefs of Staff meeting of 7 October 1943.

113. These were JP (43) 325 (Final), 6 October 1943, Operation BUCCANEER; JP (43) 337 (Final), 6 October 1943, An Advance through Moulmein and the Kra Isthmus in the Direction of Bangkok; JP (43) 350 (Final), 6 October 1943, Air Lift to China; and JP (43) 351 (Final), 6 October 1943, Operations in South East Asia in 1944. (The BUCCANEER–FIRST CULVERIN combination and recommendation appeared in the last of these four papers.)

114. CAB 79.65.240: Minutes of Chiefs of Staff meeting of 7 October 1943, and discussion of JP (43) 351 (Final), 6 October 1943, Operations in South East Asia in 1944. (This paper is also given in CAB 84.57.)

115. CAB 79.66.254: Minutes of Chiefs of Staff meeting (attended by the War Cabinet and by Smuts) of 19 October 1943, and discussion of JP (43) 351 (Final), 6 October 1943, Operations in South East Asia in 1944.

116. CAB 79.65.242: Minutes of Chiefs of Staff meeting of 8 October 1943, and discussion of JP (43) 350 (Final), 6 October 1943, Air Lift to China. (This study

had been authorized by JP (43) 350 (TofR), 2 October 1943, Reduction of Air Lift to China.) CAB 79.66.244: Minutes of Chiefs of Staff meeting of 11 October 1943, and discussion of JP (43) 325 (Final), 6 October 1943, Operation BUCCANEER. CAB 79.66.246: Minutes of Chiefs of Staff meeting of 12 October 1943, and discussion of JP (43) 298 (Final), 8 October 1943, Operations Southward from Northern Burma, and of JP (43) 337 (Final), 6 October 1943, An Advance through Moulmein and the Kra Isthmus in the Direction of Bangkok. In addition: CAB 79.66.251: Minutes of Chiefs of Staff meeting of 16 October 1943, and discussion of JP (43) 352 (Final), 13 October 1943, Air Operations against Japan, and of JP (43) 369 (Final), 15 October 1943, Operations in Upper Burma. (All papers 298–339 given as CAB 84.56, 340–364 as CAB 84.57, and 365–399 as CAB 84.58.)

117. CAB 79.66.255, CAB 122.107637, and W.O. 106.4618a.103: Minutes of Chiefs of Staff meeting of 20 October 1943. CAB 79.66.257 and CAB 122.1976.38: Minutes of Chiefs of Staff meeting of 22 October 1943. CAB 79.67.262: Minutes of Chiefs of Staff meeting of 28 October 1943, and discussion of JP (43) 385 (Final), 27 October 1943, Operations in South East Asia. See also CAB 122.1076.40: Memorandum of 22 October 1943 from Hollis to Churchill and memorandum of 23 October 1943 from Churchill to Chiefs of Staff, given respectively as Annex 2 and Annex 1 to COS (43) 655 (0), 24 October 1943, South East Asia Command: Future Operations.

118. BROOKE 3.A.X: Brooke diary entry of 29 October 1943. CAB 79.67.263, CAB 79.67.264, and W.O. 106.4618a.118a: Minutes of Chiefs of Staff meetings of 29 October 1943.

119. CAB 105.57.915 and W.O. 106.4618a.118: Signal of 29 October 1943 from War Cabinet Office to Joint Staff Mission.

120. W.O. 106.4618a.105: Unsigned memorandum, dated 21 October 1943, prepared for a conference to be held on 22 October 1943. The DMO's refusal to place the paper before Brooke was noted on the twenty-third and initialed "WL."

121. CAB 105.68.364: Signal of 8 October 1943 from Joint Planning Staff London to Joint Planning Staff Washington.

122. CAB 119.81.B4: Signal of 22 September 1943 from GHQ India to War Cabinet Office.

123. CAB 105.85.39: Signal of 14 October 1943 from Dill to War Cabinet Office.

124. CAB 105.71.142: Signal of 7 October 1943 from Joint Staff Mission to War Cabinet Office.

125. CAB 105.71.361, 370, and 373: Respectively signals of 18, 23, and 24 October 1943 from Joint Staff Mission to War Cabinet Office. CAB 105.85.41: Signal of 20 October 1943 from Dill to War Cabinet Office.

126. CAB 122.1076.41: Minutes of meeting of the Military Committee, Joint Staff Mission, of 30 October 1943. (The view was justified: as late as 12 November the Joint Planning Staff was ordered to prepare a paper on the assumption that it would take two years after the German defeat to complete

that of Japan. [See CAB 84.59: JP (43) 402 (0) (TofR), 12 November 1943, Munitions for the War against Japan]. A similar provision, which was stretched to three years, was provided in JP (44) 17 (Final), 8 February 1944, Manpower for the War against Japan. See CAB 84.60.])

127. W.O. 106.4618a.125: Signal of 30 October 1943 from Noble to Brooke.

128. CAB 105.44.1291 and CAB 122.1076.4.2: Signal of 30 October 1943 from Joint Staff Mission to War Cabinet Office.

129. W.O. 106.4619.142: Briefing note prepared on signal of 30 October 1943 from Joint Staff Mission to War Cabinet Office for attention of the Chiefs of Staff. CAB 79.67.265 and CAB 122.1076.44: Minutes of Chiefs of Staff meeting of 1 November 1943.

130. CAB 122.1076.52: CCS 390, 7 November 1943, Future Operations in South East Asia. (That the paper was presented in Combined Chiefs of Staff form, and hence immediately available to the Americans, means that representation by the Joint Staff Mission must have had some effect in London.)

131. CAB 105.85.54: Signal of 8 November 1943 from Dill to War Cabinet Office.

132. Unless, of course, the proposal was made verbally, and off-the-record between 29 October and 1 November 1943, which was quite likely. Brooke's statement that the Americans had to be told of the British wish to cancel BULL-FROG, and London's instruction to the Mission to proceed with the proposal as ordered, obviously related to formal presentation. See, respectively, CAB 79.67.265 and CAB 122.1076.44: Minutes of Chiefs of Staff meeting of 1 November 1943. CAB 122.1076.46: Signal of 5 November 1943 from War Cabinet Office to Joint Staff Mission.

133. Hayes, *History of the Joint Chiefs of Staff*, 499.

134. CAB 105.71.384: Signal of 29 October 1943 from Joint Staff Mission to War Cabinet Office.

135. CAB 105.71.392 and CAB 122.1075: Signal of 2 November 1943 from Joint Staff Mission to War Cabinet Office.

136. Hayes, *History of the Joint Chiefs of Staff*, 502.

137. CAB 105.57.932: Signal of 5 November 1943 from War Cabinet Office to Joint Staff Mission.

138. CAB 119.18.42: Signal of 17 October 1943 from South East Asia Command to War Cabinet Office. CAB 119.18.47 and W.O. 106.4618a.110: Signal of 27 October 1943 from the Joint Planning Staff Delhi to Joint Planning Staff London.

139. But JP (43) 360 (E) & (O) (TofR), 9 October 1943, Merchant Shipping Requirements for the War against Japan, had stated, "No major change in the general strategy for the defeat of Japan, such as might be involved by a transfer of the British effort from south east Asia . . . to the Pacific under the Twelve-Month Plan, is likely to take place." (See CAB 84.57.) It seems, therefore, that the failure, if such it was, was one of strategic imagination, not of means.

140. Certainly in the wake of the 7 October decision, the staffs were heavily committed to a series of feasibility studies, most obviously in the form of JP (43) 360 (E) & (O) (TofR), 9 October 1943, Merchant Shipping Requirements for the War against Japan; JP (43) 190 (E) and JP (43) 360 (E) (Supplementary TofR), 14 October 1943, Landing Ship and Craft Requirement, 1944–1945; JP (43) 372 (E) (TofR), 19 October 1943, Amendments to Plan BUCCANEER; and JP (43) 373 (E) (TofR), 18 October 1943, Operation FIRST CULVERIN. In addition, five other papers, all concerning operations in Southeast Asia and India's capacity as a base were completed between 9 October and 2 November. See CAB 84.57 and 58.

141. CAB 105.71.384: Signal of 29 October 1943 from Joint Staff Mission to War Cabinet Office.

142. BROOKE 3.A.X: Brooke diary entries of 7 and 8 October 1943.

143. CAB 105.85.49: Signal of 29 October 1943 from Dill to War Cabinet Office.

144. W.O. 106.4618a.125: Signal of 30 October 1943 from Noble to Brooke.

CHAPTER TWO
AN UNREASONABLE THING TO DO

1. The cancellation of PIGSTICK seems to have been an extraordinarily complicated business. The immediate decision, which was taken for reasons of timing, was made by South East Asia Command, and was effected by 11th Army Group on 4 January 1944. (W.O. 203.1490.27: Signals of 4 January 1944 from 11th Army Group to XIV Army and 33rd Corps.). But while London had decided to recommend PIGSTICK's cancellation to the Americans by this time, cancellation was not formally decided upon until the fourth and this decision was confirmed on the sixth. (W.O. 203.1488: Minutes of Executive Planning Section [Blue] staff meetings of 4 and 6 January 1943.) American agreement to PIGSTICK's cancellation was known to the Joint Staff Mission by the sixth (see CAB 138.3.191: Minutes of Military Committee meeting of 6 January 1944), but on the eighth the Chiefs of Staff received a signal from Churchill, who was on holiday in North Africa, ordering PIGSTICK's retention. It was not until the tenth that PIGSTICK was finally discarded in favor of CUDGEL. (CAB 79.69.6 and 7: Minutes of Chiefs of Staff meetings of 8 and 10 January 1944 respectively.)

2. W.O. 203.1490a and W.O. 203.1492.101: Signal of 30 January 1944 from 11th Army Group to Supreme Allied Commander South East Asia.

3. See, for example, W.O. 203.1489: PIGSTICK, General Planning, with special reference to Items 2a (EPS [Blue] Note, 11 December 1943, Amphibious Assistance to 15th Corps Operations. Paper also given as W.O. 203.1490.14): 35a (CPS Paper No. 22, 26 December 1943, Progress of Planning for Operation PIGSTICK. Paper also given as W.O. 203.1490.19a); and 42a (Memorandum of 28 December 1943 from MGGS South East Asia Command to Commander-in-Chief XIV Army).

4. Louis Allen, *Burma: The Longest War, 1941–1945* (London: Dent, 1986), 166.

5. This view was expressed by Col. Riley Sunderland, who served in the China-Burma-India theater and was the coauthor of the U.S. Army's official histories of this command, in conversation at Williamsburg on 11 February 1989.

6. Hayes, *History of the Joint Chiefs of Staff*, 543–68, being the title and content of chapter 21 of her book.

7. Between December 1941 and November 1943 the U.S. Navy commissioned seven fleet, eight light, and thirty escort carriers: in the next thirteen months another seven fleet, one light, and thirty-eight escort carriers were commissioned.

8. CAB 122.1074.42: Minutes of the Combined Staff Planners meeting of 28 November 1943 and discussion of CPS 86/5, 27 November 1943, British Naval and Air Forces Available for the War against Japan in 1944. (Paper also given in CAB 88.55.) This meeting took place before the cancellation of BUCCANEER.

9. CAB 122.1072.2: CCS 417/2, 23 December 1943, Overall Plan for the Defeat of Japan, Report from the Combined Staff Planners.

10. ADM 205.35: Memorandum of 2 February 1944 from Director of Plans to First Sea Lord: Statement of Forces that were to be sent to the Far East in Accordance with present Admiralty Planning. (The memorandum was forwarded to the prime minister that same day.)

11. CAB 79.70.54: Minutes of Chiefs of Staff meeting of 21 February 1944 and discussion of JP (44) 47 (Final), 19 February 1944, South East Asia Command: Future Operations, Report of the Directors of Plans.

12. CAB 80.79.114: COS (44) 114 (0), 1 February 1944, Overall Policy for the Defeat of Japan, Minute from the Prime Minister. Annex: Signal of 23 January 1944 from British Admiralty Delegation (Joint Staff Mission) to Admiralty.

13. CAB 119.17.53 and F.O. 954.7.20: COS (44) 195 (0), 23 February 1944, South East Asia: Future Operations. CAB 79.77.236 and F.O. 954.7.160: Minutes of Chiefs of Staff meeting of 14 July 1944. ADD 52577 and BROOKE 3.A.XI: Respectively diary entries of Cunningham and Brooke for this day. CAB 79.79.268 and CAB 119.181.18a: Minutes of the second of three Chiefs of Staff meetings held on 9 August 1944.

14. CAB 80.81.193, CAB 119.17.50 and CAB 122.1077.42: COS (44) 193 (0), 22 February 1944, South East Asia Command: Future Operations. (This paper was submitted by the AXIOM Mission in response to a Chiefs of Staff paper of the same title but which was not formalized, confusingly, until the next day as COS (44) 183 (0). This paper is given as CAB 80.80.183, CAB 119.17.48 and CAB 122.1077.44.) CAB 79.76.64, CAB 119.17.62 and CAB 119.153.10: Minutes of Chiefs of Staff meeting of 26 February 1944.

15. CAB 80.80.168 and CAB 119.17.33: COS (44) 168 (0), 16 February 1944, Operations in South East Asia and the Pacific. CAB 80.81.195, CAB

119.17.53 and F.O. 954.7.20: COS (44) 195 (0), 23 February 1944, South East Asia: Future Operations.

16. CAB 79.70.48 and CAB 119.17.35: Minutes of Chiefs of Staff meeting of 14 February 1944. CAB 80.80.166, CAB 119.17.31 and PREM 3.148.4.163: COS (44) 166 (0), 15 February 1944, Strategy in South East Asia: Paper submitted by Supreme Allied Commander, South East Asia. CAB 80.81.1,95, CAB 119.17.53 and F.O. 954.7.20: COS (44) 195 (0), 23 February 1944, South East Asia: Future Operations.

17. CAB 119.17.2 and 7: Signals of 1 and 7 January 1944 from South East Asia Command to War Cabinet Office. CAB 80.80.166, CAB 119.17.31 and PREM 3.148.4.163: COS (44) 166 (0), 15 February 1944, Strategy in South East Asia: Paper submitted by Supreme Allied Commander, South East Asia. CAB 80.81.192: COS (44) 192 (0), 22 February 1944, Operations in Burma. CAB 80.81.193, CAB 119.17.50 and CAB 122.1077.42: COS (44) 193 (0), 22 February 1944, South East Asia Command: Future Operations. (The line adopted in these papers and signals was that CULVERIN was the means of avoiding a Burma commitment, but at the Chiefs of Staff meeting of 14 February 1944 the AXIOM Mission provided the argument in reverse, namely that without CULVERIN a Burma commitment was inescapable. See CAB 79.70.48 and CAB 119.17.35. What is also interesting is that Stilwell also argued for CULVERIN in terms of a South East Asia Command role: on the question of the form of CULVERIN he favored an attack on Malaya without the preparatory assault on Sumatra. This argument, however, was not set down on paper in the form of a letter to Mountbatten until 5 August 1944, and by then circumstances had changed very substantially from those that had pertained in February. See CAB 119.147.77.)

18. F.O. 954.7.26: Signal of 25 February 1944 from Roosevelt to Churchill. CAB 79.73.133: Minutes of Chiefs of Staff meeting of 25 April 1944 and discussion of CSA (44) 40 (0), 21 April 1944, Potentiality of India as a Base. CAB 99.29.60–62: Minutes of sixth Chiefs of Staff meeting of the OCTAGON serial of 9 September 1944.

19. CAB 79.71.65, CAB 119.153.12 and 15: Minutes of Chiefs of Staff meeting of 28 February 1944 and discussion of JP (44) 55 (Final), 27 February 1944, Strategy for the Defeat of Japan. (Paper also given as CAB 119.174.128. See, also CAB 80.81.207 and CAB 119.174.131: COS (44) 207 (0), 1 March 1944, Strategy for the War against Japan.)

20. CAB 79.76.207: Minutes of Chiefs of Staff meeting of 23 June 1944 and discussion of JP (44) 106 (Revised Final), 21 June 1944, Manpower One Year after the Defeat of Germany. ADD 52577: Cunningham diary entry of 26 July 1944.

21. CAB 79.71.81: Minutes of Chiefs of Staff meeting of 9 March 1944 and discussion of PHP (43) 36A (Final), 7 March 1944, Military Occupation in South East Europe. ISMAY.IV.POW.I: Letter of 14 March 1944 from Ismay to Pownall. CAB 79.75.174: Minutes of Chiefs of Staff meeting of 27 May 1944,

Annex I. PREM 3.63.8.25: Letter of 27 May 1944 from Churchill to Curtin. CAB 79.75.178: Minutes of Chiefs of Staff meeting of 1 June 1944 and discussion of PHP (44) 31 (Final), 25 May 1944, and of PHP (43) 36 (Final), both papers entitled Military Occupation in South East Europe. CAB 79.75.185, CAB 79.76.194, CAB 119.14.101, F.O. 954.7.133 and PREM 3.63.6.22: Minutes of Chiefs of Staff meetings of 8 and 15 June 1944 respectively.

22. CAB 79.71.65 and CAB 119.153.12: Minutes of Chiefs of Staff meeting of 28 February 1944 and discussion of JP (44) 55 (Final), 27 February 1944, Strategy for the Defeat of Japan. (Paper also given as CAB 119.174.128.) CAB 80.81.207 and CAB 119.174.131: COS (44) 207 (0), 1 March 1944, Strategy for the Defeat of Japan.

23. PREM 3.164.5.148: Signal of 23 December 1943 from War Cabinet Office to Joint Staff Mission. CAB 119.174.142: Letter of 6 March 1944 from Ransom to Mallaby. CAB 119.174.143: Memorandum of 6 March 1944 from Directors of Plans to Chiefs of Staff.

24. Anthony Gorst, "The Politics of Strategy: The Development of the British Pacific Fleet in 1944." Master's thesis, London School of Economics, 1981, 10–11.

25. See, with respect to Australia alone, PREM 3.63.8.144: Signal of 8 October 1943 from Curtin to Dominion Office. CAB 79.69.10: Minutes of Chiefs of Staff meeting of 13 January 1944 and discussion of JP (43) 418 (Final), 7 January 1944, Australian Manpower. CAB 79.74.148 and CAB 119.14.10: Minutes of Chiefs of Staff meeting of 8 May 1944 and discussion of JP (44) 130 (Final), 7 May 1944, Australian War Effort. CAB 119.180.187: Letter of 24 May 1944 from Mallaby to Sugden. CAB 119.180.223 and F.O. 954.7.143: Signal of 4 July 1944 from Curtin to Dominion Office. See also Gorst, "Politics of Strategy," 25.

26. F.O. 954.7.29: Memorandum of 29 February 1944 from Churchill to Chiefs of Staff. F.O. 954.7.37: Foreign office internal memorandum of 10 March 1944. ADD 52564: Somerville diary entry of 11 March 1944. CAB 79.77.239 and F.O. 954.7.160: Minutes of Chiefs of Staff meeting of 14 July 1944 and discussion of COS (44) 553 (0), 13 July 1944, War against Japan: British Programme, of COS (44) 623 (0), 13 July 1944, The Capture of Amboina and of an unlisted and undated paper entitled Disposition of the Indian Army. Additional comments are provided in ADD 52577 and BROOKE 3.B.XII for diary entries of 13 July 1944 of Cunningham and Brooke respectively. Also CAB 79.79.265 and CAB 119.181.17b: Minutes of the second War Cabinet meeting of 8 August 1944.

27. F.O. 954.7.7: Signal of 18 January 1944 from Halifax to Foreign Office. CAB 66.47.111: WP (44) 111, 16 February 1944, The Future of Indo-China and other French Pacific Possessions.

28. CAB 79.77.239 and F.O. 954.7.160: Minutes of Chiefs of Staff meeting of 14 July 1944 and discussion of COS (44) 553 (0), 13 July 1944, War against Japan: British Programme, of COS (44) 623 (0), 13 July 1944, The

Capture of Amboina and of an unlisted and undated paper entitled Disposition of the Indian Army. CAB 80.85.654 and CAB 119.16.10: COS (44) 654 (0), 25 July 1944, Future Operations in South East Asia Command. CAB 79.79.265 and CAB 119.181.17b: Minutes of second War Cabinet meeting of 8 August 1944. CAB 99.29.119: JS (OCTAGON) 9 (Final), 9 September 1944, Course of Action in the War against Japan.

29. CAB 80.79.123: COS (44) 123 (0), 5 February 1944, Plan for the Defeat of Japan. CAB 79.70.54 and CAB 119.17.46: Minutes of Chiefs of Staff meeting of 21 February 1944 and discussion of JP (44) 47 (Final), 19 February 1944, South East Asia Command: Future Operations, Report of Directors of Plans, and of JP (44) 50 (Final), 20 February 1944, Transport Aircraft and Long-Range Penetration Groups in South East Asia Command. CAB 119.17.56: JP (44) 53 (Final), 24 February 1944, South East Asia Command: Future Operations.

30. PREM 3.164.6.120: Signal of 10 March 1944 from Churchill to Roosevelt. PREM 3.164.6.119: Signal of 13 March 1944 from Roosevelt to Churchill. CAB 105.85.160 and PREM 3.164.6.117: Signal of 14 March from Dill to Churchill. F.O. 954.7.132: Foreign Office internal memorandum of 15 June 1944.

31. The exact length of time needed to complete the transfer of forces and administrative resources from Europe to the Far East varied depending on service, the scale of movement, level of required preparation, and location and facilities of bases. The eighteen-month estimate referred to naval needs and Australian bases. See ADM 199.1376: Memorandum of 11 September 1944 from Head of Military Branch, Admiralty, to Second Sea Lord. See also ADM 199.1384: Examination of Potentialities of Australia as a Base for R.N. Forces, Report of 2 November 1944.

32. The PIGSTICK question came before the Chiefs of Staff first on 20 December 1943 and then on another five occasions before the events of January 1944 set out above. See CAB 79.68.310, 313, 315, 318, 320 and 323: Minutes of Chiefs of Staff meetings of 20, 23, 24, 27, 29 and 31 December 1943 respectively.

33. CAB 80.78.71 and CAB 122.1072.20: COS (44) 71 (0), 24 January 1944, Plan for the Defeat of Japan, Minute from Prime Minister. CAB 80.81.214: COS (44) 214 (0), 3 March 1944, Overall Plan for the Defeat of Japan: Communications to the Dominions. CAB 79.71.76 and CAB 119.153.24: Minutes of Chiefs of Staff meeting of 6 March 1944.

34. CAB 79.69.2 and CAB 122.1072: Minutes of Chiefs of Staff meeting of 4 January 1944.

35. CAB 105.68.454: Signal of 3 January 1944 from Joint Planning Staff London to Joint Planning Staff Washington.

36. CAB 105.68.464: Signal of 10 January 1944 from Joint Planning Staff London to Joint Planning Staff Washington.

37. Planning for the implementation of the SEXTANT amphibious program was initiated by COS 66/44 of 22 January 1944. See ELLIS.3. Appendix 23.)

38. CAB 79.69.17, CAB 119.93.12 and CAB 122.1072.18: Minutes of Chiefs of Staff meeting of 20 January 1944 and discussion of JP (43) 419 (Final), 13 January 1944, Landing Ships and Craft, 1944–1945.

39. CAB 79.69.8 and CAB 122.1072.13: Minutes of Chiefs of Staff meeting of 11 January 1944 and discussion of draft signal.

40. CAB 119.17.2 and W.O. 106.4619.212a: Signal of 1 January 1944 from South East Asia Command to War Cabinet Office. CAB 119.17.7: Signal of 7 January 1944 from South East Asia Command to War Cabinet Office. (These two signals contained proposals that followed one of 21 December 1943 in which Mountbatten had told Churchill that he, Mountbatten, was "delighted ... you continue in favor of JUNIOR CULVERIN in October/November." See W.O. 06.1619.144.)

41. CAB 79.68.313: Minutes of Chiefs of Staff meeting of 23 December and discussion of JP (43) 429 (Final), 17 December 1943, Preparations for the War against Japan.

42. CAB 79.69.19 and CAB 122.1072.19: Minutes of Chiefs of Staff meeting of 21 January 1944 and discussion of CCS 417/2, 23 December 1944, Overall Plan for the Defeat of Japan, Report from the Combined Staff Planners.

43. CAB 80.78.51 and CAB 119.202.191: COS (44) 51 (0), 17 January 1944, Japanese Intentions in South East Asia, Minute from Prime Minister. Raymond Callahan, *Burma, 1942–1945* (London: Davis-Poynter, 1978), 96–97.

44. BROOKE 3.B.XI: Brooke diary entry of 18 January 1944.

45. CAB 69.6.14: Minutes of War Cabinet meeting of 19 January 1944. (W.O. 106.4619.234 provides a Joint Planning Staff briefing paper for this meeting which carries arguments not noted in the minutes.)

46. John Ehrman, *History of the Second World War: Grand Strategy,* vol. 5, *August 1943–September 1944* (London: H.M.S.O. 1956), 425–27.

47. BROOKE 3.B.XI: Brooke diary entry of 19 January 1944.

48. CAB 80.78.71 and CAB 122.1072.20: COS (44) 71 (0), 24 January 1944, Plan for the Defeat of Japan, Minute from Prime Minister.

49. CAB 105.57.948: Signal of 13 November 1943 from Joint Planning Staff London to Joint Planning Staff Washington.

50. CAB 79.69.24 and CAB 122.1074.21: Minutes of Chiefs of Staff meeting of 26 January 1944 and discussion of COS (44) 71 (0), 24 January 1944, Plan for the Defeat of Japan, Minute from Prime Minister.

51. CAB 80.78.70: COS (44) 70 (0), 24th January 1944, Relation of FIRST CULVERIN in Autumn 1944 to our agreed Pacific Strategy. See also Annex II of this paper.

52. W.O. 203.4995.2: Memorandum of 3 April 1944 from Axiom Mission to Supreme Allied Commander South East Asia, Report of the AXIOM Mission, Section I, 5 February to 4 March 1944.

53. F.O. 954.6.711: Signal of 25 November 1943 from Mountbatten to Eden. W.0. 203.1484.7a: Signal of 6 December 1943 from Mountbatten to Chiefs of Staff.

54. PREM. 3.164.6.120: Signal of 10 March 1944 from Churchill to

Roosevelt. PREM 3.164.6.119: Signal of 13 March 1944 from Roosevelt to Churchill.

55. CAB 119.17.24: JP (44) 45, 15 February 1944, Operations in Malaya.

56. CAB 119.17.15: Signal of 1 February 1944 from Supreme Allied Commander South East Asia to War Cabinet Office. CAB 119.17.25: JP (44) 41, 12 February 1944, CULVERIN.

57. ADD 52563: Letter of 3 February 1944 from Somerville to Cunningham. CAB 80.80.162, CAB 119.17.30, and CAB 122.1077.25: COS (44) 162 (0), 14 February 1944, Future Operations in South East Asia Command. (This paper was a letter of 4 February 1944 from Mountbatten to the Chiefs of Staff.) ISMAY.IV.SOM.6: Letter of 5 February from Somerville to Ismay.

58. CAB 119.17.23: JP (44) 46, 15 February 1944, Operations in the Sunda Strait area.

59. W.O. 106.4620.284: JIC (44) 63 (0), 15 February 1944, Japanese Reaction to CULVERIN.

60. CAB 80.79.114: COS (44) 114 (0), 1 February 1944, Overall Policy for the Defeat of Japan.

61. CAB 80.79.114: COS (44) 114 (0), 1 February 1944, Overall Policy for the Defeat of Japan, Minutes from Prime Minister.

62. CAB 80.79.123 and CAB 122.1072.25: COS (44) 123 (0), 5 February 1944, Plans for the Defeat of Japan.

63. CAB 79.70.32 and CAB 122.1072.23: Minutes of Chiefs of Staff meeting of 3 February 1944 and discussion of JP (44) 32 (Final), 2 February 1944, Plans for the Defeat of Japan.

64. CAB 80.79.123 and CAB 122.1072.25: COS (44) 123 (0), 5 February 1944, Plans for the Defeat of Japan.

65. CAB 79.70.32 and CAB 122.1072.23: Minutes of Chief of Staff meeting of 3 February 1944 and discussion of JP (44) 32 (Final), 2 February 1944, Plans for the Defeat of Japan.

66. CAB 80.79.123 and CAB 122.1072.25: COS (44) 123 (0), 5 February 1944, Plans for the Defeat of Japan.

67. As the planners noted in a briefing paper prepared for the Chiefs of Staff and dated 20 February 1944, the demands of the various operations sought by South East Asia Command would involve the emptying of the strategic reserve and a need to be successful in every undertaking in order to avoid being over-committed. See W.O. 106.4620.229. (It is not clear, however, how over-commitment could have been avoided even in the event of success.)

68. CAB 80.81.195, CAB 119.17.53, and F.O. 954.7.20–21: COS (44) 195 (0), 23 February 1944, South East Asia: Future Operations. (Dening's paper was dated 17 February 1944 and by the time that it entered the Chiefs of Staff files it had been endorsed by Eden and Churchill.)

69. But such a narrow definition of British national interest could be made by the American high command and used by it as a justification for a British involvement in the Pacific war. This, ironically, was to happen.

70. CAB 80.80.166, CAB 119.17.31, and CAB 122.1077.25: COS (44) 166 (0), 15 February 1944, Strategy in South East Asia Command.

71. CAB 119.17.27 and PREM 3.148.168–79: SAC (44) 7, 12 February 1944, Strategy in South East Asia Command. (The justification for CULVERIN in terms of the diversion of enemy forces to Southeast Asia was denied by the planners with the argument that by the winter of 1944–1945 the Japanese would have lost strategic mobility and the means to undertake any significant re-deployment of forces between theaters. See W.O. 106.4620.284: JIC (44) 63 (0), 15 February 1944, Japanese Reaction to CULVERIN.)

72. Or at the expense of the airlift to China. In his signal of 24 February 1944 to the War Cabinet Office Mountbatten reversed the latter, arguing that the airlift to China could only proceed at the expense of CULVERIN. See CAB 119.14.52.

73. The point made by Stilwell in a memorandum to Mountbatten, dated 31 January 1944, that was submitted in the form of an enclosure to Mountbatten's letter of 4 February 1944 to the Chiefs of Staff.

74. CAB 122.1077.26: CCS 452/6, 17 February 1944, Operations in South East Asia. CAB 105.45.1519, CAB 119.17.37 and CAB 122.1077.27: Signal of 17 February 1944 from Joint Staff Mission to War Cabinet Office.

75. F.O. 954.7.26–27: Signal of 25 February 1944 from Roosevelt to Churchill.

76. CAB 80.80.168 and CAB 119.17.33: COS (44) 168 (0), 16 February 1944, Operations in South East Asia and the Pacific, Observations by Prime Minister on COS (44) 123 (0).

77. CAB 80.80.178 and CAB 122.1077.32: COS (44) 176 (0), 19 February 1944, Operations in South East Asia Command, Minute from the Prime Minister to the Chiefs of Staff.

78. CAB 80.80.162, CAB 119.17.30, and CAB 122.1077.25: COS (44) 162 (0), 14 February 1944, Future Operations in South East Asia Command.

79. CAB 79.70.55 and CAB 119.202.220: Minutes of Chiefs of Staff meeting of 22 February 1944. CAB 105.58.1175 and CAB 122.1077.49: Signal of 25 February 1944 from War Cabinet Office to Joint Staff Mission.

80. CAB 105.68.516: Signal of 15 February 1944 from War Cabinet Office to Joint Staff Mission.

81. CAB 79.70.48, CAB 119.17.35, and CAB 122.1077.25: Minutes of Chiefs of Staff meeting of 14 February 1944. (This meeting was attended by Churchill, Eden, Ismay, Lumsden [from South West Pacific Command], the AXIOM Mission, and the Chiefs of Staff. From the minutes, which are notoriously discreet in such matters, the meeting seems to have been a somewhat turbulent one.)

82. W.O. 203.1608.19: Signal of 17 February 1944 from War Cabinet Office to South East Asia Command.

83. W.O. 106.4620.292 and 293: Memoranda of 20 February 1944 from M.I. 2 to DDMI and from M.I. 17 to M.O. 12 respectively.

84. W.0. 106.4620.283: Notes of meeting between AXIOM Staff officers

and MO 12, dated 16 February 1944. (The immediate deficit was two corps headquarters, three divisions and virtually all the specialist troops needed for this operation. W.O. 106.4620.290: Paper of 17 February 1944, First Thoughts on Prime Minister's Observations, presumably COS (44) 168 (0).)

85. W.O. 106.4620.290: Unsigned paper of 17 February 1944, First Thoughts on Prime Minister's Observations.

86. W.O. 106.4620.294: Memorandum of 20 February 1944 from SD 2/SD 5 to MO 12. W.O. 106.4620.296: Memorandum dated 20 February 1944 prepared by QMG on the subject of base facilities in India.

87. CAB 84.61: The JP (44) 53 (S) (TofR) file indicates that AXIOM was asked by the Chiefs of Staff to record its views of COS (44) 183 (0) (Draft) and hence on this subject, on 21 February 1944.

88. CAB 79.70.60, CAB 119.93.21 and CAB 119.153.9: Minutes of Chiefs of Staff meeting of 25 February 1944 and discussion of JP (44) 53 (Final), 24 February 1944, South East Asia Command: Future Operations.

89. CAB 80.81.193, CAB 119.17.50 and CAB 122.1077.42: COS (44) 193 (0), 22 February 1944, South East Asia Command: Future Operations. Comment by the Axiom Party on COS (44) 183 (0).

90. CAB 79.70.54, CAB 119.17.46 and CAB 122.1072.26: Minutes of Chiefs of Staff meeting of 21 February 1944 and discussion of JP (44) 47 (Final), 19 February 1944, South East Asia Command: Future Operations, Report of Directors of Plans. (This paper is also given as CAB 84.612 and CAB 119.17.43.)

91. CAB 79.70.58 and CAB 119.17.54: Minutes of Chiefs of Staff meeting of 24 February 1944 and discussion of COS (44) 195 (0), 23 February 1944, South East Asia: Future Operations.

92. BROOKE 3.B.XI: Brooke diary entry of 14 February 1944.

93. BROOKE 3.B.XI: Brooke diary entry of 21 February 1944.

94. CAB 80.80.183, CAB 119.17.48 and CAB 122.1077.44: COS (44) 183 (0), 23 February 1944, South East Asia Command: Future Operations.

95. Samuel Eliot Morison, *History of U.S. Naval Operations in World War II:* vol. 7, *Aleutians, Gilberts and Marshalls, June 1942–April 1944* (Boston: Little, Brown, 1964), 315–52; vol. 8, *New Guinea and the Marianas, March 1944–August 1944* (Boston: Little, Brown, 1953), 27–41.

96. CAB 119.153.1: Minutes of Chiefs of Staff meeting of 23 February 1944. (These minutes, plus certain others in this episode, are not included in the CAB 79 file.)

97. ADM 199.1452: Commander-in-Chief Ceylon's war diary. S. Woodburn Kirby et al., *History of the Second World War: The War against Japan,* vol. 3, *The Decisive Battles* (London: H.M.S.O., 1961), 379, gives the number of Catalina squadrons as three.

98. ADM 199.1388: Eastern Fleet war diary.

99. CAB 119.17.25 and PREM 3.148.4.180.202: JP (44) 41, 12 February 1944, CULVERIN. CAB 80.80.183, CAB 119.17.48 and CAB 122.1077.44: COS (44) 183 (0), 23 February 1944, South East Asia Command: Future Operations.

100. This signal is not on file but its timing and contents can be determined by the reply. The Admiralty's signal was timed 2357 GMT on 23 February 1944. (This information was supplied by David Brown in a letter of 2 November 1984.)

101. CAB 119.153.4: JP (44) 54 (Final), 24 February 1944, Appreciation of Move of Japanese Fleet.

102. ADM 199.1452: Commander-in-Chief Ceylon's war diary.

103. ADM 199.1479: Naval air weekly summary, 23 October 1943.

104. CAB 80.79.114: COS (44) 114 (0), 1 February 1944, Overall Policy for the Defeat of Japan, Minute from the Prime Minister. CAB 119.17.49.2: Minutes of Chiefs of Staff Meeting of 26 February 1944.

105. SHIPS' COVERS: 481.E. Docket LXXI, 2 March 1944.

106. ADM 199.1480: Naval air weekly summary, 19 February 1944.

107. Information supplied by David Brown in letter of 2 November 1984.

108. PREM 3.164.6.136: Naval Intelligence memorandum of 1 March 1944: Re-organization of the Japanese Fleet.

109. CAB 119.153.4: JP (44) 54 (Final), 24 February 1944, Appreciation of Move of Japanese Fleet.

110. CAB 119.153.7, CAB 119.153.16 and PREM 3.164.1.52: COS (44) 202 (0), 28 February 1944, Move of the Japanese Fleet. This paper was the authorized version of JP (44) 54 (Final), and the arguments it contained were to be used at the meeting of 26 February 1944.

111. The *Richelieu* file is CAB 199.156b. Private information suggests that the Admiralty questioned the fitness of certain of her senior officers for the positions they held and believed that relations between officers and men in some divisions were somewhat delicate. The ship was also very political, being violently anti-Gaullist, and she had little love for the Royal Navy.

112. See CAB 66.47.111: WP (44) 111, 16 February 1944, The Future of Indo-China and other French Pacific Possessions.

113. CAB 80.81.249: COS (44) 249 (0), 13 March 1944, French Participation in Far Eastern Strategy. This paper states that the Free French had raised the question of their involvement in the war against Japan with the British on 29 September 1943 and again on 21 October, 3 November, and 17 December. Churchill noted that Britain "should adopt a negative and dilatory attitude," and to a subsequent request for a mission to Headquarters South East Asia Command he noted, "It would be better to delay. One can always concede." See F.O. 954.7.60. The bulk of material, French Participation in the Far East War, is to be found in CAB 119.111.

114. CAB 119.153.23 and PREM 3.164.1.40: Signal of 4 March 1944 from War Cabinet Office to Joint Staff Mission.

115. ADM 53.118914: *Athene*'s log, 24 February 1944.

116. CAB 119.153.3: JIC (44) 75 (0), 24 February 1944, Japanese Naval Moves. (This Joint Intelligence Committee view of proceedings was seconded by a South East Asia Command appreciation sent by signal to London on the twenty-fifth. See CAB 119.153.5 and PREM 3.164.1.64.)

117. CAB 119.153.6 and PREM 3.164.1.57: Signal of 26 February 1944 from War Cabinet Office to both Joint Staff Mission and South East Asia Command.

118. CAB 79.70.60 and CAB 119.153.9: Minutes of Chiefs of Staff meeting of 25 February 1914 and discussion of JIC (44) 75 (0), 24 February 1944, Japanese Naval Moves, and JP (44) 54 (Final), 24 February 1944, Appreciation of Move of Japanese Fleet.

119. BROOKE 3.B.XI: Brooke diary entry of 24 February 1944.

120. CAB 80.80.168 and CAB 119.17.33: COS (44) 168 (0), 16 February 1944, Operations in South East Asia and the Pacific, Observations by Prime Minister on COS (44) 123 (0).

121. CAB 119.17.49: Paper IV, Minutes of staff conference held at 1200 on 25 February 1944.

122. CAB 119.17.49: Paper III, Minutes of staff conference held at 1500 on 25 February 1944. (The "within a fortnight" schedule was later amended to a 15 March deadline. See CAB 79.71.87 and CAB 119.93.25: Minutes of Chiefs of Staff meeting of 16 March 1944 and discussion of signal of 15 March 1944 from Dill to War Cabinet Office. Signal is given as CAB 105.85.160 and CAB 119.174.160b.)

123. BROOKE 3.B.XI: Brooke diary entry for 25 February 1944.

124. F.O. 954.7.28: Signal of 25 February 1944 from Churchill to Roosevelt. (Consideration of plans for the campaign in Upper Burma and the Ledo Road project took up a considerable part of the AXIOM discussions. The British misgivings about the Ledo Road project are provided in W.O. 203.1537.5a.)

125. F.O. 954.7.34: Signal of 3 March 1944 from Roosevelt to Churchill.

126. CAB 79.71.67, CAB 119.153.7, and F.O. 954.7.29: Minutes of Chiefs of Staff meeting of 29 February 1944 and discussion of COS (44) 202 (0) (Final), 28 February 1944, Move of the Japanese Fleet. (Paper also given as CAB 80.81.202 and CAB 119.153.16.)

127. CAB 119.153.11: Signal of 26 February 1944 from War Cabinet Office to Joint Staff Mission.

128. ADM 199.1452: Commander-in-Chief Ceylon's war diary.

129. ADM 53.118914 and ADM 53.119.377: Respectively the March 1944 logs of the *Athene* and *Engadine*.

130. ADM 199.1452: Commander-in-Chief Ceylon's war diary. (Eight of these squadrons had to be sent to southern India for want of adequate naval air facilities in Ceylon, a comment on the island's unpreparedness. The *Richelieu* was involved in five operations before being relieved by the *Howe* on 3 August 1944.)

131. ADM 199.454: Letter of 4 March 1944 from Dorling to McCormick.

132. ADM 199.340: Operation DIPLOMAT. See also ADM 53.119578–79, ADM 53.120305–6, ADM 53.120376–77, and ADM 120677–78: March and April 1944 logs of the *Illustrious, Queen Elizabeth, Renown,* and *Valiant* respectively.

133. ADD 52564: Somerville diary entry of 3 April 1944.

134. Ibid., Somerville diary entry of 2 March 1944.

135. Information supplied by Vice Admiral Sir Kaye Edden (in March 1944 Somerville's operations officer) in conversation at Bosham, Hampshire, on 7 June 1984, and confirmed by David Brown in conversation in London on 21 June 1990.

136. G. Herman Gill, *The Royal Australian Navy, 1942–1945* (Canberra: Australian War Memorial, 1968), 388–90.

137. ADM 199.340 and 341: Operation COCKPIT and Operation TRANSOM respectively.

138. ADM 199.340: Operation COCKPIT. (See ADM 53.119578 for the log of the *Illustrious* and ADD 52564 for Somerville's relevant diary entries. Also, Historical Section, Admiralty, *Naval Staff History, Second World War, War with Japan*, vol. 4, *The South East Asia Operations and the Central Pacific Advance*, B.R. 1736(50)(4), 1957, 209–10, for an account of this operation.)

139. For the main developments in this story, see CAB 119.153.31: Memorandum of 12 March 1944 from Lambe to Directors of Plans. CAB 119.153.32: Memorandum of 15 March 1944 from Sugden to Lambe. CAB 119.153.36: JP (44) 116 (0), 22 March 1944, Air Strike against the Japanese Fleet. CAB 119.153.38: JP (44) 80 (0), 29 March 1944, Air Strike against the Japanese Fleet at Singapore. SHIPS' COVERS: 481-E. Docket XXX, 27 April 1945, deals with the problems of incompatibility between Avengers and British torpedoes. (Information about release mechanism problems was provided by Dr. John Sweetman in a letter of 12 March 1985 to this student.) The first landing on a carrier by a twin-engined combat aircraft, a Mosquito VI on the carrier *Indefatigable*, took place on 25 March 1944: though there had been plans for conducting carrier trials with the Mosquito it appears that the Japanese move to Singapore added a certain urgency to proceedings. In July 1944 618 Squadron RAF, having qualified for carrier operations, was reequipped with Barracudas in the escort carrier *Rajah*. It had been trained for the HIGHBALL role, using the Malaya for target practice. It was then reequipped with Mosquito IV and XVI before being embarked in the Fencer and Striker and sailed from Britain to Australia in October 1944 with a view to its being used in operations against Japanese shipping. See Norman Polmar, *Aircraft Carriers: A Graphic History of Carrier Aviation and Its Influence on World Events* (London: Macdonald, 1969), 313.

140. It is not clear from the minutes of this meeting to which move Churchill referred, and it seems that there was no discussion of whether any move was either possible or desirable.

141. CAB 119.17.49: Part II, Minutes of staff conference held on 26 February 1944.

142. F.O. 954.7.29–30: Unlisted memorandum of 29 February 1944 from Churchill to Chiefs of Staff.

143. The Twelve-Month Plan notwithstanding. But as late as March 1944 the naval member of the Strategical Planning Section noted in a draft of JP (44) 46 that the defeat of Japan was not foreseen until autumn 1948. See CAB 119.93.30.

CHAPTER THREE
ALICE-IN-WONDERLAND

1. CAB 79.71.87, CAB 119.93.35, and CAB 119.174.160b: Minutes of Chiefs of Staff meeting of 16 March 1944, and examination of signal of 15 March from Dill to War Cabinet Office. (Signal also given as CAB 105.85.164.)

2. CAB 80.81.207 and CAB 119.174.131: COS (44) 207 (0), 1 March 1944, Strategy for the War against Japan.

3. CAB 80.81.223 and CAB 119.174.135: COS (44) 223 (0), 5 March 1944, Strategy for the War against Japan. CAB 80.81.233: COS (44) 233 (0), 7 March 1944, Movement of the Japanese Fleet.

4. BROOKE 3.B.XII: Brooke diary entry of 7 March 1944.

5. W.O. 106.4620.342: Draft, dated 7 March 1944, of paper in reply to Churchill's unlisted memorandum of 29 February 1944.

6. CAB 119.174.143: Memorandum of 6 March 1944 from Directors of Plans to Chiefs of Staff.

7. CAB 79.71.78 and CAB 122.1072.30: Minutes of Chiefs of Staff meeting of 8 March 1944, and discussion of JP (44) 62 (Final), 7 March 1944, Strategy for the War against Japan, and JP (44) 63 (Revised Final), 8 March 1944, Overall Plan for the Defeat of Japan: India and Australia as Bases.

8. BROOKE 3.B.XII: Brooke diary entry of 8 March 1944.

9. CAB 79.71.79: Minutes of Chiefs of Staff meeting of 8 March 1944, and discussion of what the minutes defined as one Joint Planners and four Chiefs of Staff reports, two minutes from the prime minister covering COS reports, two notes, both with minutes covering COS reports, one note with minutes and two unnumbered papers. (For obvious reasons these are not listed here.)

10. This deadline was noted in JP (44) 71 (Final), 26 March 1944, Administrative Guidance for Supreme Allied Commander South East Asia and Commander-in-Chief India, but this fact must have been known well before this paper was finalized and discussed by the Chiefs of Staff on 30 March 1944. See CAB 79.72.104 and CAB 122.1078.29.

11. Not least because the mission was to proceed to Australia from India by sea. See CAB 79.72.93: Minutes of Chiefs of Staff meeting of 21 March 1944.

12. CAB 119.186.10: Signal of 22 March 1944 from Curtin to Churchill.

13. Interestingly, Somerville noted in his diary on 22 March 1944 that the deception of 9 March had proved unsuccessful. (See ADD 52562.) Although his previous comments were concerned with the problems that AXIOM had encountered in Washington, the available evidence suggests that the deception to which he referred concerned the Chiefs' of Staff decision on 9 March to proceed with the mission-to-Australia formula. See CAB 79.71.80 and CAB 122.1072.30a.

14. Eden saw this when he noted on a Foreign Office internal memorandum of 9 March 1944 that the Pacific option "now goes into cold storage while a mission explores Australia." See F.O. 954.7.36.

15. PREM 3.148.4.151–53: Memorandum of 15 March 1944 from Hollis to Churchill.

16. BROOKE 3.B.XII: Brooke diary entry of 13 March 1944. CAB 84.61 and CAB 119.17.69: JP (44) 72 (0) (TofR), 14 March 1944, Reconsideration of the CULVERIN Plan.

17. PREM 3.164.6.120: Signal of 10 March 1944 from Churchill to Dill.

18. ISMAY.IV.POW.1: Letter of 14 March 1944 from Ismay to Pownall.

19. This was further confirmed in the form of the instruction to produce a new CULVERIN plan. In thus directing the planners, Churchill ordered that Allied technological superiority over the Japanese should be employed in the form of an "artificial battlefield," in order to economize on manpower and bring the operation within the realms of the possible. This somewhat obscure but well-recorded episode is given only this passing reference but it would seem to confirm that at this stage Churchill was seeking any means whereby the Indian Ocean option could be kept alive.

20. CAB 119.79.49: JP (43) 376, 19 October 1943, Preparation of India as a Base. (This was a conclusion reached about arrangements for ANAKIM, but it applied equally to CULVERIN in the 1944 discussions.)

21. CAB 80.85.622: COS (44) 622 (0), 18 July 1944, Deployment of British Forces in India and the Indian Ocean.

22. Dharma Kumar, ed., *The Cambridge Economic History of India*, vol. 2, *c. 1757–c. 1970* (Cambridge: Cambridge University Press, 1983), 500–501. See also Ehrman, *History of the Second World War*, 5:466–69.

23. CAB 119.79.97: JAP (44) 24 (TofR), Potentialities of India as a Base. (This undated paper appears to be have been issued between 1 and 7 April.)

24. CAB 119.79.106: Draft, dated 15 April 1944, of a Joint Administrative Planning Staff paper, Potentialities of India as a Base, which was to be sent to the Ministry of War Transport. CAB 79.72.272 and CAB 119.181.S.21: Minutes of Chiefs of Staff meeting of 11 August 1944, and discussion of CSA (44) 91 (0), 7 August 1944, Preparation of India as a Base for Overseas Operations.

25. CAB 119.79.52: Signal of 19 October 1944 from Pownall, Somerville, and Pierse to War Cabinet Office.

26. Callahan, *Burma*, 95.

27. CAB 99.29.60–62: Minutes of the sixth Chiefs of Staff meeting of the OCTAGON serial, 9 September 1944.

28. CAB 84.6.35: Minutes of Joint Planning Staff meeting of 23 April 1943.

29. Reports of the incident and of the damage to the port are given in ADM 1.16065, ADM 1.16317, and ADM 199.1438. Somerville also provided diary comment on the incident: see ADD 52564. See also Kirby et al., *History of the Second World War*, 3:314–15. The reports differ in matters of detail, but it seems that fires burned in the city until 1 May and at their height could be seen from a distance of 75 miles. On 20 April Mountbatten sent a signal to

Ismay stating the incident would "not effect [*sic*] the mounting of amphibious operations . . . if they should be required." With the statement that this was unofficial but might interest the prime minister, this signal can only be described as mischievous. It seems that Ismay did not forward the signal, at least not before the twenty-fifth. See W.O. 106.4621.463 and 509.

30. CAB 119.79.108: JAP (44) 24 (Final), 15 April 1944, Potentialities of India as a Base.

31. CAB 79.72.104: Minutes of Chiefs of Staff meeting of 30 March 1944, and discussion of JP (44) 17 (Final), 24 March 1944, and of JP (44) 71 (Final), 26 March 1944. Both papers entitled Administrative Guidance for Supreme Allied Commander South East Asia and Commander-in-Chief India.

32. CAB 84.58 and CAB 119.79.49: JP (43) 376 (Final), 19 October 1943, Preparation of India as a Base.

33. CAB 80.82.384: COS (44) 384 (0), 1 May 1944, Labor Problems in Ceylon. CAB 80.83.392: COS (44) 392 (0), 3 May 1944, Labor Problems in Ceylon. (At this same time Ceylon was experiencing an increasingly serious food shortage and was in the middle of a constitutional crisis that rendered the political situation on the island somewhat volatile. See CAB 80.83.397: COS [44] 397 [0], 5 May 1944, Ceylon: Political Situation. An interesting sidelight on the situation in Ceylon was provided by Somerville in his diary entry of 9 March 1944 after a visit to Puttalam airfield in Ceylon. He expressed amazement at the amount of thieving of equipment in India, but noted that while Italian prisoners worked well, were thoroughly reliable, and were well liked, they had recently become restive because their pay was no longer enough to buy luxury items. They were paid 2s. 11d. (70c) a week. See ADD 52564.) CAB 79.75.171, CAB 122.1072.46a, and CAB 122.1075.77a: Minutes of Chiefs of Staff meeting of 25 May 1944.

34. CAB 79.71.78: Minutes of Chiefs of Staff meeting of 8 March 1944, and discussion of JP (44) 63 (Revised Final), 8 March 1944, Overall Plan for the Defeat of Japan: India and Australia as Bases. (Paper is also given as CAB 84.61 and CAB 119.174.149.) See also CAB 119.79.108: JAP (44) 24 (Final), 15 April 1944, Potentialities of India as a Base.)

35. CAB 99.28: PMM (44) 2, 3 May 1944, Conduct of the War against Japan. (This was a paper presented by Curtin at the Dominions Prime Ministers' Conference.)

36. CAB 66.47.140: WP (44) 140, 1 March 1944, Report for the month of January 1944 for the Dominions, India, Burma, and the Colonies and Mandated Territories.

37. PREM 3.63.8.144: Signal of 8 October 1944 from Curtin to Dominion Office.

38. PREM 3.63.8.144: Signal of 8 October 1943 from Curtin to Dominion Office. PREM 3.63.8.73: Resume of Anglo-Australian conference held at Chequers on 21 May 1944.

39. CAB 99.28: Resume of fifth meeting of the Dominion Prime Ministers' conference, 3 May 1944.

40. PREM 3.164.6.130: Memorandum of 4 March 1944, Docking Facilities available to Naval Force in Far East from Alexander to Churchill.

41. CAB 66.47.140: WP (44) 140, 1 March 1944, Report for the month of January 1944 for the Dominions, India, Burma, and the Colonies and Mandated Territories.

42. CAB 80.81.214: COS (44) 214 (0), 3 March 1944, Overall Plan for the Defeat of Japan: Communication to Dominions. (This paper was discussed by the Chiefs of Staff on the sixth. See CAB 79.71.76 and CAB 119.153.24.)

43. BROOKE 3.B.XI: Brooke diary entry of 25 February 1944.

44. PREM 3.63.8.144: Signal of 8 October 1943 from Curtin to Churchill.

45. ADD 52577: Cunningham diary entry of 3 May 1944.

46. ADD 52563: Letter of 3 January 1944 from Somerville to Cunningham.

47. CAB 80.83.467, CAB 119.180.190, and PREM 3.160.4: COS (44) 467 (0), 27 May 1944, Strategy for the War against Japan, Minutes of Anglo-Australian conference of the previous day. See also CAB 99.28: Resume of meeting of the Dominion Prime Ministers' Conference, 3 May 1944, and BROOKE 3.B.XII: Brooke diary entry of 26 May 1944.

48. BROOKE 3.B.XI: Brooke diary entry of 12 January 1944.

49. ISMAY.IV.SOM.5.1: Letter of 19 January 1944 from Somerville to Ismay. BROOKE 3.B.XI: Brooke diary entry of 14 February 1944. ADD 52564: Somerville diary entry of 4 March 1944.

50. ADD 52564: Somerville diary entry of 13 April 1944.

51. CAB 119.180: Unnumbered paper, dated 27 June 1944, from Canadian government to Dominion Office.

52. PREM 3.63.6.76 and PREM 3.63.6.74: Respectively, signals of 22 September 1943 and 20 January 1944 from British High Commissioner in New Zealand to Dominion Office. CAB 80.80.170 and PREM 3.63.6.51–53: COS (44) 170 (0), 18 February 1944, New Zealand Manpower.

53. W.O. 106.4620.321: War Office memorandum, dated 29 February 1944, prepared for inclusion in JP (44) 207 (0) (Revised Draft).

54. CAB 66.47.111: WP (44) 111, 16 February 1944, The Future of Indo-China and other French Pacific Possessions. F.O. 954.7.29: Unlisted Churchill memorandum of 29 February 1944.

55. F.O. 954.7.37: Foreign Office internal memorandum of 10 March 1944.

56. PREM 3.164.5.122: Letter of 3 March 1944 from Cherwell to Churchill. PREM 3.164.5.82 and PREM 3.260.12.23: Minutes of Defence Committee meeting of 3 April 1944.

57. John Winton, *The Forgotten Fleet* (London: Michael Joseph, 1969), 278–79.

58. PREM 3.164.5.68: Directive of 9 April 1944 from Churchill to the Admiralty. See also Ehrman, *History of the Second World War,* 5:476–78.

59. ADM 205.35: Memorandum of 10 March 1944 from Churchill to the Admiralty.

60. PREM 3.164.5.82 and PREM 3.260.12.23: Minutes of Defence Committee meeting of 3 April 1944.

61. CAB 80.83.398: COS (44) 398 (0), 5 May 1944, Shipping Implications of the Far Eastern Strategies.

62. CAB 79.71.81: Minutes of Chiefs of Staff meeting of 9 March 1944, and discussion of PMP (43) 36A (Final), 7 March 1944, Military Occupation in South East Europe.

63. CAB 99.27: COS (44) 62, 3 April 1944, Policing of Europe During the Continuance of the War with Japan and Afterwards.

64. March 1944 also witnessed staff talks between the RAF and AAF on the subject of British participation in the final attack on Japan. It seems that British planning had considered sending forty squadrons, half of which were to be tanker, for this effort, but that the RAF concluded that in a race for bases it was certain to come off second best to an AAF that planned to have 14,000 aircraft available for the final phase of operations. Although planning continued throughout 1944 and 1945 and ground elements were sent to the Pacific before the Japanese war ended, it seems that the idea of any real RAF role in the Pacific was discounted after March 1944. See CAB 119.14.106: Memorandum from RAF Director of Plans to Joint Planning Staff, Deployment of the RAF in the War with Japan, dated 18 August 1944.

65. CAB 79.73.135 and CAB 122.1072.41: Minutes of Chiefs of Staff meeting of 26 April 1944, and discussion of CSA (44) 38 (0) (Revised Final), 24 April 1944, Potentialities of India as a Base. The basic point had been outlined at the Chiefs of Staff meetings of 20 and 21 January and in COS (44) 70 (0) of 24 January 1944. See, respectively, CAB 79.69.17, CAB 79.69.19, and CAB 80.78.70.

66. ADM 167.120: Minutes of Board of Admiralty meeting of 10 December 1944, and discussion of paper, Manpower Required for the War against Japan. Paper also given as ADM 167.121. (The details set out here were related directly to decisions made at OCTAGON and which could not be known at this time, but since August 1943 the board had been aware of the manpower problems it faced in trying to raise a task force for the Pacific. For related matter, see DC (S) (44) 10, 8 February 1944, Provision of Shipping and Supply and Maintenance of the Fleet in the War against Japan, given as CAB 79.71.79. CAB 80.80.149: COS (44) 149 (0), 10 February 1944, Manpower for the War against Japan. CAB 79.71.81: Minutes of Chiefs of Staff meeting of 9 March 1944, and discussion of PMP (43) 36a (Final), 7 March 1944, Military Occupation in South East Europe. A later and detailed definition of the manpower problem was provided in JP (44) 106 (Final), 6 June 1944, Manpower one year after the Defeat of Germany. See CAB 84.62.

67. ADM 167.119: Memorandum, dated 10 August 1943 and prepared by Second Sea Lord, The Manning Position in 1944.

68. ADM 167.120: Minutes of Board of Admiralty meeting of 10 December 1944, and discussion of paper, Manpower Requirements for the War against Japan. Paper given as ADM 167.121. (The basic details were obviously known well before December 1944.)

69. CAB 80.81.255 and CAB 119.93.24: Letter of 9 March 1944 from Sinclair to Alexander included in COS (44) 255 (0), 14 March 1944, Landing Ships and Craft Requirements for 1944–1945. (Within two weeks these figures had been revised in a manner that accentuated the disparity of strength between Britain and the United States. COS [44] 279 [0], 22 March 1944, Landing Ship and Craft Requirements for 1944–1945, Ministry of War Transport. Report stated that between April 1944 and autumn 1945 Britain would produce 80 LSTs to the 590 LSMs and 755 LSTs that the United States would build. This paper confirmed that Britain simply could not afford the loss of merchant tonnage that diverting resources to the production of assault shipping on the scale needed for planned operations would involve. See CAB 80.81.279 and CAB 119.93.29.)

70. CAB 80.81.301: COS (44) 301 (0), 1 April 1944, Landing Ship and Craft Requirements for 1944–1945, The LST Position, Ministry of War Transport, Report. (Given the larger overheads involved in the Far East, the scale of establishment for an amphibious division there was greater than for an equivalent division in northwest Europe.)

71. ELLIS, 3, Chapter 30: Appendices 14 and 23.

72. At this time, however, the planning targets, based upon the premise of a German defeat by October 1944, was for the raising in Australia by 1 July 1945 of an amphibious force with 119 landing ships and 310 major and 1,100 minor landing craft, in addition to a fleet of four battleships, five fleet, five light fleet, and twenty-four escort carriers, twelve cruisers, sixty destroyers, one hundred escorts and another hundred minesweepers, and thirty-eight submarines, plus a fleet train of ninety-four auxiliaries. See CAB 80.83.469: COS (44) 469 (0), 27 May 1944, Administrative Parties for Australia, Directives.

73. CAB 119.38.115: Annex to signal of 28 November 1943 from Lumsden to War Cabinet Office.

74. CAB 119.17.2 and CAB 119.17.7: Respectively, signals of 1 and 7 January 1944 from Mountbatten to War Cabinet Office.

75. A briefing paper prepared for a planners meeting of 8 March 1944 cast doubts upon future imperial preponderance in the southwest Pacific theater and advised caution in the use of this argument. See W.O. 106.4620.348.

76. CAB 119.174,142: Letter of 6 March 1944 from Ransome to Mallaby.

77. CAB 79.72.107 and CAB 122.1078.30: Minutes of Chiefs of Staff meeting of 1 April 1944. CAB 84.62 and CAB 119.174.160.N: JP (44) 93 (S) (TofR), 1 April 1944, War against Japan: Alternative Proposal.

78. CAB 105.85.182 and W.O. 106.4621.425: Signal of 31 March 1944 from Dill to War Cabinet Office.

79. PREM 3.164.6.120: Signal of 10 March 1944 from Churchill to Roosevelt.

80. CAB 79.73.122, CAB 119.174.160.S, and CAB 119.187.1: Minutes of Chiefs of Staff meeting of 14 April and discussion of JP (44) 93 (Final), 12 April 1944, The War against Japan: Alternative Proposal. CAB 84.62: JP (44) 104 (S) (TofR), 14 April 1944, Occupation of Borneo. (This paper indicates that the formal authorization of this study was given at the second Chiefs of Staff meeting on the fourteenth.)

81. ADD 52577: Cunningham diary entry of 10 April. (Although this matter commands only *en passant* consideration at this point, the significance of this decision for the British effort in the Far East was considerable. Without a resident assault force in the Indian Ocean, all British amphibious options in the Far East were rendered dependent upon the release of forces from OVERLORD. SEXTANT had envisaged forces being freed from OVERLORD in and after September 1944, but the postponement of NEPTUNE from May to June 1944, when combined with the needs of overhauls, movement to the Far East, and training, rendered problematical any Indian Ocean option before April 1945, the onset of the monsoon in effect making this the last month when such operations were possible before November.

82. CAB 79.71.87 and CAB 119.174.160.B: Meeting of Chiefs of Staff of 14 March and discussion of signal of 11 March 1944 from Dill to War Cabinet Office. Signal also given as CAB 105.85.156. (The detailed outline of the revised American timetable was given by Dill to the War Cabinet Office in signals of 14 March 1944: see below. The meeting of the Joint Chiefs of Staff that gave effect to this revision was held on the twelfth, two days after Nimitz had attended a Combined Chiefs of Staff meeting.)

83. CAB 79.72.100 and CAB 122.1078.27: Minutes of Chiefs of Staff meeting of 25 March 1944, and discussion of JP (44) 77 (Final), 23 March 1944, Plans for the Pacific War. (This paper is also given as CAB 84.61 and CAB 119.174.160.D.)

84. This had been anticipated even before the acceleration of the American program in a memorandum that noted that lack of assault shipping would prevent CULVERIN in spring 1945 but "by autumn 1945 or spring 1946 CULVERIN . . . would be overtaken by events." See W.O. 106.4620.348a: Memorandum of 9 March 1944 from M.O. 12 to Director of Plans.

85. CAB 105.85.160 and PREM 3.164.6.117–18: Signal of 14 March 1944 from Dill to War Cabinet office.

86. CAB 105.85.156: Signal of 11 March 1944 from Dill to War Cabinet Office.

87. W.O. 106.4621.434: Memorandum of 11 April 1944 from M.O. 12 to Director of Plans on JP (44) 93 (S) (Draft) for meeting to be held that day.

88. CAB 119.174.160.S and CAB 119.187.1: JP (44) 93 (Final), 12 April 1944, The War against Japan: Alternative Proposals.

89. CAB 105.86.76: Signal of 30 March 1944 from Joint Staff Mission to War Cabinet Office.

90. ADD 52563: Letter of 10 March 1944 from Cunningham to Somerville.

91. CAB 105.85.182: Signal of 31 March 1944 from Dill to War Cabinet Office.

92. CAB 119.17.65, CAB 122.1078.7, and W.O. 106.4620.335: Signal of 3 March 1944 from Joint Staff Mission to War Cabinet Office. (Obviously there were a number of "controversial subjects," not just CULVERIN, relating to South East Asia Command, and these were cited in what was a review of issues at the meeting of 3 March: none, however, commanded more than *en passant* consideration at this stage of proceedings. See CAB 122.1078.6: Minutes of Combined Chiefs of Staff meeting of 3 March 1944.)

93. CAB 105.85.152: Signal of 6 March 1944 from Dill to War Cabinet Office.

94. CAB 105.71.528: Signal of 6 March 1944 from Joint Staff Mission to War Cabinet Office.

95. CAB 105.71.529: Signal of 7 March 1944 from Joint Staff Mission to War Cabinet Office.

96. CAB 105.85.154: Signal of 8 March 1944 from Dill to War Cabinet Office.

97. CAB 105.85.155: Signal of 10 March 1944 from Dill to War Cabinet Office and Supreme Allied Commander South East Asia.

98. CAB 105.85.171: Signal of 21 March 1944 from Dill to War Cabinet Office. (These problems concerned Imphal and the refusal of the Chinese to make any offensive effort in Yunnan. The American dimension to this problem made its way to the Chiefs of Staff in the form of COS [44] 318 [0], 4 April 1944, Operations in Burma, Employment of Chinese Forces. See CAB 80.82.318.)

99. CAB 105.85.164: Signal of 15 March 1944 from Dill to War Cabinet Office. (This would seem to suggest that Somerville's comments about "the deception of 9 March" referred to events in London rather than to events in Washington.) CAB 122.1166: Signal of 15 March 1944 from Joint Staff Mission to War Cabinet Office. (This signal stated that the issue of CULVERIN would not be raised until authorization from London was forthcoming, i.e., the British high command was to approve CULVERIN before it could be considered by the Combined Chiefs of Staff.)

100. W.O. 203.4995.2: Report on AXIOM Mission, Section II, Report submitted to Supreme Allied Commander South East Asia, dated 3 April 1944.

101. CAB 122.1166: Signal of 1 March 1944 from Wedemeyer to Mountbatten.

102. CAB 105.45.1589 and W.O. 106.4620.387: Signal of 21 March 1944 from Joint Staff Mission to War Cabinet Office.

103. This figure is the author's. The planners' own figures indicate overall requirement as 5.3 divisions for a CULVERIN in spring 1945, but that in reality this was four divisions. See W.O. 106.4620.407a: Memorandum of 26 March

1944 from Executive Planning Section to PD(Q). W.O. 106.4620.376: Memorandum of 18 March 1944 from GS(P) to M.O. 12. The difference between the totals seems to be the result of not calculating seven commandos and three long-range penetration groups in terms of division equivalents. It was the lack of these specialized formations that was seen as one of the major obstacles to meeting force-level targets for CULVERIN. See W.O. 106.4620.377: Memorandum of 18 March 1944 from M.O. 12 to GS(P). Whatever the real total, it compares to the seven assault and three garrison divisions that CULVERIN needed under the terms of SAC (44)7 as presented by the AXIOM Mission.

104. CAB 84.61 and CAB 119.17.70: JP (44) 72 (Revised Draft), 19 March 1944, Reconsideration of the CULVERIN Plan. (A Second Revised Draft was submitted on the twenty-second but withdrawn.)

105. CAB 119.17.77: EPS (44) 510, 25 March 1944, Operation CULVERIN. (This seems to be a feasibility study of JP [44] 72 [0] [Revised Draft]. This is not completely clear and it may be that more than one CULVERIN plan was under consideration at this time. For the purposes of this thesis it is assumed that this and the previous paper were related.)

106. CAB 119.17.86: Memorandum of 6 April 1944 from Hollis to Capel-Dunn.

107. The Joint Staff Mission, in preparing for the AXIOM discussions in Washington, on 4 March 1944 asked South East Asia Command if the force-level calculations for CULVERIN were genuine. (See CAB 122.1166: Signal of 4 March 1944 from Joint Staff Mission to South East Asia Command.) Somerville questioned the basis of the CULVERIN calculations, though it is not exactly clear to which set of figures he referred. He noted CULVERIN requirements as four fleet, two light fleet, and eighteen escort carriers, plus no fewer than eighty naval air squadrons, and that between them Colombo and Trincomalee could handle no more than four fleet and eight escort carriers. (See ADD 52564: Somerville diary entry of 30 March 1944.)

108. CAB 119.180.227: Memorandum of 8 July 1944 from Directors of Plans to War Cabinet Office.

109. W.O. 106.4620.376: Memorandum of 18 March 1944 from GS(P) to M.O. 12.

110. BROOKE 3.B.XII: Brooke diary entry of 17 March 1944.

111. BROOKE 3.B.XII: Brooke diary entry of 21 March 1944.

112. W.O. 203.4995.2: Report on AXIOM Mission, Section III, Report submitted to Supreme Allied Commander South East Asia, dated 8 April 1944.

113. The order to halt all CULVERIN planning was issued by 11th Army Group on 26 April 1944. See W.O. 203.1609.3a.

114. W.O. 203.4995.2: Report on AXIOM Mission, Appendix E, Minutes of meeting of 5 April. Report to Supreme Allied Commander South East Asia, dated 18 April 1944.

115. Ibid.

116. CAB 119.17.88: Minutes of Joint Planning Staff meeting of 5 April 1944.

117. CAB 119.174.162: Memorandum prepared for Captain Buzzard, RN, dated 16 April 1944.

118. CAB 119.174.161: Paper prepared by the Strategical Section of the Joint Planning Staff and dated 17 April 1944. (It seems that at the same time South East Asia Command was considering the possibility of its being ordered to complete the reconquest of Burma in terms of the seizure of Rangoon by airborne assault. See ADD 52564: Somerville diary entry of 14 April 1944. Given AXIOM's continuing presence in London, however, there must be the possibility that these two matters had a common source.)

119. These objections, indeed, were precisely those raised by the American high command when ANAKIM was presented later, in a rechristened form, for its consideration.

120. The basic arguments set down in the memoranda of the sixteenth and seventeenth were consolidated in JP (44) 109 (S) (Draft), 18 April 1944, The War against Japan: Further Examination. See CAB 119.174.163.

121. ADD 52562: Somerville diary entry of 26 March 1944.

122. W.O. 203.4995.2: Report on AXIOM Mission, Section III, Report submitted to Supreme Allied Commander South East Asia, dated 8 April 1944.

123. F.O. 954.5.57: Signal of 14 April 1944 from Churchill to Roosevelt. (These studies were conducted under JP [44] 102 [S] and [E] [TofR], which, issued on 11 April 1944 and entitled The Capture and Use of Certain Islands, anticipated a formal directive being issued as a result of the staff conference of 8 April. Among the islands considered were Simalur, Nias, Batu, Christmas Island, and Timor. The final report was delivered on the sixteenth. See CAB 84.62.)

124. CAB 119.174: Unnumbered enclosure, Undated and unsigned memorandum. (Private information indicated to this student that an unrecorded Foreign Office meeting on the Far East question was held on 20 April 1944, and this memorandum was a summary of its conclusions.)

125. F.O. 954.7.31–32: Foreign Office internal memorandum, dated 1 March 1944. (This danger was recognized in a signal of 9 February from the Joint Staff Mission to the Chiefs of Staff on 9 February 1944 and submitted as a report two days later. This signal also recorded that Noble had raised the question of British problems in operating in the southwest Pacific with an unreceptive King, but Leahy had proved more accommodating and had suggested that the British move forces to the theater in every expectation that problems thereafter would resolve themselves. Just what significance may be placed on these comments is unclear but may have been important in the subsequent calculations of the Chiefs of Staff. See W.O. 106.4620.274a.)

126. F.O. 954.7.37: Foreign Office internal memorandum, 10 March 1944.

127. F.O. 954.7.81–89: Foreign Office internal memorandum, dated 22 May 1944, Political Considerations affecting Far Eastern Strategy (Summary). (The cover note of this document indicated that it could be used either as a minute from Eden to Churchill or as a brief for the prime minister's forthcoming meeting with the Defence Committee. There is no clear indication to which meeting

this refers, but it seems most likely that it was the conference with the Australian delegation to the Dominion Prime Ministers' conference that was held on the twenty-sixth.)

128. F.O. 954.7.81–89: Foreign Office internal memorandum, dated 22 May 1944. Commentary of Butler, dated 23 May 1944, on Foreign Office Internal memorandum, dated 22 May 1944, Political Considerations affecting Far Eastern Strategy. (Summary).

129. Ibid. Commentary of Cavendish-Bentinck, dated 23 May 1944, on Foreign Office internal memorandum, dated 22 May 1944, Political Considerations affecting Far Eastern Strategy (Summary). Eden wrote, "Very true," against this observation on the twenty-ninth. (It could be noted, however, that the original paper was more accurate than this analysis if only because manpower did not become the critical consideration because of Japan's unexpectedly early surrender: the paper noted the extent to which postwar considerations and calculations *vis-à-vis* the United States should determine British policy.)

130. But squaring the circle was possible with the type of logic displayed by Jacob with the argument that the manpower shortage made CULVERIN mandatory, a point that not surprisingly defeated at least some members of the War Cabinet Office and planning staffs. See CAB 119.180.187: Letter of 24 May 1944 from Mallaby to Sugden.

131. PREM 3.164.5.158–60: Signal of 23 December 1944 from War Cabinet Office to Joint Staff Mission.

132. PREM 3.164.5.150–51: Signal of 7 January 1944 from War Cabinet Office to SEXTANT (i.e., from Hollis to Churchill).

133. PREM 3.164.5.149: Signal of 10 January 1944 from Churchill to Admiralty.

134. Such an answer clearly invites the suspicion that the Admiralty knew full well that its logistical demands were problematical.

135. PREM 3.164.5.145–48: Memorandum of 19 January 1944 from Admiralty to Prime Minister.

136. PREM 3.164.5.145–48: Memorandum of 31 January 1944 from Churchill to Chiefs of Staff.

137. CAB 70.7 and PREM 3.164.5.133–41: DC 3(44) 10, 8 February 1944, Provision of Shipping for the Supply and Maintenance of the Fleet in the War against Japan.

138. PREM 3.164.5.131–32: Memorandum of 14 February 1944 from Churchill to Admiralty.

139. PREM 3.164.5.122–23: Memorandum of 3 March 1944 from Cherwell to Churchill.

140. PREM 3.164.5.119: Memorandum of 6 March 1944 from Ismay to Churchill. (This point was endorsed again by the Ministry of War Transport. See PREM 3.164.5.88–89 and PREM 3.260.12.24–25: Memorandum of 3 April 1944 from Jacob to Churchill.)

141. PREM 3.164.5.112–15: DC (S) (44) 15, 16 March 1944, Provision of

a Fleet Train. (This warning was repeated in the Jacob memorandum of 3 April 1944.)

142. PREM 3.164.5.82 and PREM 3.260.12.23: Minutes of meeting of Defence Committee of 3 April 1944.

143. CAB 80.82.307, CAB 119.93.39, and PREM 3.164.5.90–94: COS (44) 307 (0), 1 April 1944, The Fleet Train.

144. CAB 79.73.135 and CAB 122.1072.41: Minutes of Chiefs of Staff meeting of 26 April and discussion of CSA (44) 38 (0) (Revised Final), 24 April 1944, Shipping Implications for Far Eastern Strategies. CAB 79.73.136: Minutes of Chiefs of Staff meeting of 27 April 1944, and discussion of JP (44) 83 (Final), 25 April 1944, Shipping Implications for Far Eastern Strategies.

145. CAB 80.83.396 and CAB 119.174.173: COS (44) 396 (0), 4 May 1944, The War against Japan: Summary of Various Courses. (This paper had been ordered on 21 April 1944 as JP [44] 117 [S] [TofR] and had been submitted on 1 May 1944 as JP [44] 117 [Final].)

146. ADD 52577: Cunningham diary entry of 10 April 1944.

147. CAB 119.160.21: JP (44) 110 (S), 19 April 1944, Modification of Terms for Calculation of Shipping. Enclosure: draft of JAP (44) 22 (4PD).

148. CAB 119.174.160.S and CAB 119.187.1: JP (44) 93 (Final), 12 April 1944, The War against Japan: Alternative Proposals.

149. CAB 79.74.159 and CAB 119.180.181: Minutes of Chiefs of Staff meeting of 16 May 1944.

150. CAB 119.180.182: Memorandum of 17 May 1944 from Directors of Plans to Chiefs of Staff.

151. CAB 119.180.184: Minutes of Chiefs of Staff meeting of 18 May 1944 with Directors of Plans.

152. The question of a new directive to South East Asia Command was partly provoked by the continuing problems of priority between the airlift to China and ground operations in India and Burma and of Stilwell's ambiguous role in this theater. The question apparently came before the Chiefs of Staff for the first time on 23 March 1944. (See CAB 79.72.97: Minutes of Chiefs of Staff meeting of 23 March 1944.) The question was one that spluttered during April and only attracted serious consideration after 1 May 1944 (see CAB 79.73.140: Minutes of Chiefs of Staff meeting of 1 May 1944, and discussion of JP [44] 107 [0], 27 April 1944, Burma, Appreciation by Supreme Allied Commander South East Asia) as a result of American pressure (see CAB 80.83.401: COS [44] 401 [0], 5 May 1944, Operations in South East Asia Command). The directive's terms were effectively settled on 26 May 1944. (See CAB 122.1078.78: CCS 452/12, 26 May 1944, Strategy in South East Asia Command.) The directive was finally approved by the Combined Chiefs of Staff, and London so informed, on 2 June 1944. (See CAB 122.1078.85 and 86: Respectively the minutes of the Combined Chiefs of Staff meeting of 2 June 1944 and signal of that date from the Joint Staff Mission to War Cabinet Office.) The directive was issued to South East Asia Command on 3 June 1944.

(See Hayes, *History of the Joint Chiefs of Staff*, 582; and S. Woodburn Kirby et al., *History of the Second World War: The War against Japan*, vol. 4, *The Reconquest of Burma* [London: H.M.S.O., 1965], 1.) It can be seen, therefore, that this was one more Far East problem that beset the Chiefs of Staff at this time, and it proved a difficult one. Churchill and SEAC sought to retain an amphibious option, and SEAC also sought discretion to exploit whatever success was achieved at Imphal, Kohima, and Myitkyina: as the Chiefs of Staff noted, as they sought to avoid the amphibious option, such discretion would spell an end to any Indian Ocean amphibious operation in 1944. It seems that various cross currents were at work and the Chiefs of Staff were involved in May in trying to keep Churchill and Mountbatten apart. (See CAB 80.83.401: COS [44] 401 [0], 5 May 1944, Operations in South East Asia Command.)

153. See, for example, CAB 80.83.405 and CAB 122.1078.60: COS (44) 405 (0), 7 May 1944, Draft Directive to Admiral Mountbatten, Minutes from the Prime Minister.

154. CAB 80.83.405: COS (44) 405 (0), 7 May 1944, Draft Directive to Admiral Mountbatten.

155. ADD 52577: Cunningham diary entry of 8 May 1944. CAB 79.74.149 and CAB 122.1076.63: Minutes of Chiefs of Staff meeting of 8 May 1944, and discussion of COS (44) 405 (0), 7 May 1944, Draft Directive to Admiral Mountbatten. It may be noted, moreover, that at this point what should have been the routine question of Somerville's replacement as commander in chief of the Eastern Fleet had arisen to complicate matters. Somerville's replacement was actively sought by Mountbatten and Pownall amid allegations of Somerville's disloyalty to Mountbatten (see ISMAY.IV.POW.4.2: Letter of 28 April 1944 from Pownall to Ismay), though this seems to have been, at least in part, a blind for an attempt by Mountbatten to assume direct control of combined operations (see ELLIS, 3, Appendix 23: COD 66/44 of 5 February 1944, Annex I.) and over the Eastern Fleet. (See ADD 52577: Cunningham diary entries of 31 May and 7 June 1944.) Churchill first sought to block Somerville's departure because of the admiral's alleged enthusiasm for CULVERIN (see ADD 52577: Cunningham diary entry of 2 April 1944) and thereafter tried to insist that his nominated successor, Fraser, should be questioned in order to ascertain his views about CULVERIN. In the end Churchill tried to insist upon Tovey's appointment. (See ADM 205.35 file for exchanges between Churchill and Alexander between 19 April and 27 May 1944.) Churchill seems to have dropped his opposition to Fraser's appointment on 2 June after Mountbatten indicated he would not oppose Fraser's appointment, drawing from Cunningham the comment that "if Mountbatten thinks that Fraser is going to be easier than Somerville to deal with he will have a rude awakening." (See ADD 52577: Cunningham diary entry of 2 June 1944.)

156. CAB 79.73.133 and CAB 119.14.86: Minutes of Chiefs of Staff meeting of 25 April 1944, and discussion of CSA (44) 40 (0), 21 April 1944, Potentiality of India as a Base. As if, at this stage of proceedings, the British

high command did not have problems enough in dealing with these issues, the air lift to China presented additional complications. It was at this time that the Joint Chiefs of Staff sought to place this effort (Operation DRAKE) under the executive control of Arnold and under American as opposed to British and thence Allied authority.

157. CAB 80.83.401 and CAB 122.1078.53: COS (44) 401 (0), 5 May 1944, Operations in South East Asia Command.

158. The line of the Chindwin was acceptable as the limit of a British advance into Burma even as late as September 1944. See CAB 99.29.50–53: Minutes of Chiefs of Staff meeting of 6 September 1944 with Directors of Plans.

159. CAB 119.15.270: JP (45) 20 (Final), 16 January 1945, Exploitation of CAPITAL.

160. CAB 80.83.398: COS (44) 398 (0), 5 May 1944, Shipping Implications of Far Eastern Strategies. (This was one of two papers, the other being COS [44] 396 [0], 4 May 1944, The War against Japan: Summary of Various Courses, that were sent to the Joint Staff Mission on 8 May 1944 under the cover of Dill's "eyes only." See CAB 122.1078.61.)

161. CAB 79.71.78: Minutes of Chiefs of Staff meeting of 8 March 1944, and discussion of JP (44) 62 (Final), 7 March 1944, Strategy for the War against Japan and JP (44) 63 (Revised Final), 8 March 1944, Overall Plan for the Defeat of Japan: India and Australia as Bases.

162. ADM 199.1383: Basing U.K. forces in Australia, Reports by the Australian Chiefs of Staff, Part 1: Report by the Australian Chiefs of Staff to the Australian Government, 23 August 1944.

163. ADD 52577: Cunningham diary entry of 3 May 1944. PREM 3.63.8.106: Memorandum of 1 May 1944 from Ismay to Churchill.

164. BROOKE 3.B.XII: Brooke diary entries of 10 and 11 May 1944.

165. BROOKE 3.B.XII and F.O. 954.7.81–89: Respectively Brooke diary entry of 26 May 1944 and Eden comment of 29 May 1944 on Foreign Office memorandum of the twenty-third.

166. CAB 79.75.171, CAB 122.1072.46a, and CAB 122.1078.77a: Minutes of Chiefs of Staff meeting of 25 May and discussion of COS (44) 449 (0), 23 May 1944, The War against Japan. (The reason for the Chiefs' of Staff reticence seems to have been an awareness that this paper, which is given as CAB 80.83.449, CAB 122.1072.46, and F.O. 954.7.76–77, set out all too clearly the differences within the British high command. The paper also raised the issue of future command arrangements in the southwest Pacific theater and that this was certain to provoke Curtin's resistance. The paper also assumed an Australian involvement in the Middle Strategy and raised questions about Australian facilities, but these were matters that were unlikely to cause much offense.)

167. PREM 3.160.4.135 and PREM 3.160.4.136: Memoranda exchanged on 25 May 1944 between Ismay and Churchill.

168. CAB 80.83.467, CAB 119.180.190, and PREM 3.160.4: COS (44)

467 (0), 27 May 1944, Strategy for the War against Japan. (This paper is the minutes of the meeting of the twenty-sixth.)

169. ADD 52577 and BROOKE 3.B.XII. Respectively the Cunningham and Brooke diary entries of 18 May 1944.

170. CAB 119.180.184: JP (44) 140 (Final), 20 May 1944, War against Japan: New Project. (Paper also given in CAB 79.74.166.)

171. PREM 3.164.6.105: Signal of 21 May 1944 from Churchill to Somerville. (The PREM 3.164.6 file contains a considerable exchange of memoranda between Churchill and Alexander on the subject of reconnaissance of various targets, mostly in the South West Pacific theater, by British submarines. Alexander told the prime minister in the course of this exchange that reconnaissance reports on most of the targets could be secured from the theater command and not via Roosevelt or by unilateral British action in an American area of responsibility. The exchange lasted between the twenty-first and thirty-first, with one last flourish on 9 June. Obviously this effort by Churchill was a considerable one, though not wholly directed to the Indian Ocean.)

172. CAB 80.83.467, CAB 119.180.190, and PREM 3.160.4: COS (44) 467 (0), 27 May 1944, Strategy for the War against Japan.

173. BROOKE 3.B.XII: Brooke diary entry of 22 May 1944.

174. PREM 3.160.4: Memorandum of 22 May 1944 from Ismay to Churchill. Though not dated and issued until the next day, COS (44) 449 (0) was enclosed with this memorandum.

175. CAB 80.83.449, CAB 122.1072.46, F.O. 954.7.76–80, and PREM 3.160.4: COS (44) 449 (0), 23 May 1944, The War against Japan.

176. PREM 3.63.8.73–75: Revised minute, dated 23 May 1944, of Chequers meeting of 21 May 1944. (According to this record the British and Australian service chiefs were to have met on the twenty-second, but there seems to be no record, not even in the Brooke diaries which contain distinctly unflattering references to Curtin and the "drink-sodden" Blamey on 1 and 5 May and comments on other meetings with the Australians on 10, 11, and 12 May, that this meeting took place. But either the minute of the Chequers meeting is incomplete or there was another, unrecorded, conference at this juncture because it was at this time that another Anglo-Australian dispute was finally resolved. This concerned the British request, made two months earlier, to send a mission to Australia in order to assess the support facilities that would be available for British forces in the Dominion. Because this dispute lies outside the mainstream of events and its recounting would threaten the continuity of presentation, its outline is provided separately in the appendix to this chapter: suffice to note that it seems that the matter was resolved at this stage of proceedings.)

177. CAB 119.180.187: Letter of 24 May 1944 from Mallaby to Sugden.

178. CAB 122.1072.46: Cover note, enclosure being COS (44) 449 (0), of 24 May 1944, sent to Redmond. Writer not identifiable.

179. It was on the twenty-fourth, however, that Churchill ordered that Curtin and the Australian delegation should be informed of the main features

of the options discussed by the British high command but clearly warned that British priorities had not been decided. See PREM 3.160.4: Minutes of Chiefs of Staff meeting of 24 May 1944.

180. CAB 119.180.187: Letter of 24 May 1944 from Mallaby to Sugden.

181. CAB 119.187.7: Undated and unsigned memorandum, being a preliminary draft of JP (44) 104 (S).

182. CAB 119.174.161: Paper prepared by the Strategical Planning Section of the Joint Planning Staff and dated 17 April 1944.

183. CAB 119.187.8: JP (44) 104 (S) (Draft), 10 May 1944, Occupation of Borneo.

184. The Middle Strategy file in the PRO is CAB 119.187. Its docket lists nineteen enclosures, of which six proved traceable. The totals of references and files do not include signals sent under the CAB 105 serial. The files containing Middle Strategy/Modified Middle Strategy material consulted in the preparation of this argument were: ADD 52577; BROOKE 3.B.XII and XIII; CAB 79.72–79; CAB 80.83–86; CAB 99.29; CAB 119.174, 180–82, 186–87; CAB 122.1072; ISMAY.IV; and PREM 3.160.4.

185. CAB 119.187.9: JP (44) 104 (S) (Revised Draft), 24 May 1944, Occupation of Borneo.

186. CAB 119.17.86: Memorandum of 6 April 1944 from Hollis to Capel-Dunn.

187. ISMAY.IV.POW.3: Letter of 27 May 1944 from Ismay to Pownall.

188. W.O. 106.4621.462: Memorandum of 18 April 1944 from Army Director of Plans to ACIGS(0).

189. W.O. 106.4621.487: Minute on JP (44) 117 (S) (Draft) prepared for meeting of 30 April 1944.

190. W.O. 106.4621.475: Internal memorandum of 22 April 1944 from M.O. 12 to G1 M.O. 12 covering JP (44) 117 (S) (Draft) dated 18 April 1944.

191. W.O. 106.4621.484: Memorandum of either 27 or 29 April 1944 from M.O. 12 to M.O. 1 on preliminary draft of JP (44) 104 (S).

192. CAB 84.63 and W.O. 106.4621.490: JP (44) 117 (Final), 1 May 1944, War against Japan, Summary of Various Courses.

193. BROOKE 3.B.XII: Brooke diary entry of 18 May 1944.

194. PREM 3.63.6.16: DO (44) 12, 24 June 1944, Employment of New Zealand Forces. See also BROOKE 3.B.XII: Brooke diary entry of 15 June 1944, and CAB 79.76.194, CAB 119.14.101, CAB 122.1072.50, F.O. 954.7.133–36, and PREM 3.63.6.22–30: Minutes of Chiefs of Staff meeting of 15 June 1944. Among items discussed at this meeting were those concerning New Zealand, its being noted that there had been twelve sets of talks between the British and the dominion delegation at the Prime Ministers' conference.

195. CAB 79.72.93 and CAB 79.72.97: Respectively the minutes of Chiefs of Staff meetings of 21 and 23 March 1944. CAB 119.186.10: Signal of 22 March 1944 from Curtin to Churchill.

196. CAB 79.72.100: Minutes of Chiefs of Staff meeting of 25 March

1944, and discussion of CSA (44) 27 (0), 23 March 1944, Revised Arrangements for Administrative Parties for Australia, and JP (44) 77 (Final), 23 March 1944, Plans for the Pacific War.

197. CAB 79.73.124 and CAB 79.74.128: Respectively the minutes of the Chiefs of Staff meetings of 15 and 19 April 1944 and, at the latter, discussion of CSA (44) 38 (0), 17 April 1944, Potentialities of Australia as a Base: Final Report.

198. CAB 80.83.442: JP (44) 442 (0), 20 May 1944, Potentialities of Australia as a Base. (The mission's head, Rear Admiral Daniel, left Noumea for Australia on 28 April and submitted a preliminary report on 10 May 1944.)

199. PREM 3.63.8.73–75: Revised minutes, dated 23 May 1944, of Chequers meeting of 21 May 1944. CAB 79.74.166, CAB 122.1072.45, and CAB 122.1078.75a: Minutes of Chiefs of Staff meeting of 22 May 1944.

200. CAB 79.74.169: Appendices I and II to the minutes of the Chiefs of Staff meeting of 24 May 1944.

201. CAB 80.83.442: COS (44) 442 (0), 20 May 1944, Potentialities of Australia as a Base.

CHAPTER FOUR
THE ORIGINAL PURPOSE

1. PREM 3.160.4: Memorandum of 6 June 1944 from Ismay to Prime Minister, as covering note to COS (44) 489 (0), 5 June 1944, The War against Japan.

2. CAB 79.75.177 and CAB 122.1078.83a: Minutes of Chiefs of Staff meeting of 31 May 1944, and discussion of COS (44) 455 (0), 25 May 1944, Expansion and Distribution of Fleet Air Arm Squadrons during the Second Quarter of 1944.

3. By April 1945 the numbers had shrunk to three British and two Indian divisions.

4. CAB 79.75.181 and CAB 122.1072.476: Minutes of Chiefs of Staff meeting of 3 June 1944, and discussion of JP (44) 140 (Final), 20 May 1944, War against Japan: New Project, and JP (44) 156 (Final), 1 June 1944, The War against Japan, Aide Memoire. (It was the second of these papers that was finalized as COS [44] 489 [0], 5 June 1944, The War against Japan. See CAB 119.180.198 and F.O. 954.7.120–21.)

5. CAB 84.64: JP (44) 142 (Final), 22 May 1944, Possible Operations in the Far East. (This paper noted that a review of operations in Lower Burma, northern Borneo, Formosa and northern Sumatra (!) was presently in hand.)

6. This paper does not seem to have been discussed by the Chiefs of Staff: it must be assumed, therefore, that its conclusions were not encouraging and in the preparations for the meetings with the Australians the planners abandoned the study.

7. CAB 84.63: JP (44) 148 (S) (TofR), 27 May 1944, The War against Japan, British Effort.

8. CAB 84.63 and CAB 119.180.193: JP (44) 148 (Final), 31 May 1944, The War against Japan: British Effort. (This paper set out, apparently for the first time, a program that involved the use of Australian troops.)

9. CAB 79.75.181 and CAB 122.1072.476: Minutes of Chiefs of Staff meeting of 3 June 1944, and discussion of JP (44) 140 (Final), 20 May 1944, War against Japan: New Project, and JP (44) 156, 1 June 1944, War against Japan: Aide Memoire. (Paper also given as CAB 119.180.195.)

10. CAB 79.75.178 and CAB 122.1072.47a: Minutes of Chiefs of Staff meeting of 1 June 1944, and discussion of PHP (43) 36 (Final), 10 February 1944, and PHP (44) 31 (Final), 25 May 1944, both papers entitled Military Occupation in South East Europe.

11. CAB 119.180.184: Minutes of Chiefs of Staff meeting of 18 May 1944 with Directors of Plans. (Since the effect of this was to bring the Amboina option to the forefront, there must be a suspicion, no more, that also at work was the Admiralty planners' view that Britain should cater for operations that were within its reach rather "any supposedly ideal object which cannot . . . be maintained." See ELLIS, 3, Appendix 23: Draft memorandum of 11 May 1944.)

12. BROOKE 3.B.XII: Brooke diary entry of 1 June 1944. (Cunningham's diary carried no reference to this meeting.)

13. BROOKE 3.B.XII: Brooke diary entry of 14 June 1944.

14. CAB 105.72.34: Signal of 15 June 1944 from Joint Planning Staff Washington to Joint Planning Staff London.

15. CAB 122.1078.90b: Minutes of Combined Chiefs of Staff meeting of 11 June 1944. (One wonders whether there was an irony intended in the question: the minutes of the meeting seem to suggest a somewhat tense atmosphere.)

16. ADD 52577: Cunningham diary entry of 11 June 1944.

17. BROOKE 3.B.XII: Brooke diary entry of 14 June 1944.

18. ADD 52577: Cunningham diary entry of 14 June 1944.

19. For the basis of the Chiefs of Staff argument, see CAB 79.76.194, CAB 119.14.101, CAB 122.1072.50, F.O. 954.7.133–36, and PREM 3.63.6.22–30: Minutes of the Chiefs of Staff meeting of 15 June 1944, and discussion of JP (44) 162 (Final), 13 June 1944, Organization and Command in South East Asia. (Also given as CAB 84.63.)

20. ADD 52577 and BROOKE 3.B.XII: Respectively the Cunningham and Brooke diary entries of 15 June 1944.

21. CAB 79.75.190, CAB 119.93.52, and CAB 119.1072.49.29: Minutes of Chiefs of Staff meeting of 12 June 1944, and discussion of Minute of Prime Minister on JP (44) 156, 1 June 1944, War against Japan: Aide Memoire.

22. CAB 84.62: JP (44) 109 (S) (Draft), 18 April 1944, War against Japan, Further Examination.

23. F.O. 954.7.117: Foreign Office internal memorandum of 2 June 1944 and accompanying minute from Butler to Cardogan of same date.

24. F.O. 954.7.126–29: Memorandum of 10 June 1944 from Sinclair to Eden.

25. CAB 79.76.194 and F.O. 954.7.133–36: Minutes of Chiefs of Staff meeting of 15 June 1944.

26. Churchill, however, raised the issue with Roosevelt at the OCTAGON conference. See PREM 3.63.6.9: Memorandum of 15 September 1944 from Churchill to OCTAGON Party.

27. F.0. 954.7.132: Foreign Office internal memorandum of 15 June 1944.

28. F.O. 954.7.122: Foreign Office internal memorandum of 6 June 1944.

29. Despite its date, it seems that the memorandum was drafted on the ninth and thus before the outcome of the talks with the Joint Chiefs of Staff was known.

30. CAB 122.1072.50a and F.O. 954.7.130–31: Memorandum of 12 June 1944 from Foreign Secretary to Prime Minister. Also given as CAB 80.84.525: COS (44) 525 (0), 15 June 1944, The War against Japan.

31. CAB 79.76.198 and CAB 119.1072.51: Minutes of Chiefs of Staff meeting of 17 June 1944, and discussion of COS (44) 525 (0), 15 June 1944, The War against Japan.

32. CAB 79.76.204: Minutes of Chiefs of Staff meeting of 22 June 1944, and discussion of JP (44) 204 (Final), 22 June 1944, War against Japan: British Programme.

33. CAB 84.64: JP (44) 166 (Final), 21 July 1944, War against Japan: British Programme. (The paper was accepted as COS [44] 553 [0], 22 June 1944, War against Japan: British Programme. See CAB 80.84.553 and CAB 119.180.212.)

34. CAB 119.180.213: Minute of 24 June 1944 from Prime Minister to Chiefs of Staff.

35. CAB 119.180.214: Undated and unsigned memorandum, for use as a Chiefs' of Staff aide memoire, on the subject of Churchill's minute of 24 June 1944. (This memorandum appears to be either a paper that was superseded by or a preliminary draft authorized by JP [44] 175 [0] [TofR], 26 June 1944, Middle Strategy, Operational Examination.

36. CAB 79.76.216 and CAB 119.1072.54: Minutes of Chiefs of Staff meeting of 30 June 1944, and discussion of COS (44) 216 (0), 30 June 1944, War against Japan: British Programme.

37. CAB 79.76.209 and F.O. 954.7.140: Minutes of Chiefs of Staff meeting of 26 June 1944, and discussion of signal from Lumsden to War Cabinet Office of 24 June 1944. (Lumsden also sent to a letter to Mallaby pointing out the implications of MacArthur's plans for CULVERIN, FIRST CULVERIN, and any Bay of Bengal operation. See CAB 119.180 Unnumbered.)

38. CAB 119.180.223 and F.O. 954.7.143–44: Signal of 4 July 1944 from Curtin to Churchill.

39. It is unclear, however, if the contents of Curtin's signal were known to the Chiefs of Staff before what should have been the crucial, and deciding, war cabinet meeting of 6 July 1944. The contents of the signal were set out in

JP (44) 179 (Final), 6 July 1944, British Contribution in the Far East, Mr Curtin's Views (see CAB 84.64), and the lateness of the meeting of that day suggests that the service chiefs did know of the signal. In any event the meeting of the sixth proved indecisive. It was not until the eighth that they discussed it in their routine meeting. See CAB 79.77.227 and CAB 122.1072.54b.

40.   CAB 119.186.82a: Signal of 29 May from Liaison Headquarters (of visiting British mission?) to War Cabinet Office.

41.   CAB 79.77.223: Minutes of Chiefs of Staff meeting of 6 July 1944, and discussion of COS (44) 553 (0), 22 June 1944, War against Japan: British Programme.

42.   ADD 52577: Cunningham diary entry of 5 July 1944.

43.   BROOKE 3.B.XII: Brooke diary entry for 6 July 1944.

44.   CAB 79.77.225, CAB 119.1072.54a, and F.O. 954.7.148–50: Minutes of Chiefs of Staff meeting of 6 July 1944, and discussion of COS (44) 553 (0), 22 June 1944, War against Japan: British Programme.

45.   BROOKE 3.B.XII: Brooke diary entry of 10 July 1944.

46.   CAB 79.77.229 and F.O. 954.7.151: Minutes of Chiefs of Staff meeting of 10 July 1944.

47.   CAB 80.85.596: COS (44) 596 (0), 6 July 1944, Force of LCI(L) for South West Pacific.

48.   CAB 79.77.226: Minutes of Chiefs of Staff meeting of 7 July 1944, and discussion of COS (44) 596 (0), 6 July 1944, Force of LSI(L) for the South West Pacific.

49.   CAB 79.77.230 and CAB 122.1072.56a: Minutes of Chiefs of Staff meeting of 11 July 1944.

50.   CAB 79.77.235: Minutes of Chiefs of Staff meeting of 14 July 1944.

51.   CAB 80.85.615: COS (44) 615 (0), 11 July 1944, Availability of LSI(L) in the Far East, Memorandum by the First Sea Lord. CAB 80.85.644: COS (44) 644 (0), 21 July 1944, Availability of LSI(L).

52.   CAB 80.83.407: COS (44) 407 (0), 8 May 1944, Provision of LST for the War against Japan. CAB 80.84.500 and CAB 119.93.51: COS (44) 500 (0), 6 June 1944, Production of LST. CAB 79.76.205 and CAB 122.1072.52: Minutes of Chiefs of Staff meeting of 22 June 1944.

53.   Cunningham informed King on 16 July 1944 that the required ships, along with one LSH, were to leave from the United Kingdom in Convoy UC 32 on 2 August, acknowledgment being made by King on the seventeenth. The exchange of signals is given as PREM 3.164.6.89 and 88. (As a footnote to this episode, it is worth noting that the LSH was none other than the *Lothian*, and the sorry story of her passage to and time in the Pacific Ocean is to be found in Bill Glenton's *Mutiny in Force X* [London: Hodder and Stoughton, 1986].)

54.   The issue was discussed by the Chiefs of Staff three days later, but it was one of which the service chiefs had been painfully aware for some time. See CAB 79.75.185: Minutes of Chiefs of Staff meeting of 8 June 1944, and discussion of JP (44) 106 (Final), 6 June 1944, Manpower one year after the Defeat of Germany.

55. CAB 80.84.498: COS (44) 498 (0), 5 June 1944, Assault Lift for the War against Japan.

56. With lift for one division left in the Indian Ocean, this refers to Pacific capability. See CAB 80.85.617: COS (44) 617 (0), 11 July 1944, Requirements for LSF. (The *Antwerp* was converted during 1944 as one of the two ships required in this role.)

57. CAB 79.77.230 and CAB 122.1072.56a: Minutes of Chiefs of Staff meeting of 11 July 1944.

58. CAB 84.64: JP (44) 175 (0) (TofR), 26 June 1944, Middle Strategy, Operational Examination.

59. CAB 79.77.233 and CAB 122.1072.56b: Minutes of Chiefs of Staff meeting of 13 July 1944, and discussion and approval of JP (44) 175 (Final), 11 July 1944, The Capture of Amboina, as COS (44) 623 (0).

60. CAB 119.180.227: Memorandum of 8 July 1944 from Directors of Plans to War Cabinet Office.

61. ADD 52577: Cunningham diary entry of 14 July 1944. (This entry was extremely rude about Churchill and his ministerial colleagues. Cunningham continued, "The attitude . . . of the politicians . . . is astonishing. They are obviously frightened of the Americans laying down the law as to what is to happen when Japan is defeated to the various islands and other territories. This appears to be quite likely if the Americans are left to fight Japan by themselves. But they will not lift a finger to get a force into the Pacific. They prefer to hover around the outside and recapture our rubber trees." From the minutes this seems to have been less than fair to Attlee and Eden.)

62. BROOKE 3.B.XII: Brooke diary entry of 14 July 1944.

63. CAB 79.77.236, CAB 122.1072.58a, and F.O. 954.7.160–63: Minutes of Chiefs of Staff meeting of 14 July 1944, and discussion of COS (44) 553 (0), 22 June 1944, War against Japan: British Programme, COS (44) 623 (0), 13 July 1944, The capture of Amboina, and unnumbered paper, Disposition of the Indian Army.

64. CAB 79.77.238 and CAB 122.1079.8a: Minutes of the Chiefs of Staff meeting of 17 July 1944. (The Joint Staff Mission was informed of the recall of Mountbatten that same day. See CAB 105.60.175 and CAB 122.1079.8.)

65. CAB 119.180.232: Memorandum of 18 July 1944 from Future Planners Section to Joint Planning Staff.

66. CAB 119.180.231: Minutes of meeting of Joint Planning Staff of 18 July 1944. (Presumably the SECOND CULVERIN plans were reconsidered over the weekend.)

67. CAB 79.78.242, CAB 119.181.(S-3), and CAB 122.1079.8b: Minutes of Chiefs of Staff meeting of 20 July 1944, and discussion of prime minister's memorandum D230/4 of 18 July 1944.

68. CAB 119.181.(S-1): Minutes of meeting of Joint Planning Staff of 19 July 1944.

69. CAB 84.64: JP (44) 193 (S) (TofR), 19 July 1944, Operations against Malaya.

70. Ibid.: JP (44) 194 (S) (TofR), 20 July 1944, Bay of Bengal Strategy.

71. CAB 105.46.130: Signal of 11 July 1944 from Joint Staff Mission to Chiefs of Staff. (This signal provided the outline of CCS 417/3 which had set out the need for an invasion of Japan, rather than its blockade and bombardment, as the means of enforcing its surrender.)

72. The Joint Planning Staff was ordered to examine the change under the terms of JP (44) 184 (S) (TofR), 12 July 1944, Overall Objective in the War against Japan, and it submitted its final report on the twenty-fourth. See CAB 84.64. The Joint Staff Mission reported that Duncan, the U.S. Navy's Director of Plans, had advised that it was anticipated that the Japanese would put out peace feelers and the change was the means of closing the door on those who might want to accept these overtures. The JSM view was that three needs, to commit America's allies, to guard against the possibility of Roosevelt not being reelected, and to prepare the U.S. public for the losses that would be incurred in this operation, were behind the change. See CAB 119.180.243: Signal of 20 July 1944 from Joint Staff Mission to Chiefs of Staff.

73. CAB 84.64 and CAB 119.180.252: JP (44) 192 (S) (TofR), 19 July 1944, Kyushu. (The instruction was withdrawn on 2 August 1944.)

74. CAB 122.1079.9, 10, 11, and 12: Respectively signals 205, 206, 207, and 208 of 23 July 1944 from South East Asia Command to War Cabinet Office. (The alternatives were presented as Y and Z in Signal 205, and Signal 208 defined Y and Z as CHAMPION and VANGUARD respectively. Somewhat confusingly, both were subsequently renamed, CHAMPION becoming CAPITAL and VANGUARD becoming first LIMELIGHT and later DRACULA. For the purposes of simplicity, throughout the period when they were under discussion, i.e., until the start of OCTAGON, these operations are referred to as CHAMPION and VANGUARD. Signals 205, 206, and 207 were consolidated and presented to the Joint Chiefs of Staff as CCS 452/17, 31 July 1944, Plans for Operations in Burma. See CAB 122.1079.15.)

75. CAB 199.181.(M-1): Signal of 26 July 1944 from Mountbatten to War Cabinet Office.

76. The first South East Asia Command paper to deal with an assault on Rangoon was considered as JP (44) 149 (Final), 27 May 1944, Recapture of Rangoon, which included SEAC War Staff (44) 25 (Draft) of 9 April 1944, which was during AXIOM's second visit to London. See CAB 84.63.

77. CAB 80.85.654 and CAB 119.16.10: COS (44) 654 (0), 25 July 1944, Prime Minister's Minute: Future Operations in South East Asia Command.

78. The second of the meetings on the ninth continued into the early hours of the tenth. See BROOKE 3.B.XII: Brooke diary entry for 9 August 1944.

79. At this time Churchill was scheduled to go to Italy on 9 August 1944. Given the need for pre-OCTAGON consultations with the Americans, this was clearly the deadline for a decision. See BROOKE 3.B.XII: Brooke diary entry of 4 August 1944.

80. As Churchill knew at least by 7 August 1944, that is, before the crucial

meetings of the eighth and ninth. The minutes of the Chiefs of Staff meeting with Mountbatten on the seventh record that the latter noted that Churchill had been informed of the views of South East Asia Command. See CAB 79.79.262, CAB 119.16.21, and CAB 122.1079.20a.

81. Kirby et al., *History of the Second World War,* 4:3–6, states that the CHAM-PION-VANGUARD formula was proposed by South East Asia Command planners on 14 July 1944 and that on the twenty-ninth 11th Army Group issued orders for preparations for a major offensive in Upper Burma and minor operations in the Arakan. It also states that on 1 August Giffard informed his subordinates that CHAMPION would be executed and the respective claims of it and VAN-GUARD would be decided in September. This was more or less what was decided and what happened, but on what basis Giffard could have made such an analysis, and how these events fit into the overall pattern of events as they unfolded elsewhere, is not known to this student.

82. CAB 79.78.254: Minutes of Chiefs of Staff meeting of 1 August 1944, and discussion of signal of 14 July 1944 from Joint Staff Mission to Chiefs of Staff.

83. CAB 84.64: JP (44) 198 (E) (TofR), 25 July 1944, Operations in Burma.

84. CAB 79.79.259, CAB 119.111.32, and CAB 122.1079.19: Minutes of Chiefs of Staff meeting of 4 August 1944, and discussion of JP (44) 198 (Final), 2 August 1944, Operations in Burma.

85. CAB 79.79.261: Minutes of Chiefs of Staff meeting of 5 August 1944.

86. ADD 52577 and BROOKE 3.B.XII: Respectively the Cunningham and Brooke diary entries of 7 August 1944.

87. CAB 79.79.262, CAB 119.16.21, and CAB 122.1079.20a: Minutes of Chiefs of Staff meeting of 7 August 1944, and discussion of COS (44) 701 (0), 6 August 1944, Use of Amphibious Resources in South East Asia, JP (44) 194 (Final), 6 August 1944, Bay of Bengal Strategy, and JP (44) 204 (Final), 6 August 1944, Operations in Burma: Requirements and Provision. (This meeting was divided into three parts, Mountbatten and Wedemeyer being excluded from the first and third sessions. The matters noted here arose in the first session. Future references to this meeting are cited as CAB 79.79.262 only and give session.)

88. Kirby et al., *History of the Second World War,* 4:5, disputes this.

89. CAB 80.86.701, CAB 119.181.(S-17a), and CAB 122.1079.19a: COS (44) 701 (0), 6 August 1944, Use of Amphibious Forces in South East Asia.

90. CAB 79.79.262: Minutes of Chiefs of Staff meeting of 7 August 1944, second session attended by Mountbatten and Wedemeyer.

91. ADD 52577: Cunningham diary entry of 7 August 1944.

92. CAB 79.79.262: Minutes of Chiefs of Staff meeting of 7 August 1944, third session.

93. ADD 52577: Cunningham diary entry of 7 August 1944. CAB 79.79.262: Minutes of Chiefs of Staff meeting of 7 August 1944, third session.

94. CAB 80.86.703 and CAB 119.16.22: COS (44) 703 (0), 7 August 1944, Operations in Burma, Aide Memoire for the Chiefs of Staff.

95. BROOKE 3.B.XII: Brooke diary entry for 26 July 1944. (The comment referred to a meeting with Churchill devoted to the manpower position, the needs of industry, the postwar requirements of Europe, and the demands of the Japanese war. The minutes of this meeting are elusive, and the only detail is provided by Cunningham in his diary observation of that date in which he noted that Britain would be caught by these various conflicting claims. The First Sea Lord also noted that Britain had undertaken to fight alongside the United States in the Pacific and to be self-sufficient into the bargain. The latter, he recognized, was impossible. See ADD 52577.)

96. ADD 52577: Cunningham diary entry for 8 August 1944.

97. CAB 79.79.264 and CAB 119.16.25: Minutes of Chiefs of Staff meeting of 8 August 1944, held between 1100 and 1330. (This was the second Chiefs of Staff meeting of the day, the first, which began at 1030, being the preliminary to this meeting with Churchill, Attlee, Eden, and Lyttleton. The first meeting is recorded under CAB 79.79.263.)

98. ADD 52577: Cunningham diary entry for 8 August 1944.

99. CAB 79.79.265 and CAB 119.181.(S-17b): Minutes of Chiefs of Staff meeting of 8 August 1944, held between 1600 and 1830.

100. CAB 79.79.266 and CAB 119.181.(S-17c): Minutes of Chiefs of Staff meeting of 8 August 1944, held between 2230 and 0100 of the 9th.

101. CAB 79.79.267: Minutes of Chiefs of Staff meeting of 9 August 1944, and discussion of annexed Aide Memoire Draft Policy (Basis for Discussion).

102. CAB 79.79.268 and CAB 119.181.(S-18a): Minutes of Chiefs of Staff meeting of 9 August 1944, begun at 1230.

103. The Brooke package was very close to the proposals in an aide memoire, dated 7 August 1944, that had been prepared for Cunningham. See CAB 119.181.(M-10).

104. ADD 52577: Cunningham diary entry for 9 August 1944.

105. BROOKE 3.B.XII: Brooke diary entry for 9 August 1944.

106. CAB 79.79.269 CAB 119.181.(S-19) and CAB 122.1072.68: Minutes of Chiefs of Staff meeting of 9 August 1944, held between 2230 and 0130 on the tenth.

107. As Cunningham noted in his diary on 10 August 1944. See ADD 52577.

108. Perhaps significantly, at the Chiefs of Staff meeting with Mountbatten on the fifth Brooke had noted that current thinking was that Germany might be defeated by October. See CAB 79.79.261. It is hard to give a precise form to what was clearly a hope, expectation, or confidence during August that the European war would end with the current campaigning season. See, for example, CAB 79.79.280 and CAB 119.16.40.

109. Or, as a later staff paper summarized the matter, Britain could not

sustain its existing commitment in Southeast Asia and at the same time assume an amphibious role in the southwest Pacific and a naval role in the central Pacific. See CAB 99.29.119–23: JS (OCTAGON) 9 (Final), 9 September 1944, Courses of Action in the War with Japan.

110. This draft is given as CAB 119.16.30.

111. CAB 79.79.270, CAB 119.16.28, CAB 119.181.(S-20) and CAB 122.1079.21b: Minutes of Chiefs of Staff meeting of 10 August 1944, and discussion of JP (44) 206 (Final), dated 7 August 1944, and JAP (44) 63 (Final), dated 5 August 1944, both entitled Potentialities of Australia as a Base for the Middle Strategy.

112. CAB 119.186.93: Signal of 28 July 1944 from British Mission (in Australia) to War Office.

113. CAB 119.16.26: Memorandum of 9 August 1944 from Metcalfe (Ministry of War Transport) to Mallaby. (This warning was supported by a memorandum of 1 September 1944 from the Ministry of War Production to the War Cabinet Office that indicated that the end of the war in Europe would not necessarily result in the release of shipping for the war in the Far East. [See CAB 119.16.42.] Without going into this lengthy and complicated issue, the demands of forces of occupation in Europe, the need to repatriate imperial forces, and the transfer of American forces to the United States en route to the Pacific war meant, paradoxically, that the demands on British shipping would increase rather than decrease with the end of the war in Europe, with obvious implications for British operations. See also BROOKE 3.B.XII: Brooke diary entry of 6 September 1944.)

114. CAB 119.160.21: JP (44) 110 (S), 19 April 1944, Modification of Strategic Bases for Calculation of Shipping for Far East, Note by the Strategical Planning Section. This paper noted, without dissent, that this was the conclusion drawn in JAP (44) 22 (Fourth Preliminary Draft) which had been completed between the fifteenth and nineteenth but which is not on file.

115. BROOKE 3.B.XII: Brooke diary entry of 10 August 1944.

116. ADD 52577: Cunningham diary entry of 10 August 1944.

117. CAB 105.61.243, CAB 119.16.33a, CAB 119.181.(S-22), CAB 122.1079.21, and F.O. 954.7.173–76: Signal of 12 August 1944 from Chiefs of Staff to Joint Staff Mission. (The delay in finalizing the text of this signal was no doubt related to the fact that, according to Cunningham's diary entry of the eleventh, "In a closed session Ismay told us that he was just raving last night and absolutely unbalanced. He cannot get over having not had his way over ANVIL." See ADD 52577.)

118. CAB 122.1079.23: Signal of 14 August 1944 from Joint Staff Mission to Chiefs of Staff.

119. CAB 105.47.204: Signal of 18 August 1944 from Joint Staff Mission to Chiefs of Staff.

120. CAB 79.79.274, CAB 119.16.33, and CAB 119.181.(S-26): Minutes of Chiefs of Staff meeting of 14 August 1944. (Cunningham recorded that two

letters Mountbatten proposed to send to Marshall were suppressed by the Chiefs of Staff. See ADD 52577: Cunningham diary entry of 14 August 1944.)

121. Within another week Mountbatten raised the question of CULVERIN or a similar operation against Malaya in October 1945, his justification being that it was essential to recover Singapore should an armistice with Japan come in 1945. See CAB 80.86.758: COS (0) 758 (0), 22 August 1944, Operations in South East Asia Command.

122. BROOKE 3.B.XII: Brooke diary entry of 17 August 1944.

123. Ibid.: Brooke diary entry of 18 August 1944.

124. CAB 79.79.262: As proposed in JP (44) 204 (Final), 6 August 1944, Operations in Burma: Requirements and Provision, VANGUARD involved an airborne landing by one division on D day and a seaborne landing by one brigade on D+2; three divisions being airlanded between D+2 and D+14; and four divisions and two brigades being landed by sea on and after D+21.

125. CAB 80.86.758, CAB 119.181.(S-36), and CAB 122.1079.39a: COS (44) 758 (0), 22 August 1944, Operations in South East Asia Command, Memorandum by Supreme Allied Commander.

126. CAB 80.86.739: COS (44) 739 (0), 17 August 1944, Operations in South East Asia Command, Memorandum by Supreme Allied Commander.

127. CAB 79.79.278, CAB 119.16.36, and CAB 119.181.(S-27): Minutes of Chiefs of Staff meeting of 17 August 1944, and discussion of JP (44) 210 (Final), 16 August 1944, Proposed Operations in South East Asia Command. (The main line of argument developed by the Directors at this meeting was that CHAMPION and VANGUARD were not complementary but in rivalry, and that the real choice was between investing all resources in VANGUARD or canceling the operation. The paper stated that first-phase CHAMPION would require resources needed for VANGUARD and that the resources needed for the two operations were unlikely to be available in March 1945 or, if available, were unlikely to be in position at this time. The logic seems irrefutable.)

128. CAB 122.1079.22 and CAB 105.46.198: Respectively signals of 13 and 14 August 1944 from Joint Staff Mission to War Cabinet Office. The British proposals were formally presented as CCS 452/18, 15 August 1944, British Participation in Far Eastern strategy. See CAB 119.1079.25.

129. CAB 105.61.261 and CAB 122.1079.27: Signal of 18 August 1944 from Chiefs of Staff to Joint Staff Mission. (With such deficiencies it is hard to understand Brooke's attitude in the discussions with the planners on the seventeenth.)

130. CAB 105.47.204: Signal of 18 August 1944 from Joint Staff Mission to Chiefs of Staff. CAB 122.1079.29a: Signal of 18 August 1944 from Wedemeyer to Mountbatten. (Also see CAB 138.3.278: Minutes of meeting of Military Committee, Joint Staff Mission, of 18 August 1944.)

131. CAB 122.1079.30: Signal of 18 August 1944 from Joint Staff Mission to Chiefs of Staff.

132. CAB 122.1079.25e: Signal of 17 August 1944 from Joint Planning

Staff Washington to Joint Planning Staff London. (The current British estimate for the fleet that was to proceed to the Pacific "by mid-1945 probably [was] four battleships, six fleet, four light and fifteen escort carriers, twenty cruisers, forty to fifty destroyers, 100 escorts and a considerable fleet train, the whole consisting of a force which could make a valuable contribution to the crucial operations leading to the assault on Japan." This estimate was contained in the Combined Chiefs of Staff paper dated 15 August 1944. See CAB 122.1078.25.)

133. CAB 122.1079.44: Signal of 23 August 1944 from Joint Staff Mission to Chiefs of Staff.

134. CAB 122.1079.47: Signal of 23 August 1944 from War Office to British Army Section, Joint Staff Mission.

135. CAB 122.1079.29a: Signal of 18 August 1944 from Wedemeyer to Mountbatten.

136. Such assurances were given by both the Joint Staff Mission and, directly, by South East Asia Command. See CAB 119.181.(S-31 and -32).

137. CAB 105.47.212, CAB 119.181.(S-39) and CAB 122.1079.44: Signal of 23 August 1944 from Joint Staff Mission to Chiefs of Staff.

138. CAB 122.1080.2: Signal of 1 September 1944 from Joint Staff Mission to Chiefs of Staff. The American reply was given as CCS 452/21, 31 August 1944, Plans for Operations in Burma. See CAB 122.1079.51. The American answer had been anticipated by the Joint Staff Mission. See CAB 122.1079.50: Minutes of the Military Committee meeting of 31 August 1944.

139. CAB 80.86.758: COS (0) 758 (0), 22 August 1944, Operations in South East Asia Command. (The War Office estimated 22 September because of ramifications for CHAMPION [see W.O. 203.1541.53: Memorandum of 1 September 1944 from Ops 2 to BGS] but 1 October prevailed as the cut-off date for VANGUARD.)

140. CAB 119.13.5: Signal of 29 August 1944 from South East Asia Command to War Cabinet Office. CAB 80.87.803 and CAB 122.1080.11: COS (44) 803 (0), 3 September 1944, Provision of WACO gliders for Supreme Allied Command South East Asia, Memorandum by Chief of Air Staff.

141. CAB 119.13.19a: Signal of 4 September 1944 from South East Asia Command to War Cabinet Office.

142. CAB 119.181.(M-11): Memorandum of 8 August 1944 from Mallaby to the Directors of Plans.

143. CAB 119.13.22 and 24: Respectively signals of 4 and 5 September 1944 from Joint Planning Staff London to South East Asia Command.

144. BROOKE 3.B.XIII: Brooke diary entry of 5 September 1944. Cunningham noted the same day, "It takes little to raise his vengeful temper, and he will do anything then to get the better of our allies." (See ADD 52577.)

145. CAB 84.65 and CAB 119.13.16e: JP (44) 231 (Final), 3 September 1944, Release of Forces from Europe for South East Asia Command. (This study was ordered under JP [44] 231 [S] [TofR] on 31 August 1944 as the prospect of victory beckoned, but this report was accompanied by another, on

shipping resources, that effectively said that the suggested transfer was impossible. The second paper, JP [44] 224 [Final], is one to which reference will be made.)

146. CAB 119.182.3: JP (44) 232 (S), 3 September 1944, Course of Action in the War against Japan.

147. By this time, and on Churchill's insistence, VANGUARD had been renamed DRACULA. (See CAB 122.1080.1: Signal of 1 September 1944 from War Cabinet Office to South East Asia Command.) With CHAMPION also renamed CAPITAL at this time, these two operations will be given their new code names from this point.

148. CAB 119.13.28: Memorandum of 5 September 1944 from the Directors of Plans to Chiefs of Staff. (This memorandum was prepared in readiness for a planners meeting with the Chiefs of Staff on the sixth. Minute 3 is entitled Practicability of DRACULA in March 1945, and begins, "The original purpose of this discussion was. . . ." It is clear from this minute, however, that though the reference was to the meeting rather than DRACULA, what was really under review was DRACULA's practicability and neither the Istria operation nor the meeting.)

149. CAB 99.29.66 and CAB 119.13.48: Minutes of Chiefs of Staff meeting of 10 September 1944.

150. CAB 99.29.54–56: Minutes of the second Chiefs of Staff meeting of the OCTAGON serial of 7 September 1944. (This was virtually the same conclusion, *mutatis mutandis*, that had been drawn in April about the Pacific commitment.)

151. CAB 99.29.50–53, CAB 119.167.28g, and CAB 122.1080.20: Minutes of the first Chiefs of Staff meeting of the OCTAGON serial of 6 September 1944, and discussion of JP (44) 224 (Final), 3 September 1944, Major Personnel Shipping Commitments immediately following Germany's Defeat. Paper given as CAB 84.65 and CAB 119.167.28d: its calculations were that with some 1,370,000 men earmarked for transfer to India and 900,000 elsewhere in the Far East, DRACULA would tie up the entire British trooping capacity, one or both of the *Queens* excepted, for six months, while the total demand on British resources, which included Greece and Norway and the return of 3,000,000 Americans home, would take two years to clear.

152. CAB 99.29.60–62 and CAB 122.1072.78: Minutes of the sixth Chiefs of Staff meeting of the OCTAGON serial of 9 September 1944.

153. CAB 99.29.63–66 and CAB 119.153.6: Minutes of the seventh Chiefs of Staff meeting of the OCTAGON serial of 10 September 1944 and discussion of JS (OCTAGON) 9 (Final), 9 September 1944, Course of Action in the War against Japan. (At some stage it was suggested that DRACULA's employment of British forces from Egypt and the Canal Zone might allow a postponement of the 1 October deadline for the approval of this operation. In fact, the deadline for DRACULA was dependent on the movement of airborne and airlanded formations not those in the Middle East: the 1 October date, therefore, could not be changed. See CAB 99.29.130: JS (OCTAGON) 20 (Final), 13 September 1944, Mounting Forces from the Middle East for DRACULA.)

154. CAB 99.29.60–62 and CAB 122.1080.39: Minutes of sixth Chiefs of Staff meeting of the OCTAGON serial of 9 September 1944.

155. CAB 99.29.63–66 and CAB 119.153.6: Minutes of seventh Chiefs of Staff meeting of the OCTAGON serial of 10 September 1944.

156. CAB 99.29.66 and CAB 119.13.48: Minutes of eighth Chiefs of Staff meeting of the OCTAGON serial of 10 September 1944.

157. BROOKE 3.B.XIII: Brooke diary entry of 9 September 1944. CAB 99.29.60–62 and CAB 122.1072.78: Minutes of sixth Chiefs of Staff meeting of the OCTAGON serial of 9 September 1944.

158. CAB 119.13.45: Memorandum of 9 September 1944 from Chiefs of Staff to Prime Minister.

159. BROOKE 3.B.XIII: Brooke diary entry of 6 September 1944. (Planning, however, had to be continued, and seven weeks later the planning staff assessment was that six battleships, five fleet, four light fleet, and twenty-five escort carriers, and nine cruisers; seven divisions, four brigades, and twenty L.R.P.G. battalions; and thirty-six heavy bomber squadrons would be sent to the Far East with the end of the European war. See CAB 79.82.349: Minutes of Chiefs of Staff meeting of 26 October 1944, and discussion of JP [44] 255 [Final], 25 October 1944, Questionnaire from Canadian Joint Staff Mission. The logic of these figures seems elusive.)

160. CAB 105.47.265, CAB 119.153.2, CAB 122.1080.34, and F.O. 954.7.187: Signal of 9 September 1944 from Joint Staff Mission to Chiefs of Staff. (The American decision, given in CCS 452/25, 8 September 1944, British Participation in the War against Japan, Memorandum by the U.S. Chiefs of Staff, was that a British imperial task force was to operate in the southwest Pacific but that it would be able to reinforce the main American forces in the central Pacific if required. See CAB 119.153.1 and CAB 122.1080.27.)

161. CAB 119.153.7: Memorandum of 11 September 1944 from Ismay to Churchill, as annex to Minutes of Chiefs of Staff meetings of 10 September 1944. (From this memorandum it is clear that Churchill attempted to claim that he had never agreed to seeing the fleet proceed to the Pacific.)

162. There was, of course, a major altercation between the British and Australians over OCTAGON and the latter's not being consulted. See CAB 69.6.151: DO (44) 13, 20 October 1944, The War in the Pacific, for the multitude of signals that Churchill and Curtin exchanged between 12 August and 26 September 1944.

163. CAB 99.29.63–66 and CAB 119.153.6: Minutes of seventh Chiefs of Staff meeting of the OCTAGON serial of 10 September 1944.

164. CAB 99.29.67–68, CAB 119.153.8, and CAB 122.1080.43–44: Minutes of ninth Chiefs of Staff meeting of the OCTAGON serial (and the first in Quebec) of 11 September 1944, and discussion of two signals to South East Asia Command. (The request was formally submitted as CCS 452/26 [OCTAGON], 11 September 1944, British Participation in the War against Japan. See CAB 122.1080.45. The reply was given as CCS 452/27 and dated the thirteenth. See CAB 119.153.11 and CAB 122.1080.55.)

165. CAB 99.29.70, CAB 119.153.9, and CAB 122.1080.49: Minutes of eleventh Chiefs of Staff meeting of the OCTAGON serial of 12 September 1944.

166. The prime minister did say, however, that the objective of CHAMPION was Singapore, but that was rhetoric.

167. BROOKE 3.B.XIII: Brooke diary entry of 15 September 1944.

168. CAB 99.29.4–6: Minutes of Chiefs of Staff (OCTAGON) first plenary meeting of 13 September 1944. (On the fifteenth, when Churchill raised the question of the involvement of the dominions in the Pacific war, Roosevelt indicated that he welcomed Canadian involvement in the Pacific. See CAB 122.1073.24: Covering memorandum, prepared by Ismay, on COS [OCTAGON] 10, 15 September 1944, Canadian Participation in the War against Japan.)

169. CAB 99.29.14–17 and CAB 119.153.12: Minutes of third Combined Chiefs of Staff meeting of OCTAGON serial of 14 September 1944 and discussion of no fewer than eight papers, not listed here. (Two matters would seem to be worth noting *en passant*. First, though the meeting is noted for the King affair, it nevertheless endorsed the Upper Burma–Rangoon–Pacific formula with the authorization of COS 452/28, 13 September 1944, Directive to Supreme Allied Commander South Sea Asia, Memorandum by the British Chiefs of Staff, as COS 452/30. Second, according to Brooke, on the fourteenth King was not alone in trying to block the British commitment to the Pacific. It seems that Churchill tried one last time to repudiate this commitment, and in so doing provoked Ismay to tender his resignation, which was refused. This ended the matter. Brooke also noted that the Chiefs of Staff decided to get Churchill to hammer the nails into King's coffin at the final plenary session. See BROOKE 3.B.XIII: Brooke diary entry of 14 September 1944.)

170. CAB 99.29.77–79 and CAB 119.14.108: Minutes of sixteenth Chiefs of Staff meeting of the OCTAGON serial of 15 September 1944, and discussion of JS (OCTAGON) 21 (Final), 13 September 1944, British Operations in the War against Japan. (According to the final agreement the British were to send three divisions, and lift for two divisions, to the Pacific, and to raise three amphibious divisions in South East Asia Command. Given the fact that the raising of one three-division force was beyond British means, to undertake the raising of two forces raises obvious questions.)

171. It seems that the Burma issue was not allowed to divide the two allies as a result of the British willingness to meet American expectations over phase- and stop-lines for the second part of CAPITAL. The basis of agreement was established in negotiations on 31 August 1944. See CAB 105.37.234 and CAB 119.13.5: Signal of 1 September 1944 from Joint Staff Mission to Chiefs of Staff.

172. CAB 99.29.130: Memorandum of 13 September 1944 from Prime Minister to Chiefs of Staff. (Though there is a problem of timings and conflicting figures, it seems that after this memorandum was written the RAF added the requirement for another 49,000 men for DRACULA. When this happened Churchill, quite reasonably, returned to the issue of force levels in COS (44) 844 (0), 20 September 1944, Operations in South East Asia, Minute from

the Prime Minister. See CAB 80.87.844 and CAB 119.13.49. With the DRAC-
ULA requirement fixed at OCTAGON as one airborne and six other divisions, the
estimated deficit was 352,000 men. See CAB 99.29.105: JP (OCTAGON) 27
(Final), 21 September 1944, Operation DRACULA Requirements. By the twenty-
third the DRACULA total had been cut to 253,000. See CAB 80.87.848 and CAB
122.1081.3a: COS (44) 848 (x), 23 September 1944, Operations in South East
Asia, Minute from the Chief of the Imperial General Staff.

    173. CAB 122.1080.1a: Memorandum of 22 September 1944 from
Macready to Marshall.

    174. See, for example, CAB 119.13.18a: Signal of 3 September 1944 from
Chiefs of Staff to Joint Staff Mission.

    175. CAB 99.29.6–8: Minutes of Chiefs of Staff (OCTAGON) second plenary
session of 16 September 1944, and discussion of CCS 680/1, 15 September 1944,
War against Japan, Report by Combined Chiefs of Staff to President and Prime
Minister. (Paper given as CAB 99.29.41.)

    176. CAB 122.1080.1b: Memorandum of 22 September 1944 from
Macready to Marshall.

    177. CAB 122.1080.1c: Signal of 22 September 1944 from Macready to
Vice Chief of the Imperial General Staff.

    178. Somewhat surprisingly, Dill indicated that Marshall was "not so adverse
to finding American troops for northern Burma [as I had expected] in spite of the
political implications." See CAB 105.85.238: Signal of 25 September 1944 from
Dill to War Cabinet Office. This assessment, however, does not square with other
developments, two of which may be noted. On the twenty-third Churchill, in a
minute that set out his opposition to an advance beyond 200 miles to the north of
Rangoon and to an extension of second-phase CAPITAL to include the capture of
Mandalay, noted the Chiefs' of Staff receipt of the previous day's American refusal
to provide two divisions for Burma. See CAB 119.13.113: Memorandum of
23 September 1944 from the Prime Minister to the Chiefs of Staff. The minutes
of the Chiefs of Staff meeting of the twenty-fifth suggest that a firm American
decision had been given. See CAB 79.81.317. Thus the available record is con-
tradictory. While suspicion suggests that Churchill's observation is correct, it has
been assumed that "reluctance" did not mean "refusal."

    179. CAB 104.47.272: Signal of 23 September 1944 from Joint Staff
Mission to Chiefs of Staff.

    180. CAB 105.85.241: Signal of 26 September 1944 from Dill to War
Cabinet Office.

    181. CAB 79.81.324: Minutes of Chiefs of Staff meeting of 2 October
1944, and discussion of COS (44) 324 (0), 2 October 1944, and COS (44) 853
(0), 26 September 1944, both papers entitled Operation DRACULA; COS (44)
857 (0), 29 September 1944, Gliders, Glider Pilots and Transport Aircraft; and
COS (44) 869 (0), 2 October 1944, Release of LST from OVERLORD and the
Effect on Operation DRACULA.

    182. ADD 52577 and BROOKE 3.B.XIII: Respectively Cunningham and

Brooke diary entries of 2 October 1944. Brooke's entry was almost casual, Cunningham's noted with some regret.

183. CAB 105.61.371 and CAB 105.69.87: Signal of 5 October 1944 from Chiefs of Staff to Joint Planning Mission. (The letter was to the effect that to continue with DRACULA "would jeopardize other operations" and that CAPITAL should assume priority. Formal American agreement to cancellation was provided on the tenth. See CAB 119.15.149: Signal of 10 October 1944 from Joint Staff Mission to War Cabinet Office.)

184. CAB 119.182.1r: Signal of 13 October 1944 from Joint Staff Mission to War Cabinet Office. CAB 105.72.117: Signal of 17 October 1944 from Joint Planning Staff Washington to Joint Planning Staff London.

185. CAB 119.23.28: Memorandum of 3 October 1944 from Mallaby to Joint Intelligence Committee. CAB 119.15.160: Memorandum of 4 October 1944 from Sugden to Kimmins. W.O. 106.4622.602: M.O. 12 paper, dated 5 October 1944, entitled Operations in South East Asia Command. (The report requested by Mallaby was submitted, with its distinctly pessimistic conclusions, on the fourth. See CAB 119.23.30.)

186. CAB 119.23.31: JP (44) 251 (0) (Draft), 8 October 1944, Operation BUCCANEER.

187. Churchill did not. In discussion with Mountbatten and Wedemeyer one month later he endorsed a South East Asia Command provisional program that set out operations in the Arakan between November 1944 and January 1945, the Kra to be attacked between March and May, landings in Malaya to be staged in October and November, and DRACULA, with five divisions, between December 1945 and February 1946. See CAB 80.88.913 and CAB 119.15.172: COS (44) 913 (0), 22 October 1944, Operations in South Eastern Asia: Meeting at Cairo on 20 October 1944.

188. CAB 79.80.308: Minutes of Chiefs of Staff meeting of 15 September 1944.

189. As Brooke most clearly did over the Cairo program. See BROOKE 3.B.XIII: Brooke diary entry of 20 October 1944.

190. State Department [No. 7859], *Foreign Relations of the United States: Near East, South Asia, Africa and Far East, 1944* (Washington, D.C.: U.S. Government Printing Office, 1965), 5:254–56.

191. Ibid., 256–57.

192. Ibid., 177–80.

193. Cordell Hull, *The Memoirs of Cordell Hull*, vol. 2 (London: Hodder and Stoughton, 1948), 1476 and 1586.

CHAPTER FIVE

THE END OF STRIFE

1. ADM 199.196: The Eastern Fleet: Return of 12th November 1944.

(The totals exclude warships of the Eastern Fleet not in the Indian Ocean or Indian Ocean ports and shipyards.)

2. ADM 52564: Somerville diary entry of 19 April 1944. ADM 199.340: Operation COCKPIT, Historical Section, Admiralty, *Naval Staff History. Second World War:. War with Japan*, vol. 4, *The South East Asia Operations and the Central Pacific Advance*, B.R. 1736(50)(4), 1957, 209–10.

3. ADM 199.275: Operation BANQUET.

4. ADM 199.275: Operation LIGHT, Bombardment of Selected Targets at Sigli, Sumatra, by Aircraft of H.M. Ships *Victorious* and *Indomitable*, Minute of Director of Air Warfare and Flying Duties, 4 December 1944; Minute of Director of Airfields and Carrier Requirements, 22 December 1944.

5. ADD 52564: Somerville diary entry of 23 June 1944. ADM 199.340: Operation PEDAL.

6. ADM 199.275: Operation MILLET.

7. Before January 1945 the only British operations involving the use of more than one carrier were IRONCLAD (two) in May 1942, PEDESTAL (four) in August 1942, TORCH (three) in November 1942, AVALANCHE (two fleet and one light fleet) in September 1943, and TUNGSTEN (two fleet and four escort) in April 1944, plus four operations, each involving two fleet carriers, executed by the Eastern Fleet between July and October 1944.

8. ADM 199.1884: Operation CRIMSON.

9. Having left the new commander in the Indian Ocean, Power, with the unenviable task of having to tell those officers and units that were not earmarked for the Pacific that "they were bottom of the class with their destinies controlled by the Kandy constellation." Power attributed his continuing sanity to his ability to keep away from South East Asia Command headquarters. See ADD 52562: Letter of 2 November 1944 from Power to Cunningham.

10. Interestingly, before the Americans made their request the Admiralty had ruled against an attack on Palembang by the British Pacific Fleet on its way to Australia. See Memorandum of 24 October 1944 as given in ADM 205.40.

11. ADM 199.276A: Naval Air Strikes, Eastern Sumatra, Operation ROBSON, Operation LENTIL. ADM 199.555: Operation MERIDIAN, Destruction of Oil Refineries in Sumatra, Report of Proceedings, 13 January–4 February 1945. Historical Section, Admiralty, *Naval Staff History. Second World War: War with Japan*, vol. 6, *The Advance to Japan*, B.R. 1736(50)(6), 1959, 23–24, 24–29.

12. J. D. Brown, *H.M.S. Illustrious: Operational History* (London: Profile, 1971), 258.

13. *Naval Staff History*, 6:206–9.

14. ADM 199.1478: The British Pacific Fleet: Final Phase Operations, Report of 11 August 1945. ADM 199.1747: Shipping Arrangements generally in the British Pacific Fleet area, Minutes of Staff Conference held in the King George V on 12 June 1945, dated 22 June 1945; Report from Rear Admiral Destroyers to Vice Admiral British Pacific Fleet, 30 June 1945.

15. Material for this chronology is drawn from the various war diaries and

reports of the commander in chief and vice admiral, British Pacific Fleet, of the flag officers of the 1st and 11th Aircraft Carrier Squadrons, and from the ships' and flying logs of the carriers involved and from the returns and reports of their captains.

16. ADM 199.118: Commander-in-Chief's Despatches: November 1944 to July 1945, Report from the Commander-in-Chief British Pacific Fleet to the Secretary of the Admiralty, 23 November 1945. (Fraser's own comments were to the effect that while the intention of the BPF was "to engage in the most modern type of naval warfare . . . in company with its originators [sic] and prime exponents," the American "rate of striking and length of time that all units remain in the operating area are considerably beyond anything that had previously been contemplated in the British naval service.")

17. ADM 199.118: The British Pacific Fleet in Operations against Japan: Analysis, Report submitted by the Commander-in-Chief British Pacific Fleet to the Secretary of the Admiralty, 6 November 1945. (This report covered the period between 17 July and 10 August 1945, and noted that British combat and other operational losses per mission in this phase represented 2.38% and 2.00% of initial establishment, the corresponding American figures being 1.61% and 0.55%.)

18. Ibid. Also given as ADM 219.313: Directorate of Naval Operational Studies, Report No. 02/47, Air Operating Standards achieved by the British Pacific Fleet, 13 January 1947.

19. Ibid., Table 26. The main report (see n. 20 below) stated that in the final phase of operations off Japan the carriers' aircraft accounted for 447 enemy aircraft and the Americans 2,408. But in this table a detailed analysis of enemy losses to aircraft shows that British aircraft accounted for the "certain destruction" of 125 enemy aircraft, another 199 being listed as probables.

20. ADM 199.168: Naval Operations in the Far East, Serviceability in *Illustrious, Victorious,* and *Indefatigable* during Operation ICEBERG, 26 March to 25 May 1945. This report stated that the *Indefatigable* embarked a maintenance crew of 479 for an air group that numbered 73 aircraft, but that the *Wasp* needed 469 men to service a mixed group of 100 aircraft or 419 men for an all-fighter group of 110 aircraft.

21. ADM 199.1457, Part 2: Report of Experience of British Pacific Fleet from January to August 1945, Report from the Commander-in-Chief British Pacific Fleet to the Secretary of the Admiralty, 15 March 1945, Part II (Analysis), Section II (Logistic Lessons), d (Air Stores).

22. These were the fleet quartermaster branch, the shore air stations, the fleet train, and the staff of the escort carriers of the 30th Aircraft Carrier Squadron.

23. ADM 199.1741: Air Transport in the British Pacific Fleet area, Letter from Flag Officer Naval Air Stations (Australia) to Commander-in-Chief British Pacific Fleet, 6 March 1945.

24. ADM 199.118: The British Pacific Fleet in Operations against Japan: Analysis, Report submitted by the Commander-in-Chief British Pacific Fleet

to the Secretary of the Admiralty, 6 November 1945, Appendix IV, Experience gained by the 30th Aircraft Carrier Squadron, Report from Commodore Commanding 30th Aircraft Carrier Squadron to Commander-in-Chief British Pacific Fleet, 4 November 1945.

25. ADM 199.1759: Aircraft Supplies, Balloons and Equipment, Report of Commodore Air Train to Rear Admiral Fleet Train, 19 September 1945.

26. ADM 199.1457. Part 2: Report of Experience of the British Pacific Fleet, January to August 1945, Report from Commander-in-Chief British Pacific Fleet to the Secretary of the Admiralty, 15 March 1946, Part II (Analysis), Section II (Logistic Lessons), b (Logistic Support at Sea).

27. ADM 199.1769: Report of Proceedings, Fleet Train, Report of Rear Admiral Fleet Train to Commander-in-Chief British Pacific Fleet, Volume I, November 1944 to May 1945, Appendix I, Report of the Fleet Train Engineer Officer, Captain (E) J. G. Given, RN, Part I. (Also given as ADM 199.1766.)

28. ADM 199.1384: British Naval Liaison Party, Summary Number 4, Appendix A, Report of 29 August 1944.

29. ADM 199.1766 and ADM 199.1769: Report of Proceedings, Fleet Train, Report of Rear Admiral Fleet Train to Commander-in-Chief British Pacific Fleet, 7 June 1945. Volume I. November 1944 to May 1945. Appendix D. Report of the Fleet Train Armaments Supply Officer, Commander (sp) G. D. Jones, RNVR. (It would seem that Commander Jones did not agree with the prevailing view of the competence of the R.A.N. munitions branch.)

30. Ibid., Report of the Fleet Train Engineering Officer, Captain J. G. Givens, RN, Part I. (Other appendices in this volume, particularly Appendix G, provide further comment.)

31. Ibid., Appendix T. Operations of Fleet Train in Logistics Support of the British Pacific Fleet, Report of Lieutenant-Commander Everett R. Smith, USNR, 12 July 1945.

32. ADM 199.919: Report to Director of Plans from the Fleet Gunnery Officer of visit to the British Pacific Fleet, 21 May 1945.

33. ADM 199.454: Signal of 15 January 1944 from British Admiralty Delegation to Admiralty. ADM 199.1742: U.S. Pacific Fleet and Pacific Ocean Areas: Headquarters of the Commander-in-Chief, Memorandum Record of Understandings reached in Conference 17–19 December concerning Employment of the British Pacific Fleet, 20 December 1944. (The January signal stated that monthly American losses ran at 22% fighters, 16% bombers and 12% patrol aircraft: the December conference yielded the information that pilot losses ran at 10% per month and aircraft engines at 15%)

34. ADM 199.1748: Aircraft Damage Reports, Aircraft Wastage in British Pacific Fleet, March–August 1945. Report submitted by Flag Officer Naval Air Pacific to the Secretary of the Admiralty, 24 October 1945. (This report gives a total of 362 aircraft [16.8% initial establishment] lost in action and another 143 [6.6%] written off as either unfit for further service or beyond immediate repair.)

35. ADM 199.1748: Analysis of Aircraft Wastage: July-August

Operations, Report submitted by Flag Officer Naval Air Pacific to Commander-in-Chief British Pacific Fleet, 1 October 1945.

36. ADM 199.118: Battle Reports, Flying Logs and Statistical Surveys of H.M.S. *Implacable*, 6 July to 10 August 1945. (Relevant entries only.)

37. ADM 219.280: Directorate of Naval Operational Studies, Report No. 80/45, 14 July 1945.

38. ADM 219.321: Directorate of Naval Operational Studies, Report No. 10/47, 21 August 1947.

39. ADM 119.118: The British Pacific Fleet in Operations against Japan: Analysis, Report submitted by the Commander-in-Chief British Pacific Fleet to the Secretary of the Admiralty, 6 November 1945.

40. ADM 199.118: The British Pacific Fleet in Operations against Japan: Analysis, Report submitted by the Commander-in-Chief British Pacific Fleet to the Secretary of the Admiralty, 6 November 1945. Appendix IV. Experience gained by the 30th Aircraft Carrier Squadron, Report from Commodore Commanding 30th Aircraft Carrier Squadron to Commander-in-Chief British Pacific Fleet, 4 November 1945. ADM 199.1478: Report of Proceedings: July–August Operations of the 30th Aircraft Carrier Squadron, Report from the Commodore Commanding 30th Aircraft Carrier Squadron to Rear Admiral Fleet Train.

41. ADM 199.118: The British Pacific Fleet in Operations against Japan: Analysis, Report submitted by the Commander-in-Chief British Pacific Fleet to the Secretary of the Admiralty, 6 November 1945, Appendix IV, Experience gained by the 30th Aircraft Carrier Squadron, Report from Commodore Commanding 30th Aircraft Carrier Squadron to Commander-in-Chief British Pacific Fleet, 4 November 1945.

42. ADM 199.1457. Part 2: Report of Experience of British Pacific Fleet, January to August 1945, Report from the Commander-in-Chief British Pacific Fleet to the Secretary of the Admiralty, 15 March 1946, Part II (Analysis), Section II (Logistic Lessons), c (Replenishment at Sea).

43. ADM 199.1744: Periodic State of the Fleet Train, Report from the Rear Admiral Fleet Train to the Commander-in-Chief British Pacific Fleet, 11 June 1945.

44. ADM 199.118: Commander-in-Chief's Despatches: November 1944 to July 1945. Report from the Commander-in-Chief British Pacific Fleet to the Secretary of the Admiralty, 23 November 1945. (S. Woodburn Kirby et al., *History of the Second World War: The War against Japan*, vol. 5, *The Surrender of Japan* [London: H.M.S.O., 1969], 156–57, however, seems to suggest that the BPF was to serve with the 5th Fleet, but this is contradicted by E. B. Potter, *Nimitz* [Annapolis, Md.: Naval Institute Press, 1976], 380–81, and by Ray Skates in conversations of 30 January and 28 February 1990.)

45. ADM 199.1760: Signals of 15 July 1945 from Vice Admiral (Q) to Commander-in-Chief British Pacific Fleet; of 19 and 26 July 1945 from Commander-in-Chief British Pacific Fleet to Vice Admiral (Q) and Rear

Admiral Fleet Train; of 31 July 1945 from Rear Admiral Fleet Train to Commander-in-Chief British Pacific Fleet.

46. ADM 199.1457. Part 2: Report of Experience of the British Pacific Fleet from January to August 1945, Report of the Commander-in-Chief British Pacific Fleet to the Secretary of the Admiralty, 15 March 1946, Part III (Recommendations for a Fleet conducting ocean warfare), Section I (The Balanced Fleet and its Air Train and Sea Logistic Support Group).

47. *Naval Staff History,* 6:197.

48. ADM 199.118: Comments by E. S. Wood, Director of Stores, dated 1 March 1946, on Commander-in-Chief's Despatches: November 1944 to July 1945, Report from the Commander-in-Chief British Pacific Fleet to the Secretary of the Admiralty, 23 November 1945.

49. C. F. Romanus and R. Sunderland, *China-Burma-India Theater: Time Runs Out in CBI* (Washington, D.C.: Department of the Army, 1959), 138.

50. ADD 52562: Letter of 20 April 1945 from Power to Cunningham. (Mountbatten's final report as Supreme Allied Commander set the decision for DRACULA as 22 March 1945, but it seems that DRACULA was sanctioned on 2 April and the final plan of attack was approved on the seventeenth.)

51. Allen, *Burma,* 392. (The initial orders from Imperial General Headquarters for the future defense of Burma were issued to Southern Army in September, and then passed down the chain of command to Burma Area Army and its armies. See Japanese Monograph 132, *Burma Operations Record: XXVIII Army Operations in the Akyab Area.*)

52. The Arakan plan was settled on 25 October 1944: the appropriate directive was completed by South East Asia Command on 8 November and issued on the twenty-third. Under its terms there was to be an assault landing on Akyab on or about 20 January 1945 and Myebon was to be secured by amphibious assault by the end of February, but at the Mountbatten-Giffard conference of 21 December it was noted that Akyab would be attacked if the opportunity presented itself but that the existing timetable—for an assault in March—would stand for the moment. After reconnaissance established that Akyab had been abandoned, the island was occupied on 3 January 1945 (Operation LIGHTNING) and the follow-up operations were brought forward.

53. Ronald Lewin, *Ultra Goes to War* (London: Hutchinson, 1978), 139. F. W. Winterbotham, *The Ultra Secret* (London: Weidenfeld and Nicolson, 1974), 228.

54. Allen, *Burma,* 481. (It must be noted, however, that the decision to proceed with DRACULA, which was made because of the uncertainties that surrounded the advances from central Burma, may well have been taken without knowledge of Japanese intentions.)

55. *Naval Staff History,* 4:128–29.

56. ADD 52562: Letter of 2 June 1945 from Power to Cunningham.

57. It must be noted, however, that the *Ulster Queen* could not have been the source of signals intelligence for most of the campaign in Burma because she did not arrive on station until the spring.

58.   Edmund Burke: speech of 22 March 1775 on the subject of concili-
ation of the American colonies.

Appendix A.   The Eastern and East Indies Fleets

1. *Naval Staff History*, 6:22.
2. The total of sinkings, which excludes minor or local vessels, numbered
three heavy cruisers, one light cruiser, three submarines, three minelayers, eight
minesweepers, ten submarine chasers, four gunboats, five netlayers, and one
survey ship, plus nine army, ten navy, and twelve other merchantmen. Warships
accounted for seven warships and one merchantmen, submarines for twenty-
one warships and eighteen merchantmen, mines for five warships and five merchantman, carrier aircraft and shore-based aircraft each for two warships and
three merchantmen, and sabotage for one warship and one merchantman.
Interestingly, the four major Japanese units that succumbed to British action in
the Far East in 1945 fell to different forms of attack: an escort carrier to carrier
aircraft and three heavy cruisers to warships in a night surface action, to submarine attack and to sabotage.

Appendix D.   Operation ZIPPER and the British Pacific Fleet

1. S. W. Roskill, *History of the Second World War: The War at Sea, 1939–1945,*
vol. 3, *The Offensive,* part 2, *1st June 1944–14th August 1945,* provides comment
on ZIPPER on page 382. Kirby et al., *History of the Second World War,* vol. 5, part
1, Operations in S.E.A.C. (May–August 1945) allocates a number of chapters
to ZIPPER's planning and evolution, most obviously chapter 7, "Planning for the
Invasion and Defence of Malaya (May-June 1945)," 57–62, and chapter 8,
"The Mounting of 'Zipper' from India Base (July-August 1945)," 63–75.
2. *Naval Staff History,* 4:24. *Naval Staff History,* vol. 6, makes no mention
of ZIPPER.
3. Kirby et al., *History of the Second World War,* vol. 5, appendix 4, "Outline
Order of Battle for the Invasion of Japan," 444–45, and appendix 7, "The
Planned Build-up in Malaya for the First Phase of 'Zipper,'" 451–57.
4. Apparently the *City of Auckland* was the *City of Canterbury,* the *Glen Affric*
was the *Glenaffaric,* and the *Samholt* was the *Samhoult,* and the *Rivercrest* was the
River Crest.

Bibliography

PRIMARY SOURCES

MANUSCRIPTS ROOM, BRITISH MUSEUM
ADD: The Cunningham Papers
52562. Correspondence with Power
52563. Correspondence with Somerville
52564. The Somerville Diaries
52577. The Cunningham Diaries

AT CHURCHILL COLLEGE, CAMBRIDGE
AVAR: The Alexander Papers
ELLIS: The Ellis Papers

KING'S COLLEGE, LONDON
BROOKE: The Brooke Papers
3. Notes on My Life
The Brooke Diaries
A. 7 August–31 December 1943
B. 1 January–20 October 1944
ISMAY: The Ismay Papers
IV. Special Correspondence

NATIONAL MARITIME MUSEUM, GREENWICH
Ships' Covers

PUBLIC RECORD OFFICE, KEW
ADM 1: Admiralty and Secretariat Papers
16065. Explosion in Bombay Docks: Report on Damage and Loss
Suffered: Committee of Enquiry
16317. Bombay Dock Explosion: Extracts from Report
ADM 53: Ships' Logs
ADM 167: Board of Admiralty: Minutes and Memoranda
119. Board of Admiralty Memoranda, 1943
120. Board of Admiralty Minutes, 1944

121. Board of Admiralty Minutes and Papers, 1944

ADM 205: First Sea Lords' Papers

27. Correspondence with Prime Minister

35. First Sea Lords' Records

40. First Sea Lords' Meetings

ADM 199: War History Cases and Papers

118. British Pacific Fleet: Operations against Japan, 1945–1947

168. Naval Operations in the Far East and Surrender of Japanese at Singapore: Reports, 1945–1947

196. Eastern Fleet Weekly State, 1943–1945

275. Naval Operations in the Far East: Reports, 1944–1945

276a. Naval Sea and Air Operations: Reports, 1944–1945

340. Naval Operations in the Far East, 1942–1945

341. Naval Operations in the Far East, 1942–1945

454. War against Japan: Naval Operations, Requirements, 1941–1945

526. Enemy Submarine Attacks on Merchant Shipping: Reports

919. Visits to British Pacific Fleet Units by Rear Admiral 2nd Cruiser Squadron and Fleet Gunnery Officer, 1944–1945

1376. Basing of Royal Naval Forces on Australia, 1944–1945

1383. Basing of Royal Naval Forces on Australia, 1944

1384. Joint Administrative Planning Sub-committee: Report, 1944

1388. Eastern Fleet: War Diaries, 1944

1438. Flag Officer Commanding Royal Indian Navy, War Diaries, 1944

1452. Ceylon Command: War Diaries, 1944–1945

1457. Commanders-in-Chief British Pacific Fleet, Eastern Fleet, East Indies Fleet and Flag Officer Commanding 11th Aircraft Carrier Squadron: War Diaries, 1943–1946

1478. Operations against Japan: British Pacific Fleet Narrative of Events, 1945

1479. Naval Air Weekly Summaries, 1939–1944

1480. Naval Air Weekly Summaries, 1945

1741. Fleet Train Records. (Part 2). Air Transport, Logistic Support, etc., 1945–1946

1744. Fleet Train Records. (Part 5). Periodic States of the Fleet Train, etc., 1945

1748. Fleet Train Records. (Part 9). Electrical Maintenance, Aircraft Damage Reports, Ships, etc., 1945

1759. Fleet Train Records. (Part 20). Transport of Lubricating Oil and Water, Fuelling and Distilling, etc., 1945

1760. Fleet Train Records. (Part 21). Principle Details of Royal Fleet Auxiliaries and Tankers, and Logistics of Various Craft, 1945

1766. Fleet Train Records. (Part 32). History of the Fleet Train, 1944–1946

1769. Fleet Train Records. (Part 36). History of the Fleet Train,

Procedures for Fleet Train with British Pacific Fleet, Memoranda and Office Notes, 1945–1946

ADM 219: Directorate of Naval Operational Studies: Reports

  280. Supply of Aircraft to the British Pacific Fleet from the Main Base

  313. Air Operations: Standards Achieved by British Pacific Fleet

  321. Replenishment of Carrier Fleet

AIR 9: Director of Plans Papers

  370. Air Plan for Defeat of Japan

  485. Capture of Andaman Islands

CAB 66: War Cabinet Memoranda

  47. War Cabinet Papers, 1944

CAB 69: War Cabinet: Defence Committee (Operations)

  5. Meetings and Memoranda, 1943

  6. Minutes of War Cabinet meetings

CAB 70: Defence Committee Minutes and Memoranda

  7. Minutes of Defence Committee (Supply) Meetings

CAB 79: War Cabinet: Chiefs of Staff Committee, Minutes of Meetings

64.	Nos. 201–226.	To 25 September 1943
65.	Nos. 227–243.	To 9 October 1943
66.	Nos. 244–260.	To 26 October 1943
67.	Nos. 261–290.	To 27 November 1943
68.	Nos. 291–323.	To 31 December 1943
69.	Nos. 1–30.	To 2 February 1944
70.	Nos. 31–60.	To 25 February 1944
71.	Nos. 61–90.	To 17 March 1944
72.	Nos. 91–112.	To 6 April 1944
73.	Nos. 113–140.	To 1 May 1944
74.	Nos. 141–170.	To 25 May 1944
75.	Nos. 171–190.	To 12 June 1944
76.	Nos. 191–216.	To 30 June 1944
77.	Nos. 217–240.	To 18 July 1944
78.	Nos. 241–260.	To 4 August 1944
79.	Nos. 261–285.	To 23 August 1944
80.	Nos. 286–310.	To 18 September 1944
81.	Nos. 311–340.	To 17 October 1944
82.	Nos. 341–370.	To 5 November 1944

CAB 80. War Cabinet: Chiefs of Staff Committee, Memoranda: (0) Series

73.	1943.	Nos. 451–500.
74.		Nos. 501–560
75.		Nos. 561–650
76.		Nos. 651–750

77.   Nos. 751–801
78. 1944. Nos. 1–100
79.   Nos. 101–133
80.   Nos. 134–190
81.   Nos. 191–305
82.   Nos. 306–390
83.   Nos. 391–471
84.   Nos. 472–580
85.   Nos. 581–666
86.   Nos. 667–778
87.   Nos. 779–894

CAB 84. War Cabinet: Joint Planning Committees
Minutes and Memoranda
   6. Minutes of JPS Meetings. 1943
JPS Planning Papers and Memoranda
   53. JP (43) 80 to JP (43) 204
   55. JP (43) 205 to JP (43) 297
   56. JP (43) 298 to JP (43) 339
   57. JP (43) 340 to JP (43) 361
   58. JP (43) 362 to JP (43) 399
   59. JP (43) 400 to JP (43) 445
   60. JP (44) 1 to JP (44) 44
   61. JP (44) 45 to JP (44) 73
   62. JP (44) 74 to JP (44) 114
   63. JP (44) 115 to JP (44) 162
   64. JP (44) 163 to JP (44) 202
   65. JP (44) 203 to JP (44) 238

CAB 88. War Cabinet: Combined Chiefs of Staff and sub-committees
   3. Combined Chiefs of Staff: Minutes of Meetings, Nos. 101–139.
      9th July–31st December 1943
   55. Combined Staff Planners: Memoranda, Nos. 64–100. 20th March
      1943–23rd February 1944

CAB 99. War Cabinet: Commonwealth and International Conferences
   27. Preparations for the Dominion Prime Ministers' Conference
   28. Dominion Prime Ministers' Conference, London, 1944
   29. OCTAGON Record of Proceedings on board *Queen Mary* and at
      Quebec, 1944

CAB 105. War Cabinet Office, Telegrams
From Joint Staff Mission to Chiefs of Staff
   43. Nos. 1001–1200. June–September 1943
   44. Nos. 1201–1400. September 1943–January 1944
   45. Nos. 1401–1651. January–April 1944
   46. Nos. 1–200. April–August 1944
   47. Nos. 201–400. August–November 1944

From Chiefs of Staff to Joint Staff Mission
    57. Nos. 801–1000. September–December 1943
    58. Nos. 1001–1200. December 1943–March 1944
    59. Nos. 1201–1294. March–April 1944
    60. Nos. 1–200. April–July 1944
    61. Nos. 201–400. July–October 1944

From Joint Planning Staff London to Joint Planning Staff Washington. Red
    68. Nos. 255–573. May 1943–April 1944
    69. Nos. 1–295. April 1944–March 1947

From Joint Planning Staff Washington to Joint Planning Staff London. Blue
    70. Nos. 1–262. January 1942–June 1943
    71. Nos. 263–565. July 1943–April 1944
    72. Nos. 1–347. April 1944–July 1946

From Joint Staff Mission to Chiefs of Staff
    85. Dill telegrams. Nos. 16–293. September 1943–January 1945

From Joint Staff Mission to War Cabinet Office
    86. Nos. 1–200. January 1944–January 1945

CAB 119. Joint Planning Staff Files
    13. Operation DRACULA—Plan for the Capture of Rangoon: Discussions at OCTAGON Conference. Part 1. 1944
    14. Plan DRAKE and MATTERHORN—Plans for Air Operations against Japan. Part 2. 1944
    15. Operation ROMULUS: DRACULA and CAPITAL—Plans for Future Operations in Burma, 1944–1945
    16. Operation ROMULUS: DRACULA and CAPITAL—Plans for Future Operations in Burma, 1944
    17. Operation CULVERIN—Plans for Operations against Northern Sumatra, Discussion with the AXIOM party, 1943. (South East Asia Command staff visiting UK.)
    18. Operation CULVERIN—Plans for Operations against Northern Sumatra, discussion with the AXIOM party, 1943–1944
    21. Operation SCEPTRE—Plans for Advance on Bangkok, 1943
    22. Operation TRIUMPHANT—Plans for Reconquest of Burma, 1943–1944
    23. Operation BUCCANEER—Plans for Recapture of Andaman Islands, 1943–1946
    38. Proposed Operations in South East Asia: Reports and Assessments, 1943
    79. Preparations for Operations against Japan from Indian Bases, 1943–1944
    81. Plans for the Direct Capture of Singapore and Recapture of Burma, 1943

93. Landing Ships and Craft: Future Requirements and Provisions, 1944–1945

111. French and Dutch Participation in the War against Japan, 1944–1945

153. Participation of British and French Naval Forces in War in the Pacific, 1944–1945

155. Provision of Munitions and Manpower for War against Japan, 1943–1945

160. Far Eastern Strategy: Shipping Implications, 1944–1945

162. Provision of Landing Craft for the Far East, 1944–1945

167. Redeployment of Resources for the War against Japan after the Defeat of Germany, 1943–1944

174. Strategy for the War against Japan, 3 February–9 May 1944

180. Overall Strategy for the War against Japan, 16 May–23 August 1944

181. Overall Strategy for the War against Japan, 1944

182. Overall Strategy for the War against Japan, 1944–1945

186. Potentialities of Australia as a base in the war against Japan, 1944–1945

187. Proposals for the Establishment of a Base in Borneo, 1944–1945

202. Operations in South East Asia Command, 1 January–25 May 1944

CAB 122. British Joint Staff Mission Washington: Office Files, 1944

1072. Plans for the Defeat of Japan, 1943–1944

1073. Plans for the Defeat of Japan, 1944–1945

1074. Plans for the Defeat of Japan, 1943

1075. Defeat of Japan within One Year of Defeat of Germany, 1943

1076. Future Operations in South East Asia Command, 23 August–24 November 1943

1077. Future Operations in South East Asia Command, 25 November 1943–29 February 1944

1078. Future Operations in South East Asia Command, 1 March–29 June 1944

1079. Future Operations in South East Asia Command, 3 July–31 August 1944

1080. Future Operations in South East Asia Command, 1–21 September 1944

1081. Future Operations in South East Asia Command, 22 September–30 October 1944

1156. Move of the Japanese Fleet to Singapore, 1944

1166. AXIOM, 1944

CAB 138. British Joint Staff Mission Washington: Minutes and Memoranda

3. Minutes of Meetings Nos. 1–52, 1944

F.O. 954. The Avon Papers

6. The Far East. 1942–1943

7. The Far East. 1944–1945

PREM The Prime Minister's Office: Operational Papers

3.63.6. New Zealand Manpower, September 1943–September 1944

3.63.7. Employment of New Zealand Land Forces against Japan, August 1944–January 1945

3.63.8. Australian Manpower and War Effort, October 1943–April 1945

3.148.4. Strategy in South East Asia Command: CULVERIN operation (Sumatra) (AXIOM papers), February–March 1944

3.160.4. The "Middle" Strategy, May–June 1944

3.163.7. The British Pacific Ocean Force, September–October 1943

3.164.1. Move of Japanese Fleet to Singapore, February–April 1944

3.164.5. British Fleet Train, December 1943–July 1945

3.164.6. Various, November 1943–July 1945

3.167.7. Pacific War Council, 1942

3.260.12. American Production of LST for British Use against Japan, April 1944

3.324.29. Naval Manpower, May–July 1944

W.O.106. Directorate of Military Operations and Intelligence, Papers. (South East Asia Command section.)

4618a. Future Operations: Chiefs of Staff Planning and Strategy, etc., January–November 1943

4619. Future Operations: Chiefs of Staff Planning and Strategy, November 1943–February 1944

4620. South East Asia Command, Future Operations, February–March 1944

4621. South East Asia Command, Future Operations, March–August 1944

4622. Future Operations: Planning and Strategy, August 1944–January 1945

W.O.203. Military Headquarters, Far East. (Allied Land Forces, South East Asia.)

1484. Operation BULLFROG, Planning, November 1943–January 1944

1488. Operation PIGSTICK against Arakan Coast, EPS Meetings, November 1943–January 1944

1489. Operation PIGSTICK, Planning and Alternative Planning, December 1943–January 1944

1490. Operation PIGSTICK, Planning, December 1943–February 1944

1492. Operation CUDGET, Planning Directives, January–March 1944

1541. Operation CAPITAL, Planning Papers and Appreciations, August–September 1944

1608. Operation CULVERIN, General Planning, December 1943–March 1944

1609. Operation CULVERIN for Capture of North Sumatra, Transport Planning, April 1944

4995. Reconsideration of the CULVERIN Plan to Seize and Hold North Sumatra: Visit of AXIOM Party to Far East [*sic*] to Discuss Alternative Plans, January–April 1944

NAVAL HISTORICAL BRANCH, MINISTRY OF DEFENCE
CHRISTISON, Lt. Gen. Sir Philip. *Royal Indian Navy Amphibious Operations in Burma, 1942–1945.* Report lodged in the Burma, 1942–1945 file
Office of Flag Officer, Force "W." No. 80L/22/1944. Force "W" Orders. Operation "Zipper," 2 August 1945.

SECONDARY SOURCES

Published
Allen, Louis. *Burma: The Longest War, 1941–1945* London: Dent, 1986.
Brown, J. D. *H.M.S. Illustrious: Operational History.* London: Profile, 1971.
Callahan, Raymond. *Burma, 1942–1945.* London: Davis-Poynter, 1978.
Churchill, Winston S. *The Second World War,* vol. 5, *Closing the Ring.* London: Cassell and Co., 1952.
Craven, Wesley Frank, and James Lea Cate, eds. *The Army Air Force in World War II,* vol. 5, *The Pacific: MATTERHORN to Nagasaki, June 1944 to August 1945.* Chicago: University of Chicago Press, 1953.
Ehrman, John. *History of the Second World War. Grand Strategy,* vol. 5, *August 1943–September 1944.* London: H.M.S.O. 1956.
Gill, G. Herman. *The Royal Australian Navy, 1942–1945.* Canberra: Australian War Memorial, 1968.
Hayes, Grace Person. *History of the Joint Chiefs of Staff in World War II: The War against Japan.* Annapolis, Md.: Naval Institute Press, 1982.
Hull, Cordell. *The Memoirs of Cordell Hull,* vol. 2. London: Hodder and Stoughton, 1948.
Kirby, S. Woodburn, et al. *History of the Second World War: The War against Japan.* Vol. 3, *The Decisive Battles.* London: H.M.S.O., 1961.
———. Vol. 4, *The Reconquest of Burma.* London: H.M.S.O., 1965.
———. Vol. 5, *The Surrender of Japan.* London: H.M.S.O., 1969.
Kumar, Dharma, ed. *The Cambridge Economic History of India,* vol. 2, *c. 1757–c. 1970.* Cambridge: Cambridge University Press, 1983.
Lewin, Ronald. *Ultra Goes to War.* London: Hutchinson, 1978.
Matloff, Maurice, and Edwin M. Snell. *Strategic Planning for Coalition Warfare, 1943–1944.* Washington, D.C.: Department of the Army, 1959.
Morison, Samuel Eliot. *History of U.S. Naval Operations in World War II,* vol. 7, *Aleutians, Gilberts and Marshalls, June 1942–April 1944.* Boston: Little, Brown, 1964.

———. Vol. 8, *New Guinea and the Marianas, March 1944–August 1944*. Boston: Little, Brown, 1953.

Polmar, Norman. *Aircraft Carriers: A Graphic History of Carrier Aviation and Its Influence on World Events*. London: Macdonald, 1969.

Potter, E. B. *Nimitz*. Annapolis, Md.: Naval Institute Press, 1976.

Romanus, C. F., and R. Sunderland. *China-Burma-India Theater: Time Runs Out in CBI*. Washington, D.C.: Department of the Army, 1959.

State Department. [No. 7859.] *Foreign Relations of the United States: Near East, South Asia, Africa and Far East, 1944*, vol. 5. Washington, D.C.: U.S. Government Printing Office, 1965.

Winterbotham, F. W. *The Ultra Secret*. London: Weidenfeld and Nicolson, 1974.

Winton, John. *The Forgotten Fleet*. London: Michael Joseph, 1969.

Unpublished

Gorst, Anthony. "The Politics of Strategy: The Development of the British Pacific Fleet in 1944." Master's thesis, London School of Economics, 1981.

Historical Section, Admiralty. *Naval Staff History. Second World War. War with Japan*, vol. 4, *The South East Asia Operations and the Central Pacific Advance*. B.R. 1736(50)(4). 1957.

———. Vol. 6, *The Advance to Japan*. B.R. 1736(50)(6). 1959.

EXCLUSIONS FROM THE BIBLIOGRAPHY

Only those primary and secondary sources used to sustain the text of this work have been included in this bibliographical section: other sources that were consulted but which did not yield source material have been denied inclusion. The bibliography, therefore, has some notable exclusions, not least, except for Churchill's *The Second World War*, vol. 5, *Closing the Ring* (London: Cassells, 1952), of all biographical accounts written about or by individuals involved in the decisionmaking process. Churchill's volume, however, was used only with respect to the prime minister's movements and not for documentary purposes, and those reasons that dictated so sparing a use of this selective and unreliable work as a secondary source similarly precluded certain other notable biographical works being used as reference sources. It would nevertheless be correct to note certain biographical accounts that were consulted in the preparation of this work and to state the specific reasons for their having been discarded for reference purposes.

Sins of omission, the product of convenient amnesia, precluded consideration of Cunningham's *A Sailor's Odyssey: The Autobiography of Admiral of the Fleet Viscount Cunningham of Hyndhope* (London: Hutchinson, 1951), Ismay's *The Memoirs of General the Lord Ismay* (London: Heinemann, 1960), and George Mallaby's *From My Level: Unwritten Minutes* (London: Hutchinson, 1965).

Cunningham, on page 598, devotes just twenty-seven lines to the 1944 discussions on policy for the war against Japan. Mallaby, whose postwar destruction of his diaries represents a major loss to historians, seems almost to delight in his avoidance of matters of substance in his account. Ismay similarly provides little, not even an account of his offer of resignation at OCTAGON, though the accuracy of Brooke's account of this incident was confirmed by Ismay in a letter to Eden which is given, without date, by Ronald Wingate on page 112 in *Lord Ismay: A Biography* (London: Hutchinson, 1970), and which is repeated on page 277 of Denis Richards's *Portal of Hungerford: The Life of Marshal of the Royal Air Force Viscount Portal of Hungerford* (London: Heinemann, 1977). With respect to other episodes and aspects of Far Eastern issues in 1944, neither of these two biographies could provide much for this book.

The limitations of Richards's biography is perhaps surprising, but in the story of a long career in public service the Far Eastern issues of 1944 were marginal, and presumably a similar consideration explains why the most recent and authoritative biographies of two of Churchill's most important colleagues, Kenneth Harris's *Attlee* (London: Weidenfeld and Nicolson, 1982) and Robert Rhodes James's *Anthony Eden* (London: Weidenfeld and Nicolson, 1986), make no reference to Far Eastern issues in 1944. Somewhat surprisingly, Philip Ziegler's *Mountbatten: The Official Biography* (London: Collins, 1985) represents scarcely any improvement, and its account (281–82) of the transactions of August 1944 is both superficial and erroneous, and attributes to Mountbatten an importance and influence that he did not possess. It must be noted, however, that Ziegler's biography examines the Indian Ocean option and places it in its correct theater setting.

Martin Gilbert's *Winston S. Churchill*, vol. 7, *Road to Victory, 1941–1945* (London: Heinemann, 1986) provides an examination of Far Eastern issues, but its main contribution lies in its placing of these issues in their wider context. Its attention to the British high command's immediate preoccupation in the opening months of 1944 with such complicated problems as Poland's future, relations with the Soviet Union, the internal affairs of Italy and Yugoslavia, the Free French, and with the problems of OVERLORD, future bombing policy, ANVIL, and the failure of the Anzio landing reduces the Far Eastern issues to the status of small change, as indeed they were to Britain at this time. But in his somewhat fragmented account of Far Eastern issues Gilbert makes no mention of the Middle/Modified Middle Strategy episode and makes no serious examination of the high command's arguments. Moreover, what might be a suggestion (712) that Churchill's minute of 17 March 1944 initiated what became the Middle Strategy endeavor may well be substantiated by the closed files at Gilbert's disposal, but not by the documents consulted in the preparation of this work. John Colville's *The Fringes of Power: Downing Street Diaries, 1939–1945* (London: Hodder and Stoughton, 1985) confirms the distractions, particularly domestic political distractions, of early 1944, but in its accounting of issues is never anything more than a lightweight irrelevance.

John Kennedy's *The Business of War: The War Narrative of Major-General Sir John Kennedy* (London: Hutchinson, 1957) presents problems of an altogether different kind. The summaries of 5 April 1944 (322–23), and of 14, 19, and 24 July, 4, 10, 13, and 15 August, and 19 September (336–39) provide detailed critiques of issues and the development of the argument within the British high command, but three considerations preclude reliance upon this source.

By their very nature, Kennedy's comments were undocumented, normally took the form of summaries of several days' proceedings and, at least in part, were not necessarily firsthand accounts. Moreover, some of Kennedy's analyses provide genuine problems of understanding and interpretation. In the 10 August summary Kennedy gives the impression that he harbored no doubt that Britain would be able to release six divisions from Europe for the war in the Far East once Germany was defeated. This may be so, but this author stands by the conclusion that the release of such numbers could not have been anything other than problematical. More seriously, in the 19 September summary of the OCTAGON proposals and decisions Kennedy wrote, "We are to embark upon . . . the second-best course. . . . We really do not know whether the Americans would have agreed to our original suggestion, because it was never put to them seriously."

Given Kennedy's opposition to CULVERIN and Indian Ocean options and his support for the Pacific commitment, it is somewhat difficult to deduce what had been the preferred course and thus what had not been seriously put to the Joint Chiefs of Staff.

Such were the more important of the biographical works consulted in the preparation of this thesis and the reasons for their not have been used as secondary sources.

Index

Note: Single-page, and in the chronologies single-month, entries have not been included in this index: ships and places identified only in the orders of battle similarly have been excluded. Conferences, operations, and ships excepted, subheadings are given for subjects with more than twelve entries unless of singular theme. Names of operations have been given in small capitals.

About the Author

H. P. Willmott is a senior research fellow with the Institute of War and Society at De Montfort University and a member of the faculty at the Royal Military Academy Sandhurst. A visiting lecturer at Temple University and the University of Memphis in 1989–90, he taught naval history in the Department of Military Strategy and Operations at the National War College in Washington, D.C., between 1992 and 1994.